Marketing Operations
2002–2003

Marketing Operations 2002–2003

Karen Beamish

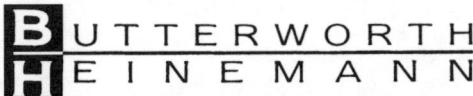

OXFORD AMSTERDAM BOSTON LONDON NEW YORK PARIS
SAN DIEGO SAN FRANCISCO SINGAPORE SYDNEY TOKYO

Butterworth-Heinemann
An imprint of Elsevier Science
Linacre House, Jordan Hill, Oxford OX2 8DP
225 Wildwood Avenue, Woburn MA 01801-2041

First published 2002

Copyright © 2002, Elsevier Science Ltd. All rights reserved

No part of this publication may be reproduced in any material form (including
photocopying or storing in any medium by electronic means and whether
or not transiently or incidentally to some other use of this publication) without
the written permission of the copyright holder except in accordance with the
provisions of the Copyright, Designs and Patents Act 1988 or under the terms of
a licence issued by the Copyright Licensing Agency Ltd, 90 Tottenham Court Road,
London, England W1T 4LP. Applications for the copyright holder's written
permission to reproduce any part of this publication should be addressed
to the publisher

British Library Cataloguing in Publication Data
A catalogue record for this book is available from the British Library

ISBN 0 7506 5707 3

For information on all Butterworth-Heinemann publications
visit our website at www.bh.com

Typeset by Integra Software Services Pvt. Ltd, Pondicherry, India
www.integra-india.com
Printed and bound in Italy

Contents

Preface	**Welcome to the CIM Coursebooks**	ix
Unit 1	**Introduction**	1
	Introduction	1
	The marketing planning process (syllabus section 1.1–1.2)	1
	Managing marketing relationships (syllabus section 1.3)	2
	Marketing operations in context (syllabus section 1.4)	2
	Understanding the aims and objectives of marketing operations and achieving your learning outcomes	4
	The importance of reading	6
	Approaching the Marketing Operations examination	6
	An overview of the strategy and planning hierarchy	7
	Corporate planning – what is it?	8
	Marketing strategy – what is it?	10
	Planning – what is it?	11
Unit 2	**The marketing audit**	16
	Introduction	16
	Conducting a marketing audit	16
	Stage 1 – Analysis of the macro environment	20
	Stage 2 – Analysis of the micro environment	26
	Identifying key opportunities	36
Unit 3	**Marketing planning, implementation and control**	40
	Introduction	40
	How to take the marketing audit to the planning process	41
	Stage 3 – The setting of objectives	42
	The balanced scorecard	44
	Gap analysis	47
	Formulation of the marketing strategy	49
	Market segmentation and competitive positioning	55
	The role of a marketer in positioning	66
	The marketing plan	66
	Implementation of the marketing plan	67
	A supportive and effective marketing structure	71
	The control process	75
Unit 4	**Theories of communication**	82
	Introduction to promotional operations in the context of the marketing mix	82
	The marketing mix in the context of marketing operations	82
	The communications process	83
	Communications theory	84
	The process of adoption	88
	Targeting decision makers	91
	Profiling marketing segments for promotional activities	92
	Push and pull strategy	92
	Promotional operations and the planning framework	93
	Aims and objectives of the promotional communications process	94
Unit 5	**Promotional operations**	96
	The promotional mix	96
	Advertising	98
	Advertising media characteristics	99
	The role of advertising in the product life cycle	101
	Advertising and the marketing mix	103
	Confusion marketing	104

	Campaign planning	107
	The agency	109
	Campaign evaluation	113
	Sales promotions	116
	Sales promotions techniques	117
	Retailer to consumer sales promotions	118
	Manufacturer to consumer sales promotions	118
	Evaluation of sales promotions	120
	Public relations	121
	Marketing information to underpin public relations activities	123
	Public relations and attitude change?	123
	Public relations techniques	124
	Evaluation of public relations activities	126
	Direct and interactive marketing	127
	Objectives of direct marketing	128
	Database marketing	129
	Direct marketing techniques	130
	Telemarketing	131
	Internet marketing	133
	Evaluation of direct marketing techniques	135
	Sponsorship	136
	Evaluation of sponsorship	138
	Personal selling	138
	Opening and closing a sale	140
	Evaluating sales performance	140
Unit 6	**Product operations**	**143**
	Product operations	143
	Branding	146
	Brand values	147
	Packaging	152
	Product management	153
	The product life cycle	153
	Managing the product life cycle	156
	Product portfolio planning tools	158
	New product development	162
	The new product development process	163
	The product adoption process	165
Unit 7	**Price operations**	**168**
	Introduction	168
	Price perception and the customer	169
	Perspective of price and the organization	169
	Pricing in relation to demand	169
	Influences on price	170
	Correlating price with value	171
	Strategic pricing determinants	172
	Price sensitive markets as a determinant	174
	Pricing objectives and strategies	177
	Strategic pricing	178
	Tactical pricing strategies	178
	Eight stages to establishing a price	180
	The route to setting higher prices	180
Unit 8	**Place operations**	**183**
	Introduction	183
	Influences on distribution	184
	Marketing issues for distribution	185
	Distribution channels	185

	Channel members	185
	Why use intermediaries?	187
	The distribution channel and the customer	188
	Selecting the channels of distribution	189
	Intermediary selection criteria	190
	The balance of power within the distribution channel	190
	Vertical channel integration	192
	Horizontal channel integration	193
	Physical distribution management (PDM)	193
	Push and pull strategies	194
	The impact of the Internet on channel decisions	195
	Evaluating channel effectiveness	199
Unit 9	**Managing marketing relationships**	**201**
	Introduction	201
	Relationship marketing	202
	From transactional to relationship marketing	202
	The scope of marketing relationships	204
	Planning for relationship management	205
	Customer retention management	208
	Key account techniques to aid customer retention management	210
	The marketing mix for customer retention management	213
	Relationships with outside suppliers	214
	Different types of outsourced relationships	214
	The advantages and disadvantages of outsourcing	215
	Supplier selection	215
	The agency brief	216
	Evaluation and control	217
	Building supplier relationships	217
	Managing internal marketing relationships	218
	Relationship marketing with the wider public and society	220
	Marketing and social responsibility	221
	Legislation	222
	The rise in consumerism	223
	Social response to consumerist pressure	223
	Ethical issues for consumers and marketers	224
	Ethical implications for the marketing mix	224
	Codes of ethics	226
	Chartered Institute of Marketing's Code of Practice	226
	The CIM code of ethics	226
	The enforcement of the Code of Practice within CIM	227
	Proactive, reactive or passive strategies for deploying ethics and social responsibility at a corporate level	228
	The relationship marketing plan	229
Unit 10	**Industrial/business-to-business and services marketing**	**232**
	Business-to-business marketing	232
	Characteristics of business/industrial buying behaviour	233
	Organizational buying	233
	Understanding the nature of business-to-business buyers	234
	Market segmentation for organizational marketing	236
	The buying and decision-making process in organizational markets	236
	The decision-making process	237
	The buying centre – the decision-making unit	238
	Relationship marketing in organizational markets	239
	Competitive tendering	240
	The marketing mix for organizational marketing	240
	Summary	243
	Marketing of services	244

	Services defined	244
	The structure of the services sector	244
	Service characteristics	245
	The uncertainties of service	246
	Meeting customer expectations	247
	The services mix	248
	The marketing mix in the context of services	249
	The key components of designing a services mix	250
	The importance of service quality	251
	Implementing a quality culture	252
	Monitoring and evaluating service	253
Unit 11	**Charity and not-for-profit marketing**	**257**
	Charities – non-business marketing	257
	Marketing planning for charities	259
	Marketing segmentation and targeting for charities	259
	Marketing planning and control	260
	What is a non-profit-making organization?	261
	Not-for-profit marketing versus profit marketing	262
	The motivational factors influencing not-for-profit marketing and profitable organizations	263
	Marketing planning for not-for-profit marketing	263
	Managing the marketing mix – charities and not-for-profit marketing organizations	264
Unit 12	**International marketing**	**270**
	Introduction	270
	Why go international?	270
	Levels of international marketing	271
	The international marketing environment	272
	Know your markets	276
	Understanding the external marketplace	277
	Understanding consumer and business buying behaviour	277
	International research	278
	Developing an international marketing information system	279
	Acquiring primary research	282
	Potential barriers to entry	285
	The implications on marketing plans	285
	Globalization	288

Appendices

1 Guidance on examination preparation	291
2 Answers and debriefings	302
3 Curriculum information and reading list	319

Index   324

Preface
Welcome to the CIM Coursebooks

An introduction from the academic development advisor

This year has seen the continuation of our commitment to ensure that the CIM Coursebooks are kept up to date and relevant for the forthcoming session. This is deemed as essential as the dynamics of the global market are forever changing, often in a way most unexpected and indeed not anticipated – as no doubt you will have all experienced, especially in the wake of September 11th.

Over the past few years there have been a series of syllabus changes initiated by the Chartered Institute of Marketing to ensure that their qualifications continue to be relevant and of significant consequence in the world of marketing, both within industry and academia. As a result Butterworth-Heinemann and I are continuing to rigorously revise and update the Coursebook series in order to make sure that every title is the best possible study aid and accurately reflects the latest CIM syllabus.

The ongoing updates and revisions to the series include both restructuring and the inclusion of many new mini cases and examples to support the learning and assessment process. The authors are accomplished writers and have been commissioned both for their CIM course teaching and examining experience and their wide general knowledge of the latest marketing thinking.

We are certain that the coursebooks will be highly beneficial to your study, providing you with structure, direction, relevant examples and assessment opportunities that will enable you to focus on acquiring the broad range of theory and concepts required to underpin the examination and continuous assessment process.

The editorial team and authors wish you every success as you embark upon your studies.

Karen Beamish
Academic Development Advisor

How to use these coursebooks

Everyone who has contributed to this series has been careful to structure the books with the exams in mind. Each unit, therefore, covers an essential part of the syllabus. You need to work through the complete coursebook systematically to ensure that you have covered everything you need to know.

This coursebook is divided into units each containing a selection of the following standard elements:

- **Objectives** tell you what part of the syllabus you will be covering and what you will be expected to know, having read the unit.
- **Study guides** tell you how long the unit is and how long its activities take to do.
- **Questions** are designed to give you practice – they will be similar to those you get in the exam.
- **Answers** (at the end of the book) give you a suggested format for answering exam questions. *Remember* there is no such thing as a model answer – you should use these examples only as guidelines.
- **Activities** give you a chance to put what you have learned into practice.

- **Debriefings** (in the back of the book) shed light on the methodologies involved in the activities.
- **Exam hints** are tips from the senior examiner or examiner which are designed to help you avoid common mistakes made by previous candidates.
- **Study tips** give you guidance on improving your knowledge base.
- **Insights** encourage you to contextualize your academic knowledge by reference to real-life experience.
- **Definitions** may be used for words you must know to pass the exam.
- **Summaries** cover what you should have picked up from reading the unit.

While you will find that each section of the syllabus has been covered within this text, you might find that the order of some of the topics has been changed. This is because it sometimes makes more sense to put certain topics together when you are studying, even though they might appear in different sections of the syllabus itself. If you are following the reading and other activities, your coverage of the syllabus will be just fine, but don't forget to follow up with trade press reading!

The coursebook in a glance

Unit	Objectives	Summary
Unit 1 Introduction	Marketing Operations is the mainstay and module of the Advanced Certificate in Marketing. It is the backbone of marketing, and builds clearly upon the Fundamentals of Marketing at Certificate level and firmly underpins Planning and Control and Integrated Marketing Communications at Postgraduate Diploma level. In this unit you will: • Understand the basis and focus of the Marketing Operations Coursebook • Gain a brief insight into issues relating to the planning process, relationship marketing and the context of marketing operations • Understand the nature of the CIM Learning Outcomes, and what you should achieve through your studies • Be encouraged to read more broadly around the marketing operations area • Focus on the nature of the examination	As many markets reach maturity, organizations are working significantly harder to achieve and retain sustainable competitive advantage. The varying dynamics of devising strategies and plans require careful and sensitive management, as the organization, i.e. 'the corporate group' of business functions seeks to achieve its organizational objectives. Essentially there are many strategic marketing issues that need to be addressed in respect of the future success of an organization and their product/services portfolio. Ideally organizations will need to focus on the brand values, brand statements, product/services portfolios, customer services, supply chains and of course customers and consumers. Developing a strategy and associated plans that are innovative, competitive and sustainable is a tremendous challenge. Ultimately the most successful measure of performance is said to be customer satisfaction. Without satisfied customers the organization will struggle to remain competitive and remain at the

Unit	Objectives	Summary
	• Understand the process of marketing planning at an operational level.	leading edge in the marketplace, and the challenge will never be fully realized.

According to Nigel Pearcy –author of *Market-Led Strategic Change*, you can tell if a company has a strategy and knows where it is going and develops the capability to get there. He suggests 'this is something that stands behind planning and systems and structure - strategy is more fundamental'.

It is, therefore, clear to see that strategies and plans give focus, structure, outcomes and a planned destiny for the organization. Every organization should have a pathway mapped out that takes their organization to a state of competitive strength.

In Unit 2 'The marketing audit' of this book we look very closely at the setting of appropriate objectives, and the development of appropriate strategies, but prior to looking at this, it is essential to understand the planning framework and where it all fits together. |
| Unit 2 The marketing audit | The main focus of this particular unit relates to the development of the marketing strategy and the overall planning focus. The learning outcomes associated with this particular unit will enable you to:
• Conduct a basic marketing audit, considering internal and external factors
• Look closely at the 'macro' and 'micro' elements of the marketplace
• Analyse internal capability
• Undertake a SWOT analysis.

This unit will serve to provide you with some of the analytical tools of the trade, for ensuring sufficient analysis is undertaken and used to underpin the marketing decision-making process and overall strategy development. | As a result of studying through this unit, you will hopefully have a clear perspective of the importance of undertaking a thorough, structured and objective marketing audit, in order that you understand the marketing environment in which your organization operates.

It is of primary importance that both macro and micro factors are analysed and that subsequently a clearly defined strategy may be developed based on sound management information and reliable forecasts derived that represent anticipated market share and future potential sales.

While it is essential to understand the macro environment, the micro environmental issues must be addressed in order that an organization is well poised to respond to changing market conditions. An organization should analyse in |

Unit	Objectives	Summary
		depth, the issues related to their internal relationships, customer relationships, supplier relationships and stakeholder relationships and ultimately be prepared for the demands that they might place upon it.
		Additionally it will be of considerable importance to ensure that the organization has the capacity to respond to the driving force of change, by creating an appropriate infrastructure. The infrastructure should be based on highly-skilled employees, appropriate levels of financial investment, adequate resources, technological soundness, ultimately ensuring that the customer is at the centre of the business, that the organization is marketing oriented and customer focused.
		In order that organizations can successfully develop an appropriate marketing strategy that underpins the corporate objectives and goals, then the marketing audit is a vital ingredient of the overall strategy and planning hierarchy and process.
Unit 3 Marketing planning, implementation and control	During this unit, we will be looking at *developing marketing objectives and strategies*. The learning outcomes associated with this particular unit are: • Developing marketing objectives and strategies • Developing marketing objectives as simple goal statements with links to the mission statement • Understanding how marketing strategy defines target markets (from segmentation bases and profiles) and achieving differential advantage and desired brand positioning • Gap analysis and the Ansoff matrix • Implementation of the marketing plan • Barriers to implementation	This has been a particularly extensive unit, focusing on the broad range of issues associated with planning. However, again, you are reminded that while you have been provided with an insight into the notion of marketing planning, the basis of marketing operation is to look at marketing at an 'operational' level. • During the text we have looked closely at taking the marketing audit to the planning process • Setting different types of objectives • Segmentation, targeting and positioning • Strategy development • Implementation of the marketing plan. The influence and importance of marketing planning must never be

Unit	Objectives	Summary
	• Allocations of budgets, tasks and responsibilities • Control implications • Alternative ways of managing marketing activities including internal marketing implications. This unit will provide you with basics in order that you understand the process of marketing planning at an operational level, and that you are also able to develop marketing objectives and plans at an operational level.	underestimated, it is vital to the success of the organization. There is endless academic writing in relation to this particular subject area, while many are a slight variation on a theme, there is a core at the heart of planning that never actually changes. It is very important to read around the subject wherever possible and gain a real insight into the major driving forces behind the planning processes and what makes planning such a vital activity.
Unit 4 Theories of communication	This particular subject area has been divided across two units, the theory of communications and the practice of communications, i.e. 'promotional operations'. This unit concentrates on the theory of marketing communications which may not necessarily be new to you. You may have indeed covered communication theories in other contexts. However, it is essential that you are able to utilize communication models in respect of marketing and promotional operations, creating synergy and consistency in line with the objectives of the marketing plan. This particular unit covers theories of communications: single step, two-step, multi-step and adoption models.	The focus of this particular unit, was to provide you with an overview of the essential communication and adoption models that might assist you in the development of appropriate promotional mix programmes, in order that they effectively communicate with the customer in a way in which they will relate to. One of the key objectives of any promotional operational programme will be to ensure that ultimately, potential customers adopt the product offering and are converted to the brand, in a way that can establish long and loyal relationships in years to come. This particular element, will very much underpin the Unit 'Promotional operations', contextualizing promotional communications in the planning process, and will prepare you to put into an operational context, the tools of the promotional mix.
Unit 5 Promotional operations	Now that you have a full underpinning knowledge of the marketing planning process, it is time to look at how the marketing mix is applied in context of the implementation process. The learning outcomes associated with this particular unit are: • To understand the need to integrate marketing mix tools to achieve effective implementation of plans	This unit has been particularly extensive as it seeks to provide an overview of the key components of the promotional mix. One of the critical success factors of implementing the promotional operations plan, will be the degree of synergy and integration that exists between each of the promotional mix elements. It is clear that the mix elements are indeed complementary to each other,

Unit	Objectives	Summary
	• Select and justify the use of one or more promotional techniques for a particular marketing context. It is therefore important to understand the basis of the indicative content that underpins this particular unit and how it will form the basis of your study in relation to 'promotional operations'. • Advertising techniques • Sales promotion techniques • Public relations techniques • Direct and interactive communications • Sponsorship • Personal selling techniques. Should you continue through to the Postgraduate Diploma in Marketing, this particular unit underpins the strategic implications of Integrated Marketing Communications.	some of them are more effective and efficient in terms of targeting volumes, while other elements have a key strength in developing customer relationships in the long term. Ultimately, the key success factor for any promotional mix, will be its ability to meet the marketing objectives and bridge the successful implementation of the marketing strategy. Promotional planning in complete isolation of the marketing plan, could be catastrophic, untargeted and a complete waste of valuable resources. At an operational level, you are likely to be involved in the development and implementation of promotional plans. Therefore you will need to clearly identify the direct objectives, relate them back at all times to the marketing plan, undertake an integrated approach of promotional mix tools to optimize the effectiveness of a combined campaign and of course evaluate the implementation for measurement of success.
Unit 6 Product operations	This particular unit will be focusing very much on the role of the product in implementing the marketing plan and will, therefore, focus on product operations. The following learning outcomes will be addressed within this unit: • Understand the needs to integrated marketing mix tools to achieve effective implementation • Select an appropriate integrated mix (4Ps) for a particular market. The indicative content underpinning the learning outcomes for product operations is • The nature of products, components and life cycles	The product is the very core of what the organization is about; the product is the purpose. The product on its own is worthless, but carefully managed, branded and packaged, the benefits it provides and the satisfaction it will achieve are the key factor to its overall success. The main aim of any organization should be to create products that customers need, want and expect, always ensuring quality, innovation, customer delight and value are at the core of their strategy development and business activity. It is of primary importance that the organizations create a differential between themselves and their competitors, through the successful planning implementation of a brand and product strategy, that places them in a uniquely differentiated and

Unit	Objectives	Summary
	• Brand management: brand values, brand planning and threats to the brand • Product portfolio, product mix • New product development.	competitive position. However, the critical success factor in establishing product and brand success, is ensuring that an integrated approach is taken toward the utilization of the marketing mix. This will be a marketing imperative. As marketers, we are becoming increasingly aware of the speed of change, resulting in shorter life cycles, faster levels of innovation, rapid speed of products to market, accelerated diffusion and excessive competition. With the added impetus of global marketing, new technologies, the importance of product development, product innovation and robust product planning is providing the most significant challenge of the 21st century – where do we go from here?
Unit 7 Price operations	During this particular unit, you will be focusing on the importance of pricing operations, and the implications and impact of pricing upon other activities within the marketing mix. The learning outcomes associated with price are in line with the other units relating directly to the marketing mix and include: • Understanding the need to integrate marketing mix tools to achieve effective implementation of plans • Select an appropriate integrated marketing mix. The indicative content of the syllabus underpinning those learning outcomes in the context of price is: • The importance of price and its determinants • Pricing models for decisions based on cost competition and demand • Pricing objectives and method • Adapting the price for the marketing mix.	The price element of the marketing mix leaves marketers aiming to balance all of the eggs in the basket, to achieve the ultimate blend of price, quality and perceived value. A balanced marketing mix will ensure the customer is getting the right product in the right place, at the right time, for the right price. Customers are very fickle today and clearly understand that they have significant choice and indeed power, in the marketplace and that they have significant influence upon supply and demand. Prices will vary according to what people are prepared to pay in different situations. Different prices might also reflect what customers can pay or are prepared to pay. However from a management perspective, you are challenged to consider, is price simply what the customer will pay, or is it a more flexible marketing tool than just that? In order to understand the influence of price on the customers and competitors, a marketer must understand

Unit	Objectives	Summary
		the need for significant ongoing research into the state of the external environment and the activities of competitors and gain a key understanding of buyer behaviour and expectations.
		The critical success factors in relation to price, are to maintain the organizational objectives, yet endeavour to remain sensitive to the needs of the customers, ensuring that you can address their long-term needs, including the further development of new and innovative additions to the product range and lines. The key to price is to link the product quality and the clear indication of value for money from the organization to the customer.
		Pitching the price at the right level may be the difference between profit and loss or survival and failure, as pricing will reflect the long-term profitability and market share. Therefore in order to achieve a marketing oriented approach to pricing the organization should take into account a broad range of factors • Marketing strategy • Value proposition • Price-quality relationships • Competitive pricing • Costs • Ability to negotiate higher prices • External market forces • The affects of globalization • Product line pricing.
Unit 8 Place operations	Place operations highlights the importance of distribution as a key factor in achieving the ultimate marketing mix. It is the final component and relates to ensuring that customers are able to gain access to and purchase their chosen product. The basis of this unit reflects the same principal learning outcomes as the other marketing mix units; in	The process of distribution is costly, complex and logistically challenging and will often involve many different groups of people or organizations. Right through the 1990s and continuing on into the 21st century, there has been a significant shift in distribution patterns, including the ongoing demise of many traditional middlemen. More and more organizations are merging, developing

Unit	Objectives	Summary
	terms of understanding the need to integrate the marketing mix tools and achieves effective implementation of plans. From a place perspective, the indicative content reflects the following: • Distribution channels • Consumer and business-to-business (business-to-business will appear later in the text) • Criteria to select and evaluate alternative channels of distribution.	alliances and utilizing and pooling resources where possible, always looking at ways in which they can be more cost-effective, and expanding into broader geographical, in fact global markets. As the external marketing environment is so competitive organizations have to find ways of increasing their market share and obviously, increasing profits for shareholders. Selection of the appropriate channel decision can give organizations the competitive edge over others by reaching customers in new and more innovative ways, particularly with the increasing use of the Internet. Developing relationships between suppliers and customers is the essence of long-term customer loyalty, should the marketing mix break down as a result of poor distribution strategy and management, then customers will go elsewhere. Physical distribution management is a phenomenal task; it is complex, costly and critical. It has many facets, but its key role is getting the products to the customers, when and where they demand them. One thing all organizations should bear in mind is that it is highly unlikely that customers will 'beat a path to their door'. The marketplace is vast so is the amount of choice, ensuring your product is visible when it should be will be one of the keys to marketing success.
Unit 9 Managing marketing relationships	The key to success within any marketing environment will relate to the realization that managing marketing relationships will be the key to long-term customer loyalty and customer retention. Additionally, it will also reflect the necessity to manage each market differently in order to optimize customer relationships and the associated benefits. This unit is broken into four parts, which in essence reflects the structure	The move from transaction marketing to relationship marketing has meant that the marketing planning process has now taken on a new set of dynamics. It is no longer purely based around developing a marketing mix to meet organizational goals it is now much broader in perspective, and the task much bigger. Essentially, organizations who are truly committed to developing a relationship marketing approach will

Unit	Objectives	Summary
	and content of the indicative content of the syllabus • Relationships with customers • Relationship with outside suppliers • Internal marketing relationships • Relationships with the wider public and society. NB: Relationship marketing will also be part of your studies within Marketing Customer Interface, but there is a greater concentration of the scope of relationship marketing within the Marketing Operations syllabus, from the point of view of covering a broader scope of audience.	need to be supported by structure, culture and overall organizational climate that will enable each of the functional business units within the organization to align and co-ordinate themselves to develop a integrated approach to the achievement of the overall marketing objectives of every market. Principally the role of the relationship marketing plan is to ensure that there is a synergy, consistency, coherence and cohesiveness and a 'pan-company' approach to the implementation of the marketing plan.
Unit 10 Industrial/ business-to-business and services marketing	This unit is one of three units looking at the application of marketing in a number of given contexts, in order that you understand the broad diversity of marketing, given different situations, different markets and different customers. The learning outcome underpinning this unit, is therefore: • To understand and appreciate the marketing operations process and how it can be delivered through multiple relationships. The indicative content of the syllabus is therefore as follows: • Distinguish characteristics of business versus consumer markets • Business buyer behaviour, factors affecting buyer behaviour and business decisions • Marketing mix differences • Basic characteristics of services • The extended marketing mix • Importance of service quality. This unit will be separated into two parts – one for business-to-business	Marketing to organizations and industries is different in practice from consumer marketing, but uses the same principles. The demand is managed differently and the buying process has to be accepted as it is. Quite often the delivery in the time promised is more important than price alone. The range of marketing opportunities is very wide and the range of products can be bewildering. The buyers are professionals, and their motives for buying are quite different from those of consumers. Instead of looking at their own individual needs they will be accountable to the organization for making the right purchase decision in order for the supply chain to function satisfactorily. The 4Ps can still apply to marketing to organizations but with a different emphasis. Distribution of some products is similar to that for consumer goods, but there are also some quite big differences. There is a stronger need to maintain a competitive edge, because of the professionalism of the buyers and the competitors.

Unit	Objectives	Summary
	and the other reflecting upon services marketing.	The importance of services in the modern economy is shown by the fact that Britain, and most other developed countries, are now service economies, with more than 50 per cent of gross spending being on services and 64 per cent of the workforce employed in services.
		Services have to be marketed but there are more differences than similarities with the marketing of products. The problems arise from the features of services – their intangibility, inseparability from the provider, perishability and the impossibility of stocking up for future sale. There is also the potential variation of quality due to the fact that people, who vary in performance day by day, provide the services.
		The marketing mix for services includes the 4Ps of product marketing, with the addition of people, physical evidence and the process or methods of providing the service. However the importance of the eleven elements of design should not be underestimated.
		Ultimately, as with all marketing strategies, plans and implementation of various marketing mixes, the customer and the quality to the product and service provision should be a matter of 'exellence'.
Unit 11 Charity and not-for-profit marketing	The basis of this unit looks at the role of marketing within charities and not-for-profit organizations. The profile of charities and the work that they undertake has risen significantly in the last 10 years. Originally charities did not involve themselves heavily in the function of marketing, however as there is more and more work to undertake, and more and more competition in respect of gaining charitable donations and grants, they have had to implement a more marketing-oriented approach, a competitive stance in order to survive	Planning and controlling go together, and in this respect there is no basic difference between the activities of normal commercial organizations and those of charities and non-profit-making organizations.
		The big difference for charities is their dependence on the unpaid work of volunteers; you cannot make the same demands on volunteers that you can make on employees. Also, you do not have the power to threaten them with dismissal – many employees tolerate the job because

Unit	Objectives	Summary

and undertake the work they feel destined to do.

The purpose of this unit is to link with the learning outcome:

- Demonstrate the adaptation of marketing operations principles in a variety of contexts.

The indicative content of the syllabus underpinning this learning outcome is:

- Objectives differ from consumer/industrial markets
- Target markets (donors, volunteers, clients)
- Marketing mix differences (product usually ideas and services rather than goods, short distribution channels, approach to pricing, promotion emphasis on PR and face-to-face fund raising)
- Performance hard to measure.

they need the money, either now or in the future, so they cannot walk out. It is almost impossible to estimate the value of volunteer workers, and controlling them is a matter of good organization and the appropriate expressions of gratitude for their help. If you see a charity putting on a big party, don't grumble – the people in there probably deserve a lot more than they get.

There is probably more need for charities to be seen to be using their money wisely than there is for commercial companies, as a donor who thinks that money is being wasted may not feel like giving money next time round. Donations to such television marathons as Children in Need improved when some of their successful projects were shown in the course of the marathon programme.

The marketing philosophy is now becoming a permanent feature of not-for-profit-making organizations. It has been necessary to introduce marketing gradually, so as to highlight a 'customer-centred' focus, which had not previously been noticeable.

Typically, all customers are better educated, better informed and are not shy about asserting their 'rights and entitlements', therefore, in the context of charities and not-for-profit organizations, the power of the customer (Porter's Five Forces) is not to be underestimated. Introducing a marketing philosophy into charities and not-for-profit-making organizations is now of primary importance.

The most significant benefits that marketing can give the public sector organization are in the provision of managed information, effective use of promotional mix. The value of advertising, PR and sponsorship had already shown immeasurable success in increasing the availability of

Unit	Objectives	Summary
		funds. We have seen this in the case of Red Nose Day and the Children in Need Appeal, where millions and millions of pounds are generated in a one-day event.
		The total income for charities and not-for-profit organizations is significant. In the case of McDonalds, $300 million has been used to improve medical support and aid for children in need, therefore the necessity to plan and control the use of these funds is vital.
		The same applies to smaller local charities, as locally involved participants will want to see their donations appropriately used, in order that they might be encouraged to contribute to these organizations in the future.
Unit 12 International marketing	With the ongoing evolution of global markets, it is of primary importance that the function and practice of marketing in an international context is considered. The basis of the learning outcome underpinning this module is to demonstrate the adaptation of marketing in a variety of contexts. The underpinning indicative content, i.e. the syllabus areas to be covered include: • Identifying marketing information needs • Marketing environment, managing the differences • Structure choices: exporting, licensing, joint ventures, trading companies and direct ownership. Necessary adaptation to the marketing mix.	The issues relating to international marketing and globalization are considerable. But the key to its success is to remember the purpose of marketing. It is critical to the organization not to see international markets as a special project or view them in isolation. Critical to any decision in relation to international marketing is sufficient information on which to base a decision. Organizations should never underestimate the power of market research in giving them a snapshot of the bigger picture. The picture will tell a range of stories, relating to the many different facets of the country, which is when the organization identifies whether or not to globalize or localize. Because marketing is dynamic and ever changing and because of the growing participation of the Internet in the marketing environment today, globalization will continue to be an objective for which many organization should strive. To remain competitive the organization will need to make a number of

Unit	Objectives	Summary
		major decisions based on who their market is, where their market is, the status of the economy of their markets and the opportunities they present.
		Staying ahead of the competition will be critical, therefore for many years to come, many organizations will increasingly need to develop and use a range of marketing information, market entry strategies and overall marketing strategies to keep the balance between globalization and localization and customer satisfaction.

About MarketingOnline

With this year's coursebooks Butterworth-Heinemann is offering readers free access to MarketingOnline (www.marketingonline.co.uk), our premier online support engine for the CIM marketing courses. On this site you can benefit from:

- Tutorials on key topics every two weeks during the term, comprehensive revision support material and access to revision days from Tactics – the highly acclaimed independent trainer for CIM courses.
- Fully customizable electronic versions of the coursebooks – annotate, cut and paste sections of text to create your own tailored learning notes.
- Access to the e-Library – electronic versions of eight classic BH marketing texts to enrich and extend your knowledge.
- Instant access to specimen papers and answers, as well as other extra material and weblinks related to the coursebooks.
- Capacity to search the coursebook online for instant access to definitions and key concepts.

> **Logging on**
>
> Before you can access MarketingOnline you will first need to get a password. Please go to www.marketingonline.co.uk where you will find registration instructions for coursebook purchasers. Once you have got your password, you will need to log on using the onscreen instructions. This will give you access to the various functions outlined below.

Using MarketingOnline

MarketingOnline is broadly divided into six sections which can each be accessed from the front page after you have logged on to the system:

1. **The coursebooks**: buttons corresponding to the three levels of CIM marketing qualification are situated on the home page. Select your level and you will be presented with the four coursebook titles for each module of that level. Click on the desired coursebook to access the full online text (divided up by chapter). On each page of text you have the option to add an electronic bookmark or annotation by following the onscreen instructions. You can also freely cut and paste text into a blank word document to create your own learning notes.

2. **The e-Library**: click on the 'BH Library' button on the front page to access the eight titles in the e-Library. Again you can annotate, bookmark and copy text as you see fit.

3. **Revision material**: click on the 'Revision material' link and select the appropriate CIM level and coursebook to access revision material.

4. **Useful links**: click on 'Useful links' to access a list of links to other sites of interest for further reading and research.

5. **Glossary**: click on the 'Glossary' button to access our online dictionary of marketing terms.

6. **Discussion**: click on the 'Discussion' button to access our various online noticeboards. All users can access and put up entries on our public noticeboard using onscreen instructions. If your college has registered as a MarketingOnline user you may also have access to your own 'Tutor Group Discussion' where you can interact with your fellow students and tutors.

If you have specific queries about using MarketingOnline then you should consult our fully searchable FAQ section – again, this is accessible through the appropriate link on the front page of the site. Please also note that a **full user guide** can be downloaded by clicking on the link on the opening page of the website.

Unit 1 Introduction

Objectives

Marketing Operations is the mainstay module of the Advanced Certificate in Marketing. It is the backbone of marketing, and builds clearly upon the Fundamentals of Marketing at Certificate level and firmly underpins Planning and Control and Integrated Marketing Communications at Postgraduate Diploma level.

In this unit you will:

- Understand the basis and focus of the Marketing Operations Course Book
- Gain a brief insight into issues relating to the planning process, relationship marketing and the context of marketing operations
- Understand the nature of the CIM Learning Outcomes, and what you should achieve through your studies
- Be encouraged to read more broadly around the marketing operations area
- Focus on the nature of the examination
- Understand the process of marketing planning at an operational level.

Introduction

The Marketing Operations module within the Advanced Certificate has a very clear focus and is based upon three key overall concepts:

- The Marketing Planning Process (syllabus sections 1.1 and 1.2)
- Managing Marketing Relationships (syllabus section 1.3)
- Marketing Operations in Context (syllabus section 1.4).

A brief insight into each of these components appears below. You might find it useful at this stage to look closely at the CIM syllabus, which can be found either in your Student Manual or the CIM website at www.cim.co.uk, as this will put your study into context.

The marketing planning process (syllabus section 1.1–1.2)

This element of the text focuses on the process of effectively 'doing' marketing. It looks at the concepts and applications of 'the marketing planning process', from the marketing audit through to developing objectives and marketing strategies. One of the key success factors of marketing is the successful utilization and integration of the marketing mix. The marketing mix is a set of tools for the trade; if they are not carefully managed, in a co-ordinated and defined way, then the strategy may crumble and the process may fall apart.

Organizations will often be found analysing their capabilities, assessing their true position and overall potential in the marketplace, both home and abroad. This analysis provides the foundations of the planning process, which are critical to the direction of the organization in the future.

Malcolm McDonald, Cranfield University School of Management, defines the overall purpose of planning at this stage as follows:

> *The overall purpose of marketing planning and its principal focus is the identification and creation of sustainable competitive advantage. (Quoted in Dibb, Simkin, Pride and Ferrell, Marketing Concepts and Strategies, p. 689, 2001)*

Implementing the marketing plan is probably one of the most challenging and often fraught areas of business strategy. Each division and department will be involved in fighting for their share of the budget and appropriate resource allocations, in order to achieve the objectives that are the fundamental basis of the future success of the organization. Ultimately this can often result in one of the most dramatic changes of all, i.e. change in the organizational structure. It is necessary to consider carefully the nature, structure and culture of any organization, in order that it can clearly meet the challenges to achieve a sustainable competitive advantage and remain at the heart of the marketplace.

Managing marketing relationships (syllabus section 1.3)

Relationship marketing is a really exciting, dynamic and futuristic area, with many challenges inherent within it. Achieving a sustainable competitive advantage may very often rely on successful relationships with all components of the organization, from suppliers through to the ultimate consumer and, of course, stakeholders. As you will know from experience, relationship building is likely to be a very complex and long-term process with so many components to be managed. In a nutshell, therefore:

> *The purpose of marketing is to establish, maintain, enhance and commercialise customer relationships. (Quoted in Payne, Christopher, Clark and Peck, p. 3, 1998)*

Marketing appears to be becoming increasingly complex as customers and consumers are continually demonstrating empowerment in their decision making and purchasing process. They are exercising choice in every aspect of their life; they know that their demands should be central to an organization's business objectives and strategy, that their marketing, quality and service levels must be beyond 'excellence'. Included in that is the 'perfect relationship'. Achieving this means having the customer at the heart of the organizations, being marketing oriented, customer oriented and ultimately relationship oriented.

Structuring an organization, its systems and processes, to meet the relationship marketing objectives is a significant task, with more and more organizations moving from the 'transactional' focus to the 'relationship' focus of marketing. A well-known fact in business is that retaining customers is more cost-effective than attaining new customers – but structuring the organization to achieve this can prove to be a major undertaking!

Marketing operations in context (syllabus section 1.4)

This syllabus has been designed and structured in a logical way to provide marketers with an understanding of the different concepts applicable to operational marketing management. Marketers are required to develop a range of transferable skills that aid creativity, innovation and the potential to exploit and develop new marketing opportunities.

In order that you can successfully achieve some elements of this, the CIM syllabus, and this text in association with it, has presented you with an opportunity to look at marketing in a range of different contexts. Therefore the latter part of your studies will see you starting to apply the 'process' and 'relationship' elements of marketing operations, into a range of contextual situation, such as:

- Industrial/business-to-business marketing
- Services marketing

- Charity and not-for-profit marketing
- International marketing.

Being able to apply marketing in different contexts is vital to your own individual success and continuing professional development. You will be in a much stronger position to add value to your own position within the organization as well as to the organization as a whole.

At this early stage of your studies, it is useful to highlight how these concepts can actually work in practice.

> **Case history**
>
> **The Easy Group**
>
> One of the greatest success stories of recent years is Stelios Haji-Ioannou and the 'Easy Group'. According to *Marketing Week*, the 'Easy Group is flag-waver for branding' and is described by *EuroBusiness* as Europe's most successful brand since Richard Branson's Virgin. Haji-Ioannou has clearly taken a planned approach to ensuring this high level of success for his organization, and has achieved a strong positioning for easyJet, 'the Web's favourite airline'.
>
> Haji-Ioannou is famous for single-handedly revolutionizing low-cost air travel in Europe and has made a significant fortune in the process.
>
> Haji-Ioannou's vision is to provide what the consumer wants, wherever they want it. Clearly he has played a game as good as the one he talks. His brand translated into reality immediately, with some 3 per cent of Britons initially having heard of the airline, and 90 per cent of Europeans recognizing the brand and some 18 million passengers flying with easyJet annually within five years.
>
> Whilst 2001 proved to be a devastating year for the airline industry, easyJet continued to thrive and grow, producing results completely contrary to the rest of the global airline business.
>
> The Easy Group consists of:
> - easy Jet
> - easy Rentacar
> - easy Everything
> - easy Value.
>
> (Other ventures include easyFinance and easyHotels).
>
> In essence the complete 'travel solutions package' for 'Easy' customers has been achieved.

Easyjet extends across all consumer and business sectors, meeting a variety of customer needs, from corporate business through to the individual consumer, with an increasingly innovative product/services portfolio that can see the brand being continually stretched.

This is a prime example of the success of a sound planning basis, taking into consideration all of the components of the marketing plan and developing customer relationships in the context of the 'travel' services industry.

Like people, organizations are far from perfect, and the Easy Group will be no exception. Within many businesses it is clear to see that while the concept is good, the reality has scope for improvement. The purpose of your studies is to prepare you to add value to your organization, with a combination of knowledge, understanding and application abilities and skills that could really make the difference, make them stand out from the crowd and achieve 'sustainable competitive advantage'.

Understanding the aims and objectives of marketing operations and achieving your learning outcomes

Having read the CIM syllabus overview for Marketing Operations, it is clear that the syllabus is broken down into three tiers:

- Aims and objectives
- Learning outcomes
- Indicative content and weighting.

Understanding the role of each of these areas is quite important, as together they culminate in the acquisition of the knowledge and understanding that underpins the examination process.

Aims and objectives

The aims and objectives clearly explain the basis of your learning and what that learning is designed to achieve. It is this basis that this text seeks to promote:

- To build on your knowledge and understanding of marketing fundamentals
- To enable you to apply modern marketing theory to the understanding and solution of practical marketing problems and situations
- To provide a sound understanding of the process of marketing planning, analysis, strategy and implementation
- To provide a sound understanding of the marketing mix tools that contribute towards the effective implementation of marketing strategy
- To enable you to evaluate the relative effectiveness and costs of elements of the promotional mix, providing underpinning operational knowledge for progression on to the Postgraduate Diploma in Marketing
- To explore the multiple relationships which need to be formed and maintained to enable successful and ongoing exchange in the marketplace
- To examine the need to adapt marketing operations to a variety of different contexts.

Table 1.1 provides a list of key learning outcomes, linked to the units of study, so that it is clear to see how the coursebook provides you with the underpinning knowledge and understanding to support a successful outcome to your studies, and of course the all-important examination. This should provide you with a useful reference for structuring your learning.

Learning outcomes

Table 1.1 Learning outcomes/unit guide

Learning outcomes	Study units/syllabus reference
Conduct a basic marketing audit, considering internal and external factors	Unit: 2 – Syllabus reference: 1.1.1
Understand the process of planning at an operational level	Units: 1, 2 and 3 – Syllabus reference: 1.1 (1.1–1.3)
Develop marketing objectives and plans at an operational level	Units: 1, 2 and 3 – Syllabus reference: 1.1.2

Understand the need to integrate marketing mix tools to achieve effective implementation of plans	Units: 4–8 – Syllabus reference: 1.2 (1.2.3–1.2.4)
Select and justify the use of one or more promotional techniques for a particular marketing context	Units: 4, 5 and 10–12 – Syllabus reference: 1.2.1 and 1.4.1, 1.4.2, 1.4.3 and 1.4.4
Demonstrate the adaptation of marketing operations principles in a variety of contexts	Units: 10–12 – Syllabus reference: 1.4.1, 1.4.2, 1.4.3 and 1.4.4
Understand and appreciate the marketing operations process and how it can be delivered through multiple relationships	Unit: 9 – Syllabus reference: 1.3.1 (1.3.1–1.3.4)
Select an appropriate integrated mix (4Ps or 7Ps) for a particular marketing context	Units: 4–8 and 10–12 – Syllabus reference: 1.2 (all points) and 1.4 (all points)
Communicate ideas effectively in a variety of formats: reports, articles, presentations in preparation for both the workplace and examinations	Appendix 1: Guidance on examination preparation

All learning outcomes are designed in order than you can apply marketing in practice in a range of different contexts

You will notice that there has been mention of how Marketing Operations might potentially underpin your future studies and progression through to the Postgraduate Diploma. Figure 1.1 illustrates how Marketing Operations will provide you with a sound basis when studying for the Diploma examinations. This should reinforce to you the opening description of Marketing Operations as the 'backbone' or the fundamental element of marketing.

Figure 1.1 Links with the postgraduate diploma

Indicative content

The third and final tier of the syllabus is the indicative content and weighting. This explains in detail the different elements of the syllabus that you will cover to achieve the learning outcomes. These have been referenced in Table 1.1 for your information.

You should endeavour to familiarize yourself with these key syllabus points as they form the basis of the examination process. The examination questions are formulated by the CIM Senior Examiners and are written with a clear focus upon the indicative content. There is more on examinations later in this book.

The importance of reading

While you might be taking the Marketing Operations module with the sole objective of achieving the Advanced Certificate in Marketing, hopefully you will broaden your horizons considerably along the way.

In order to do this, you should not only use this particular course text, but also read around the subject. CIM have clearly specified a range of recommended reading texts, which are listed in your Study Manual and also in *Curriculum information* of this text. Many of the texts within the reading list have been used to develop this book and you are encouraged to read and follow-up on these and the other references interspersed throughout this text and extend your knowledge.

In addition, you should regularly read various journals, such as *Marketing Week*, *Marketing* and *Campaign*, which have international accessibility, particularly *Marketing Week*, through www.mad.com. Other suggestions are *The Economist* and broadsheet papers, in particular the weekend versions and equivalents of the *Financial Times* and the *Sunday Times*. Here you will see a range of useful and relevant examples of how all of the components of marketing impact on everyday business in your own country. One of the most useful resources is *Marketing in Business*, the CIM magazine, where you will find many useful case studies that will consolidate your learning.

As e-commerce plays such a pivotal role in everyday life, you will also find a range of different websites referenced. It is recommended that you visit them where appropriate and in the context in which they have been offered. A useful journal to support aspects of e-commerce in relation to marketing operations is *connectis* – Europe's e-business magazine.

> **Study tip**
>
> As part of your studies you will be continually referring to a range of promotional activities and international references.
>
> To assist you in preparing for the examination you are advised to set up two separate information files. One is for keeping cuttings relating to marketing mix activities, in respect of both consumer and business-to-business marketing. In the second file, you should keep a range of international-based marketing cuttings.
>
> It is recommended that you follow developments closely in two or three countries and record events over a period of time.
>
> These would be particularly useful when answering examination questions that say 'in a country of your choice' or indeed a 'company of your choice'. With a file of cuttings to fall back on at revision time, you have a range of examples to use.

Approaching the Marketing Operations examination

As already suggested, the examinations are written based upon the very detailed indicative content. Furthermore they are clearly focused on ensuring that you can achieve the specified 'learning outcomes' referenced earlier in this unit. It is vitally important, therefore, that you pay close attention to the requirements of the syllabus and learning outcomes, in order that you can successfully attempt the CIM examinations. Any one element of the syllabus could be tested, therefore 100 per cent coverage must be achieved through your studies.

Preparation for the examinations is essential – www.marketingonline.com provides some generic guidelines on exam preparation, in addition to past CIM examination papers and specimen answers. In addition to this, the Senior Examiner's comments are included. This gives you an indication of the strengths and weaknesses of a range of specimen answers. All of this is provided to help you and support you through the examination process.

CIM provide you with a range of exam preparation tools within their website. You will be provided with web addresses, passwords and usernames upon completion of your student registration process. There is also plenty of help and support through the 'marketingonline' facility.

The exam paper questions will be mostly practical in nature, in that the questions will ask you to take on a role, possibly solve a problem, prepare a presentation, write briefing notes, develop an outline plan or devise the basis of a strategy. Many of the questions will ask you to put different concepts from within marketing operations into practice. Again, refer to past papers to conceptualize how the exam paper will look when your turn comes to take the examination.

Questions will be naturally challenging at this level, and will not require you to regurgitate knowledge but to apply it into real-life situations or scenarios. This is a key requirement at Advanced Certificate level. You are about to prove to the Senior Examiner that you can 'do marketing' at an operational management level. Therefore avoid superficial answers and get straight to the thrust of the question.

An overview of the strategy and planning hierarchy

The backdrop to the planning process

In the last two decades, the function of marketing has had an increasing influence upon the strategic development of the organization, achieving a much more favourable position, more on a par with the other business functions. This has been an uphill battle, one that has seen marketing gaining a very prominent position in the 1980s, and subsequently being diluted in the early 1990s as a result of the economic recession. Ever since, marketing as a business function has had to fight back in order to establish its position at the heart of the corporate planning process.

Essentially, the marketing function may play a pivotal role in feeding information upwards, to provide substance, guidance, direction and vision to support the corporate planning process. In turn, the significant work that the marketing function undertakes plays a major role in establishing a vision and mission for the organization, a sense of direction as to where it is heading in the short, medium and long term.

To put this into context, it is necessary to understand and conceptualize the strategy and planning hierarchy (Figure 1.2). This highlights the route that strategy and planning takes from the corporate strategy stage down to the marketing function and through to marketing tactics. For example, it is likely as a marketing director that you will have a significant input to the strategic decision-making process, this is commonly known as 'bottom-up planning'. Your role would include providing the board and the corporate strategy team with appropriate levels of information to support corporate level decision-making. Subsequent to this, you would also have a vital role in then taking the corporate objectives and corporate strategy, and translating them into marketing objectives and marketing strategy (Figure 1.2).

Figure 1.2 Strategy and planning hierachy

Further down the strategy and planning hierarchy (Figure 1.3), marketing operations start to play a pivotal role in implementing the marketing plans, through a tightly defined marketing programme. This is known as bottom-down planning.

At this stage it is appropriate to consider the various tiers of the strategy and planning hierarchy in a little more detail, in preparation for your studies in Unit 2, 'The marketing audit'.

Corporate planning – what is it?

Corporate planning starts at the very top of the organization. It provides clearly defined objectives for the organization as a whole, which can then be translated down through the hierarchy to each of the business functions, inclusive of marketing, human resources, finance, and the operations departments. In turn, each of these business functions has responsibility to deliver the overall corporate objectives, meeting the corporate mission and corporate vision of the organization. They will also have a key role in ensuring that corporate values are deployed and understood by the internal market.

While the business functions will vary in nature, it is essential that they each work together, developing an innovative and integrative approach to delivering corporate objectives. No business unit should work in isolation of the other functional units; ignoring this approach could ultimately have a detrimental effect. It amounts to planning in a vacuum.

A good example of this would be a financial services organization. You will be aware that financial services organizations such as 'Egg', First Direct Bank, American Express or MBNA rely heavily upon 'people' in order to provide the required level of service to meet customer demands and expectations. For any of the above organizations to succeed, both the human resources and marketing business functions will need to work closely together to achieve an integrated approach to fulfilling the corporate objectives.

Read the case history below and then undertake Question 1.1.

> ## Case history
>
> **The Egg that came first**
>
> October 1998 saw the Prudential launch 'Egg' – a financial service that was developed and tailored to meet individual needs.
>
> Egg was a new 'brand' development with a new and innovative strategy, with the main focus being on the delivery of this brand via the Internet. Egg was designed with a clear focus on utilizing the new technologies, not just providing an information based website, but clearly a transaction based website where customers could manage all of their financial needs wherever they were, whenever they wanted.
>
> Significant marketing research was undertaken and the outcome suggested that Egg would appeal to a core of 15 million people in the UK, particularly young professionals, the well-off older generation and busy younger people.
>
> Egg made its financial services available 7 days a week, 24 hours per day, by telephone, post and Internet. Within days of its launch, the website had received over 1.75 million hits and over 100,000 telephone calls were received. Personal loans were processed in 24 hours and home loans in 48 hours.
>
> The brand name was a great success. By Christmas 1998, Egg had achieved 50 per cent recall of the name 'Egg', rising to 75 per cent by the end of 1999.
>
> The Egg brand continued to grow over ensuing months to include just about every package you could think of, e.g. travel insurance, credit cards and promotional incentives such as unlimited access on the Internet and e-mail or 1 per cent off all high street purchases. Its promotional activity was considerable, including special offers.

Egg website is www.egg.com – research for information to support your case study answers.

> ## Question 1.1
>
> In the case of 'Egg', why would it have been vitally important for the marketing function and human resources function to have worked closely together?
>
> Before commencing this question it would help if you start to think about the role that marketing play's within the organization and what it is that they need to be able to function. You should think about this in the realm of both physical and human resources.
>
> You should then be able to approach this question understanding the linkages between human resources and marketing and how they might be inter-dependent on one another.

You will see that there needs to be clear co-operation between the business functions. This ensures that there is synergy between functions, in order that the brand values can be delivered and a sustainable competitive advantage achieved. Defining the service that Egg was to deliver could not be undertaken in isolation, as there was a requirement for a sound infrastructure to deliver the high level services envisaged.

Ultimately corporate planning provides focus and direction for the whole organization. It is from here that the infrastructure of the organization to support the corporate requirements is shaped, formed, structured and organized in a way that will ensure ultimate customer satisfaction and high performance and profitability for the organization.

Marketing strategy – what is it?

In this Unit the words strategy and planning often appear linked together in the same sentences. Clearly, however, they are not one and the same, and therefore they be must differentiated.

Marketing strategy – a strategy indicating the specific target markets and the types of competitive advantages that are to be developed and exploited. (Dibb, Simkin, Pride and Ferrell, p. 656, 2001)

As a strategy, marketing seeks to develop effective responses to changing marketing environments, by defining market segments, developing and positioning product offerings for those target markets. (Webster 1997, from Hooley, Saunders and Piercy, p. 7, 1998)

Strategy is the matching of the activities of an organization to the environment in which it operates and to its own resource capabilities. (Johnson and Scholes, 1988)

On close examination of these definitions, it is clear to see that they have a common thread. This marketing strategy should create a sense of vision and direction. Nigel Piercy (1997) states that:

Strategy is all about doing best what matters most to the customer.

and

Finding new and better ways of looking at important things to get some leverage for changing the way things are done.

Marketing strategy provides the basis of a framework for meeting organizational needs and customer wants in an integrative and innovative way. It communicates to the internal market and its external stakeholders the strategic intent of the organization, where they are going, to whom they are taking their products and services and how they propose to achieve a positive competitive market position.

When developing a strategy, the critical success factor is to ensure that the marketing strategy is robust and focuses on building long-term relationships, creating customer value and sustainable competitive advantage. This is quite important to comprehend, as while organizations are subject to constant change, and as a result often work continually on various contingency plans, there should be some consistency in approach. Therefore, a robust marketing strategy is long term, it is strategic in nature and should remain constant. The contingency approach is very much tactical, leading to changes in the marketing mix as a result of changing market conditions.

Piercy (1997) suggests, in his book *Market-Led Strategic Change*, that a robust marketing strategy should have the following characteristics:

- Focus on providing superior customer value, but recognize that no innovation offers a sustainable advantage
- Make long-term investments in relationships, with suppliers, distributors, employees and customers
- Be built around 100 per cent satisfied customers based on capabilities and motivation of their people
- Build effective supply chains and IT to deliver superior operating performance.

Therefore, the key to success is to build a strategy based on these concepts, added to which an organization must strive to ensure that they implement a learning culture, are open to change and are innovative, with a long-term commitment to developing long-lasting customer relationships. Figure 1.3 represents some of the key components of the fundamentals of marketing strategy.

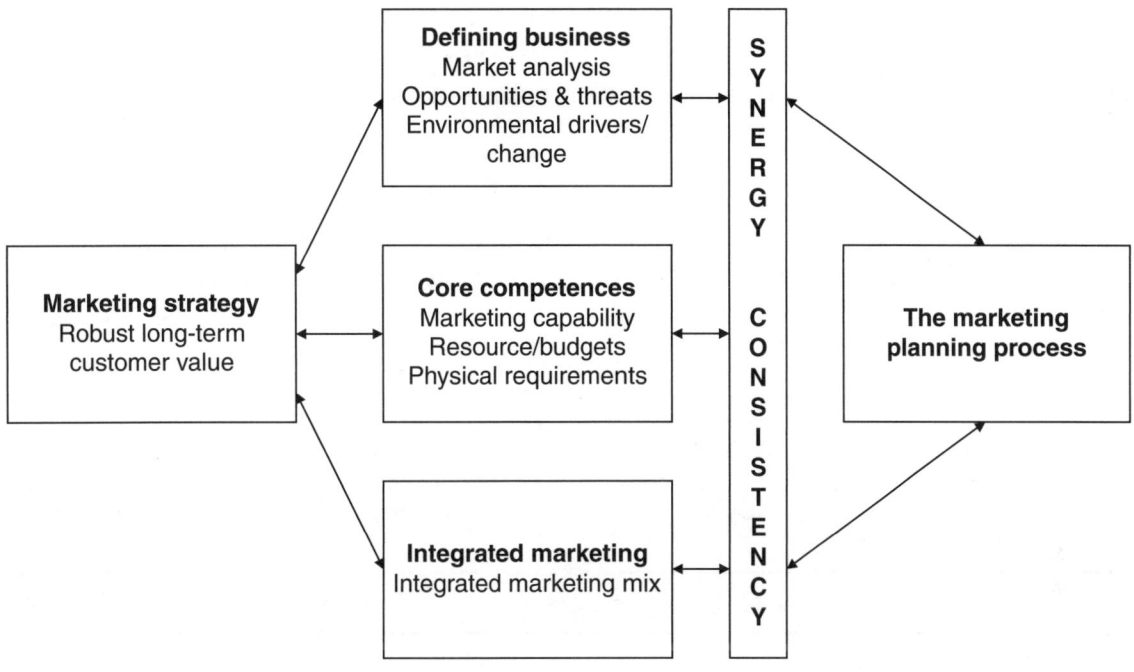

Figure 1.3 The basics of strategy (Adapted from Drummond and Ensor, 1999)

Essentially marketing strategy should identify specific segments of the market, towards which the organization's marketing activities and programmes might be aimed. It should highlight opportunities to be exploited and explicitly state the objectives required in order that the corporate goals of the organization should be achieved.

Ultimately, strategy should ensure synergy across the whole organization without exception. Critical to the success of any strategy is the need to ensure that all business functions and their underpinning activities are working to the same purpose and design, with a common vision, achieving integration and consistency in approach.

Planning – what is it?

Planning is an essential process ensuring that the defined strategy may be successfully implemented, and that the infrastructure required in order to meet the corporate and marketing objectives has been set in place. Planning provides specific direction, activities and timetables, and it creates pathways to achieving competitive advantage. Effectively it becomes a programme of events.

More and more organizations today appear to have an increasing emphasis on the importance of planning, and Johnson and Scholes (2000) suggest a number of reasons why this might be:

- Planning provides a structured means of analysing the marketplace, considering the dynamics of it and forcing managers to both question and challenge what they quite often take for granted

- Planning provides a sense of direction, and can be seen as a means of involving employees in the development of a strategy. This provides an opportunity for employees to take ownership of the overall objectives and the planned approach to achieving them
- A plan is a good way of communicating proposed actions/activities expected to be undertaken by the organization, in order that they achieve their corporate objectives
- Having a plan in place provides a sound basis for control, and presents an opportunity to regularly review the organization's progress against objectives.

While there is an emphasis on 'planning' as a key business activity at this stage, your studies will focus on 'marketing planning' at an operational level. Therefore, it is important to highlight a typical marketing planning model at this stage, so that you understand the level for which you are being prepared.

The 'marketing planning process model' in Figure 1.4 clearly illustrates how planning might take place within a typical marketing function. This model will form the basis of your study within Unit 2.

Figure 1.4 The marketing planning process

However, while the focus will be around marketing planning, it is still important to understand the 'bigger picture' of how it all fits together, including the issues and implications of planning.

Barriers to planning

While planning has many positive facets, it can also create many barriers within the organization. It is likely that the majority of people and organizations have faced considerable change as a result of newly defined strategies and have had to come to terms with some of the major repercussions of this level of change. The most prominent factor related to change is that it is almost without exception linked with cost-cutting and downsizing.

Drummond and Ensor (1999) suggested that barriers to successful planning are:

- The existing culture may not be amenable to marketing plans, particularly if the organization is not marketing oriented.
- *Power and politics* – All organizations are subject to internal politics and often as a result of this the strategic planning process becomes a boardroom battlefield, where vested interests fight each other's proposals in order to gain resources and status.
- *Analysis not action* – Many organizations waste time and energy in analysing data and developing rationales for action, but ultimately fail to act. A further element of this is 'paralysis-by-analysis', too much information, not enough direction.
- *Resources* – After years of downsizing, striving for increased efficiencies, many organizations now find themselves resource-starved. When corporate objectives are defined, it is of prime importance that organizations realistically consider the resources required, in order that they can rise to the challenge of achieving the corporate targets.
- Skills are very closely linked to the challenges of resources. One of the key components of any organization is a highly skilled workforce. As a result of the changes brought about by the economic slowdown in the early 1990s, marketing as a function was cascaded down to managers in the organization who were untrained, unskilled and unable to suddenly carry the mantle of marketing that had now been bestowed upon them. An unskilled workforce could hinder significantly the implementation of marketing plans and ultimately reduce service and performance levels overall.

Question 1.2

Stop for a moment and think about your own organization, or one that you are familiar with. Make a list of specific barriers to planning and the subsequent change that your chosen organization has experienced.

Why do you think these barriers were created?

See Answers and debriefing

The influence of 'change' upon the planning process

One of the most certain factors impacting upon the planning process in any organization is that of 'change' – change is a by-product of the modern-day world. Planning is now undertaken against the backdrop of constant change, internally and externally. Organizations are challenged to manage through a range of either predictable change or unexpected change, cyclical change or evolutionary change. Either way, the impact upon the organization can be significant, causing a slowdown in the strategy implementation process, or a diversion to develop an unexpected and unanticipated opportunity that it is essential to exploit and promote.

Of course, alternatively, change can mean that strategies and plans are no longer relevant or that they will no longer guarantee the levels of success that had previously been anticipated. One of the most recent examples of this is Marks and Spencer. In March 2001 they announced the closure of all their international branches outside the UK, marking a change in direction and overall strategy. As a result of a wide range of changes, Marks and Spencer had suffered considerably over the previous two years, with market share and associated profits reducing, against the tide of increasing competition in the high street and also on the Internet.

In today's rapidly changing environment, understanding the key drivers and forces will be of primary importance if an organization is going to be prepared to respond.

In essence, change means the future is unpredictable, more intense, more competitive, with shorter life cycles, shorter planning cycles and much uncertainty. In an environment where planning is a key activity, the challenges presented by change will intensify.

Activity 1.1

Taking your own organization, or one that you are familiar with, consider the various changes they have implemented over the past two years. Then think about the key drivers of that change – make a list of them.

Study tip

Nobody will be expecting you to produce a fully fledged strategic marketing plan as a result of study for this module. The learning outcome supporting this module is very focused on providing you with '*an understanding of marketing planning at an operational level*'. This 'Planning Overview' will have provided you with an insight into the relationship between corporate planning and marketing planning, and therefore the focus of your studies will relate to 'bottom-up' planning, i.e. operational level marketing, where the responsibility rests for the successful implementation of the marketing plan.

Drummond and Ensor (1999) describe 'bottom-up planning' thus:

Authority and responsibility for formulation and implementation of strategy is devolved. Senior marketing managers approve, and then monitor, agreed objectives.

Summary

As many markets reach maturity, organizations are working significantly harder to achieve and retain sustainable competitive advantage. The varying dynamics of devising strategies and plans require careful and sensitive management, as the organization, i.e. 'the corporate group' of business functions, seeks to achieve its organizational objectives.

There are many strategic marketing issues that need to be addressed in respect of the future success of an organization and its product/services portfolio. Ideally an organization will need to focus on the brand values, brand statements, customer services, supply chains and, of course, its customers and consumers.

Developing a strategy and associated plans that are innovative, competitive and sustainable is a tremendous challenge. Ultimately the most successful measure of performance is said to be customer satisfaction. Without satisfied customers the organization will struggle to remain competitive and remain at the leading edge in the marketplace, and the challenge will never be fully realized.

According to Nigel Piercy, author of *Market-Led Strategic Change*, you can tell if a company has a strategy and knows where it is going and develops the capability to get there. He suggests 'this is something that stands behind planning and systems and structure – strategy is more fundamental'.

It is therefore clear to see that strategies and plans give focus, structure, outcomes and a planned destiny for the organization. Every organization should have a pathway mapped out that takes their organization to a state of competitive strength.

In Unit 2 of this book, we look very closely at the setting of appropriate objectives, and the development of appropriate strategies, but prior to looking at this, it is essential to understand the planning framework and where it all fits together.

Unit 2
The marketing audit

Objectives

The main focus of this unit is on the development of the marketing strategy and the overall planning function. The learning outcomes associated with this unit will enable you to:

- Conduct a basic marketing audit, considering internal and external factors
- Look closely at the 'macro' and 'micro' elements of the marketplace
- Analyse internal capability
- Undertake a SWOT analysis

    (Syllabus reference 1.1.1)

This unit will serve to provide you with some of the analytical tools of the trade for ensuring that sufficient analysis is undertaken and then used to underpin the marketing decision-making process and overall strategy development.

Introduction

Having worked through the introductory unit, and the overview of the strategy and planning hierarchy, you should now have a good idea about the importance of marketing planning in giving structure and direction to marketing activities.

Principally, in the words of Dibb, Simkin, Pride and Ferrell (2001):

> *Marketing planning is a systematic process of assessing marketing opportunities and resources, determining marketing objectives and developing a thorough plan for implementation and control.*

Therefore, the overall purpose of the marketing plan, is to create a blueprint, a map, which provides detailed requirements of the company's marketing activities for the future. It serves a number of purposes:

- It provides a pathway along which a company may travel to reach its ultimate destination
- It provides time-lines for marketing activities to be achieved within, e.g. six months, 12 months, etc.
- It enables resources to be allocated efficiently and effectively to ensure high levels of performance are achieved
- It identifies strengths, weaknesses, opportunities and threats, all of which can be addressed, exploited and improved upon
- It ensures that the organization is marketing-oriented and customer-focused, ideally striving to meet customer needs, wants and expectations
- It may shape the organizational structure in order to achieve the corporate objective and marketing objectives
- It assists in the implementation and control of the marketing strategy.

Planning is fundamental to the successful implementation of strategy and achievement of objectives.

Conducting a marketing audit

The marketing audit is of pivotal importance to the planning process, as it provides the backbone analysis that supports both the **corporate and marketing decision-making process.**

Its primary objective is to ensure that the decision-making process is an informed one and that the organization is coming from a position of strength in respect of its knowledge of the marketplace, as opposed to 'planning in a vacuum'.

The audit seeks to provide information on two key aspects of the marketing environment, the external and internal environment, otherwise known as the 'macro' and 'micro environment' (Stages 1 and 2 of Figure 1.4).

Primarily the macro environment will provide information in relation to the external conditions in which the company operates, taking into account the following:

- The wider *political/legal* environment, not just on a local basis, but on a global basis. For example, the European Union, World Trade Organization, G7 countries, organizations such as NAFTA. (These will be addressed again in Unit 12, 'International marketing'.)
- Key *economic* factors – understanding key economic drivers that effect organizations' ability to achieve high performance and profitability.
- *Social/cultural* issues – this element will concentrate on demographics, population trends, birth rates, and life expectancy, changing life styles and family life cycles, the changing role of women.

One of the most significant influences on modern marketing, is the rapid evolution of new technologies. *Technological* factors are highly influential in today's environment and they enable high levels of innovation, create factors influencing competitive advantage and have enabled the implementation of more efficient and effective manufacturing processes and a wide range of scientific developments. The most radical change in our time is that of the Internet, the World Wide Web (WWW), the information superhighway, that is rapidly changing the way we all do business, broadening business horizons and opening up new opportunities.

The significance of understanding the macro environment should never be underestimated. Understanding important trends, anticipating change, forecasting the organization's future, measuring the impact of strategies and preparing alternative strategies (contingencies) will all be directed by the outcome of the macro environmental analysis.

The key words are: political/legal, economic, social/cultural, technological; they are the key environmental factors, more formally known as PEST. Other acronyms are used, such as SLEPT:

- **Social**
- **Legal**
- **Economic**
- **Political**
- **Technological.**

A further extension of this is STEEPLE:

- **Social/cultural**
- **Technological**
- **Economic/market competition**
- **Education/training and employment**
- **Political**
- **Legal**
- **Environmental protection.**

They are all a variation on a theme and while the latter is the basis for a more extensive macro environmental analysis, any one of these analytical tools will be helpful. However, the most important factor is that you understand the level of information and detail you may need to support the decision-making process.

No organization should ever underestimate the powerful force of external drivers within the marketplace, as they can ultimately hinder the success and indeed aid the failure of many organizations. Changing trends in the marketplace have often seen the demise of business. Take for example the recent downturn in electronic communications. As competition has intensified over the past months, many major corporations have been cutting jobs in a big way – see Table 2.1.

Table 2.1 Technology job cuts				
Date	Company	Job cuts	Scale of cut (%)
2 May 2001	Vitesse	150	12
1 May 2001	Loudcloud	120	19
30 April 2001	Comverse	400	6
29 April 2001	ECI	1,000	20
26 April 2001	Siemens	3,500	1
25 April 2001	Flextronics	7,000	10
24 April 2001	Agere	2,000	11
23 April 2001	Compaq	2,000	3
20 April 2001	Ericsson	12,000	11

Source –www.ft.com(Technology job cuts watch)

The statistics in Table 2.1 illustrate how companies need to respond to change, and also how many of the technology cuts are, as a result of increasing competition, driving down prices and ultimately profitability. Failure to address competitive rivalry and to strive to achieve competitive advantage and positioning could be catastrophic.

A further effect of this downturn in hi-tech industries is that banks are being hit by a meltdown in hi-tech deals. They experienced a devastating slump in business in the early part of 2001, and as a result only 50 per cent of the banking deals normally made were experienced.

However, possibly one of the most devastating events of all time had an impact of unprecedented measure, that is the events of 'September 11th 2001'. Whilst we can see that economic downturn has a significant impact upon the economy earlier in 2001, the events that took place in the United States of America did untold damage to many industries and many economies, not least of all the airline industry and the US economy, with tens of thousands of jobs being lost as a result. The impact of which is still being felt.

Again as a result of change in the environment in one industry, a range of industries subsequently have to respond also as the downturn may affect their ability to exploit new opportunities as originally planned. On the other hand the *'micro environment'* looks at a range of internal factors, which relate to the elements of the internal marketplace. Typically this will look at issues relating to marketing processes, suppliers, customers, competitors, stakeholders, and integral to this, issues relating to resourcing and financing the future marketing activities of the organization.

Should organizations fail to respond to changing marketing conditions, or underestimate the internal infrastructure that may be required to support the changing marketing conditions, then they may further fail to understand the changing needs of customers. In addition they may also fail to understand their customers' increasing expectations, which ultimately means failure to meet growth and profit-related objectives.

External forces are dynamic, the marketplace is volatile, and changes can be rapid. Today it appears that organizations face new levels of uncertainty, more significant threats, but also major opportunities. The key is being prepared to understand and analyse the market, and indeed respond to key drivers that are forcing such rapid rates of change.

There are two vital activities, therefore, that an organization should be involved in:

1. Environmental analysis
2. Environmental scanning.

Environmental analysis is the process of analysing, assessing and interpreting information collected through the environmental scanning process.

Environmental scanning is the process of actually collecting the information in order that the organization can understand relevant information in relation to external forces and drivers within the marketplace. See the following table.

Environmental assessment process

Continually scan the environment so that early changes can be identified and acted upon.	**Step 1** Scanning the environment
When change has been identified, the pace of change must be monitored so implications of the change are understood, opportunities and threats identified.	**Step 2** Monitoring
Forecasting change is difficult, but the information obtained as a result of monitoring should be used to measure the intensity of change.	**Step 3** Forecasting
Assess the impact of potential change on meeting customer requirements, and examine what opportunities change could present.	**Step 4** Assessment

Assessing the marketing environment

When undertaking an assessment of the marketing environment, there are critical areas of external information that might be useful to consider.

- *Market intelligence* – looking at change, potential, competitors and associated marketing activities.
- *Technical intelligence* – vital given the rapid evolution in today's technology. An examination of technological developments that would aid and improve production techniques, increasing quality and efficiency, but also allowing innovation and modernization, is essential.
- *Political/economic intelligence* – looking at political and economic shifts within the external environment.
- *Mergers/acquisitions intelligence* – in an era of ever-larger mergers and acquisitions between banks, IT organizations, communication networks, etc. it is vital that organizations assess the potential impact and how they might respond to it.
- *Supply chain intelligence* – what is the position of the supply chain in terms of supplies of raw materials, available resources, etc.

Assessing the marketing environment is a huge task, but of major importance to the future success of the organization.

Stage 1 – Analysis of the macro environment

In this section you will now be looking at the components of the macro environment and considering in more depth the issues relating to each element of ***SLEPT***.

There are a number of perceived benefits to the organization in undertaking such an activity:

- It aids the decision-making process and planning process
- It can provide a sound basis for change and evolution within the organization
- It provides a clear analysis of competitive activities and an understanding of related market share
- It enables organizations to anticipate the opportunities that change in the external environment might present
- Organizations may become more aware of emerging trends and opportunities in international markets that it may be appropriate to pursue
- Organizations may, as a result of the changing external environment, need to consider their resources, both financial and physical, in order that they may implement relevant change strategies
- It enables organizations both to foresee and consider the implications of environmental, regulatory and political change and to manage the implementation of such changes successfully
- It can assist organizations in forecasting potential supply and demand from the open market and from their supply chain.

The list could go on. What is important, however, is that understanding the key components of SLEPT is essential to an organization if it is to cope with change and, most important, respond to it.

Social

Understanding the social influences and implications on the marketing environment is of utmost importance, as organizations need to respond to the social infrastructure of their marketplace.

Social factors include issues such as:

- **Demography** – the characteristics of customers, age, sex, class, family life cycle etc., trends in age distribution.

> **Question 2.1**
>
> The population trends for the older generation, 'the grey market', are clearly highlighting that people are living much longer. What potential opportunities could this present to you, as marketing manager for a healthcare products manufacturer?

- *Society* – This reflects upon the infrastructure of society and its attitude towards many issues, i.e. religion, culture, families, the environment, green and ethical issues. (This will also be looked at under 'Environment'.)

  For example, there has been a serious decline in churchgoing in the UK, which would suggest the demise of the Anglican Church by the middle of this century. There are now fewer 19-year-olds going to church than at any time previously.

  In response to the 'Green Issue', vehicle manufacturers such as BMW have been stressing the suitability of their three series range for recycling, making them more environmentally friendly cars. This was in response to potential EU legislation that would likely have enforced the recycling of vehicles. BMW responded to this and now has 30 partner recycling plants worldwide. In doing this they have responded to the growing social and environmental awareness of their customers.

  Today we find ourselves subject to lively debate and forceful demonstrations about environmental issues. There is an increasing choir of consumer voices raising the stakes in respect of environmentally friendly practices. As there is growing social concern for the environment, the impact of which could be quite major to industry practices today, and ultimately upon organizational profitability in the future, organizations are being faced with change programmes as never before. The significance of understanding consumer power, customer needs and wants, is critical to organizational success, and therefore failure to react to the outcomes can have a high profile and catastrophic implications in the future. An example of this can be found in the Exxon case study, later in the unit.

- *Culture* – the range of variables relating to culture is extensive, and will be covered in more depth in Unit 12, 'International marketing', but they include:
    1. Language
    2. Religion
    3. Values and attitudes
    4. Law
    5. Healthcare
    6. Education
    7. Social organization.

This is possibly the most complex area of analysis that an organization might involve itself in. Values and norms will vary greatly from country to country, and will reflect different social divides.

For an organization involved in exploiting international marketing opportunities this is important to understand, as on occasions significant mistakes have been made by large organizations as a result of their lack of appreciation of the underpinning culture of their host nation.

Legal

In a culture bound by regulatory bodies, legal restraints and an increasing role played by European and international legislation, organizations will clearly need to understand the legislative nature of their own marketing environment and abide by it.

Every organization is bound by controls. For example, there are regulations concerning:
- Monopolies and mergers
- Competitive activities
- Unfair trading
- Consumer legislation
- Trade descriptions
- Health and safety
- Professional codes of conduct (for example, the Chartered Institute of Marketing).

Example

A recent headline suggests 'Gas giants face competition probe'. This particular probe focuses on a potential investigation into some of the world's biggest energy players and could include names such as BP, Conoco, BG International, Amerda Hess, Gas de France and International Power. The cause of the probe is the doubling of gas prices in 18 months, which have seen spot rates rise from 12p to 24p. These organizations have been asked to 'make sure that there are no anti-competitive practices going on'.

Source: *Observer*, May 2001

Economic

One of the key influences in any organization is the state of both the local economy and the global economy. There has been talk of economic slowdown in the USA and its potential to create a spiralling effect on economies all over the world. Historically, economic indicators have provided a basis for business cycles to move on to the next stage, effectively 'boom' or 'bust' (Figure 2.1). Obviously the impact of September 11th, is a classic example of how economic indicators can be affected by world events.

Figure 2.1 Business cycle model

Key component measures of the economy are:
- Inflation rates
- Interest rates

- Income levels
- Resources
- Gross National Product
- Gross Domestic Product
- Employment levels
- Exchange rates – currency valuation
- Consumer spending patterns.

As a marketer, it is important to understand economic factors and indicators and also how to use the information to aid your marketing decision-making and planning process.

For example, if there is a fluctuation in interest rates, then it is likely that your organization may be involved in considering increases in costs. Essentially this is like 'cause and effect'; as the interest rate rises, there will be a cyclical effect in the marketplace. The cost of living increases, the cost of borrowing increases and, therefore, the likelihood is that availability of disposable income may drop, reducing consumer spending considerably and thereby influencing a slow-down in market activity.

From the perspective of a marketer it is important to consider closely how to manage this particular element of economic change. You will be encouraged to consider how long it might take for the impact of an interest rate rise to filter through to organizational activity, how long the anticipated rise in interest rates is likely to last, and what might be the competitive responses to this economic change. Furthermore, you need to think about what will be the consumer response to this change and ultimately what it will do to consumer spending power.

The whole area of economic pressure and power is complex, but crucial to understanding the power of buyers and suppliers in the marketplace.

Political

The 21st century is experiencing a new kind of political power that is very broad and very diverse. With increasing moves towards emphasis on globalization, there is more and more influence from global politics and international driving forces. Both national and international governments are increasing their political weight, enforcing greater regulation of a range of industry sectors, in order that customers and organizations alike are protected from irregularities that can bring organizations into disrepute.

Political initiatives both home and abroad can create many opportunities, while also generating many threats into the political scene. There are political agendas in all areas of business; there is political influence in agriculture, mining and fuels, to name but a few. Take for example the recent Free Trade Agreement between Singapore and Japan, in January 2002. Here two significant political forces in the Far East came together to work out an agreement that would be politically, socially and economically beneficial to the two countries involved.

Additionally in March 2002, we saw other political forces at work between the USA and Europe as the EU aimed to fight its corner on tariffs introduced by the USA on the importation of European steel.

Key issues might include:

- Increases in taxation, reducing disposable income
- Environmental protection (a social and political issue)
- Employment law
- Health and safety
- Foreign trade agreements
- Stability of political systems (e.g. Middle East).

> **Example**
>
> Last year, the insurance services group 'Prudential' has found itself facing possible sanctions in America after 'snubbing' an international commission set up to trace insurance policies stolen or lost during the Holocaust.
>
> It is likely that Prudential will be warned by public finance officials from the USA that a withdrawal of funds will take place in America should the Prudential fail to join the 'commission' which is currently backed by both the American and Israeli governments.
>
> Failure by the Prudential to respond to this will see a significant impact upon any future efforts to enter the American insurance markets, as it is likely that they will find a number of obstacles to market entry that others might not experience.
>
> Source: *Observer*, May 2001

This is a prime example of potential political intervention that organizations should be aware of. A thorough analysis of the political environment is essential in order to understand the implications of failing to take account of political aspirations.

Political factors can also often impact in a cyclical manner, and the cause and effect scenario sees political influences cross-fertilizing with other elements of the external market analysis, as we can see in the case study of Exxon.

> **Case history**
>
> **Exxon**
>
> The 'Stop Esso' initiative will be launched by Bianca Jagger and is seen as a way that 'people' can make a difference, that assertion of consumer power can drive change within organizations.
>
> The National Consumer Council has suggested that 'undoubtedly consumers have the power to influence even a multinational either by causing enough embarrassment or by having sufficient impact on a company's bottom line.'
>
> Exxon has repeatedly declined to sign the Kyoto Treaty, which is designed to cut greenhouse gases in the USA by 5 per cent by 2010. While Exxon have taken this stance, competitors such as Shell and BP have acknowledged the need to combat global warming.
>
> More than 160 governments worldwide have now acknowledged links between fossil fuels and global warming, but in a recent statement Exxon condemned the promotion of scientifically unfounded scare scenarios.
>
> Esso in the UK have suggested that 'we are concerned that the obligations of the Kyoto protocol to reduce emission of greenhouse gases would impose dramatic economic costs throughout the developed world'.
>
> The 'Stop Esso' campaigners, however, insist that they will continue their protest until Exxon contributes towards the global warming issues and endorses the Kyoto Treaty.
>
> Source: *Observer*, May 2001

Exxon Mobil is the world's largest oil company, with a market value of somewhere in the region of $315bn, followed by Shell and BP Amoco. They are the third largest company in the world after Wal-Mart and GM. Esso UK is the British arm of Exxon.

Esso, the company who tells the world to 'put a tiger in your tank', could be brought to its knees by environmental pressure groups, who are effectively presenting the biggest demonstration by consumer activists since Barclays Bank were forced out of South Africa.

The biggest consumer boycott of all time was launched in May 2001, seeing Greenpeace and Friends of the Earth trying to force Esso and Exxon to abandon their opposition to the Kyoto climate change agreement. The two pressure groups concerned have 500,000 members in the UK branches alone, which is quite a powerful tool. If their initiative is successful Esso in the UK could experience a reduction in sales of more than £1 billion a year.

> **Question 2.2**
>
> What do you consider will be the long-term effect upon Exxon, if they continue to ignore the driving forces of change in the 'oil and related products' marketplace?

The demonstrations in respect of Exxon are socially motivated, as a result of political initiative on a global scale. Ultimately, there will be legal, economic, political and social consequences, should they refuse to change their policy to reflect the components of the Kyoto agreement.

Technological

Technology has evolved rapidly over the past 20 years and particularly in the past 10 years. Technological developments have seen improved manufacturing techniques, new and dynamic innovations and increases in efficiency and effectiveness in a way never previously imagined.

However, marketers need to understand the drive for technological change, and the need to go with the flow, to remain competitive. Decisions to improve, change or implement new technological processes must be made in order to meet customer needs and expectations. Principally, if there is a cost-effective method or process that could improve customer service and increase efficiency and effectiveness and add to the bottom line financially, then it should be the focus of serious research and development, in order to pursue the opportunity that technological advances might present.

External or 'macro' market analysis is vitally important to the development of any marketing strategy and associated plan. As a marketer engaged in operational level marketing, you may find yourself very involved in collating much of the intelligence gathered, in order that the decision-making process may be fully informed and responsive to the challenges of the external marketing environment. It will be important to call on previous knowledge gained through taking the Certificate in Marketing, and also to be aware of the importance of 'The Marketing Customer Interface', and 'Management Information for Marketing Decisions', in order that you fully understand the challenges of market scanning and intelligence gathering.

While on occasions you may collect information specifically related to developing strategies and plans, it is equally important to continue scanning the external environment, in order that change may be detected and subsequently responded to in a proactive rather than reactive way.

As you move on through your studies, and upwards to the Postgraduate Diploma, you will be well placed to consider the strategic implications of environmental change and how it could impact upon the strategic planning process in the future.

> **Study tip**
>
> This was the basis of the mini-case study question from the Marketing Operations examination in June 2000. This should highlight its importance as a key marketing issue.
>
> *Practise writing a report which explains, using relevant examples, the aspects of a marketing audit the Senior Brand Manager should monitor and how these factors may be summarized into a SWOT analysis.*

Stage 2 – Analysis of the micro environment

Analysis of the 'micro' environment is equally important; as a marketing manager you must clearly understand the issues relating specifically to your organization.

For example, you will need to consider the following components:

- Sales
- Market share
- Marketing procedures
- Profit margins
- Sales/marketing controls
- Marketing mix
- Number of employees
- Financial resources
- Physical resources
- Production – capacity and variety.

Each of these factors will in some way affect the organization's overall achievements in terms of the key marketing objectives of meeting both the needs of customers and the organization's profit requirements.

A more simplistic approach to this analysis will be to break it down into the following five key elements:

- Business
- Competitors
- Suppliers
- Customers
- Stakeholders.

Business/marketing function

When developing marketing strategies and devising marketing plans, organizations need to consider very closely the internal prerequisites for success.

In this instance, it is essential that organizations develop a strategy that primarily meets the needs, wants and expectations of their customers and that they have the resources and infrastructure within the organization to deliver their promises and meet their corporate and marketing objectives.

Ultimately, a culture appropriate to customer demands must be in place, i.e. a marketing-oriented customer-focused culture, with the customer at the centre of the business, as expressed by the Chief Executive of 'easyJet' in Unit 1.

In doing this, serious consideration should also be given to the 'internal' customer. When a newly devised strategy indicates significant change, then the reactions, attitudes and abilities of the workforce must be considered, managed and adapted to meet the overall objectives of the organization.

In order to achieve this, a tightly defined strategy must be designed, which ensures that management, research and development, production, logistics, physical and financial resources are working to the same end and 'synergy' must be prevalent in the planning process. Without the appropriate mix of resources across the organizational business functions, the corporate goals may not be achieved.

Therefore analysis of each of these functions should be considered. Undertaking a company capability profile is therefore of the essence.

A full audit should be undertaken, with full consideration being given to the following factors:

- **Managerial factors**
    - Corporate image
    - Speed of response to changing conditions
    - Flexibility of the organization
    - Entrepreneurial orientation
    - Ability to attract and retain highly creative people
    - Aggressiveness in meeting competition.
- **Competitive factors**
    - Product strengths
    - Customer loyalty and satisfaction
    - Market share
    - Use of the life cycle
    - Investment in R&D
    - High barriers to market entry
    - Advantage taken of market potential
    - Customer concentration
    - Low selling and distribution costs.
- **Financial factors**
    - Access to capital when required
    - Ease of exit from the market
    - Liquidity
    - Degree of financial leverage
    - Ability to compete on prices
    - Capital investment versus capacity to meet demand
    - Stability of costs
    - Ability to sustain effort in cyclic demand
    - Elasticity of price.
- **Technical factors**
    - Technical and manufacturing skills
    - Resource and personnel utilization

- Strength of patents and processes
- Value added to product
- Intensity of labour to produce product
- Economies of scale
- Newness of plan
- Application of new technologies
- Level of co-ordination and integration.

One way of undertaking this form of analysis is grading these areas from 1 to 5, with 1 being weak and 5 being strong. Clearly any particular element that falls under the level of 3 requires urgent attention, while factors being above 3 demonstrate room for continuous improvement.

This type of analysis is vital to the success of organizations and will ultimately enable you to identify key strengths and weaknesses, opportunities and threats within your own environment.

It is of primary importance to undertake an 'audit' of the actual 'audit process' itself, the marketing objectives and plans and the overall marketing activity including the effective integration of the marketing mix.

Marketing managers will have some responsibility for adopting existing practices and modifying plans, in order that these factors are taken into consideration at the implementation stage.

Competitors

> **Definition**
>
> *Competition*
>
> Those companies marketing products that are similar to, or can be substituted for, a given business's products in the same geographic area. (Dibb, Simkin, Pride and Ferrell, 2001, p. 56)

Very few, if any, organizations exist in isolation of competition. You have already seen, earlier in this unit, some of the effects of competition in relation to the high tech electronics industries, where as a result of intense competition, profits have declined, resulting in massive job cuts across the industry as a whole.

From the perspective of a marketing manager, in order to truly ascertain the full force of the external environment, you must consider the influence of competitive forces upon the external marketplace and your own organization. Therefore a competitor analysis is essential.

There are many components to competitive activity, and in marketing terms competitive strategies can be quite ferocious in attack. From a strategy development perspective you will probably be familiar with terms such as 'guerilla attacks' and 'offensive attacks', which indicate some of the fighting talk that underpins competitive behaviour.

In order that your organization can respond to competitor attacks, you must be familiar with the profile of your competitors and therefore must analyse their activities and behaviour quite closely.

Ultimately, competitor attacks can provide the basis of significant threats to the successful implementation of the corporate and marketing strategy.

Typical competitor analysis should include a review of the following elements:
- Marketing capabilities
- Technical capabilities

- Management capabilities
- Production capabilities
- Innovation and design capabilities.

Clearly you will need to align your own strengths and weaknesses against those of your competitors in order to identify areas of improvement in your own organization.

One of the key tools for undertaking this is a 'Company capability profile', as previously discussed. You could do this, by undertaking a SWOT analysis on your competitor. This is covered in more detail shortly, but as you will see when looking at it, there are possibilities of mapping your own capability against that of your competitors. You could potentially grade each of the components within an element and then grade your own organization against it. Not only would this provide you with a basis of understanding your competitor, but also it would highlight any opportunities to exploit their weaknesses and attack their strengths.

The main focus of most competitive attacks is on price. Competitive warfare today is most prevalent in the retail sector, with intense competition between supermarkets, making high profile headlines on a regular basis. A further example is financial services, where competition in respect of services and products offered continues to intensify on a day-to-day basis.

Case history

Time Extra!

One of the most intensively competitive markets is that of PCs. Recently PC World were threatened when Time Computers announced it was to stock other computer brands in a new venture, branded Time Extra, which it would be launching to rival PC World.

Time sealed deals with other major manufacturers, including Hewlett-Packard and Fujitsu, to sell over 1,500 products through three major channels.

Time Extra introduced a range of concessions to be rolled out in 200 UK Time Computer stores.

Over £2 million was invested on a press campaign with TV ads due to follow. The company plans to spend £30 million on marketing over the next year.

Their aim: 'customers will be able to get the best products at the lowest prices through Time Extra.'

This is a prime example of intense competition.

Source: *Marketing Week*, November 2000

In the same way that the macro environment needs continually scanning, competition needs continually monitoring. Competitor monitoring will ultimately allow organizations to identify competitor strategies clearly, enabling them to make pre-emptive strikes as opposed to reactionary measures. It may in some instances mean continual adjustment of the marketing plan, in order that competitive advantage is retained.

Porter's Five Forces – competitive analysis

It is imperative for you as a marketer to have a clear understanding not just of your competitor, but of the nature of the competitive environment, particularly if you are to succeed in developing a sustainable competitive advantage and be able to respond from a position of strength to competitor attacks.

The objectives of any organization will relate closely to profit margins, increasing market share, diversification or market penetration. In order that an organization can define the future direction of its corporate and marketing strategy, it is of primary importance that it should consider the nature of the driving forces within the marketplace, in order to understand exactly what is shaping the industry. Therefore when undertaking a micro analysis it is important that you consider the components of Porter's Forces and understand either the potential threats from within the marketplace, or the profit potential of the industry.

Porter's Five Forces model (see Figure 2.2) will be particularly helpful when undertaking a competitor analysis within the existing marketing environment. It provides a framework for an analysis of a range of micro-factors, which enables industry attractiveness to be measured and also helps organizations understand the complexity of the markets in which they operate.

Figure 2.2 The five forces model (Adapted from M. E. Porter, Competitive Strategy, The Free Press, 1980: © The Free Press/Macmillan)

The threat of competitive rivalry

Competitive rivalry within the marketplace is highly intense. Intense competition has, over the years, changed the shape of a number of industries, and as a result there has been an increasing number of mergers and acquisitions to ensure that major players within the marketplace maintain market share and superior positioning. This has been particularly prevalent in the financial services sectors, with a number of mergers between key players in the banking sector, e.g. Royal Bank of Scotland and the Halifax.

In the mining industry, concerns have been voiced as the Australian mining group BHP considered mergers with Billiton, the UK mining group (May 2001). Their aim is to create the largest diversified mining group in the world. By joining forces, they will eradicate larger forces of competition in the marketplace, and take significantly higher market share than currently achievable between the two; the long-term profits also look exceptionally healthy.

We have already seen that competition can take various shapes, as in the case of Time. Competition can be cut-throat, with ongoing price wars, as have been experienced in recent years in the food retail industry, while at the other end of the scale, competition can appear to be non-existent. However, while rivalry might seem healthy, it can have both positive and negative effects.

Organizations who succeed in competition, possibly increasing market share, through a range of activities, potentially experience a rise in profit. However, the reverse may happen; the organization might increase market share, but at the expense of their profit margins.

Key factors influencing competitive rivalry will be identified when undertaking the competitor analysis as already suggested, but key components might be:

- Stage of the product life cycle of competing products
- Use of specialized production techniques
- Liquidity of competitor
- Ability to achieve differentiation and brand loyalty
- Competitor intentions
- The relative size of the competitor
- Barrier of exit from the industry.

Understanding the balance of various forces is critical to ensuring that the organization makes the correct competitive response.

Bargaining power of suppliers

The key components of this particular element of Porter's Five Forces emphasizes the following key points:

- *The strength of the supplier brand* – i.e. is it a brand that all like organizations will want to exploit, and will this therefore increase the price of supplies?
- *The source of supply spans only a small number of suppliers* – i.e. limited sources provide the supplier with a supply and demand component in their favour: the more limited the demand, the higher the price they can charge.
- *Switching supplier* – the cost of switching suppliers can be quite high: negotiation of new contracts, establishing relationships and developing trust all cost time and resource. This can act as a deterrent to many organizations, who will want to retain their relationship with their supplier.
- *Substitute products of suppliers* – are there appropriate substitute products available?
- *Forward integration* – the threat of suppliers establishing their own production facilities.

Bargaining power of buyers

The bargaining power of buyers is likely to be quite strong in the following instances:

- *Where few buyers control a large volume of the market* – a good example of this might be that larger players in the electrical goods industry can buy large volumes of products based on economies of scale and can pass these reductions on to their customers.
- *Where there are a large number of smaller suppliers fighting for a share of the market* – again the retail industry would be a classic example of this, particularly in the food sector, i.e. grocery and meat products.
- *The cost of switching supplier is low* – the retail sector and high street are a good example of how customers who are not brand loyal will swap around to gain the best deal. This can happen where the relationship between customer and supplier is not based upon loyalty.
- *The supplier's product is a mass-market product and not necessarily differentiated* – e.g. where there are many variations on the same theme, for example, toothpaste, soft drinks, etc.

- *Strong customer power* – this involves knowledge of the market and where to attain the best deal.
- *Threat of backward vertical integration* – where the buyer goes back to the supplier, cutting out the middle man.

The threat for potential entrants

This issue looks at the obstacles to entering new markets:

- *Economies of scale* – existing organizations often have economies of scale and therefore new entrants will struggle to achieve the same competitive economies in the short/medium term.
- *Access to new distribution channels* – it may be difficult to gain access to the appropriate distribution channels, due to competitive operations and networks in the marketplace.
- *Brand loyalty* – in a brand-loyal market it might be difficult to attract new customers and therefore marketing spend could be quite considerable.
- *Capital investment* – it can be cash intensive to enter into new markets and require high levels of investment – from a competitive perspective, this would actually weaken your initial position, unless you are a cash-rich organization.
- *Competitor retaliation* – it is likely that competitors will follow suit quite closely behind, therefore competitive rivalry could be highly intensive.
- *Regulatory influence* – what is the position in respect of fair competition, monopolies and mergers. The case of Microsoft is a clear example of trying to prevent competitive rivalry.

Threat of substitutes

- *A new product or service equivalent* – a directly equivalent product, from a differing brand, may have a competitive influence. This is typical of the evolution of 'home brands', e.g. supermarket brands as a substitute in soft drinks, breakfast cereals, etc.
- *A new product replacing an existing product* – for example the DVD player replacing the VHS video player or cassette tapes being replaced by compact discs.
- *Consumer substitution* – consumer choice can be the basis of a threat, when the consumer is willing to search for substitute products; for example, when the consumer chooses a new kitchen over a new car.

Essentially the Porter framework is an opportunity for the organization to understand the holistic range of driving forces in the micro environment, which they can clearly link to the macro analysis, i.e. the SLEPT/PEST analysis.

From an audit perspective, whereby information is being collected in order that key marketing decisions are made and strategies developed, it will enable the organization to consider ultimately the following factors, that will in turn enable a full SWOT analysis to be developed, to inform the strategy development process.

- What is the likelihood of change in the marketplace, both on a macro and micro scale and what is driving that particular change?
- What is the likely response that the organization can make, in order to retain sustainable competitive advantage in the marketplace – how can they develop their weaknesses and turn them into strengths and their threats into opportunity? Ultimately what is their competitive response likely to be?
- What is the likely response of their competitor in the marketplace – how are the driving forces affecting them, what might be their likely approach – what might it do to their competitive positioning overall?

As a marketer you must consider what the likely response of your organization might be – will it be certain retaliation – will you compete on an aggressive basis, if so what is the likely challenge that you will be presented with?

A further consideration will be what will happen if you fail to act, fail to compete aggressively. What will it do to your market share, your customer base? Will you see a loss of long-term customer relationships, will your brand loyalty be challenged, will your bottom line be challenged?

Reacting competitively does not just mean reducing prices or increasing sales promotions, it means looking at the bigger picture of increased marketing budget, diversification, new product strategies, to name but a few. The biggest failing of many organizations is to attack what is an overt competitive hit by competitors, but to continue blissfully unaware of the competitive activity that is being orchestrated behind closed doors. This will then hit the organization from behind, it will not be ready for the attack, and will then have to develop a reactive marketing approach, as opposed to a pre-emptive marketing strike.

Failure to observe competitive actions will mean inconsistency in competitor attack. Losing sight of the competitor will give them a position of strength and they will ultimately be unpredictable, preventing a continuous competitive reaction from your organization.

Finally, organizations should never be complacent, and as a marketing manager, you should not be lulled into a false sense of security by the continuous monitoring of existing competition. All organizations, without exception, should also be on the look out for new entrants to the markets, who could potentially offer a competitive proposition with the development of the same or substitute products. Therefore, competitive monitoring in line with environmental scanning are critical components of a successful marketing oriented organization.

Suppliers

Supplier relationships are a further critical component to the success of any organization. It is of primary importance to many organizations to ensure consistent supplies flowing through in order to provide consistent demand for their products. Therefore, supplier analysis is vital.

This should include a review of the following:

- The basis of the supplier relationship
- The supply and demand components of raw materials
- Supplier innovations
- The relationship suppliers have with competitors
- Supply record – i.e. ability to deliver and meet demand on an ongoing basis
- Liquidity and financial stability
- Costs
- Quality
- Warranty provision
- Supply trends
- Any potential change to the supply environment – new entrants.

There is more discussion of supplier relationships in Unit 9, 'Managing marketing relationships'.

Customers

As already indicated and highlighted in the case of easyJet in Unit 1, customers should be at the centre of any business. Organizations should be customer focused, meeting customer needs and managing to deal with the evolution of ever-increasing customer power.

It is essential that customers are analysed; we must know who they are, where they are, what they are, what they want, when and how they want it. The sole focus of the marketing effort should be based around meeting customer expectations, the idea being that as an organization you can provide the right product, at the right price, communicated through the right medium and distributed to the right place at the right time.

While undertaking the Advanced Certificate in Marketing, your studies will focus on other modules, including 'Management information for marketing decisions'. Here you will look very closely at the concept of using information about your customers to support the marketing decision-making process. In addition, 'Marketing customer interface' will focus very much on the psychology of the customer, buyer behaviour, the necessity to understand the strategic importance of the customer, marketing segmentation and market research. Both these modules will underpin the analysis of customers and their buying behaviour.

The important aspect of understanding customers is being able to respond and react and to remain competitive for them, in order that you retain them as customers in the long term.

Ultimately, once customers have been segmented into particular market groups, then they can be targeted with a tailored marketing mix that meets their individual demands.

Once again this will require marketers to ensure that the infrastructure of human, physical and financial resources is in place to underpin the customer experience.

Stakeholders

The role of stakeholders in any organization seems to have an increasing influence on the way in which organizations can do business. The mini-case study on Exxon highlights how environmental pressure groups actually strive to influence the future direction of the organization overall.

Stakeholders include:

- Customers
- Suppliers
- Shareholders
- Employees
- Financiers
- Wider social community (including pressure groups).

Stakeholder influences and expectation should be understood. In the Exxon case, it would appear that they might have underestimated the potential power of the 'wider social community' and the pressure that they may bring to bear upon the organization. It is vital that the organization understands the balance of power and influence that various stakeholders might have.

For example, in many organizations, shareholders play a vital role in the decision-making process. The pending de-mutualization of Friends Provident, or the merger between the Halifax and the Royal Bank of Scotland, is reliant on the vote of the shareholders for the planned changes to succeed.

In order that your organization can provide the basis for strong relationships with stakeholders, it is necessary to understand the balance of power that they hold so that appropriate marketing mix strategies and indeed marketing communications strategies can be developed to keep them informed of the proposed changes. Effectively, you will need to know how influential they are, and how controllable they are. Currently in the case of Exxon, the demonstrations could do untold damage to the business, should Exxon fail to respond to the treaty while competitors work towards meeting the objectives of it.

For both the 'macro' and 'micro' environment, analysis is essential, as is monitoring and reacting to changes. It is important that organizations are not just reactive, but that they are proactive, managing the components in the 'micro' environment, to provide the basic infrastructure for an organization to meet the demands of its customers and the marketing environment.

There is a key marketing tool that we can use to help us bring the main elements and components of the marketing analysis together. It is commonly known as the SWOT analysis.

SWOT analysis

A SWOT analysis draws together key strengths, weaknesses, opportunities and threats that have been derived as a result of the marketing audit, i.e. the 'macro' and 'micro' analysis and assessment.

SWOT, alternatively known as 'WOTS-UP' analysis, is an important tool in enabling organizations to distil the findings of the audit into a more cohesive and succinct model. It is essential that it is used for this purpose and that it is seen as an addition to the marketing audit, not a replacement (Figure 2.3).

Strengths   Weaknesses

← CONVERT

Internal

Strengths	Weaknesses
Financial resources Product portfolio Economies of scale Technical capability Management ability Innovative design Profitability R & D Marketing intelligence	Lack of skilled labour High workforce turnover Lack of financial investment Poor internal communications Lack of management commitment Supplier relationships Lack of resources Management weaknesses Over-capacity
Global markets Investment opportunities Diversification Technology innovation Internet High quality products	Global markets Competitive activity Competitive investment Supplier desertion Substitute products Market saturation Resistance to change

External

Opportunities   Threats

← CONVERT

Figure 2.3 SWOT analysis

Figure 2.3 highlights some of the issues that you might include within a SWOT analysis and that might have been derived from the marketing audit.

The aim of the SWOT process is to enable you to *convert* weaknesses into strengths and threats into opportunities, by taking remedial action to improve existing situations and plan a programme of ongoing continuous change. Where an organization is weak in respect of a skilled workforce then it is essential that training is identified as a key objective of the internal marketing strategy and that this is underpinned by financial investment and resource.

When undertaking a SWOT analysis, you should also be aware of the differences between controllable and uncontrollable. Essentially the controllable areas are those relating to internal issues. By and large your organization does have control on 'micro' issues relating to technology, skills, investment, resources, innovations, morale, motivation, etc.

External factors, however, are often uncontrollable, and while you might be able influence their outcomes you will not be able to control it. When establishing future opportunities and how to improve upon weaknesses, you will be required to work on the controllable variables, i.e. that which you can change.

> **Question 2.3**
>
> Undertake a SWOT analysis of your own organization or one you know well, highlighting the key components of each element. Suggest how you might turn weaknesses into strengths and how you could potentially reduce the threats that affect your organization.
>
> *See Answers and debriefing*

As you can see, undertaking a marketing audit is a major task, not only in terms of the volume of analysis to be undertaken and the concepts, elements and components which you are required to understand, but also in ultimately putting the outcome of the audit into the context of strategy development and planning.

A marketer's responsibility might be to ensure that scanning and monitoring of the environment is constant and undertaken regularly. In turn, the outcomes should be used to maximize the potential of the marketing programme and adaptation of the marketing mix should be undertaken. Furthermore, remedial actions have to be taken to overcome any areas of weaknesses identified that may ultimately reduce the bottom line of the organization.

The marketing audit should not be ad hoc, but planned, co-ordinated, structured and pre-determined in nature, context and content. Without key objectives, and a planned approach taken, the marketing audit could be too extensive, too complex and ultimately meaningless, and therefore wasteful in the extreme. The marketing audit process can be costly and therefore a structured approach is an absolute.

Identifying key opportunities

Having undertaken the planned and objective audit process, you should now be armed with considerable information that will assist you in establishing the potential marketing strategy for the organization to pursue.

A marketing opportunity provides the organization with the opening to venture into new territory, perhaps a new target market, or diversification opportunity, or indeed the opportunity to launch a new product into the marketplace.

The **Ansoff** matrix (Figure 2.4) provides an opportunity for an organization to think creatively about its future, about how it can take a strength and make it a key success factor or driving force for a successful outcome in the marketplace. Principally the Ansoff matrix allows you to consider a range of four strategic options:

- Product development
- Market development
- Diversification
- Market penetration.

Products

	Existing	New
Existing	Market penetration — Low cost flights	Product development
New	Market development — Increase number of handling airports	Diversification — Hire cars, Internet cafe, Hotels

Markets

Figure 2.4 Ansoff matrix – 'easy everything' (easyJet)

The 'Easy Group' started off with the core activity of providing low-cost flights into Europe. This is their core business, and with over 18 million passengers a year flying easyJet, the Easy Group needed to establish alternative options in order that the business could grow and expand.

The Easy Group has taken a threefold route. While continuing with penetrating the existing air trasport market with low-cost flights, it is also developing the market potential to include greater accessibility of easyJet flights by increasing the number of airports handling easyJet passengers.

While flights are the core business of the Easy Group, a complementary diversification programme has been entered into, in order that a 'travel solutions' package is made available to meet the whole range of customer needs and expectations of both frequent and holiday travellers. The travel solutions business is aimed at both the corporate and consumer sectors of the business.

You can see here that taking the key strengths and opportunities available to the Easy Group, they have established a further growth strategy, which includes further market penetration, market development and diversification into new, but compatible areas of the business.

It is important to consider the basis of Ansoff at this point, by way of illustrating how you can identify core strengths and opportunities and then develop them into potential strategies. However, we will return to this in Unit 3, 'Marketing planning, implementation and control', as we consider the process of developing marketing objectives and strategies and ultimately defining the strategy and developing the plan to underpin overall achievement of objectives.

Summary

As a result of studying through this unit, you will hopefully have a clear perspective of the importance of undertaking a thorough, structured and objective marketing audit, in order to understand the marketing environment in which your organization operates.

It is of primary importance that both macro and micro factors are analysed and that subsequently a clearly defined strategy is developed based on sound management information. This will allow reliable forecasts to be derived that represent anticipated market share and future potential sales.

While it is essential to understand the macro environment, the micro environmental issues must be addressed so that an organization is well poised to respond to changing market conditions. An organization should analyse in depth the issues related to their internal relationships, customer relationships, supplier relationships and stakeholder relationships and ultimately must be prepared for the demands that each might place upon the organization.

Additionally it will be of considerable importance to ensure that the organization has the capacity to respond to the driving force of change, by creating an appropriate infrastructure. The infrastructure should be based on highly skilled employees, appropriate levels of financial investment, adequate resources and technological soundness, ultimately ensuring that the customer is at the centre of the business and that the organization is marketing oriented and customer focused.

The marketing audit is a vital ingredient of the overall strategy and planning hierarchy and process that organizations must successfully develop to underpin the corporate objectives and goals.

Further study and examination preparation

Question 2.4

June 2000, Question 1a

Go to www.marketingonline.co.uk or www.bh.com/marketing to access Specimen Answers and Senior Examiner's advice for this exam question.

Earlier in this unit, a study tip was given highlighting the importance of this area in respect of marketing operations.

Undertake Question 1a. Read the mini-case study carefully, and take on the role of Marketing Manager for Dulux and address the issues associated with the marketing audit and SWOT analysis.

June 2001, Question 2

In the role of a Marketing Analyst in a pharmaceutical company of your choice, produce a report for the Marketing Manager, which indicates how the micro environment has changed in the past 10 years and what future trends are likely. You should highlight those factors which particularly need to be taken into account when developing the long-term marketing plan.

> **Study tip**
>
> A few helpful websites for marketing audit activities
> www.ft.com
> www.tradepartners.co.uk
> www.ecola.com
> www.economist.com
> www.asiannet.com
> www.cbw.com/busbj
> www.dti.com
> www.mad.co.uk

Unit 3
Marketing planning, implementation and control

Objectives

In this unit, the focus will be on *developing marketing objectives and marketing plans*. The learning outcomes associated with this unit are:

- Developing marketing objectives and strategies
- Developing marketing objectives as simple goal statements with links to the mission statement
- Understanding how marketing strategy defines target markets (from segmentation bases and profiles), and achieving differential advantage and desired brand positioning
- Gap analysis and the Ansoff matrix
- Implementation of the marketing plan
- Barriers to implementation
- Allocations of budgets, tasks and responsibilities
- Control implications
- Alternative ways of managing marketing activities including internal marketing implications.

(Syllabus reference 1.1.2 and 1.1.3)

This unit will provide you with basics in order to understand the process of marketing planning at an operational level, and also be able to develop marketing objectives and plans at an operational level.

Introduction

In Unit 2, the concentration was on the need to undertake a planned marketing audit, so that that we clearly understood the nature and context of an organization's marketing environment.

Clearly, the marketing audit plays a pivotal role in underpinning both the corporate and marketing planning processes, effectively feeding information from the 'bottom-up' in the organization to support the corporate decision-making process.

In this unit, the focus will be on stages 4 and 5 of Figure 1.4, which has been included in former chapters. Next we will move on to look at issues associated with implementation within the organization.

In any organization, there are three key questions to be asked in ascertaining the vision and direction for the future:

Where are we now?	Stage 1 & 2 – Marketing audit
Where are we going?	Stages 3 & 4 – Marketing strategy
How are we going to get there?	Stage 5 – Marketing plan

Planning horizons

One of the major considerations expected from strategies and plans is the time horizon. In today's marketing environment, while the ideal is to have a predetermined plan for the long term, in some environments this is becoming increasingly difficult, as we have seen, in particular, in the hi-tech industries.

Typical planning horizons	
Short-term	1–3 years
Medium-term	3–5 years
Long-term	5 years and beyond

In many organizations there is an obvious friction between long-term and short-term planning horizons. In the main, short-term planning drives marketing activities at an operational level. However, the real conflict lies in the fact that it is often difficult to establish the impact that short-term objectives might have on long-term strategies. Because marketing is subject to many changes, it is fairly typical for organizations to work on the basis of short-term objectives, short-term budgeting arrangements and short-term resource allocations. Therefore, for objectives to be strategic in nature, they should be developed within a long-term timeframe. Obviously, these planning horizons will vary from writer to writer and organization to organization (see Figure 1.4).

How to take the marketing audit to the planning process

The principal objective of the marketing audit is to provide an indication of potential opportunities and threats that might exist within the marketplace, and ultimately enable the organization to move on to develop their marketing objectives and strategies.

The most effective way of providing a more succinct approach to the audit is to produce a SWOT analysis, which highlights very specific areas that should potentially be addressed through the planning process.

Essentially the analysis produced in Unit 2 highlighted some of the possible SWOT components that might be an outcome of the audit process, i.e. strengths, weaknesses, opportunities and threats.

To assist the planning process, the SWOT analysis should be substantiated with background information that underpins it and gives considerably more detail on the potential opportunities or even pitfalls that might arise in respect of developing future strategies.

Making assumptions can be a useful activity so that the organization can conceptualize the potential that a particular opportunity might present or indeed what the effect might be of not exploiting it. An organization might make assumptions based around competitive practices in relation to price levels and promotional activities or perhaps the introduction of a new product range or an addition to the product portfolio. For example, it is possible that launching a new product range will produce an anticipated growth at a rate of 10 per cent per year for two years and 15 per cent thereafter.

It is recommended that as few assumptions are made as possible, and that they are based on solid management information attained through the audit process.

> **Question 3.1**
>
> In what way does the SWOT analysis assist the planning process?

Stage 3 – The setting of objectives

As a result of the SWOT analysis and any subsequent assumptions made as a result of the marketing audit, the organization is now in the position of considering realistic marketing objectives, i.e. establishing 'where they are going'. It is hoped that these objectives will go a significant way to underpinning and achieving the corporate goals. One of the key issues relating to setting objectives is ensuring their relevance to achieving the corporate vision and mission.

Objectives should be widely understood by the organization and closely related to the organization's financial, physical and human resource capability.

Setting objectives within the organization is central to its overall effectiveness and its ability to achieve high level performance. In the words of Dibb, Simkin, Pride and Ferrel (2001):

A marketing objective is a statement of what is to be accomplished through marketing activities.

An objective is something that you want to achieve and it should have the SMART components illustrated in the following table.

S	**Specific** – objectives should be descriptive, succinct and provide clarity throughout the organization as to what is to be achieved
M	**Measurable** – objectives should clearly state tangible targets that can be measured in the future
A	**Aspirational** – objectives should be challenging but achievable, motivational and not demoralizing
R	**Realistic** – objectives should be based on sound market analysis. Financial, human and physical resources should underpin the objectives
T	**Timebound** – A timescale should be set against the achievement of each objective in order for performance measurement to be undertaken

The basis of SMART objectives is that they are simplistic, quantifiable and therefore easier to measure, monitor and control.

Primary objectives

In the first instance, many organizations will set primary objectives. These are expressed in financial terms. For example:

- To achieve 15 per cent return on equity
- To increase operating profit by 25 per cent
- To achieve ROCE of 22 per cent
- To achieve 10 per cent growth in earnings per share.

Profitability on its own is insufficient, as the key principle behind profit is ensuring that the original capital invested is being paid back at a percentage rate every year, so that ultimately the organization can then be more profit-oriented.

Non-financial objectives

While financial objectives are vitally important at the corporate level, so are non-financial objectives. For example, we have seen that many organizations have to adjust their strategies and plans in order to survive is a time of intense competition across a number of industry sectors. Therefore functional and operational objectives need to be defined in order that survival is achievable.

Functional objectives may read as follows:

- Human resources function – to increase highly-skilled element of workforce by 10 per cent
- To increase training provision to the organization by 10 per cent

- Operations function – to increase productivity by 10 per cent
- To introduce new technology programme by June 2002.

As a marketer your job is to define marketing objectives to further underpin corporate objectives in order that corporate goals might be achieved.

Marketing objectives

Marketing objectives in the main are about products and markets only. Do not get confused about marketing *objectives* being set directly in relation to pricing and advertising. Service levels are the *means* by which objectives are achieved, rather than objectives in themselves.

It is likely therefore that marketing objectives will focus on:

- Increasing sales of existing products into existing markets
- Launching new product ranges into existing markets
- Launching existing products into new markets
- Launching new products into new markets.

Then transfer these concepts into objectives and you may see some of the following quantifiable and measurable objectives. Below is a list of examples highlighting some possible objectives that could be set by an organization:

- To increase sales of the 'X' product range into the existing marketplace by 10 per cent by December 2002
- To launch Product 'Y' into China by October 2003, providing a sales turnover of £5 million by October 2004
- Increase market share of Product 'A' by 20 per cent by June 2005
- To increase customer retention by 30 per cent by June 2003.

Programme/subsidiary objectives

In particular, these relate to objectives specifically focused around the marketing sub-function, or marketing activities. This is most closely related to the marketing mix. You will note that in the Planning Process model (Figure 1.4), Stage 5 reflects upon the marketing mix, therefore these are more tactical objectives. For example, in this area, you will find specific objectives relating to pricing, the promotional mix, distribution elements or product mix requirements.

Each of these subsidiary objectives is developed specifically in relation to achieving a 'higher' level marketing objective.

For example, where an objective relates to 'penetrating the existing market and increasing market share by 10 per cent', a subsidiary objective might be to drive prices down, therefore a pricing objective may then read 'to reduce prices by 10 per cent to increase marketing penetration by June 2001'.

Whilst the focus on setting objectives will be based around 'marketing', it is essential that at a corporate level, objectives are balanced – i.e. that corporate objectives reflect across the whole organization, the idea being that the whole organization integrates, works together, consistently and with synergy, to achieve corporate goals.

Having an understanding of the 'balanced scorecard' approach to setting objectives and ensuring a balance is achieved is important.

The balanced scorecard

Figure 3.1 The balanced scorecard. (Adapted from Kaplan and Norton, 1993, 1996)

The balanced scorecard (see Figure 3.1) is a management system developed by Robert S. Kaplan and David P. Norton. The balanced scorecard provides a key link between setting objectives and measuring performance. It is a management system that provides a channel whereby abilities and knowledge held by personnel throughout the organization can be used towards achieving long-term goals.

Kaplan and Norton suggested that a balanced set of objectives should be developed and, at the same time, a complementary set of performance measures could be set alongside them.

Primarily, the balanced scorecard is a tool that guides performance and identifies key measurements in four categories:

- Financial perspective
- Customer perspective
- Internal perspective
- Innovation and learning perspective.

Financial performance

This closely aligns with the financial objectives you have already seen, i.e. it looks at factors such as those shown in Table 3.1.

Table 3.1 Adapted from Kaplan Norton (1992, 1996) and Drummond and Ensor (1999)

Strategic Objectives	Strategic Measures
Return on capital	ROCE
Cash flow	Cash flow
Profitability	Net margin
Profitability growth	Volume growth rate versus industry
Reliability of performance	Profit forecast reliability
	Sales backing

Ideally the role of the 'financial' perspective relates to seeing how the business might look in the eyes of the shareholders (i.e. stakeholder influences). The proposed strategic measures subsequently ensure both the success of the organization's strategy and also its implementation overall.

The customer perspective

Understanding the basis of the customer perspective (see Table 3.2) is vitally important, as this element reflects how the customer might perceive the business, in particular, issues such as relationships, quality, service and performance levels overall.

Table 3.2 Adapted from Kaplan and Norton (1992, 1996) and Drummond and Ensor (1999)

Strategic Objectives	Strategic Measures
Marketing share	Reflecting the proportion of business acquired in a given market (volume per customer)
Customer satisfaction	Monitoring performance criteria such as customer satisfaction index Mystery shopping
Customer retention	Tracking customers, measuring the rate at which the business retains customers or maintains ongoing relationships
Customer profitability (value for money)	Measuring the net profit of a customer, segment or target market
Customer acquisition	Measuring the rate at which a business attracts new customers

Internal perspective

The internal perspective (see Table 3.3) looks very closely at the implementation of essential internal processes required to meet customer needs and achieve ultimate customer satisfaction. The focus of this particular area will be providing the organization with the specific human resources, physical resources required and competence in order that customer satisfaction might be achieved.

This area will focus on the functional aspects of the organization:

- Marketing
- Manufacturing
- Logistics
- Quality.

Given below is an example on the basis of some possible strategic objectives and the potential strategic measures that could be implemented.

One of the key benefits of the balanced scorecard is its ability to ensure that not only objectives are developed, but also associated performance measures, by which an organization can monitor and control its achievement.

Table 3.3 Adapted from Kaplan and Norton (1992, 1996) and Drummond and Ensor (1999)

Strategic Objectives	Strategic Measures
Marketing	
Product and service development	Pioneer percentage of product portfolio
Shape customer requirements	Hours with customers on new work
Manufacturing	
Lower manufacturing cost	Total expenses per unit versus competition
Improve project management	Safety incident index
Logistics	
Reduce delivery costs	Delivered cost per unit
Inventory management	Inventory level compared to plan and output rate
Quality	Zero defects

Innovation and learning perspective

One of the key success factors of organizations today is their ability to be innovative and involve themselves in a programme of continuous improvement (see Table 3.4). This should be both in terms of business processes, manufacturing processes, research and development, product development and services delivery.

Therefore it is essential that innovation-led objectives are developed in order that an organization can strive to achieve sustainable competitive advantage in the marketplace.

Furthermore, it is of primary importance that the organization is seen to be a 'learning' organization.

Table 3.4 Adapted from Kaplan and Norton (1992, 1996) and Drummond and Ensor (1999)

Strategic Objectives	Strategic Measures
Innovate products and services	Percentage revenue from pioneer products
Time to market	Cycle time versus industry norm
Empowered workforce	Staff attitude survey
Access to strategic information	Strategic information availability
Continuous improvement	Number of employee suggestions

The balanced scorecard should broaden the horizons of managers, ensuring that they focus on a cross-section of 'balanced' objectives across all functions of the organization, in order that they create 'distinctive' objectives that will enable them to meet corporate goals and ultimately achieve sustainable competitive advantage and customer satisfaction.

Later in this unit we will be looking at barriers to implementation and issues relating to internal marketing, in respect of the planning process. One of the benefits of the balanced scorecard is that it forces management to address a broad range of issues, sometimes issues that they would previously have tried to avoid. It will also force the issues of setting realistic, SMART objectives that can be underpinned by an infrastructure providing the right resources for delivery of products and services to the marketplace.

In Unit 1, we considered the need to ensure that objectives, strategies and plans reflected consistency and synergy in respect of implementation. Effectively the balanced scorecard would go some way to redressing the balance across the organization, ensuring the successful implementation of plans both vertically and horizontally, cross-functional, top-down and bottom-up.

As you can see, setting objectives is not a simple exercise. It requires dexterity and simplicity at the same time. It requires an understanding of the context of the vision, mission and corporate goals and how they will ultimately be achieved.

Gap analysis

One of the most significant problems within many organizations is that they use objectives as a basis of forecasting what levels of performance will be, and then turn the objectives into corporate goals, as opposed to setting objectives based on forecasts.

A gap analysis is used to assist the organization with its strategy development process and in simple terms it is designed to illustrate 'where are we now' and, 'where do we want to be'.

The analysis undertaken as part of the marketing audits will tell the organization 'where they are now' and then a forecast can be undertaken that shows 'where the organization wants to be. It is then possible to identify a gap between the two.

The aim of the organization then must be to develop a marketing strategy and implement marketing plans that close the gap.

Figure 3.2 Gap analysis grid

Case history

Kellogg's Cornflakes

Kellogg's is probably one of the best known and trusted brands in the world, particularly in the branded breakfast cereals market where it has been in operation in excess of 100 years.

For decades they have been the leading light in the breakfast cereals market, with Kellogg's Cornflakes, in particular, leading the way. But like every other organization in today's volatile marketing environment, they have been subject to intense competition, and threats such as radical changes in market structure and life-style patterns.

Between 1992 and 1998 Kellogg's saw their market share in the breakfast cereals market reduce from 38 per cent to 32 per cent. In this period of time Kellogg's experienced a reduction in profit from 19 per cent to 15 per cent. Share prices fell, net profit fell and Kellogg's position as number one cereal provider in the USA was taken by General Mills and for the first time in decades Kellogg's US leadership had slipped away.

At the end of 1998, Kellogg's warned shareholders that earnings per share would fall by 15 per cent because of the actions it needed to take to restore market share. The policies they implemented centred on boosting sales, heavy spending on promotional activities, potentially to the detriment of expected profits.

For example, in 1999, in response to continued loss of market share to supermarket own-label brands, Kellogg's was involved in a serious attack on the UK cereals market, cutting prices simultaneously across its major brands by as much as 12 per cent, and at the same time as increasing its advertising budget by 40 per cent.

During that period, Kellogg's entered into a significant retrenchment programme, cutting back on high-salaried white-collar jobs both in the USA and in Europe, essentially providing savings of some $10 million a year.

They diverted the advertising spend into the Kellogg's brand name and moved it away from individual products. As a result of the ongoing difficulties faced by Kellogg's, their then Chief Executive launched a new strategy to *'fill the gap'* between declining market share and long-term planned objectives.

> The key elements of Kellogg's strategy included:
> - Leadership in product innovation
> - Strengthening their position in seven of Kellogg's largest cereals markets
> - Accelerating the growth of convenience foods with expansion of markets and distribution channels
> - Developing a more focused organization to support the growth strategy
> - Continuing to reduce costs.
>
> Source: Adapted from *Tales from the Market Place*, by Nigel Piercy (1999)

As you can see from the mini-case study above, Kellogg's could not have continued without trying to redress the balance between what was actually happening and what should have been happening, i.e. the gap. Therefore, a balanced strategy was developed. If you refer back to the balanced scorecard approach, you will notice that a balance of cross-functional issues had been addressed and would be the basis for a consistent, integrated organizational approach to achieving corporate goals.

> **Question 3.2**
>
> What are the key benefits of undertaking a gap analysis?

Formulation of the marketing strategy

Now that the objectives have been defined and the gaps identified, it is time for the organization to define, develop and shape the direction they will take in the short-, medium- and long-term time horizons which they have planned within.

The key questions that should be asked in any organization are:

- Where are we now?
- Where are we going?
- How are we going to get there?

As a strategy, marketing seeks to develop effective responses to changing marketing environments, by defining market segments, developing and positioning product offerings for those target markets.

Whilst the focus of your marketing operations is predominantly around marketing planning, it is of the utmost importance that you have a good foundation in strategy in order to put planning into context.

Strategy or tactics?

It is important that a clear understanding of the difference between strategy and tactics is established at this early stage (see Table 3.5).

Table 3.5 Adapted from Drummond and Ensor (1999)

	Strategic Marketing	**Tactical Marketing**
Time frame	Long term	Short term
Focus	Broad	Narrow
Key tasks	Defining marketing and competitive positioning	Daily marketing activity
Information and problem	Unstructured, external, speculative	Structured, internal, repetitive
Example	Market growth	Advertising

The constant theme of this text has been the necessity of developing a sustainable competitive advantage. This, of course, will be achieved through the development of appropriate marketing objectives and a marketing strategy, in order to achieve the corporate goals.

Two other key components of the strategy development are the need to achieve a strong market position through potential growth and to have a sound product/market strategy.

The next stage of this unit focuses on how, as an organization, you develop an appropriate mix of marketing strategies to retain the much-desired 'sustainable competitive advantage'.

Competitive marketing strategy

The marketing audit process should include a competitor analysis. It is important to develop a competitor profile, identifying likely competitive attacks, and have a full understanding of the various forces that will define the shape of the marketplace, through the analysis of Porter's Five Forces. This information, consolidated in the main within a SWOT analysis, will form the basis of your considered approach to developing a competitive strategy.

Michael Porter also defined a Competitive Advantage Grid based upon three generic strategies that enable an organization to closely identify the various competitive options open to them. Typically they would include:

- Cost leadership
- Differentiation
- Focus.

Michael Porter himself suggested that strategy is primarily about creating and sustaining a profitable position in the marketplace. The organization needs to identify the competitive scope available to it, considering the approach to targeting and segmenting the market, and ensure that the organization is operating in a closely defined market.

Cost leadership

One of the key competitive positions to achieve in a mass market setting is that of cost leadership within your defined industry or sector. The focus of marketing and indeed overall strategic activity at this level will relate to ensuring that a low-cost structure is implemented. In essence the organization will be looking to achieve economies of scale, cost reduction policies, zero defects, minimum expenditure on research and development and very closely defined cost-effective marketing strategies. Therefore, the organization is likely to be process driven and technologically focused.

The basic drivers of cost leadership, according to Drummond and Ensor (1999) are:

- Economy of scale – the single biggest influence on cost
- Linkages and relationships – being able to link activities together and form long-lasting customer relationships, inclusive of customer retention programmes
- Infrastructure – factors such as location, availability of skills and government support.

Differentiation

This particular strategy presents the opportunity to market products or services distinctive from those of its competitors. However, while it might be distinctive in nature, it is only competitive and purposefully different if it ultimately adds value to the overall customer experience.

The product/service should have unique features, characteristics and even benefits. It should enable the organization to achieve a degree of customer loyalty and should ultimately be a competitive response that cannot be challenged directly by any competitor.

The most likely scenario is that as a result of the differentiation it will command a premium price, that will essentially reflect the quality of the brand, design, product and high service levels.

Again Drummond and Ensor (1999) suggest that the common sources of differentiation will include:

- Product performance – does the product performance enhance perceived value from the customer perspective
- Product perception – often the perception of the product is different from the performance
- Product augmentation – extending and augmenting the product in ways that will be of value to the customer (we will look at this later under Product operations).

Focus

Interestingly the basis of competitive strategy is both cost leadership and differentiation, but instead of competing in a mass market environment, it is more likely to compete in a smaller or narrowly defined area of the market. In particular the focus will be on attractive segments or niche markets. The emphasis of a focus strategy primarily implies that the organization is focusing effort on producing products for a closely defined market. Often the products will be customized, high quality, differentiated and potentially premium priced. For example specialist clothing, or the high quality car market, e.g. Rolls-Royce, Morgans etc.

Clearly the more successful the organization is within the niche, the more likely it is to attract attention. Therefore, the emphasis of a focus strategy should be on:

- *Product and service specialism* – producing highly differentiated, possibly exclusive products to a closely defined target market
- *Geographic segmentation* – tailoring product/service needs to geographic regions, as long as the markets are commercially viable, based upon size
- *End-user focus* – the focus might be on the end user, therefore a customer profile might be more appropriate to target than an entire marketplace.

These strategies, while studied in isolation from a student perspective, are very much part of a bigger integrated corporate and marketing picture.

> **Question 3.3**
> What is the significance of differentiation when establishing a sustainable competitive advantage?

Growth strategies

While Porter offers one approach to identifying competitive strategies, it is also essential to consider Ansoff's approach. The Ansoff matrix was developed to provide linkages between both products and markets. Ansoff proposes four alternative strategies to take the product to market in order that corporate goals and related marketing objectives are achieved.

At the end of the section on 'The micro environment' in Unit 2, we looked very briefly at Ansoff to put the SWOT into context. However, now we need to consider it in the context of defining the marketing strategy, in respect of identifying options available to the organization for growth.

Ansoff's model builds on Porter's generic strategies and highlights the gap the subsidiary objectives relating to the marketing mix are used to fill.

Principally the Ansoff matrix (Figure 3.3) allows you to consider a range of four strategic options.

Products

	Existing	New
Markets Existing	Market penetration	Product development
Markets New	Market development	Diversification

Figure 3.3 Ansoff matrix

At the end of Unit 2, there was a brief reference to Ansoff. However, it is now important to consider Ansoff in the context of defining the marketing strategy.

Market penetration

The basis of the market penetration strategy is primarily to increase sales of existing products in existing markets. If you look at the top left-hand side of the matrix, you can see where this fits. To do this, the organization will need to demonstrate a high level of competitive force; they will need to be price-competitive, promotionally competitive and execute a hard-hitting advertising campaign.

The focus of market penetration will be on persuading existing customers to buy more of your products. A number of examples highlight this particular practice. Retailers offering store cards, with opening discounted rates of purchase, e.g. open a credit card account today and you will receive 10 per cent discount. The broader scope of this particular strategy is winning customers from other competitors, testing out the power of the buyers, their willingness to change. Therefore part of your strategy might be to create easy transition between the organization and its competitors.

The main problem with market penetration is that while it is appropriate now in some industries, markets are becoming increasingly saturated and therefore competitive intensity at this level is forcing some organizations to revisit their existing strategies. A full and comprehensive marketing audit should identify these emerging issues, and ongoing environmental scanning will enable organizations to take proactive actions in advance of market saturation, rather than waiting for it to happen.

Market development

Market development is an alternative growth strategy that focuses on the development of new markets for existing products (Figure 3.3, bottom left-hand side of the matrix). The aim will be to open up new geographical regions; target new market segments and find new uses for existing products.

This particular strategy draws on the creative skills of marketers to develop alternative uses for products and then devise creative and dynamic marketing programmes to underpin them. A good example of this would be Timberland Boots. In the main designed for walkers, who stalked the hills and dales, Timberland Boots are now a fashion statement. While existing customers continue to buy Timberland Boots for leisure pursuits, others wear Timberland Boots on a day-to-day basis.

Product development

Expanding and developing the product portfolio is an essential marketing activity, in order that organizations continue to move with the times and the new and more challenging expectations of their customers, i.e. the power of the customer/buyer. Product development is required to attract existing customers in existing markets to new products, or revamped, redesigned equivalents.

A good example of product development could relate to the car market. On a regular basis most popular brands extend the life cycle of their existing vehicles by giving them either a minor or major facelift. The aim is to maintain existing customers and encourage them to develop customer loyalty traits in order that they will purchase the redesigned and redefined model. Mercedes have recently revamped the Mercedes 'A' Class and also the 'C' Class range, attracting a surge of interest from the existing customer base. One of Mercedes' key success factors (KSF) until now has been their ability to retain customers and develop a long-term relationship with them. Along with Saab, they boast one of the highest customer retention records in the motor vehicle market history.

In an ideal world, a product portfolio would have a range of products that should provide something for everybody. However, this is not always possible.

Product development plays an important role in attracting new customers, opening up new markets and provides many new opportunities, but clearly the main drawback can be the level of investment required. So as a growth objective, it is one that provides the greatest strain on resources. Here the organization would need to undertake a financial analysis, including a break-even analysis, to measure how long it would take for the new product to break-even, should it be launched into the market.

Related marketing activities would clearly need to reflect a strong competitive response, in order that the product is taken to market in advance of similar competitive strikes and before the threat of substitute products arises.

The organization would clearly have to exploit the company name and brand in order that the product is given credence in the marketplace. Therefore the components of success will rely upon a good quality product, associated high service levels, and a compatible promotional and pricing strategy to give it a head start.

Diversification

Diversification potentially poses the most significant risk to the organization. This strategy is based on diversifying or moving away from the core business of the organization and looking for an alternative or complementary source of income and profit. This often results, in today's market economy, in mergers and acquisitions, as organizations seek to set up compatible business portfolios, increasing their market attractiveness and market share along the way.

This is a high-risk strategy, a move into the unknown, and one that may present threats associated with 'new entrants' in the marketplace: high investment, lack of economies of scale, and difficulties associated with distribution. Again going back to the previous point, one of the benefits of mergers and acquisitions in this sense is that some of the risk is reduced. However, this is an expensive alternative option, for many organizations it is a last resort.

While this puts a negative perspective on the benefits of diversification, there are indeed a number of success stories in the marketplace. Take for example the case of easyJet referred to in Unit 2, to see how Ansoff was used to identify potential diversification for the 'Easy Group'.

One of the principal benefits of using Ansoff is that in addition to contributing to identification of the potential direction to take in relation to developing the marketing strategy, it also focuses the mind of the organization on the future deployment of the marketing mix.

In linking Ansoff back to the SWOT analysis the potential opportunities that face an organization in the future may be identified.

Market positioning strategies

When defining market positioning strategies, it is not just about product position, it is also about positioning the organization within the marketplace. Now is the time to give the organization a competitive identity. Is the organization going to be a market leader, market challenger, market follower or a market nicher?

Market leaders

Market leaders are extremely dominant and high profile within their industry sector and target marketplace. This marketplace might be local, national or even global. It is likely that they possess significant market share. For example organizations such as Coca-Cola and Pepsi are market leaders in the 'Cola' drinks industry. They possess significant market share within the soft drinks industry.

Positioning the organization as market leader immediately leaves them open for a range of competitor attacks. These attacks are likely to be aggressive in nature, and therefore constant monitoring of the competitor activities should be undertaken in order to pre-empt any potential strikes.

Typical competitor attacks might include market expansion, aggressive and offensive attacks to regain lost market share or even defensive attacks, trying to protect existing market share from a market leader contender. You should be aware that offensive attacks are not just the market leaders attacking, but in essence any industry player in the associated market.

Market challengers

Market challengers are particularly difficult to compete with, as they are aggressive and will very much strive to take market share. In the main you will find that these organizations are fairly significant, cash rich and well resourced.

Their likely approach will be based around selective targeting of competitors or indeed an attack on the market leader. Armed with the competitor intelligence and competitor profile built during the marketing audit activities, the market challenger will know where to attack to cause the most pain and discomfort to the competing organization. Probably one of the best-known examples of this is the fight between British Airways and Virgin Air. The battle for clawing back market share has been particularly high profile and ongoing for a number of years. It is a battle that is continually fought in the spotlight of media attention. It is a long-term war of attrition, and it will take a long time before any change is evident.

Market followers

Quite often not being a market follower can be more favourable than being a market leader. Being second or third or even lower down the rankings within the target marketplace, can have a number of advantages.

The key to success here is continually 'following the leader': what ever they do, the follower duplicates. Therefore the strategy is somewhat reactive rather than proactive in context. If the prices go up, the follower puts them up. If the market leader approaches a new market then the follower effectively follows on behind.

It is very rare that the follower will challenge the leader in this particular market positioning area, unless they were absolutely sure of success.

Market nichers

As we saw from looking at the generic strategy of 'focus' earlier, nichers are known for the ability to specialize and focus on particular market segments. Their aim will be to achieve competitive advantage by differentiating their products and services, and move towards the high level, high quality markets.

When defining a marketing strategy, there are so many components that an organization and you as the marketer must consider. The essence of the message is that, strategy development cannot be undertaken in isolation, and therefore, the importance of the marketing audit must never be underestimated or ignored.

The basis of an earlier heading was 'How to take the marketing audit to planning'. Primarily you should never get to the planning process without it. You should be able to see, from the use of Porter's Five Forces, PEST and SWOT, how the information is then transferred into a decision-making pot, out of which a number of potential competitive, growth and market development strategies might be developed and defined.

While the overall basis of the strategic direction has been established, it is equally important to ensure that the specifics of the target audience are clearly understood. As a result of this, marketing segmentation is a crucial activity that must be undertaken, in order that the marketing effort is specifically focused.

> **Question 3.4**
>
> What are the key benefits in being a market follower?

Market segmentation and competitive positioning

At an operational level, segmentation, targeting and positioning are often linked together and the terms interchanged regularly.

For a marketer, there are three stages in the segmentation and positioning process, as can be seen in Figure 3.4.

SEGMENTATION Consider the basis on which to segment the market Look at the profile of people and how they break into groups Confirm the groups are valid segments
TARGETING Decide on a target strategy Decide which segments should be targeted and why?
POSITIONING Understand consumer perceptions Position products in the mind of the consumer Design an appropriate marketing mix to meet customer requirements

Figure 3.4 The process of segmentation

For the time being, however, the concentration of your study will be purely on the principles of segmentation.

> **Definition**
>
> **Segmentation**
>
> The act of dividing the market into specific groups of consumers/buyers who share common needs and who might require separate products and/or marketing mixes. (Adapted from Kotler et al., 1998)

> **Definition**
>
> **Market segmentation**
>
> Identifying the most productive bases for dividing a market, identifying the customers in different segments and development segment description. (Adapted from Hooley, Saunders and Piercy, 1998)

The aim of marketing segmentation is to assist the organization to differentiate their product/service offerings to differing groups of customers. It helps describe how marketers can divide up the market into groups of like-minded customers, at the same time as understanding the different characteristics of them and the different demands that they might make.

Marketing segmentation recognizes the differing needs of buyers and a different approach for each segment identified may subsequently be developed. This is then known as target marketing. This has grown in importance to meet the complex demands of the markets.

Therefore building on the existing stages in the segmentation process, the key steps to market segmentation may be as follows:

- *Identify the possible segments within the market* – this will consist of individuals or organizations with similar needs and preferences
- *Gather information on those market segments identified* – to do this the segments need to be accessible
- *Evaluate the attractiveness of the different segments* – they need to be large enough to be viable
- *Ascertain the competitive positioning within each of the target segments*
- *Develop variations on product/service specifications to meet the needs of individual segments*
- *Design the appropriate communications mix to meet the target market demands.*

For a market to be split into segments specific criteria must be met. These criteria clearly relate back to the decision-making process in the previous section.

- Customers must want or need the associated products or services
- Customers must assert their buying power, i.e. money, resources, etc.
- Customers must be willing to use their money and resources to buy products
- They must have the authority to buy different products.

The basis for segmenting markets

Segmenting markets is a complex issue, but is often seen as a critical factor in the successful implementation of marketing strategy.

Segmentation relates to identifying customer groups and their common characteristics. Segments are often formed based upon common customer characteristics, brand preferences and upon customer attitudes.

Segmentation of consumer markets

It is important to understand what is often termed the 'classificatory' information and 'background' characteristics of your customer. Customers have two types of characteristics that can be measured; they have objective characteristics, which relate to:

- Demographics
- Socioeconomics
- Consumer life cycle
- ACORN
- Media usage.

They also have subjective characteristics, which relate to the 'psychographics'. Psychographics look closely at various personality traits and inventories and very importantly, particularly in the 21st century, lifestyles.

Geographic segmentation

Geographic segmentation is a popular form of segmentation; for example, geographic regions of television areas are used as a form of geographic segmentation. Geographic segmentation means that the market can be broken down into areas for marketing purposes, into towns, cities, regions, countries, etc. This is particularly relevant with the tourism industry, where particular regions will be promoted as holiday and leisure destinations.

Geographic segmentation is particularly important on a global basis, as there are so many different cultures, characteristics and lifestyle requirements that need to be met. Many organizations will try, where possible, to standardize their product offerings globally, while others may try to tailor global requirements. It will very much depend upon the marketing place and the competitive elements that exist within it.

Demographic segmentation

One common area of demographics is social class. This is often a contentious issue. Let us look at some of the areas developed by the JICNAR's social grade definitions when looking at segmentation (see Table 3.6).

Table 3.6 JICNAR social grading system

Social grades	Social status	Characteristics of occupation
A	Upper middle class	High managerial/professional
B	Middle class	Intermediate managerial/administrative professional
C1	Lower middle class	Supervisory/clerical/junior/managerial/administrative/professional
C2	Skilled working class	Skilled manual labour
D	Working class	Semi-skilled and unskilled manual labour
E	Lowest level of subsitence	Widows, casual workers, state pensioners

As a marketer you should be able to recognize different market segments for any major product, for example, motor vehicles. There are a number of different cars available to suit the many and varied needs of customers and their lifestyles.

Geo-demographic segmentation

Geo-demographic factors are a combination of demographic and geographic variables which suggest that certain groups of people tend to move in circles appropriate to class and occupation, while others may move together relating to lifestyles and geographic factors. There are two particular methods in this area that should be considered, ACORN and MOSAIC.

ACORN

ACORN (A Classification of Residential Neighbourhoods – Table 3.7) is a classification system which identifies people by geo-demographics. The current ACORN system divided the UK into 17 groups, which comprise of a total of 54 different types of areas, which share common socioeconomic characteristics. The basis of this type of segmentation is recognizing that different residential areas have very different profiles of people within them and therefore the products they may need may vary from area to area. In many instances products may not even be targeted at specific groups as it is not deemed to be appropriate.

Table 3.7 ACORN consumer targeting classification (Adapted from Dibb, Simkin, Pride and Ferrell, 1997)

Category A Thriving	19.8%	1 – Wealthy achievers – suburban areas 2 – Affluent greys, rural communities 3 – Prosperous pensioners
Category B Expanding	11.5%	4 – Affluent executives 5 – Well-off workers, family areas
Category C Rising	7.6%	6 – Affluent urbanites, town and city areas 7 – Prosperous professionals, metropolitan areas 8 – Better-off executives, inner city areas
Category D Settling	22.3%	9 – Comfortable middle-aged, mature home owning areas 10 – Skilled workers – home owning
Category E Aspiring	13.7%	11 – New home-owners, mature communities 12 – White-collar workers, better-off multi-ethnic areas
Category F Striving	22.6%	13 – Older people, less prosperous areas 14 – Council estate residents – better off homes 15 – Council estate residents, high unemployment 16 – Council estate residents, greatest hardship 17 – People in multi-ethnic low-income areas
Unclassified	2.4%	

From the seven overall catagories, ACORN can then go on to identify issues relating to behaviour, personality, motives and lifestyle. These are what we termed the 'psychographics'. The 'objective' characteristics of ACORN versus the 'subjective' characteristics of personality, motives and lifestyle, serve to move the organization much closer to understanding the basis of customer needs, wants and expectations.

MOSAIC

MOSAIC is a classification system which analyses information from a variety of sources. It analyses geo-demographic data including the census (which provides housing, socioeconomic, household and age information), post code address records (to provide housing and special types of address information, e.g. non-residential addresses), the electoral role (to provide composition of households and population movement information) and the CCN files/Lord Chancellor's office (to provide information on credit searches and bad-debt risks).

MOSAIC provides three types of information as follows:
- Unit postcodes – a six or seven digit code
- Census enumeration districts – based upon census data, containing about 180 addresses in each district
- Psuedo-enumeration districts – areas created by MOSAIC using a combination of unit postcodes within an individual enumeration district.

Presently there are 58 individual neighbourhood types in the MOSAIC classification system.

Lifestyle segmentation

Lifestyle segmentation is a very complex area and is based upon the characteristics of psychographics. These are more subjective and less easy to measure than the typical traits of demographics.

The key areas of interest for a marketer would typically be:
- Social activities – leisure activities, sport, eating out, holidays, shopping habits
- Interests – music, reading, science, history, food, fashion, Internet
- Opinions – social and ethical issues, business, politics, culture, education, religion.

Clearly these characteristics will then be linked with demographics, to start establishing a clear customer profile, on which to base segmentation.

Behaviour segmentation

Behavioural segmentation relates to dividing customers, or indeed organizations, into groups based upon their purchase behaviour, frequency of purchase, attitudes towards the products/services, benefits sought and consumption patterns.

There are a variety of different ways that a market can be segmented. The process of market segmentation involves the following steps:
- Analyse and describe the market segments
- Validate segment choice by testing
- Choose an appropriate strategy for segmentation
- Develop the product or market positioning.

Dividing the market into smaller segments can often present a wide range of new and exciting opportunities for organizations, enabling them to meet more directly a wider range of customer needs, but also enabling them to remain competitive in the marketplace. Segmentation can also allow organizations to respond faster to the changing needs of the customers and also the macro-factors of the external marketing environment.

Market segmentation is therefore essential for successful implementation of marketing strategy. It can help achieve:
- Lengthening of the product life cycle
- Increased sales and profits
- Capture of some of the competitors' share of the market
- Survival of a small firm operating in a competitive market consisting of large firms
- Effective resource allocation
- Strategic marketing planning.

Business-to-business and organizational segmentation

The disciplines of marketing in a business-to-business (B2B) context are often quite different and unfortunately the segmentation techniques available to those marketing to individuals are not available to the organizational marketer. However, a particular bonus of business-to-business segmentation is perhaps the more limited size of the customer base.

For business-to-business and organizational segmentation grouping of customers can be as follows:
- Using the Standard Industrial Classifications (SIC)
- By the industry technology, e.g. chemical or electrical, etc.
- By size of organization
- By season purchasing trends
- By geographical location
- By the type of product needed.

Demographics, in a business-to-business context, assume that organizations operating in similar industries have similar needs and will exhibit similar behavioural traits.

All organizations aim to satisfy their customer needs, whether their customer is an individual or a business. As we have already identified, organizations do find it difficult to totally segment their markets for business-to-business buying because of the characteristics of the market they operate within.

Therefore, there are five key variables that organizations should consider:

- The personal characteristics of the buyers
- Situational factors
- The organizational approach to purchasing
- Operating variables – technologies, etc.
- Demographics.

Company demographics – have a slightly different approach, and are in the main far less personal. However, they do focus on areas such as company age, location, size and the likelihood of them wanting to change their product specification in the future.

Clearly these factors are highly significant, as they will indicate the volume of purchases, the ordering procedures, accessibility for delivery, etc.

Business-to-business buying should reflect the same considerations as consumer segmentation and the same approach to developing marketing plans and strategies should apply.

Further consideration of this area is included within Unit 10.

Continuous monitoring of segmentation

As with any element of marketing, segmentation, targeting and positioning should be tightly controlled and monitored, to ensure the information provided has enabled an organization to meet its corporate and marketing objectives.

Should an organization not meet its objectives, then it should review and evaluate segments selected to ensure that the profile of customers is one that matches the benefits and characteristics of the product, or indeed that the correct medium has been selected to get the message to the customer or consumer.

If the segment that has been targeted should prove to be ineffective, then further research should be undertaken and plans revised and the marketing mix strategy redefined.

Possible examples of segmentation monitoring might include measuring the sales distribution across segments, measuring advertising effectiveness, repeat sales and responses to special sales promotions.

Achieving segmentation effectiveness

Ineffective marketing segmentation can have lasting effects and be the cause of many lost opportunities. Therefore it is essential that there is clear and perceived value in the segmenting process. It is of primary importance that the appropriate segmentation characteristics are identified and that time is not wasted and investment is not lost in the selection of the incorrect or inappropriate segmenting variables. For example there is little point in segmenting a homogeneous market, as it does not provide the basis for effective segmentation.

Therefore the following criteria should be adhered to:

Specific	Clearly identified, broken down into a number of meaningful groups
Measurable	Each group should be quantifiable in order for the organization to identify opportunities and forecast the future
Achievable	The segments themselves need to achieve organizational objectives, they will therefore need to be viable groups and accessible
Realistic	What is achievable in the name of segmentation must be realistic in terms of resources, and with a clear indication that customer expectations can be met
Timebound	Appropriate segments of the market must be targeted in an appropriate and timely way and in line with the organizational objectives.

While marketing segmentation can be a very process-driven exercise, it will require a degree of commonsense and perhaps even a number of related assumptions, in order that the market can be closely defined.

Ultimately the benefits of segmentation are significant and they include:

- It allows target markets to be mapped against organizational competences
- It helps identify gaps within the marketplace
- It enables marketers to match the product/service to their customer – a basis of competitive advantage
- It provides an opportunity for mature/declining markets to identify possible growth segments
- The failure to segment can reduce competitive strength.

Targeting

> **Definition**
> **Targeting**
> The decision about which market segment(s) a business decides to prioritize for its sales and marketing efforts. (Dibb, Simkin, Pride and Ferrell, 2001)

Targeting is the process that involves evaluating the attractiveness of a range of potential market segments that have been identified in terms of being commercially viable.

Each organization has several options when deciding on which segment to specifically target:

- Organizations could concentrate of making one product for one market and having one marketing plan or programme – this is know as *undifferentiated marketing or even mass marketing*
- The organization could concentrate its efforts on one market but have a number of different versions of each product. *This is known as differentiated marketing*
- Another alternative is to have a product that meets the need of each segment within the market with a specific product – this is known as *target marketing*
- Concentrating efforts on a small and carefully chosen segment, often referred to as a niche and the basis of a '*focus*' strategy.

Targeting in essence is where we identify a number of different segments within the market, whereby a sustainable competitive advantage can be built.

In ascertaining the appropriate target market strategy the organization must take into consideration the following six components:

- Customer needs, wants and expectations
- Product market – size and structure
- Brand strength and market share
- Company capability
- Competitive rivalry
- Economies of scale – production and marketing.

The organization must, through market research, identify which is the most appropriate target, which they can effectively manage to meet the customer needs and wants, in a cost-efficient and effective way, in order that they can meet the corporate goals of the organization.

Segmentation is not an exact science, and will require a balanced view of market conditions, clear and precise criteria for assessing segmentation attractiveness and an understanding of the key components that will enable successful target marketing.

> **Question 3.5**
>
> Why is it so vital for an organization to undertake segmentation and targeting activities?
>
> What would be the effect of failing to undertake segmentation and targeting?

Positioning

Earlier on in this unit, we looked at the concept of market positioning strategies. Here we want to look at the source of positioning, starting with the product.

> **Definition**
>
> **Positioning**
>
> The act of designing an offer so that it occupies a distinct and valued place in the minds of the target customers (Kotler).

Simplistically, positioning refers to how you present your product or services to the marketplace, it is almost a state of mind, a perception, it is something you as a marketer have to create in the minds of your target audience.

When establishing a positioning strategy there are a number of steps that can be taken in preparing a positioning plan.

- Identify all of the segments within the market
- Decide which segments are the most suitable to target, based upon marketing research information
- Ensure that the organization clearly understands the customer requirements
- Develop a product or service that specifically meets the needs of the target audience
- Identify benefits, usage, user category, competitive positioning components

- Evaluate how the product/service is positioned in the eyes of the target group
- Identify an image that matches the requirements of the customer
- Promote the product to the target audience, establish relationships, aim for customer loyalty.

Pivotal to the success of positioning is the ability to differentiate your products and services from those of your competitors.

From a competitor perspective, there needs to be a comparison of competitor positioning, which means that as a marketer you should:

- Determine competitive positioning
- Examine the competitive dimensions
- Determine the customer positions
- Understand and identify the positioning decision
- Track the positioning strategy.

This will ultimately enable you to monitor competitor positioning and take the necessary retaliatory action.

Perception is a vital component of positioning strategies and therefore it is helpful for organizations to try to represent the similarities between products or services and try to ascertain what the differences are, in respect of position. The key tool to support this process is a perceptual map (see Figure 3.5).

You will see when looking at the perceptual maps that there are four perceptions to be considered:

- High price and high quality
- High quality and low price
- Low price and low quality
- High price and low quality.

Figure 3.5 Perceptual positioning map

What effectively happens with a perceptual map is that it represents similarities and differences between products/services and ultimately it highlights where products are similar/dissimilar.

As we can see here, the service offered by British Airways and Cathay Pacific is of a very high standard. The accommodation and service on board in a British Airways flight is aimed at meeting customer expectations at a high level, which is primarily the executive market. British Airways are known for their superior service in executive, business and first-class flights. But obviously this all comes at a premium. Therefore in this instance British Airways have positioned themselves as premier quality, premium priced. Cathay Pacific seek to achieve the same positioning.

At the lower end of the scale, we have Go, Ryanair and Virgin Express, in addition to easyJet. However, while easyJet position themselves at the lower end of the market, flights to Malaga for example, fall anywhere between £45 and £175, flights from London to Edinburgh fall between £68 and £228, depending upon how far in advance they are actually booked. The further in advance you book, the cheaper the flight is.

Therefore for a 'no frills' brand, they are actually positioning themselves as an economy brand, 'low-cost airline'. However, in reality their positioning is somewhere between economy and high-price, which is a slightly confused positioning. Other factors to consider with 'no frills' is the additional expenses customers incur while on flight, i.e. they add on expenses of food, drink. Of course, in terms of positioning, reliability will play a significant factor in the minds of the consumer, in respect of value for money, something for which easyJet received extremely poor publicity during the early part of 2001.

Therefore while positioning is a positive activity from both a customer and competitor perspective, it is not an exact science. In positioning your organization you are raising an expectation in relation to the level of product or service quality you might offer. The important element of that is achieving the expectations that you have established in the eyes of the consumer.

While the plotting on the perceptual map in Figure 3.5 is based upon the perceptions of customers, it is also useful to consider this from a competitor perspective. Plotting competitor positioning on a perceptual map will enable you to further understand the role and positioning of your competitors, enabling the organization to have a clear understanding of the nature of the competition and, of course, where to attack. However, remember that when you attack, positioning is something that has to be sustainable, therefore in attacking a competitor it has to be more than a short-term activity and part of a longer-term strategy to compete on product and market positioning.

The positioning alternatives

Perceptual maps should be based upon marketing research, in order that a factual presentation of the information can be plotted, and assumptions made in relation to positioning are as accurate as possible. It is not recommended that you use either expert witnesses or expert judgements, or take the very subjective approach of establishing positions on gut feel.

Ries and Trout (1998) suggest that there are three positioning alternatives available:

- *Distinctive attributes* – identify the distinctive attributes of the product and service as a source of credible positioning.
- *Fill the gaps in unfilled positions* – where there is a positional gap in the perceptional map, this may present a business opportunity to exploit.
- *Repositioning* – changes in consumer behaviour (which are quite frequent) may mean that the product life cycle could be maturing or going into decline, therefore you might need to reposition your products to attract a different market. Clearly in the instance of the above perceptual map, there is a space in the high price, low quality quadrant – *but this is not one to fill*. Of course, as a marketer, you would need to consider carefully why

the gap might exist. It would be difficult in this instance to actually conceive what would be the benefits of selling a 'high price – economy' product, as it is unlikely that customers will pay for it. Therefore this should always be addressed and the likely gaps that you might wish to exploit are the remaining three.

Think about Alco Pops. They were originally aimed at the younger end of the market – 18–25 year olds. Now they are more sophisticated perceptually and are as popular with 31–40 year olds. This is a slight repositioning in order to allow for market penetration, i.e. ensuring customer retention for the 18–25 year old market, but undertaking market development to target new markets, i.e. the 30+ more mature markets, but with the same products.

As part of the segmentation and targeting process, it is essential where possible to closely define the segmentation bases and associate it with the product/service in question. Ultimately, it is then possible to position the product clearly in a defined positioning strategy, in order to meet customer needs and expectations.

The role of a marketer in positioning

The role of a marketer will be to assist with the definition of positioning, in the context of the market, the brand and the product. As you move through this book, you will come across a number of different tools of the trade that will assist you with ascertaining positions in relation to the brand, for example the Boston Consulting Group Matrix, which will allow you to make decisions in relation to product positioning.

Positioning is all about differentiating your products and brands for your customers: what are the key characteristics and benefits that stand out – that differentiate your product/brands from those of your competitors; what characteristics do your products have that your competitors' may not. The purpose of positioning is to establish a position and perspective of your brands, products and services in the marketplace.

Clearly segmentation can therefore be a complex activity, and should always be objective in nature, i.e. very clearly defined, very specific and very focused. Subjective judgements in relation to the segmentation base and target market may lead to failure to implement any marketing strategy.

According to Hooley, Saunders and Piercy (1998): 'Segmentation and positioning researchers have indeed failed to find a single criterion which will fit all markets, despite the claims of those selling lifestyle segmentation'. Therefore the safest and most reliable way to segment, target and position your markets is through the use of product market data that enables customers to be clearly segmented into smaller groups in order that they might be specifically targeted.

Question 3.6
You have been asked by your marketing manager to develop a brief statement that clearly explains the positioning of your own company – in no more than 50 words.

The marketing plan

This section focuses upon conceptualizing the basis of a marketing plan. There are some components that we will only look at briefly within implementation, as they are the source of strategic planning and beyond the scope of the CIM syllabus for this module.

Table 3.8 Contents of the marketing plan

1. Executive summary	Key issues, current position, potential overview of the outcome
2. Corporate strategy	Corporate misson/vision and corporate goals/objectives
3. Macro/macro analysis	Market assessment Current state of the market Market trends Competitor analysis SWOT
4. Marketing objectives	Financial objectives Marketing objectives
5. Marketing strategy	Segmentation, targeting and positioning Marketing strategy Marketing programme Product, price, place, promotion
6. Implementation	Key tasks, resources, budgets, contingency plans
7. Monitoring and control	Basis of the plan and the assumptions made Key/critical success factors Benchmarking Forecasts/costs/revenue

There is no set way in which the marketing plan must be presented. Table 3.8 shows the key headings that you should cover and also the order and sequence that is logical and appropriate. Planning offers you the opportunity to present the future of the organization and its marketing activity systematically, in a way that is meaningful and clearly defined. The basis of this particular plan will provide the template by which the organization will operate in the forthcoming years and will also form the basis of a planned approach to implementation. Furthermore, it will provide the basis for measurement, monitoring and control, it will act as a benchmark of what needs to be achieved, taking the organization from where it is now, to where it wants to be in the future.

Implementation of the marketing plan

There are a number of key components that you should familiarize yourself with in respect of the implementation of marketing plans. From an organizational perspective, implementation is one of the most challenging activities you will find yourself involved in.

Nigel Piercy (1997) suggests that:

The real strategic problem in marketing is not strategy, it is managing the implementation and change.

New plans, new processes, different approaches are all components of change, and in many situations change meets with opposition and many barriers are therefore erected. You may recall from Unit 1 where we looked at those barriers and here they are again as a reminder.

- The existing culture may not be amenable to marketing plans, particularly if the organization is not marketing oriented
- *Power and politics* – All organizations are subject to internal politics and often as a result of this the strategic planning process becomes a boardroom battlefield, where vested interests fight each other's proposals in order to gain resources and status

- *Analysis not action* – Many organizations waste time and energy in analysing data and developing rationales for action, but ultimately fail to act. A further element of this is 'paralysis-by-analysis', too much information, not enough direction
- *Resources* – This is one of the most contentious issues facing many organizations, as after years of downsizing, striving for increased efficiencies, many organizations now find themselves resource-starved. When corporate objectives are defined, it is of prime importance that organizations realistically consider the resources required, in order that they can rise to the challenge of achieving the corporate targets
- Skills are very closely linked to the challenges of resources. One of the key components of any organization is a highly-skilled workforce. As a result of the changes brought about by the economic slowdown in the early 1990s, marketing as a function was cascaded down to managers in the organization, who were untrained, unskilled and unable to suddenly carry the mantle of marketing that had now been bestowed upon them. An unskilled workforce could hinder significantly the implementation of marketing plans and ultimately reduce service and performance levels overall.

There are some key ingredients that are required and vital for the successful implementation of any marketing plan, and the driving forces of change. They are:

- Strong and committed leadership
- A marketing oriented and customer-focused culture
- A supportive and effective marketing structure
- Financial and human resources
- Internal marketing – systems and processes
- Control and measurement mechanisms.

For a strategy to be successfully implemented, it is therefore important that these areas are managed effectively. If they are not, immediately a range of barriers to implementation will arise and then change becomes very difficult to manage.

Let us look briefly at the importance of each of these factors.

Strong and committed leadership

You might recall that in the first unit, there was a reference to 'top-down' and 'bottom-up' planning. In a planning environment, leadership needs primarily to come from the top. A leader therefore must demonstrate commitment at the highest level to the proposed strategy and plans. Leaders need to be effective communicators, motivators and facilitators.

The process of continuous improvement will only succeed if those in influential roles demonstrate their commitment to the process, but also ensure that they equally affect the commitment of their followers. Commitment is not a management function that can be delegated downwards, it has to be shown by actions.

Commitment is difficult to measure but it is likely that the following key factors will be present:

- A vision for the future has been developed
- The necessary resources have been committed
- When solutions to problems are found they are promptly implemented
- Barriers to change within the organization have been dismantled.

While this is a limited list, it is obvious that each relates to potential causes of conflict within the implementation process, therefore committed leadership is imperative to successful implementation of the marketing plan.

There is more to leadership than autocracy or democracy, charisma or inspiration – in the words of Sir John Harvey Jones:

'leadership is about making things happen'.

Therefore effective leadership starts at the top, with the vision for the organization, examining closely the needs of the market, creating, exploiting and capitalizing on opportunities for the organization, at the same time as ensuring that it achieves competitive advantage.

Marketing oriented and customer-focused culture

The 'marketing concept' in the words of Kotler *et al.* (1998):

> *Holds that achieving organizational goals depends on determining the needs and wants of target markets and delivering the desired satisfactions more effectively and more efficiently than competitors do.*

Reflecting on the different facets of marketing you have already examined, it is clear that marketing is increasingly dynamic and if you and your organization are going to succeed then you need to ensure that you take into most serious consideration the expectations of your customer.

Organizations will need to be marketing oriented, which means that there must be a clear focus throughout the whole organization on the customer needs and the wants and how these needs are met constantly.

Marketing orientation consists of five key facets:

- Customer orientation
- Competitor orientation
- Integrated functional co-ordination
- Organizational culture
- Long-term profits.

To enable the marketing concept to continue to evolve and for marketing orientation to develop within organizations, organizations, big or small, should pay serious consideration to the following:

- Create customer focus throughout the business
- Listen to the customer
- Define the nature of the organization's key abilities, i.e. what they are good at
- Target customers precisely
- Manage profitability
- Make customer value the guiding star
- Let the customer define loyalty – how many times they may wish to repeat business
- Measure and manage customer expectations
- Build customer relationships and loyalty
- Commit to continuous improvement
- Manage the marketing culture.

For culture change to be implemented successfully, the following components must be at the forefront:

- Innovation must be highly valued
- Leadership must be an activity not just a function
- Shared values and rewards
- A learning organization
- Empowerment.

Ultimately, change in the context of marketing should be planned, consistent and incremental.

Strategy implementation can be a complex period full of conflict and recriminations. Cultural change must create something that did not exist before. The careful crafting of the 'internal marketing plan' may ease the situation.

Internal marketing

It is clear from everything we have seen so far that change is the one factor that is here to stay. It is also evident that the implementation of a new corporate strategy and indeed a new marketing plan may also require change within the organization.

The basis of internal marketing is focusing on the relationship that exists between the organization and its employees, often couched in terms of the 'internal customer'. It has been suggested on many occasions that the successful implementation of the marketing plan hinges upon treating internal staff like 'customers', hence the link with the internal customer.

> **Definition**
>
> **Internal marketing**
>
> The application of marketing internally within the company, with programmes of communication and guidance targeted at internal audiences to develop responsiveness and a unified sense of purpose among employees. (Dibb, Simkin, Pride and Ferrell, p.731, 2001)

Nigel Piercy (1997), suggests that:

> *'Marketplace success is frequently largely dependent on employees who are far removed from the excitement of creating marketing strategies'.*

Therefore it is highly important that the internal marketing programme bridges the information gap between the strategy development team through to technical engineers, customer services staff, production and finance, to name but a few, so that essentially they are fully informed about the direction of the organization.

Internal marketing plays a pivotal role in ensuring that the organization is marketing and customer focused, the components of which have already discussed in the previous section. It is based upon a programme of communications externally that ultimately demands a positive response from the employees, i.e. buy-in and commitment to the newly-formed strategy and planned changes that are due to be implemented.

One of the critical success factors of internal marketing is its ability to break down the various barriers to planning that were evident earlier in this unit. Its prime objective is to ensure that a more positive attitude is formed towards the organization and its vision and that productivity, effectiveness and efficiency will increase.

Internal marketing can go a long way to achieve the two key factors important to planning: 'synergy' and 'consistency'. These factors will come from a workforce in tune, integrated and committed to achieving the corporate vision.

Successful implementation of an integrated market plan will be based upon employees understanding the concepts and philosophy of the organization and that they will understand the mission and corporate goals. It may enable employees to feel part of the organization, responsible for its achievement.

One of the key components of an internal marketing programme is therefore communication. Internal marketing is, as suggested earlier, a communications programme. There are a number of steps that an organization can take in order to achieve internal synergy and employee co-operation:

- Creating an internal awareness of the corporate aims, objectives and overall mission
- Determining the expectations of the internal customer
- Communication to internal customers

- Changes in tasks and activities
- Internal monitoring and control.

As with the external marketing plan, the internal plan ultimately needs the same components:

- Internal vision
- Aims and objectives
- Internal marketing strategy
- Segmentation, targeting and positioning
- Marketing programme to include all elements of the marketing mix
- Implementation
- Monitoring and control of the success or failure of execution.

It is as important to segment your market internally as it is externally, as the basis and the focus of the message will need to be tailored to the particular audience, potentially fitting their contribution and that of their departments into the context of the proposed change.

The key aim of the marketing plan must therefore be the successful motivation and retention of the internal customer in order that the organization can meet the needs of the external market. The marketing mix will be the tools with which to achieve it.

Later on in this book in Unit 8, 'Place promotions', we will be looking at 'Managing marketing relationships' and we will examine this particular area in a lot more depth, looking at the techniques involved in internal marketing. Ultimately if internal marketing is implemented effectively it will have something to offer in achieving the level of strategic change the organization may want.

> **Question 3.7**
>
> What is the importance of communication to the 'internal marketing process' and why?

A supportive and effective marketing structure

For a marketing strategy to be successfully implemented it will rely on an infrastructure to be in place that will deliver the corporate goals in an efficient and effective way. At the end of the day the sign of a good leader is one who ensures that the organization is structured in a way that gets the job done.

Therefore it is essential that you are fully aware of the different ways of organizing the marketing activities.

Typically the structure of the organization might be functional, by territory or product based.

Figure 3.6 Departmentalism by function

Figure 3.7 Departmentalism by territory

Figure 3.8 Departmentalism by product

The functional organization

The functional organization (see Figure 3.6) typically defines each of its business functions, from which each functional unit will have a management line of control established. In terms of marketing it is likely that this is headed up by the Director of Marketing, down to a range of functional specialisms including sales, product development and market research. This will allow for the marketing team to work on an integrated basis, undertaking a range of marketing activities on a day-to-day basis.

The territory-based organization

This is quite a useful structure for organizations who trade internationally, or particularly in the retail sector, where there may be independent marketing activities undertaken in each territory (see Figure 3.7). However, this is formally known as decentralized management. This is where the business management functions are devolved to the regional centre of activity, whereby they will be responsible for their own 'territory' budget, resources and marketing activity, albeit still in line with meeting the corporate goals and objectives.

This is more typical of large organizations, and where cultural differences are significant enough to perhaps require a different approach.

While on occasions territory management is decentralized, it can also be centralized, whereby the organization does have regional offices, but the management functions are all co-ordinated from a central point. In the main, the regional office will have little autonomy over its overall business dealings and would be responsible for the day-to-day running of the business only.

The product-based organization

Organizations such as Philips, Pepsi, Coca-Cola, Lever to name but a few, work on a product-based structure (see Figure 3.8), whereby different brands and products are managed as separate business units. Each brand is individually accountable for its own performance, although it is still aligned to and responsible for meeting the overall corporate goals. In a product-based organization, product managers will have responsibility devolved down to them and be expected to ensure that their particular brand and product range delivers in line with corporate expectations.

Each brand/product unit will be responsible for defining and implementing their own marketing plans and are likely to have budgetary and management responsibilities. However, they also have the responsibility of ensuring that each of their brands/products retains their position and competitive advantage in the marketplace.

Other organizational structures include *matrix management*, whereby the responsibility of the marketing manager can potentially cut across all business functions. As the role of marketing has evolved over time, it encroaches more and more on other business functions in order that an integrated and co-ordinated approach is undertaken to achieve the corporate goals.

Customer-based structures are also quite prevalent, particularly in organizations involved in financial services, whereby customers and products might be linked together and therefore the organization is run in such a way as to be able to ultimately manage and retain customers.

Whatever the structure of the organization, it is vitally important that the lines of communication are clearly defined, in order that from an internal perspective employees clearly understand the purpose and direction of the structure and ultimately their contribution overall.

Financial and human resources

One of the key successes of good vision and leadership, is the ability to produce the resources to get the job done. By resources we mean the money, the people and the place, in which the marketing activities can be successfully implemented.

Today resources appear to be one of the most scarce commodities in the workplace and quite often one of the key barriers to implementation. This is as a result of resources actually being budget-driven. However, when strategies are being defined and planned, resource implications must be considered as part of the overall process.

For the organization to function it needs people and finance, so for the marketing strategy to be successful it is of primary importance to ensure that the whole infrastructure is in place.

Human resources

From a human resource perspective, it will be essential that the organization has the appropriate mix of management and technical skills required for implementation of the marketing plan. A team of multi-skilled marketers will be critical to successful implementation. You will learn about this within Effective Management for Marketing, where you will look at issues relating to being an effective marketing manager, appropriate recruitment, selection and teambuilding strategies.

As a marketing manager you will have responsibility for managing the marketing team, ensuring the implementation of the process, through the successful management of tasks.

Financial resources/budgets

The processes of strategic planning and budgeting are very closely linked. In real terms, having a budget means that you are able to execute and implement a very carefully laid plan in a very controlled way, as budgeting is probably the most common control mechanism of any planning process. The concentration of theory in relation to this subject will arise as you study for Management Information for Marketing Decisions. Therefore you will not be asked to produce a budget as such in this examination. It is essential, however, that you understand the concepts and the importance of them.

When developing a plan and setting a budget, often the full picture of the situation can be unclear. This may be as a result of missing or inaccurate information. But in any case, the budget allocation process will ensure that an indication of the resources required to make the plan work is considered, together with the financial implications of the plan. Much of the information formulated within the budget is based on forecasts, and there is an important difference between the two.

From this a budget will be defined. The budget is a financial plan demonstrated in quantitative terms. It is likely that the budget will show volumes as well as values, over a set period of time, which in most organizations is one year. Budgets may be prepared for the various activities undertaken by the firm or they may be for products, locations and organizational functions, such as marketing, sales, administration, research and development, production, etc.

In setting a budget, you have a control mechanism, a tool to quantify plans, co-ordinate activities, highlight areas of critical importance and assign responsibilities.

According to Drummond and Ensor in their book *Strategic Marketing* (1999), budgeting seems to highlight two key points. First, they suggest that budgeting is about resource allocations and secondly, budgeting is a political process, hence the need for negotiation and bargaining, to secure the resources necessary to achieve the proposed plan.

Effectively what we are seeing is that a budget must be prepared to allocate resources in order to achieve marketing objectives. It should contain estimates of costs of implementing the plan; costs of each functional area of the organization; and, in respect of marketing, costs of research, advertising, sales and other promotional mix activities.

A budget is effectively a financial plan of action, for an identified period of time. It is essential that the budget be developed in line with both corporate and marketing objectives. For the purpose of sales and marketing, it may include a number of project areas that have been planned for a year ahead.

It is important to understand that a plan is effectively worthless without any control element. Control will be achieved by comparing actual figures against budget figures, and the variance can then be calculated.

Budgeting can play the role of a motivational tool, when managing people who are involved in marketing activities. While organizations should be customer driven, in many instances they are budget driven and achieving objectives, within time and within budget, is a key motivational factor, for which personnel are often rewarded.

Budgeting must not be carried out in isolation from corporate objectives or other business functions, otherwise the budget becomes ineffective, as it does not take on the realism of the situation and what can be effectively achieved corporately. This could result in lack of focus or direction.

Budgeting is critical for measuring both the performance of the organization and of individuals. Budgeting and performance can play a very significant role in personnel appraisal processes, where the budget versus the actual can be the basis of an individual achieving their employment objectives for the period. Within the organization as a whole, the same applies. It is critical that sales and production targets are met, and the only realistic way in which this can be measured effectively is by measuring actual performance against budgeted performance.

From this you will see that human and financial resources are essential to the successful implementation of the marketing plan and provide the basis of a benchmark of performance.

The control process

The final component of the planning processes that it is necessary to comprehend is the need to control.

In order that the goals of the organization are met, continual monitoring of the business functions within the organization must be undertaken.

Monitoring and control effectively contains four key activities:

1. Development or adjustment of marketing objectives
2. Setting of performance standards
3. Evaluation of performance
4. Corrective action.

In Figure 3.9 you can see the planning cycle, which includes two lines of arrows, each line pointing in opposite directions. The purpose of this is to highlight the importance of planning, which is going in one direction, i.e. forward and onward, and control, which is continually going backwards and checking what has happened so far and essentially establishing whether the plan reached its targets step by step throughout the process. Ideally, if the targets are not being met, then clearly the planning process may need to be revised.

Figure 3.9 The marketing planning cycle

The first stage in the process after setting the objectives, by which performance will be measured, is setting performance standards. *Performance standards are principally the level of performance against which actual performance can be compared.* In the main, performance standards are presented in the form of budgets. The sole purpose of this will be to ensure that the amount of money given over to expenditure is not exceeded and that the proposed targets for income and profit are actually achieved.

There are a number of techniques that can be employed in this area, but basic and generic principles apply. There are a number of organizational methods of measuring performance overall, such as *performance appraisal/evaluation* which includes measurement and control of staff performance. This consists of reviewing performance, giving feedback and counselling if necessary.

In addition to this there is *benchmarking*, which ensures that the organization develops an ongoing process of measuring processes and achievements against key performance indicators, such as competitors and best practice standards.

Monitoring and measuring performance is a critical element of business and therefore every organization must find effective ways of ensuring that plans and budget appropriations are met, or revised accordingly, and that they underpin the corporate, business and marketing objectives.

As control is an important part of the planning process, it is critical to manage it in a way that is transparent and meaningful. Therefore for the purpose of ease, it is likely that the budget will be broken down into a number of smaller areas, often termed *cost centres*. For each of these, planned income and expenditure are monitored and compared with the actual results.

In many organizations, each function, i.e. marketing, personnel, production, becomes a cost centre. Splitting the budget on this basis enables an overview of how each division is performing against the plan and where the variances lie, giving an opportunity to identify each variance and potentially move towards a contingency plan if necessary, depending on the cause of the variance.

For example, typical headings on a monthly or annual budget report would be as shown in the following table.

INCOME BUDGET – Marketing and Sales Division					
Income	Actual Year	Month	Budgeted Amount	Variance Under	Variance Over
Sales					
Interest earned					
Sales commission					
Licence fees					
Royalty payments					
Property rentals					
Total Income					

EXPENDITURE BUDGET – Marketing and Sales Division					
Income	Actual Year	Month	Budgeted Amount	Variance Under	Variance Over
Sales					
Rent					
Advertising					
PR					
Sales promotions					
Travel					
Sales commission					
Total Expenditure					

Variance analysis

One of the main things that control is likely to expose is constant variances from the planned budget. For example, when your sales are planned for £300K for the first quarter and they are only £200K in this session, then this is a variance from the actual budget.

Variance analysis is commonly used along with budgetary control. What it seeks to do is to compare the planned budget and then the variance is examined in order for the difference between the two to be established. It is a little like looking for a cause and effect.

Variance analysis is not confined to price or volume either. It can include variance on profit achieved, budgeted costs and change in potential market size.

The key to this control tool is to be fully aware that very often variance in budgets is inevitable and can mean that changes to the existing plan, be they contingency or fully fledged changes, are for the duration of the plan.

Budgetary control

In essence, budgetary control involves financial control of the whole business through a system of budgets. It consists of:

- Preparation of budgets
- Measuring actual performance
- Comparing actual results with budget results
- Taking corrective action if necessary.

Other methods of measurement and control might relate to *customer satisfaction surveys*. These may be carried out at peak points during the control process or monitored on an ongoing basis. It is essential that the organization identifies whether or not they are meeting customer expectations, needs and wants, and if not what remedial action might be required.

Brand awareness is a further example of measuring marketing effectiveness. You may recall in the case of Egg and easyJet, that brand awareness was one of the key success factors, in particular the speed at which brand awareness increased.

Case history

'accenture' – Who??????

Brand awareness is vital to the success of many organizations. One of the big branding stories of all time is that of Anderson Consulting. Anderson Consulting is a company of management consultants that has just had to ditch what a brand expert suggested was worth £5 billion.

The enforced stripping of the company's name followed an acrimonious split between Anderson Consulting and Arthur Anderson (auditors). This has literally pulled down the curtain on nearly 94 years of corporate history, which has resulted in Andersons being one of the best-known management consulting companies on record.

Now known as 'accenture', the organization is one of Europe's biggest companies, with annual revenues of £16 billion, employing over 65,000 staff across 54 countries.

However, 'accenture', facing a UK flotation pending of some £50 billion, which apparently has the global stock markets in a frenzy, appears to have one key problem. Up until early in 2001, nobody had ever heard of it.

'accenture' has been renamed, rebranded, redefined and reborn. They are running some 6,000 TV commercials, 250 UK poster sites in addition to taking out commercials during the American Superbowl season – all a very expensive proposition.

The sub-head line of a recent article in relation to 'accenture' stated 'the new appellation has to stick – failure is impossible to comprehend'.

The results of the name change are impossible to quantify. Arthur Anderson consultants now work for a company no one has heard of. That is a tough pill to swallow. The eyes of the corporate world are now on 'accenture'.

Source: *EuroBusiness*, March 2001

This shows a very strong need for the highest level of measurement and evaluation of brand awareness. This brand name change for such a prestigious organization is a tremendous risk to the future growth and development, therefore its profile is 'critical', indeed the brand name will be a 'critical success factor'.

Both these measures are vital to the measurement of the organization's performance. High levels of customer satisfaction and brand awareness are vital to the achievement of corporate goals. Should there be a decline in either of these key areas, then the organization may have to take remedial action, particularly at the marketing mix level.

Effectiveness of the marketing mix

Other units of this text focus closely on marketing mix operations, and how to plan and implement the marketing mix taking an integrated approach. Therefore understanding key components of measuring the marketing mix will be essential in the long term. Some of the potential performance standards might be based upon price, whereby the effects of a particular pricing policy will be measured.

Organizations such as easyJet and Go will frequently undertake promotional activity to generate interest and awareness in the brand. It will be vital, therefore, to monitor the response to the promotional campaign, in order that future successes or failures are identified in relation to the marketing mix.

Competitor performance

Many of these factors are internal analysis components. It is therefore essential that while monitoring your own performance you also continually monitor that of your competitors. This can be done through scanning the press, but also from obtaining financial information in relation to their performance.

Typical competitor comparisons will be based upon the original financial factors relating to their organization, such as financial objectives provided in Figure 3.4. Going back to the capability profile will allow you to monitor the performance of your own organization against your competitor quite effectively and again will also highlight the need for pre-emptive or reactive strikes.

For an effective control process to be implemented, the marketing manager should consider ways of developing and maintaining effective marketing control processes.

Information is the key to monitoring and measuring marketing success effectively. The quality, quantity and speed of information will be critical.

The control process should be designed to enable a flow of information that will quickly allow a marketing manager to identify the difference between the planned and actual performance, i.e. the variance, and therefore the manager should be able to make informed decisions about any possible remedial changes. Should control procedures trigger a change in the overall plan, or even part of the plan, the full implications of the change must be carefully considered and, ultimately, carefully communicated.

Effective marketing control therefore hinges on quality, quantity and speed of information. The biggest single factor that inhibits the control process is that areas such as environmental changes, time lags between marketing activities and their outcomes and, more seriously, the cost of marketing activities, are often difficult to determine. This means that careful budget monitoring and control is essential.

Corrective action

Implementation of marketing strategy very rarely goes directly to plan, as external driving forces, time-lags, competition and economic downturn may all change the pace at which the organization's growth can be achieved.

As a result of this many organizations will have to take varying forms of corrective action. In the main this is required when a performance standard falls below what is termed as a 'tolerable' level. For example, if sales are in decline at an unsustainable rate, then corrective action may have to be taken.

> **Case history**
>
> **Wal-Mart Sounds US warning**
>
> Wal-Mart, the world's largest retailer and owner of Asda in the UK, has recently predicted that trading in its core US operation is likely to remain subdued for a further period of at least three months.
>
> After a lacklustre first quarter of the year, which saw net income rise at just 4 per cent, the retailer suggested that US consumer confidence was mostly to blame.
>
> Due to a slowdown in the US economy, Wal-Mart had to reduce its forecasts for the year. This in essence was unexpected.
>
> Source: *The Times* May 2001

As a result of the downturn in the US economy, you will notice that Wal-Mart had to revise their forecasts for the year. This is one of many corrective actions that business will have to take. If you recall in Unit 2, 'The marketing audit', the hi-tech industries have taken significant corrective action to try to get back on track, but that has also amounted to the loss of many jobs to achieve it.

Corrective actions can take the form of:

- Revised forecasts
- Revised sales targets
- Increased advertising
- Competitive responses
- Price reductions or increases
- Repositioning of products
- Marketing development strategies.

These are only a few, but it gives you an insight into the potential for change, in extenuating circumstances, when the organization can effectively no longer 'tolerate' the market conditions.

This probably brings us back to a key learning point in respect of setting objectives, developing strategies and plans. Objectives always need to be achievable, and it may be that in many instances the reason for the failure to meet performance standards is the lack of realism in the original objectives set, and perhaps failure to resource the implementation programme satisfactorily.

Summary

This has been a particularly extensive unit, focusing on the broad range of issues associated with planning. However, again, you are reminded that while you have been provided with an insight into the notion of marketing planning, the basis of marketing operations is to look at marketing at an 'operational' level. In the text we have looked closely at:

- Taking the marketing audit to the planning process
- Setting different types of objectives
- Segmentation, targeting and positioning
- Strategy development
- Implementation of the marketing plan.

The influence and importance of marketing planning must never be underestimated; it is vital to the success of the organization. There is endless academic writing in relation to this particular subject area, but while many are a slight variation on a theme, there is a core at the heart of planning that never actually changes. It is very important to read around the subject wherever possible and gain a real insight into the major driving forces behind the planning processes and what makes planning such a vital activity.

Further study and examination preparation

Extending knowledge
Recommended reading

You may find it useful to read Chapters 21–23 of *Marketing Concepts and Strategies*, 4th European edn by Dibb, Simkin, Pride and Ferrell (2001). (This is on the CIM recommended reading list.)

Study tip

Operational level marketing will focus quite clearly on involvement in the marketing audit, preparing the audit for strategy development, and thereinafter providing information to support the decision-making process, that ultimately culminates in the development of the marketing mix programme.

At an operational level, you will be expected to define, based upon the key strategic marketing objectives presented to you, a marketing strategy and tactical marketing plan, i.e. define a marketing programme based upon the marketing mix.

The mini-case study question for June 2000 is a good indicator of the level of marketing planning you will be challenged with in a marketing operations examination.

Question 3.8

June 2000, Question 1b

Go to www.marketingonline.co.uk or www.bh.com/marketing to access Specimen Answers and Senior Examiner's advice for this exam question.

June 2001, Question 6

Go to www.marketingonline.co.uk or www.bh.com/marketing to access Specimen Answers and Senior Examiner's advice for this exam question.

Unit 4
Theories of communication

Objectives

Introduction to promotional operations in the context of the marketing mix

This particular subject area has been divided across two units, the theory of communications and the practice of communications, i.e. 'promotional operations'.

This unit concentrates on the theory of marketing communications which may not necessarily be new to you. You may have indeed covered communication theories in other contexts. However, it is essential that you are able to utilize communication models in respect of marketing and promotional operations, creating synergy and consistency in line with the objectives of the marketing plan.

This particular unit covers theories of communications: single step, two-step, multi-step and adoption models.

(Syllabus reference 1.2.1)

The marketing mix in the context of marketing operations

The marketing mix is a set of tools that provides the basis of implementation of the marketing plan. The promotional tools provide the means by which an organization communicates with potential and existing customers about their products, services, distribution outlets and overall prices.

For many organizations, the marketing mix provides a basis for the organization to develop its marketing strategies, plans and tactics. They will take the marketing mix and develop a marketing strategy that will enable them to meet customer needs, be highly competitive both in terms of proactive and reactive competition and allow them to differentiate on brand, products and services and position themselves successfully against competitive equivalents.

The principal approach to marketing should be based around three key ingredients, i.e. integration, co-ordination and communication. This applies to the design and development of the marketing mix as well as every aspect of the planning process, with synergy and consistency as critical success factors to the overall implementation of the plan.

The marketing mix cannot be developed in a vacuum or in isolation of the other elements. For example, an organization cannot develop a quality, value-added product/service without due consideration to the cost of the product and how they can charge that to the customer. Organizations will then have to give due consideration to how they will distribute it. Then of course, how do they communicate with their customers to inform them of the existence of the new product or service.

For a truly marketing-oriented, customer-focused organization it is of primary importance to understand the impact of each element of the marketing mix upon customers and their perspectives of the organization.

In order to provide a clearer understanding of customer responses and reactions to the marketing mix, it is useful to consider the key components of the 7Cs model as shown in Figure 4.1.

Organizational perspective of the marketing mix		Customer perspective of the marketing mix
PRODUCT	=	CUSTOMER VALUE
PRICE	=	COST
PLACE	=	CONVENIENCE
PROMOTION	=	COMMUNICATION
PHYSICAL EVIDENCE	=	CONFIRMATION
PEOPLE	=	CONSIDERATION
PROCESS	=	CO-ORDINATION AND CONCERN

Figure 4.1 The 7 Cs of the marketing mix

This model provides you with a framework of reference when identifying customer expectations of the organization's marketing mix. For example:

- The customer does not buy the product/service, but the value that the product/service provides
- The price of the product/service is not the customer issue, but how much it will cost them
- What is important to the customer is not the method of distribution, but the convenience of the product for purchase
- The customer perspective is not the promotion but how the messages are communicated to them
- The customer is not concerned with the surroundings or physical evidence, but wants confirmation of their assumptions
- Customers are not concerned with people involved in providing services, but that consideration is provided when purchasing
- Finally, customers are not concerned with the process, but that efforts are co-ordinated to meet their requirements.

It might appear that the main focus of the 7Ps is very much on the services aspect of marketing, however, it is becoming extremely clear that more and more products and services are integral and reliant on one another. What is important is the 'customer experience' – this will require an integrated approach of some or all of the marketing mix elements simultaneously and not in isolation.

The communications process

The role of communications in marketing is often seen as one of the most dynamic, explosive and exciting areas of marketing. With the growing impact of the Internet, the challenges of finding the most creative and effective method of communication are endless. It provides the flow of information that effectively meets the needs and wants of the customers in a forum or framework to which they might respond.

Communication is an exchange process, which provides the opportunity to inform the potential customer about the offerings of the organization, at the same time acting as a channel of encouragement to existing customers to keep purchasing, i.e. it is a tool for customer retention.

You can be forgiven for thinking that communication theories and processes might be easy to implement, but it can be one of the most challenging tools to work with, as communication often sets the tone of the relationship, provides clarity, direction and the opportunity for action.

At the same time poorly managed or poorly staged communication can form the basis of conflict, misinterpretation of the facts and cause customers to consider and question the validity of the communication and of the organization itself.

Therefore, the basis of communication as identified by Chris Fill (1999) provides an opportunity upon which to consider the formula, structure and purpose of any communication. Ideally, therefore the basis of promotional operations communication should be as illustrated in Figure 4.2.

DIFFERENTIATE product and services

REMIND and reassure customers and potential customers

INFORM and

PERSUADE targets to think or act in a particular way

Figure 4.2 Adapted from Fill, 1999

Communications theory

Simplistically, a communication process involves sending messages to the target audience. It is usual that the message provides the audience with the opportunity to respond and for feedback, whereby, again in simplistic terms, the sender provides the receiver with a feedback mechanism, a response opportunity in order that they can perhaps demonstrate their overall intent or actions. Communication in a marketing context therefore must be a two-way process.

In order that you fully understand the implications of marketing communications, it is essential to understand a number of communications models: single-step, two-step, multi-step and adoption models.

Single-step – 'The communication loop'

Figure 4.3 The single-step communication model

Sender: The sender is the source of the message, i.e. the organization – they ascertain the need to communicate with the customer and will then through the encoding process, identify the appropriate basis of communication.

Encoder: Encoding the actual message, its content and intended meaning into a symbolic format that can be transmitted and understood by the target audience; symbolic format being appropriate words, pictures, images or music that the customer might identify with and be attracted by.

Channel: The method by which the message is communicated, e.g. TV, radio, the Internet.

Decoding: The customer actually understanding the symbolic format that was transmitted – i.e. associating with the symbols, words or images used.

Receiver: The target audience – the customer, the organization, the audience for which the message was intended.

Feedback: The response the receiver makes – their communication back to the actual source of the message.

Noise: Background noise, interference, distortion of the message, its content and meaning, making it difficult for the receiver to interpret, understand and respond to the message accordingly – overcoming noise is of the essence in order to gain successful feedback.

Figure 4.3 illustrates a communications loop, whereby the sender uses the method of encoding, i.e. developing a message and symbolic reference to which a customer might react, in order to ascertain the best method of communication to send a message to their potential or existing customers. To do this, they must have a detailed understanding of their target audience, their consumer behaviour and responses in relation to promotional activity.

The 'one-step communication loop' above has frequently being criticized for its simplistic approach to marketing communications. Although it provides the basis for communications planning and the basis for the customer to respond, it fails to take into account personal influences upon the communication process; what might inhibit them from responding and why. What are the key influences upon the decision-making process and where might the key 'influences' emerge from?

To clarify, noise levels do not take into account opinion leaders and the role they might play in underpinning the decision-making process of the customer, but are related more to forms of interference or distraction from absorbing the content of the communication. They could be distracted by somebody calling them away at the critical point in the advertisement, or for example, by a competing message being presented in close proximity of the original message.

Two-step communication model

This particular model is more adept at considering the inadequacies of the one-step communication model, as it takes into account the role played by opinion leaders in the interpretation of 'mass' messages to a 'mass' audience. Katz and Lazarsfeld (1995) developed the two-step model of communication illustrated in Figure 4.4, which incorporates the influence of opinion leaders.

Figure 4.4 Two-step communication model

This model represents the fact that opinion leaders might be able to directly reach various target groups, and either reinforce the message being transmitted by the sender or alternatively they may have a negative influence upon the customer group. Therefore, it is vital to consider the role of the opinion leader in preparing appropriate communications that will have a positive influence on both groups.

Opinion leaders play a significant role in our everyday decision-making. They can include the media, subject specialists magazines such as *Which?*, who bring influence to bear on the decision-making of anything from computers to motor vehicles, washing machines, etc. They will provide opinions, weightings and ultimately a significant influence upon the decision-makers, particularly those who need confidence and reinforcement of their behaviour and of their decisions.

Opinion leaders can take many forms, for example, pressure groups. They may force us to consider very careful the basis of our decision-making. They will ensure that we consider not only what the product has to offer, but perhaps some of the principles of the organization that is providing it to us, and perhaps the basis of their supply chain.

With both invasive and investigative media, customers and consumers are coming to realize that there is no such thing as a 'pure' or 'value-free' offer, which makes them concentrate very seriously on the broader aspects of their decision-making process.

Behind every brand, product and service offering lie the people who are making decisions and choices in a more informed way, and according to priorities, motives and perhaps personal goals.

Increasingly customers are getting to know more about the product and perhaps the ethos of the organization. In some instances, customers will even want to establish a relationship between themselves and their suppliers based upon trust.

As we see through Porter's Five Forces, customer power is significant and they are exerting their power more and more by making informed decisions. Where high profile brands are concerned, customers want to be reassured that promises will be met. Can they really deliver what they say?

Opinion leaders are playing a more and more significant role in responding to customers' thirst for knowledge. They are individuals who are predisposed to receiving information and then using it to influence others.

Opinion leadership manifests itself through a number of channels, in advertising, public relations, editorials, journals, pressure groups to name but a few.

For marketers therefore, the role of opinion leaders should never be underestimated and they should never be excluded from a communications agenda.

It is important as an organization, therefore, for you not just to have customers and consumers, but also to have friends and supporters, who may, to your advantage, be opinion leaders, who will exert positive influence upon your organization. This will be vitally important as you, along with your competitors, are in a desperate race for competitive edge.

It is also important that you have an understanding of the role of opinion formers. Effectively they are people who exert personal influence because of their authority, status, education or perhaps association with the product or service offering. They are likely to provide information and to advertise and in some instances make take on roles as 'expert witnesses', i.e. they use their experience and expertize to justify particular situations in relation to various products. A good example of this could relate to the outbreak of 'Foot-and-Mouth Disease' in the UK. As a result of this outbreak, serious consideration was given to introducing a programme of vaccinations in order to combat further spread of the disease both nationally and internationally. A number of veterinary surgeons and scientists were then asked to undertake research to consider the impact of this proposed programme and its likely success. Clearly they acted as expert witnesses and expert 'opinion formers'.

The influence of opinion formers is quite significant and can act as a vehicle to reinforcing the credibility of products and services, or indeed the validity of such products can actually be questioned and found to be deficient in some areas.

In order that organizations can 'win friends and influence people' they will often seek support through lobbying in addition to various other activities to win the opinion formers' support.

Question 4.1

Discuss with examples the differences between opinion leaders and opinion formers.

The multi-step communication model

Figure 4.5 Multi-stage communication model

The basis of this model (see Figure 4.5) relates to the exchange of information and opinions between the opinion leaders/formers and target groups. Effectively everybody who is communicated to as a receiver then influences another. The process of communication here is also two-way. However, one thing to bear in mind is that opinion formers can also have some communication with the sender, in respect of providing research and expertize in relation to specialist subjects, at the same time as influencing perceptions in the minds of opinion leaders and the target audience. It is a complex web of intrigue and communications that needs careful planning.

Again an exchange of personal influences is undertaken, whereby a range of shared experiences, knowledge, perceptions, reflections and recommendations are provided in order to reinforce the purchase decision or indeed to reverse it.

Potential influences upon the decision-making process and therefore the process of communication and adoption, are categorized into three key areas:

Personal	Demographic, situational and level of involvement
Psychological	Perception, motives, learning, attitudes and personality
Social	Roles and family, reference groups, social classes, culture.

Dealing with the vast range of influences will stretch the minds of anybody involved in promotional operations, as in essence your communication has to reach and influence those people who are in the main predisposed to this type of information exchange. Sometimes this might mean a move away from the typical approach to targeting very specific customers for a particular product or service range and instead concentrating effort and resources on reaching those individuals or groups who indeed bring influence to bear on customers and consumers.

> **Question 4.2**
>
> Explain with examples, the differences between the two-step and multi-step communication theory models.

The process of adoption

Equipped with some understanding of the three key communication models, it is necessary to consider the next stage of communications theory, which concentrates directly on how, having prepared the communication or message and encoded this message, you actually influence customers to adopt your product or service.

The key to success in this particular area is to target each stage of the consumer decision-making process (Figure 4.6) in order to continually reinforce the customers' decisions as they go. However, in order to do this successfully, it will be essential to understand and consider some of the external influences that might hinder their adoption of the product.

Figure 4.6 Possible influences on the decision process (Adapted from Dibb, Simkin and Ferrel, 1997)

Another imperative is that you clearly understand the basis of decision-making units, how they are structured, and what active role they play in the decision-making process. This assists you as the marketer to know more about the basis of profiling and targeting specific influences in the decision-making process.

The consumer decision-making unit (DMU)

Decision-making for the consumer is not exclusive to one person, it can involve a wide range of influences and influencers. The DMU is a term used to describe the various people or members involved in the decision-making process. It is useful marketing information to know who and how many people are involved in the decision-making process. The various people in the decision-making unit will have different roles in decision-making.

There are five consumer buying roles that must be considered:

- Initiator
- Influencer
- Decider
- Buyer
- User.
- *The initiator* – is the person who effectively identified the problem, i.e. the need to buy the product or service. The initiator will most likely suggest the need to buy this product to other people.
- *The influencer* – is the person or people to whom the initiator will likely turn for advice and guidance on the purchase. This could be a family member, a friend or an expert in the area. A good example could be the purchase of a personal computer for the home. This is quite a significant purchase and one that involves a lot of technical detail. An influencer could guide you on the mechanics of the PC and the functions you may need it to perform for you.
- *The decider* – is the person who will give the go-ahead to purchase the product. This could be the initiator or the influencer. This person will decide what to buy, how much to pay, where to buy it from and what additional service or warranty requirements may be needed.
- *The buyer* – is the person who makes the purchase, the individual who then gets involved in the exchange process between the customer and the organization.

There are a number of models that represent the way in which a range of promotional activities within the promotional mix seeks to persuade customers to purchase. A somewhat aged model, known as AIDA and designed in 1925 by Strong, developed stages which advertising may go through to attract the customer's attention. Then in the 1960s the hierarchy of effects model was developed by Lavidge and Stiner. This represents the process by which advertising was thought to work and assumed that customers may go through. After that, in 1978 McGuire developed a further model known as the Information Processing Model.

Figure 4.7 demonstrates the phase each model takes a customer through to engage their attention towards the product.

These are three commonly used models, which in essence have common denominators, each one trying to ensure that they optimize the possibility of the customer actually adopting their chosen product. There are other models, such as DAGMAR, which works on the basis of:

- Action
- Conviction
- Comprehension
- Awareness
- Unawareness.

Alternatively there is also the adoption model, which again is very similar to the above with the key components relating to:

- Awareness
- Interest

- Evaluation
- Trial
- Adoption.

In respect of promotional operations, they are to focus the minds of those involved to prioritize and order the various communication objectives against the different stages in the decision-making process. This is necessary in order that the organization exploits every available opportunity to attract the customer's attention with the ultimate objective of securing a purchase.

AIDA (Strong)	Hierarchy of effect (Lavidge and Stiner)	Information processing model (McGuire)
	Awareness	Presentation
		Attention
Attention	Knowledge	Comprehension
Interest	Liking	Yielding
Desire	Preference conviction	Retention
Action	Purchase	Behaviour

Figure 4.7 Adoption models

There are three key types of objectives associated with the links between adoption models and consumer decision-making processes, they are cognitive objectives, affective objectives and behavioural objectives.

- **Cognitive** being objectives related to providing information that creates both knowledge and awareness of the particular products. Within the models above, this particular area will be linked with *attention, knowledge, action, awareness or unawareness*. Essentially this would be at the problem recognition and information search stage of the consumer decision-making process.
- **Affective** objectives are those that will be determined with a view to actually developing or indeed changing customers' and consumers' attitudes to the product or service offering. With respect to the hierarchy models this will be linked clearly to desiring the product, evaluating alternatives, developing a form of conviction in relation to the product, or indeed a preference or liking. This would clearly link directly with the evaluation of alternatives within the decision-making process.
- **Behavioural** objectives are designed to ensure that the customer acts in a positive way and actually purchases the product. Clearly this is the ultimate phase, whereby you aim to achieve action, adoption and purchase – the 'purchase decision' within the consumer buying decision process. These are the higher level objectives within the hierarchy.

A further consideration in relation to adoption in respect of communications is that of the process of diffusion and innovation (Figure 4.8). It is essential that great care is taken over the rate at which sales occur, the speed at which they occur and the level of market penetration that occurs, as this will determine the nature and longitude of the communications plan.

Figure 4.8 Innovation and diffusion process

It is likely that innovators are probably those who are in the 'B' range of social class as suggested in JICNAR (see Unit 3). It could be likely that they as innovators speed up the process of diffusion through their actions and potentially by word of mouth. Clearly this will then need to be supported by a range of other communications tools in order that the opportunity to speed up the diffusion process is optimized and exploited.

Targeting decision makers

We looked at market segmentation and targeting within Unit 3, 'Marketing planning, implementation and control'. To remain competitive and cost-effective for both marketing and promotional operations, it is critical to profile and target your audiences and hence communicate with them very specifically, ensuring that all messages are relevant at that particular point in the decision-making process. It is also important to ensure that the messages are meaningful in a way that will pull decision-makers towards the product and a long-term loyal relationship.

However, targeting decision-makers at the right time can be a very complex process, particularly in a business-to-business (B2B) setting. It is therefore of primary importance that you ensure that all communications, at each stage of the decision-making, and for meeting each element of the overall marketing strategy, are specifically targeted and provide the basis of synergy and consistency in terms of the overall implementation.

Example – Black and Decker

Black and Decker developed three distinct product ranges each one targeted to different channels. They used the Quantum brand at the heavy DIY end of the market, Black and Decker for major multiples and De Walt aimed at trade buyers and contractors. Different promotions and incentives are made available to each target market.

Profiling marketing segments for promotional activities

It has already been suggested that segmenting markets in relation to promotional activities can be a complex process. However, whatever the range of variables that the organization uses in order to establish target groups of customers, it is essential that they establish a clear understanding of the characteristics of the individuals within the group before ultimately defining their make-up.

> **Definition**
>
> **Profiling**
>
> Profiling is the task of building up a fuller picture of the target segments. (Dibb, Simkin, Pride and Ferrell, 2001)

Profiling is achieved by taking a group of what is commonly known as descriptors, based around traditional segmentation criteria, i.e. demographics, geographics and socio-economics of the target group, and seeking to understand how these descriptors match against the variables established to identify customer needs and wants. The idea is that while some of the customer base might have matching demographics, their socio-economics might differ and result in differing customer needs. It is essential that you profile customers in this way, to highlight as many similarities as possible, in order to maximize the potential impact of a fully integrated marketing mix.

A good example of this would be the motor vehicle market. While most 30–45-year-olds possess a car, the needs associated with this car will differ significantly. Therefore in the context of promotional needs the targeting of cars in the upper range, such as high level specification Mercedes or BMWs, might require a different promotional mix to those who are looking for a low-cost family saloon. Typical profiling strategies will ensure that the differences between target groups are identified to maximize the potential of the promotional mix.

This then allows for very specific targeting in promotional terms, and allows the organization to define its approach on either a mass media basis, or indeed a concentration strategy or even a focus strategy approach to promotional activities.

Push and pull strategy

Prior to moving on to look at the intricate detail of the promotional mix, and how the promotional tools are used to implement the marketing strategy, it is essential that you understand the nature of 'push and pull' strategies.

Push strategy

This is where the manufacturer effectively takes the decision to concentrate their communications effort on the members of the distribution channel, i.e. the wholesaler and retailers. This means that the wholesalers may possess a significant amount of stock that they need to move on from a particular manufacturer and therefore they in turn promote the products to the end user and customer.

The basis of this particular strategy is that the manufacturer is promoting directly to the suppliers, and the products are, therefore, pushed down the line by the different members of the channel. By the same token, the promotional activity is also pushed down the line in parallel with the product. In this instance it is highly unlikely that the manufacturer will therefore have any direct contact with the customer.

Pull strategy

This strategy operates in contrast to the push strategy, in that it requires the manufacturer to create demand for the product through direct communication with the customers. From here it is likely that the retailers might identify and perceive the demand for this product and that it is essential in the interest of serving their customers. They might then demand the product from their supplier/wholesaler. This effectively sees the product being pulled up the line by consumer demand, i.e. the consumer is pulling it to market and being pulled by the manufacturer.

However, on this occasion it is likely that the promotion and communications activity will be working in the opposite direction from the product, and therefore the communication relates to pulling the product to market, effectively developing a strong consumer demand.

Of course, in reality, manufacturers will involve themselves in both push and pull situations, in order to assert as much influence as possible on the supply chain and the customer.

Promotional operations and the planning framework

Figure 4.9 Promotions and the planning framework

It is important to understand the role of promotional operations and the role it plays in terms of the implementation of the overall marketing strategy. Figure 4.9 provides an insight into where promotional operations will fit into the planning hierarchy.

Aims and objectives of the promotional communications process

You will probably by now realize that the process of product adoption is a high level objective – for any component of the promotional activity and the promotional mix. Therefore it is essential that you translate this into five key communication effects:

Category needs	The perception and understanding of the actual customer needs
Brand awareness	The ability of the consumer to identify and associate with a particular brand and differentiate from another brand
Brand attitude	This relates to the consumer's particular observations, view and perceptions of the brand – cognitive beliefs
Brand purchase intention	Once the category needs have been identified – the brand purchase intention follows
Purchase facilitation	The purchase activity needs to be facilitated by the organization, by ensuring that the product is available at the right price and the right place – this in essence is the manifestation of the integrated marketing mix.

These aims break down into a number of more specific promotional objectives that the promotional operations activity will seek to achieve in order to meet the corporate goals and marketing objectives and also to ensure successful implementation of the marketing strategy.

Possible communications objectives will therefore include:

- Clarification of customer needs
- Increasing brand awareness
- Increasing product knowledge
- Improving brand image
- Improving company image
- Increasing brand preference
- Stimulating search behaviour
- Increasing trial purchases
- Increasing repeat purchase
- Increasing word-of-mouth recommendation
- Improving financial position
- Increasing flexibility of the corporate image
- Increasing co-operation from the trade
- Enhancing the reputation with key stakeholders
- Building up management ego.

Source: Based on Delozier, 1976

Ultimately, any activities that you undertake as part of the promotional operations process will therefore be aiming to achieve one or more of the above promotional objectives, reflecting very much the nature of the key marketing objectives and strategy.

The critical success factors associated with achieving the aims of the promotional communication process relate to specifically targeting customer groups through a clearly defined profiling process.

In the same way that short-term and long-term objectives are an issue within the marketing strategy framework, so they are in terms of promotional activity, as the promotional strategy will be shaped and determined by those objectives. However, it is likely that much of the promotional activity will be based on short-term activity, but in the context of the broader picture of the long-term achievement of goals.

Summary

The focus of this unit was to provide an overview of the essential communication and adoption models that might assist you in the development of appropriate promotional mix programmes, in order that they effectively communicate with customers in a way that they will relate to.

One of the key objectives of any promotional operational programme will be to ensure that, ultimately, potential customers adopt the product offering and are converted to the brand, in a way that can establish long and loyal relationships in years to come.

This underpins the next unit on 'Promotional operations', contextualizing promotional communications in the planning process, and will prepare you to put into an operational context the tools of the promotional mix.

Further study and examination preparation

Question 4.3

Categorize the objectives below into cognitive, affective, behavioural and corporate.

1. Clarification of customer needs
2. Increasing brand awareness
3. Increasing product knowledge
4. Improving brand image
5. Improving company image
6. Increasing brand preference
7. Stimulating search behaviour
8. Increasing trial purchases
9. Increasing repeat purchase
10. Increasing word-of-mouth recommendation
11. Improving financial position
12. Increasing flexibility of the corporate image
13. Increasing co-operation from the trade
14. Enhancing the reputation with key stakeholders
15. Building up management ego

Source: Based on Delozier, 1976

Unit 5
Promotional operations

Objectives

Now that you have a full underpinning knowledge of the marketing planning process, it is time to look at how the marketing mix is applied in context of the implementation process.

The learning outcomes associated with this unit are:

- To understand the need to integrate marketing mix tools to achieve effective implementation of plans
- To be able to elect and justify the use of one or more promotional techniques for a particular marketing context.

It is therefore important to understand the basis of the indicative content that underpins this unit and how it will form the basis of your study in relation to 'promotional operations'.

- Advertising techniques
- Sales promotion techniques
- Public relations techniques
- Direct and interactive communications
- Sponsorship
- Personal selling techniques.
  (Syllabus reference 1.2.1)

Should you continue through to the Postgraduate Diploma in Marketing, you will find this unit underpins the strategic implications of Integrated Marketing Communications.

The promotional mix

The promotional mix will now be the heart of this unit, whereby we will be looking at how it is used in a direct way in order that the organization can communicate with its various target audiences.

Tools of the promotional mix

There are many elements of the promotional mix, which are used as a way of communicating messages to customers. They are summarized as follows:

- Advertising
- Packaging
- Merchandising
- Personal selling
- Sales promotion
- Direct marketing
- Public relations
- Sponsorship
- Exhibitions
- Internet.

These tools form the basis of the promotional mix and they are deliberately selected for their ability to attract customers, fulfil their desire for information and ultimately persuade them to adopt the products. However, in this unit, we will be looking at advertising, sales promotions, public relations, direct and interactive marketing communications, sponsorship and personal selling.

Choosing the ultimate promotional mix is a complex task, that requires skill, creatively matching the profile of the customer and the target group with a promotional mix that will essentially attract them to the product. Of course the complexity of the exercise will differ based upon the market, certainly from a B2B (business-to-business) perspective, it is highly complex given the number of people involved in the decision-making process.

It has been suggested on a number of occasions that the key to success in implementing the ultimate promotional mix is understanding customers and their characteristics, something that is a consistent theme to implementation of communications and promotional objectives.

However, the success of any promotional campaign will impinge upon the integrated approach to using the promotional mix.

Integrated marketing communications

Integrated marketing communications is growing in impetus and importance in marketing today as more and more organizations realize the importance of taking a more structured, ordered and integrative approach to their marketing communications activities.

In the simplest form, it involves the integration and cohesion of all elements of the marketing mix. A campaign that is integrated is planned, it is uniform in terms of its design, and it shares a USP and communicates the same message in a co-ordinated way. By combining more than one element of promotion, the message that is communicated is more powerful.

For example, Walkers Crisps have been involved in implementing an integrated campaign. This has been both on TV and poster advertising. In addition to that, they are developing a consistent approach to advertising, using key personalities to identify with their products. As a result of this, Walker's market grew by 21 per cent, while the crisp market generally rose only by 11 per cent.

Another prime example was Häagen-Dazs. They demonstrated an effective use of integrated marketing communications when entering the UK market. They positioned their products as luxury, fashionable food for adults and used a number of key personalities to promote the product for them. They gave themselves a quality positioning and used quality press in which to advertise. The net effect: they are a main player in the ice cream market in the UK today.

As customers, we require a variety of different communication and promotional activities to fulfil our need to know about products and services and then to purchase them. So while this course is predominantly about advertising, you must consider the need to integrate and co-ordinate all of your marketing and communications/promotional activities.

Communications plans can only be successfully developed if the key factors within the marketing plan are clearly defined, identified and developed.

According to Chris Fill, in his book *Integrated Marketing Communications, 1999*:

> *Integrated marketing communications cannot be achieved just by saying the same message through a variety of tools; the marketing mix is also a strong communicator.*

Integrated communications are mostly likely to occur when organizations attempt to enter into a co-ordinated dialogue with their various internal and external audiences. The communications tools used in the dialogue and the message sent should be consistent with the organization's objectives and strategies.

Integrated marketing communications often means different things to different people, but in the main the view is that it should embrace the marketing mix, the promotional mix, internal communications and all those who contribute to the overall marketing communications process.

This means that PR, advertising, direct mail, trade promotions, consumer promotions, packaging, point-of-sale signage, brochures, literature, merchandise, websites and sponsorship all have their own individual role, but all achieve the corporate and marketing objectives for the brand.

There are a number of driving forces at work encouraging the growth in integrated marketing communications. From the organizational perspective, there is the need for improved efficiency, rapid growth in global marketing, co-ordinated brand development and competitive advantage and the organization's drive to provide direction and purpose for the brand.

From the market-based perspective, drivers include better-educated audiences, cost of media and greater amounts of information – 'message clutter', competitor activities, growth in relationship marketing and the growth of networks, collaborations and alliances.

Communication-based drivers include technological advances such as the Internet, databases, new segmentation techniques, message effectiveness, more consistent brand images and the need to build brand reputations to provide clear identities.

As we move on it is essential that while you look at each element of the promotional mix in isolation, to understand its role in the promotional operations process, you should also look at ways of maximizing the mix potential by integrating it and aligning it with other promotional tools in order to optimize the marketing effort.

Advertising

Advertising is one of the most influential forms of communication within the promotional mix, and the one that perhaps has the most impact upon our everyday lives. It does not matter where we go during a day, it is likely that we are bombarded either by radio, billboard, TV, cinema or banner advertising on a regular basis.

> **Definition**
> **Advertising**
> Advertising is a paid form of non-formal communication that is transmitted through mass media such as television, radio, newspapers, magazines, direct mail, public transport vehicles, outdoor displays and the Internet.

It is likely that advertising will serve a number of purposes in terms of communicating with both individual and organizational customers. It is used to meet a number of specific marketing and promotional objectives as you have already seen, but its main emphasis is to inform, persuade and remind customers to purchase products and services.

Ideally advertising is used to promote products and services, but it is also a source that creates long-term images and perspectives of the organization. It is likely that there have been a number of adverts that stick in your mind, that have impacted upon you in a direct way, created an image and perception in your mind.

Take for example 'Orange Tango' – being 'Tangoed' became a way of life for young people for a long time as a result of the orange coloured man running around and slapping an unsuspecting person in the face. It is probably one of the most successful advertisements in achieving 'recall'.

Advertising objectives

You will see later in this unit where advertising objectives actually come into play, and how they break down into different categories. Advertising objectives should be SMART in the same way that marketing objectives are SMART and they should relate directly to achieving the marketing objectives overall. It is therefore likely that advertising objectives will reflect some of the following components:

- Promoting product, organizations and services
- Stimulating demand for products
- Competitive advertising – offensive/defensive advertising
- Increasing sales (growth)
- Educating the market – brand and product awareness
- Increasing the use of product and services (market development)
- Reminding and reinforcing (market penetration)
- Reducing fluctuations.

For example a typical advertising objective could be to increase sales by 10 per cent from £500K to £550K by the end of June 2001. A further example, perhaps as in the case of Egg or easyJet, is to increase brand awareness from the existing 70 per cent to 100 per cent within 12 months to June 2002.

However, there is a fine line between advertising to create sales and advertising to create awareness and each of these will require a different approach in order to achieve the long-term goals of the organization.

It is quite clear that one of the key tools of the promotional mix to support the sale of products is advertising. This is particularly so for consumer-based products, where advertising serves to create an awareness of the product, its characteristics, its image and buying habits.

A good example to demonstrate how consumer-based products interact with advertising is chocolate. A low involvement, low unit-price bar of chocolate would not, of course, warrant an investment in personal selling to the millions of consumers who purchase it on a day-to-day basis. In this situation it is much more likely that the emphasis would be through some form of advertising, or even sponsorship through advertising. Sponsorship-based advertising is becoming increasingly common, with organizations such as Cadbury sponsoring the UK soap opera *Coronation Street*, for example.

It is critical that you understand the impact of advertising and the role it plays on the product, and the link between the advertising campaign and the different stages of the product life cycle. However, it is also important that first you understand the appropriate media and their characteristics and how therefore they can be used.

> **Question 5.1**
>
> Why is it important to define advertising objectives?

Advertising media characteristics

As a marketer it is not expected that you will become a media expert, however it is important that you understand how it can be used and how the impact can be potentially measured.

We have already looked at the importance of profiling and targeting the audience precisely, and in doing this it will be vital that in parallel you understand the nature of the most appropriate media for that target audience.

		TV	Radio	Cinema	Press				Posters	Direct Mail
					Daily, Evening and Sunday	Regional	Magazines			
A U D I E N C E	Audience size	Some wastage, large and national (some international)	National and tightly segmented local coverage	Small, no national coverage	Large and mostly national	Small, no national networks	Mostly national (and international)		National coverage is difficult	Large national and international
	Audience type	Few 15-24 year olds	Many housewives, commuters	Many 15-24 year olds	Socio-economic	Geographic segments	Lifestyle segments		Commuters, car drivers etc.	Any target available
	Audience state of mind	Relaxed and passive TV couch potato = visual wallpaper	Background/audio wallpaper	Captive audience - willing suspension of disbelief	Deliberately read		Relaxed and involved with magazine			
C O S T S	Cost of production	High	Low	High	Low-Med.	Low	Low-Med.		Med.	Low
	Minimum cost of space	High	Low	Low	Med.	Low	Low-Med.		Low-Med.	High but can experiment in small quantities
	Average cost per thousand	Low less than £2	Very low less than £1		Low-Med. £8	Med. £30	Med. £12-70			High £500
	Extra advantages	Adults credibility to product or company	Transportable medium	High impact and captive audience						

Figure 5.1 A summary of media characteristics (Adapted from Smith, 1998)

Clearly one of the gaps in Figure 5.1 relates to the new technologies in direct and interactive communications. However, we will look at this a little later in this unit.

The role of advertising in the product life cycle

Introduction

This is the stage where the product is actually launched into the marketplace and where a significant amount of investment is made in creating an awareness of the product. This is often referred to as *pioneering* advertising.

It is likely that the role of advertising will be to ensure that the product name and benefits become known and spread quickly among the target market, possibly supported by sales promotions, e.g. coupons, sampling, etc. to help encourage customers at least to trial the product.

This might be an extremely intense period of advertising as early sales will be essential in order to enable some return on investment (ROI) as soon as possible. The ultimate aim will be to ensure that buyers can see how the product might relate to them and stimulate them sufficiently to consider its use or consumption.

Case history

Heinz Green Sauce

Heinz Green Sauce, EZ Sauce, was initially launched in the USA and once sales became successful the decision was taken to undertake some market development and launch the product in the UK via TV advertising.

As with many other advertising campaigns these days, consumers will be encouraged to find out more about the product through logging on to the Heinz website. Heinz felt that their core condiment portfolio needed a 'boot up the backside'. This product was aimed particularly at the younger generation. Heinz spent some £5 million on promotional activity as part of an overall £30 million on global brand repositioning.

Growth

Advertising may become a little less tense at this stage as the product effectively begins to find its own impetus and both retailers and consumers possibly start making repeat purchases. There will be a little less emphasis on creating awareness and providing information about the 'new' product. More emphasis will be placed on repeat purchase, image and developing a long-term relationship, effectively building loyalty.

However, the organization should be aware of the pending competitive attacks that might emerge at this stage, as competitors may be launching their version of the same product. It is here that advertising has a role to ensure that the customer can differentiate clearly between brands, i.e. that the advertising campaign clearly relates to objectives requiring brand awareness and brand attitude.

Advertising will therefore be used to generate the message of differentiation. As a result of this the key message that advertising will be seeking to send is that of brand image. It is likely that organizations will also be developing and implementing *'competitive advertising'* strategies to ensure that the unique benefits of their products are communicated to the customer.

> **Case history**
>
> **Heinz Green Sauce**
>
> Taking the example of Heinz again, they should, accordingly to Paul Von Bergen, managing director of youth marketing agency Chemistry, be trying to:
>
> - Focus on increasing usage and portion size
> - Invest in different promotions that are relevant to different audiences
> - Emphasize the simplicity of the product
> - Learn from Coca-Cola.
>
> According to Peter Knapp, creative director of Landor Association, Heinz should
>
> - Continue to invest in the credibility of the Heinz brand with proven long-term reputation
> - Welcome green Ketchuppers to the club – 'with relish'
> - Beware of budding ketchup Picassos.

Maturity

The role of advertising takes on a different dimension at the maturity stage of the product life cycle, involves very defensive advertising aimed at maintaining customers and holding on to market share. Many competitors may now be in the marketplace and therefore there is a serious threat to market share for a particular organization. To combat this threat a range of *competitive* and *comparative* advertising is likely to be undertaken.

Advertising will focus very much on reminding customers of the benefits of the product and service, encouraging them to continue to repeat purchase of the product, but it also provides an opening for customer relationship advertising to achieve customer retention.

It is possible that many organizations that reach the maturity stage for their products may actually take the opportunity to either reposition their products somewhat or re-launch a modified version. This will mean that for the brand to be revitalized there is likely to be a more aggressive and intensive period of advertising entered into again. The car industry is a typical case of this, as they often seek to make minor cosmetic alterations to the exterior of a vehicle and then re-launch it.

Decline

Should a product reach decline it is often beyond redemption and therefore it is about moving the product on and making room for the new one. Therefore the majority of advertising and sales promotion will be based on *reminder and reinforcement* advertising and sales promotion to keep it going a little longer, but eventually it will become obsolete. The majority of organizations at this stage would be looking more to investing funds into the next product launch.

Looking at the product life cycle in this way does assume that a product has a typical life cycle and declines and disappears from the market altogether. In fact in the case of Heinz, this could not be further from the truth, as Heinz was born many years ago and EZ Sauce is indeed the first variation on the traditional red sauce for over 124 years.

Many products will be revamped, modified and relaunched, as suggested in the maturity stage. If this does happen then clearly there will be a need to revise the whole communication plan to communicate the message based around the new and improved product and brand.

When considering the development of a communications plan, the product life cycle does have limitations, and these must be considered, as the last thing any organization wants is to hasten the demise of their product. Therefore it is always critical to look at a range of environmental factors to support the planning process and never look at the product life cycle in isolation of other factors.

Advertising and the marketing mix

Advertising is used to support many elements of the marketing mix, but in most instances the product and brand are the key focus to advertising activities.

Advertising for both distribution and retailing is very much related to the 'push' and 'pull' strategies that we discussed earlier. In essence an organization at this stage may be developing a strategy related to increasing the number of outlets it has, e.g. a marketing objective may have been set to increase the number of retail outlets by 15 per cent within a 12-month period.

Advertising will be focused on encouraging retailers to stock their products. In this situation, advertising will be very closely linked to a high level of promotional activity to support the advertising and give an incentive for distribution outlets to stock their products.

A good example of this is electrical wholesalers, who are encouraged by organizations such as MK, Mitre and Crabtree to sell their products on to electrical retailers. They will therefore advertise in trade media and quite possible offer incentives for wholesalers to carry stock.

A push strategy would often include a range of personal selling, trade (sales) promotions, advertising and direct marketing, in addition to public relations.

For a retail outlet, a pull strategy would be developed. The key to developing this is to create an awareness of the brand and its associated product and encourage customers to purchase from them.

Advertising on this occasion will take several forms, such as TV, radio, press advertising and possibly a big poster campaign. Clearly the level of advertising will be based on the budget available both through the manufacturer and the retailer.

Quite often in retailing situations some promotional support will be available from the manufacturer, such as various brochures, point-of-sale display materials and merchandising support. Again this is very relevant with the sale of electrical goods. Organizations such as Philips or Electrolux offer keen incentives to their retail outlets and distributors to sell their products.

As a marketing communications planner you will need to undertake the following activities in this area:

1. Liaise with channel members to ensure that stock is available
2. Be aware of the needs of the channel and how and when they need communications support
3. Provide consistency for all communications
4. Ensure that all members of the channel support and are empowered by the message the advertisement seeks to deliver.

Repositioning through advertising

Taking a more strategic perspective, advertising can also be used to reposition a product and redefine it in the mind of the customer. Quite often this happens in response to competitive pressures and therefore both aggressive and defensive advertising is likely to be used in order to improve or at least sustain a competitive position.

Positioning is the definition of how and where the brand is going to compete: what particular virtues does the product possess, what are the benefits it offers and when can it best be used?

The most likely approach to this would be opening up new segments of the market to operate within, either based on a benefit usage or possibly geographical or demographic segments.

Ultimately, the brand repositioning will need to provide an even stronger point of differentiation for consumers. Advertising must represent how the brand is meant to fit into its market. It must represent the truth about the brand and offer benefits that are strong enough to encourage customers to buy.

Advertising and its influence on price

The role of marketing communications is informing the target market about the price of a product or service offering. This can be undertaken through advertising in addition to the other elements of the promotional mix, e.g. personal selling, promotions, etc.

There will be many instances when buyers will be concerned with the price of their purchase. However, they may not consider the price in isolation, indeed you will most likely consider it in respect of the product, its size, shape, smell, colour and overall benefits.

Organizations must be aware that price can in fact inhibit purchase of products and services for many people and therefore a pricing strategy needs to be reflected in the communications undertaken by an organization. The customer/consumer has thus a clear understanding of the cost impact upon them.

Price issues will vary from product to product and target group to target group, but the prominence that price receives will depend upon a number of factors:

- Target group
- Level of involvement
- Attitude to risk
- Complexity and technical nature of the product/service
- The importance of price to the decision-making process.

Therefore with this in mind, the design of an advertisement and its emphasis on price will very much be based on the target audience, positioning of the product and the competitive position the product has in the marketplace.

Confusion marketing

One of the key trends emerging from the integration of advertising and pricing implementation process of the marketing mix, is 'confusion marketing'.

Increased competition has found each of us as consumer, continually battling through a mass of information in terms of advertising, promotions, special offers and so on. Each is aimed at persuading us that a product or services package is the best. Unfortunately this mass of information can often serve to confuse us, and in some instances sadly, this appears to be the ultimate objective – confusion marketing.

A recent article in *Marketing Business* quotes a representative from the Consumer Association as saying 'strong brands have a major incentive to confuse customers, as it forces them to make decisions based on brand value, not on value for money. In some areas there is confusion because the product is complex, but in others the complexity is invented purely to stifle competition.'

In the same article veteran marketer Drayton Bird, founder of the Drayton Bird partnership, laments that confusion marketing is often the rule and not the exception. Typical examples of confusion marketing are mobile phone companies, car dealers, airlines, and credit cards.

According to *Marketing Business*, March 2001, confusion marketing plays on people's emotions and insecurities about changing brands. It is a way of creating inertia in your customer market.

One of the prime examples of all time is British Telecom. They have apparently developed confusion marketing as a deliberate strategy and an effective counterattack when competitors are trying to woo customers away. However, BT have in their defence denied that they have ever set out to deliberately confuse their customers.

> ### Case history
>
> **British Telecom fights back!!**
>
> BT's famous Friends and Family scheme, one of the most popular schemes of modern day times, and also one the most admired discount packages – is apparently a classic case of confusion marketing.
>
> Friends and Family offers provide saving on 10 of the most regularly used telephone numbers. However, BT are secure in their knowledge that these numbers are probably local call numbers and therefore the amount of discount achieved is somewhat limited and actually costs BT very little.
>
> Confusion marketing, whether or not it was deliberate, has therefore helped BT hang on to far more customers that they could have expected, especially with the number of aggressive market entrants to the phone market. According to a MORI survey fewer than 12 per cent of UK residential customers have switched away from BT.
>
> However, BT have, in response to this, tried to simplify its offers under a single discount brand 'BT Together'. This has replaced most of the existing consumer calling packages and now allows customers to make unlimited calls in return for a monthly flat fee. There are still several choices, but the system is designed to overcome 'confusion'.
>
> Other initiatives to overcome accusations of 'confusion marketing' include Oftel's Price Comparison Website and www.phonebills.org.uk. This site actually calculates the cheapest supplier according to the user's typical usage. According to a BT representative, this independent arbiter of value shows BT performing consistently well compared to its rivals.
>
> Source: *Marketing Business*, March 2001

It is essential that when combining advertising and pricing as an integrated approach to the marketing mix, issues such as the impact of confusion marketing are carefully thought through as they can often form the basis of legal actions and reproach by significant competitors.

> ### Question 5.2
>
> Why is it important to integrate advertising with other elements of the promotional mix?

Creative advertising

Adverts are usually designed to exploit either rational or emotive emotions of the customer. Rational appeals will enable a logical argument to be formulated that persuades the customer to act in a certain way, while emotional appeals will seek to reinforce the logic of the message. For example, many TV advertisements for toilet cleaners or disinfectants include men in white coats telling us that our toilets, baths, sinks, etc. are full of germs. This could instill an element of fear into some people, which then leads into the emotional appeal – that 'Domestos – kills all known germs dead'.

A similar approach is taken with disposable nappies/diapers, where the rational element explains how 'Sam will get a sore bottom', from wet diapers and the emotional appeal is whereby if you wear a particular brand of nappy, this problem will cease to exist.

Fear is quite a common factor of creative appeals, where advertisers will play on the emotions of their customers.

These are negative emotional appeals in a way, but positive emotional appeals are also important, playing to customers need to pamper themselves, or do something different, even outrageous. A good example of this could be L'Oreal – *'because I'm worth it'* or Allure perfume – *'difficult to define, impossible to resist'*. Other emotion-based slogans include:

Company	Slogan
Durex	Feeling is everything
Nokia	Connecting people
Peugeot	The drive of your life
Swatch	Time is what you make it
Toyota	The car in front is a Toyota
Vauxhall	Raising the standard
Source: Brassington and Pettitt, 2000	

Advertising can be creative, emotional, rational or product centered, all of which are used to persuade the customer to buy the product. Its design should enable it to speak to us in a way to which we can all relate.

Product-oriented advertising

It is likely that on this occasion advertising will focus on issues such as the features and attributes of the product and their importance to the target audience, for example with a car the advertisement may discuss the safety factors or the style and performance of a vehicle.

Customer-oriented advertising

Here, advertising is focused on what the consumer personally gains through using a particular product. These kinds of advertisements may talk about the benefits of purchasing a product, such as saving money, fear avoidance, security enhancement, self-esteem, image, to name but a few areas. Customer-oriented advertising may often be very people-focused including humour, sex, music, animation, etc. to create an exciting message.

Question 5.3
In what way does advertising support the other elements of the promotional mix?

Campaign planning

Planning for an advertising campaign is a complex process, often very involved, drawn out and resource intensive.

As regards the campaign itself, it is likely that it will involve a predetermined theme but communicated through a series of different messages in different media, carefully chosen for maximum impact on the target audience. The campaign will need to be managed carefully and synergy of advertisements will need to be planned. Campaigns will run over various lengths of time, from the quick burst or seasonal burst to the drip-drip approach that goes on over a long period of time, in some instances for many years.

Regardless of the time period of the campaign, it needs careful planning and the client and agency need to be able to work together and move from stage to stage assessing each situation as it arises and making a range of important decisions.

Figure 5.2 clearly explains the stages in an advertising campaign.

Figure 5.2 The campaign planning process

Setting campaign objectives is a very strategic role and will involve a series of meetings to ensure that the campaign objectives link clearly to the marketing and corporate objectives from which they actually evolve. It is sensible to point out at this stage, however, that the other strategic component of the campaign is the budget. This will most likely have been set within the budgeting round and it is therefore likely that the budget appropriation has been defined in advance of the campaign commencing.

Advertising is highly creative, and will therefore include a number of creative brainstorming sessions, both internally before the brief is issued and externally in preparation for the pitch. Within an agency there will be a range of activities being undertaken, preparing to meet the brief, both creatively and strategically, with an advertising campaign that is SMART. They will be asking themselves a range of questions, for example:

- What is the role of advertising in this campaign?
- What is it expected to achieve?
- Who is the target audience?
- What is the single most important thing we should convey?
- What is the brand called?
- Why do people want to buy it?
- Why should people buy it?
- What is the proposition?

The creative process

From answering these questions the creative process gets underway. The creative team will want to know, in particular, what it is about the brand that justifies the proposition. What are its key characteristics? What if anything is physically unusual about the product or even the service? Do people have a special relationship with the brand? Or is there anything special about the people who use it?

> ### Case history
>
> **Virgin Megastores – £7 million advertising campaign – the creative process at work**
>
> Virgin Megastores focused on consumers' 'bizzare obsessions' with their favourite types of music in a £7 million TV, press and outdoor advertising campaign that was launched in late-2000.
>
> The eight-month campaign was to include a new advertising strapline 'Virgin Megastores - whatever turns you on'.
>
> The advertisements were created by TBWAS London, and were planned to focus on the emotional appeal of music. The aim of Virgin was to differentiate their approach, not focusing on price or value, but indeed focusing on 'celebrating musical passions'.
>
> The advertisements were to be placed in *Q Magazine*, VH1, MTV, ITV and Channel 4.
>
> Source: *Marketing Week*, November 2000

The agency

There are a number of different agency types that you should first of all be familiar with.

Full service agencies

Full service agencies provide a complete range of services and, in general, they are probably the most popular type. The range of services includes:

- Creative skills
- Artwork
- Media buying
- Public relations
- Direct marketing
- Market research.

A number of well-known agencies such as Saatchi & Saatchi, Leo Burnett and J.Walter Thompson offer full service provision.

There are a number of advantages to a full service provision. For many organizations it means that there is an additional resource with which to work, to share ideas and responsibilities. Working with a full service agency will see a huge pool of skills under one roof that can be drawn on as needed; new, different perspectives on the communication problem may be gained, which ultimately will contribute towards the corporate and marketing objectives of the organization being achieved.

For an organization preferring an integrated marketing communications approach, using a full service agency means that all of the elements of the promotional mix can be managed under one roof, almost like a supermarket, and the marketing communications operation then becomes easier to manage and control. Moreover, from a security angle there is less chance of sensitive information leaking out into the competitive domain.

One key disadvantage to a full service agency on the other hand is 'having all your eggs in one basket'. We all know within business that this can be a dangerous way to operate and within the volatile world of advertising, this must be considered. For example, if an organization is channelling all of its marketing communications through one agency, should the relationship break down and the contract be breached in any way the organization could have every element of the promotional mix left high and dry, with no agency to manage the process for them.

Therefore, in a full service agency it is critical to have a relationship built around quality, trust and understanding. This is imperative for the successful implementation of the marketing communications strategy.

The type of customers that use full service agencies in the main will be organizations who have significant budgets, but possibly little internal resource to support the co-ordination of the advertising campaign. You will possibly find a large multinational organization using a full service agency, who will then co-ordinate their global activities and guarantee a consistent approach.

Limited service agencies

Limited service agencies tend to specialize in particular elements of the marketing communications process. For example, an advertising agency may specialize the level of artwork and creative skill and therefore focus on the design and development of advertisements. They will then rely on significant information being provided by their client to enable them to meet the brief. Another agency may specialize in media buying and therefore be able to achieve a high level of competitive advantage to enable a more effective use of the advertising budget.

The key advantage to using limited service agencies is that an organization can shop around to get the best skills to suit a range of marketing communication activities. It also gives scope for some in-house work which then goes to a limited service agency for specialist elements of the marketing communications strategy.

'A la carte' agency

Many organizations seem to want greater flexibility and choice in the way in which the advertising is managed. To do this they need to have a broad range of options, which do not necessarily come from a full service approach; rather they want to select a range of services from a range of different specialist agencies. While this gives choice and the desired flexibility, it takes a lot of time, effort and commitment to manage the potential number of relationships involved.

For example, Lloyds TSB gave their Internet bank advertisements to Saatchis but they also appointed a company called Inter-focus to work on their strategy for the launch and handle the direct marketing and customer relationship management for the project.

Another good example is Wrigley. They took the decision to expand their Web activity across Europe. To do this they decided to manage the project via a joint committee of marketers from Wrigley operations in the UK, Sweden and Germany. The company's local operations spent time talking to a handful of new media houses. The key here is that Wrigley's works with a number of agencies and in this case they have chosen to work with a different agency specially to deal with their Web activity.

An 'a la carte' agency would be able to help resolve this problem by co-ordinating the range of specialist agencies for you. For example, an organization preparing for a launch of a new product may require market research, sales promotions and perhaps on this occasion their launch will take place at an exhibition. The a la carte agency would act on behalf of the organization, take away the brief, define their role and then outsource the remainder of the work, across a broad range of other specialist agencies. The a la carte agency then co-ordinates the project activities.

Over the years there has been some erosion of the status of full service agencies, with a resultant decline in numbers and the emergence of companies specializing in media planning and buying, sometimes known as 'media buying shops' or 'media independents'. Effectively this means that an agency is buying in services to support a project that has been outsourced to them.

Agency selection criteria

Choosing an appropriate advertising agency is a very time-consuming process; it is not simply a matter of choosing the agency which is capable of producing the best advertising campaign, but choosing an agency which is creative, which has something your own organization does not possess.

When selecting an agency it is important that you establish your own criteria, based around the aims and objectives of the advertising process, and the demands of the remaining elements of the promotional mix.

Therefore the following questions should be addressed:

- Do the agency fully understand the requirements of a brief?
- Do they know and understand how to use market research?
- Is their strategic thinking sound?
- Is their thinking imaginative and creative?
- Are they professional and businesslike?
- Can they work with senior people?
- Are their capabilities high in all key areas, management, strategy, creative media?
- Do they work well as a team?
- Is their creative work of a high quality?
- Is their work confined to TV or does it go across all media?
- Does this include below the line activities, new media?
- Can they offer an integrated communications approach?

- How do they propose to evaluate the campaign?
- Can they work internationally?
- What is their attitude towards costs? – Will they work effectively to reduce costs?
- How will they relate to our media-buying agency?
- Will they fit with our working practices?
- How important to them will our account be?

(White, 1999)

> **Question 5.4**
>
> What are the advantages of using a full service-advertising agency over a limited service agency?

Managing the agency relationship

Running an agency relationship can be quite complex. Once an agency relationship has been established it will be likely that both the marketing team and the agency team hit the ground running, establishing day-to-day operational teams, systems, contracts and reporting lines.

At the same time that this is all going on, the agency team will be wanting to learn everything they can about the organization, its business, product and services portfolio. It will want to be conversant with your supply chain and wanting to review all available market research in order that they have a full understanding of the organization and its purpose.

The most important element to establish within an agency relationship is a communication line and a day-to-day communication contact.

Other key components of building a successful relationship will include:

- Structuring agency contracts
- Formalizing contacts
- Day-to-day meetings
- Major meetings
- Critical review points
- The budget for advertising expenditure.

The budget will be central to the agency/client relationship. Setting a budget will be a difficult process, but it is essential to establish the budget as a sound and robust basis to work from.

The brief

The success or failure of the implementation of the advertising campaign can depend on the creative brief, but they are not easy to write.

- *Current situation* – the history of the brand, previous campaign successes (or failures) and the reasons for mounting the new campaign.
- *Promotional objectives* – having set your marketing objectives (often expressed in terms of sales volume), you then have to address the promotional objectives. These will vary according to your overall plans, but could include:
    1. To encourage product trial
    2. To raise awareness levels
    3. To encourage direct sales
    4. To increase distribution outlets.

- *Target markets* – a good definition of the target market will include not only socioeconomic details (e.g. age, class, sex), but also psychographic information on users. This will have a bearing on the nature and tone of the promotional activity, its overall focus and content.
- *Product/service* – in providing your agency with a detailed brief, this section is very important. It should include any original research results or focus group research to establish what the perceived benefits are, so that these can be promoted strongly, both visually and in words.
- *Budget* – The budget should be carefully planned with consideration given to your total budget as often it includes funds not only for the cost of the media, but also for the production of promotional material.
- *Competitors* – You should know your competitors and their products as well as you know your own. Make it your business to find out and include the results of your findings in your brief.
- *Timescales* – This should include the start date of the campaign and the period over which it is to run. Media scheduling will play a vitally important role at this stage, with the need to establish the consistency of the campaign in terms of the 'drip-drip' approach or indeed the necessity for a 'burst' style campaign.
- *Drip* being a campaign that pans out over a period of time on a consistently timed basis.
- *Burst* being a campaign that is executed in a concentrated burst of time, e.g. every 4 weeks a run of advertisements is executed.

The creative team will be responsible for the direction of the artwork, ensuring that visualization and copywriting match the needs of the organization and would be meaningful and attention grabbing to the target audience.

From the advertising agency perspective, every opportunity must be taken to send a message that is succinct, effective, dynamic, exciting, meaningful and able to incite 'action'. Technology today allows for a highly creative range of opportunities to convey the message in positive way. The use of multimedia campaigns is likely to be a very attractive option and more effective than a single medium.

Advertising is big business and therefore advertising briefs require careful handling. For large corporations the basis of agency relationships is something that the media watch closely and it is often managed very much in the public domain.

Case history

Toyota hands GRP £4.5 million regional brief

Toyota is to move its £4.5 million advertising account into Glasgow based Guy Robertson Partnership. The account, which includes TV, radio, press and direct marketing, will be handled by full service agency GRP from January 2001 onwards.

Case history

Siemens picks W & K for £70 million global advertising account

Siemens is attempting to boost its position in the mobile phone market. It ranks first in Germany, but only sixth worldwide, trailing behind market leaders Nokia, Motorola and Ericsson.

> Previously, Siemens had started a global TV and print campaign in May 2000 which used Seimens 'Be inspired' strapline. In addition to this Siemens signed a £3 million sponsorship deal with the FA Premier League earlier in the year and sponsors Formula One motor racing.

Campaign evaluation

Campaign evaluation is a vital component of the advertising activity. The findings and results of the process are invaluable in providing feedback that could result in improvements for future advertising campaigns.

The primary role of evaluation is to ensure that the planned and executed advertising campaign has achieved its overall objective both in terms of the campaign itself and also how it relates back to the achievement of the corporate and marketing objectives of the organization.

The secondary role of evaluation is to ensure that the advertising campaign has been executed efficiently, that advertisements have been displayed or gone live, when planned, in the right media, at the right place and at the right time.

Measuring advertising effectiveness is mainly the role of marketing research, as was established much earlier on in your studies. The research will provide guidance on development, and it will also provide the opportunity to plot future trends.

There are two key elements to advertising evaluation: pre-testing and post-testing.

Pre-testing

You may already be familiar with the term 'market testing', whereby a product is taken to a small segment within the target market to test it out. Is it usable? Does it meet with customer expectations? Would you buy it? Why would they buy it? etc. Well, advertising works in exactly the same way.

Advertisements should realistically, when time and resource allow, be pre-tested prior to release into the public domain. This is particularly important with TV advertising and it is necessary for the regulatory bodies to view and confirm that the advertising is appropriate for broadcasting.

Tests are structured around various stages of the development of the advertisement. They begin with the initial concept, i.e. a storyboard, where a sample will comment and try to relate the message to the scenario set.

Further on into the process, a 'rough' video may be produced; an advertisement, or even a virtual advertisement, helped by the use of IT, will be prepared, the idea being that it will give a flavour of the actual advertisement. Again this is tested. This particular test allows for final adjustments to be made to the creative side, the message and the overall image of the advertisement prior to launch. In many instances, further testing will take place at each stage of the advertisement's development, until it is actually ready for release.

Different approaches to pre-testing

Approaches to pre-testing include activities such as copy testing, i.e. preparing print copy and asking an invited audience to respond. You may also ask them to undertake a readability test and get them to give their views. Hall and theatre testing is another approach, where pre-prepared advertisements and TV programmes are shown to invited audiences to gain a response. This can be quite a complex exercise where target consumers are invited to the theatre or hall or even a test laboratory, and they may respond by telephone a few days after the viewing, when they have had time to review it and see if the message can be recalled. Or alternatively, prior to the programme, the consumers' demographic and attitudinal details are recorded and they are then asked to state their preference from a range of products. Clearly, in both instances, this will enable advertisers to understand something about the way in which their customers may respond to the advertising campaign.

Much of the work will involve direct, face-to-face discussions, either in focus groups or on a one-to-one basis. In some of these situations physiological measures are taken, such as pupil dilatation or eye tracking or even skin response, with the use of electrodes. Such are the lengths some research or pre-testing agencies are prepared to go to.

Pre-testing requires both quantitative and qualitative data, which are obtained through primary and secondary means.

All of these, while valid and necessary tests, should be approached with some element of caution. Test conditions are often artificial, and audiences will respond very differently to seeing advertisements in artificial situations than they would in their own home.

Evaluation criteria

There are a number of key criteria for this method of evaluation. It includes identification of the following key factors:

- Level of interest
- Level of intelligibility
- It is likeable?
- Level of information included
- Believability
- Ability to induce trials
- Potential distribution outlets.

Case history

Kenco Coffee pre-test

Kenco, who moved to the instant coffee market, wanted to know three main things about their proposed print advertisement:

- Its ability to generate awareness and interest
- The message take-out
- Whether the Kenco instant brand would be perceived.

The interest factor was found to be present and the Kenco brand was also perceived. The artwork, however, needed to be improved, as it did not look as if there was a jar of coffee in the cafetière or the grinder. This meant that the instant aspect was not communicated.

Work was undertaken to highlight the jar and the tag line was reworked.

Source: *Integrated Marketing Communications*, Fill, 1999

Question 5.5

As an advertiser, what would be the benefit of undertaking a pre-test of an advertisement?

Post-testing

Post-testing can be complex, time-consuming and is more costly than pre-testing. While pre-testing can be somewhat artificial, post-testing is more realistic, as consumers respond to the test, having received the advertisement in the comfort of their own surroundings.

There are a number of methods of post-testing including inquiry tests, recall tests, recognition tests and single-source data. Other tests include tracking studies, which have been previously mentioned, financial analysis and likeability.

Recall testing

Recall tests are designed to assess the recall strength of the advertisement. The approach is very similar to that taken in hall and theatre testing, but this time the customers will be tested on their impressions and perceptions, not their behaviour, opinions, attitudes or the advertising effect. It is likely that this test would involve several hundred customers who were exposed to the advertisement.

Recognition tests

Recall tests are based purely on the ability of the customer to remember what was within the advertisement. With recognition testing, customers will be asked if they recognize the advertisement. This is very common with press advertising.

In many instances it is likely that recognition tests will often be carried out within homes and will be undertaken in a minimum of 200 households. This measures four particular areas:

- Did the customer remember seeing the advertisement?
- Did they see it and associate it?
- Did they read at least 50 per cent of the advertisement?
- Did they remember the brand name or logo?

Single-source data

With the assistance of new technologies, it is now possible to correlate consumer purchases with advertisements. This is known as *single-source data*. It involves a controlled transmission into a home where advertisements have been sent and whose every purchase is monitored through a scanner in the supermarket. These tests are quite costly and involve a significant number of people. A good example of this is Central TV, which set up Adlab in the mid-1980s. This involved a consumer panel of 1,000 housewives, each recording their media consumption and where, when and what they purchased.

Tracking studies

Tracking studies can be undertaken by interviewing a large number of people on a regular basis, with a view to collecting data about buyers' perceptions of advertisements and how they might be affecting buying behaviour. Measuring the impact of an advertising campaign while it is running, does give the opportunity for contingency action to be taken should something go wrong.

Other forms of tracking can be done through the use of EPOS – the electronic point of sale. EPOS measures stock turnover and can produce records that identify trends in purchase that can then be correlated against the advertising campaign. This may provide evidence to suggest that sales did or did not fluctuate as a result of the advertising campaign over a period of time. This information could provide the basis for additional sales promotions to be developed or even reminder-based advertising to be implemented.

Further examples include coded responses for response-based advertising, where the customer may be asked to provide a reference number, or there may be one already on the reply form. This will measure where the advertisement was observed and assists in the choice of media in the future.

The process of advertising is complex, extensive, expensive, exciting and dynamic. It has many components, and although it is only one of the elements of the marketing mix, it is the one that is most absorbing in terms of learning. However, as suggested at the start, it is one of a range of promotional activities that are undertaken in order to 'adopt' and 'retain' customers in the long term.

Sales promotions

Sales promotions traditionally are complementary to advertising. They are used to reinforce and encourage customers to trial the product and then to purchase. Sales promotion provides a range of short-term tactical measures to induce sales of particular products or services. Its aim is to provide extra value to the product or service, creating the extra impetus to purchase products that we might not normally buy.

> **Definition**
>
> **Sales promotions**
>
> A range of tactical marketing techniques designed within a strategic marketing framework to add value to a product or service in order to achieve specific sales and marketing objectives.

Sales promotion should be part of a planned approach and very much an integral part of the marketing communications planning framework. It should be planned and executed in parallel with associated advertising and possible public relations campaigns.

Marketers will therefore rely upon sales promotions to enhance the performance of other components of the promotional mix. Again this reinforces the nature of an 'integrated marketing communications' approach to promotional activity.

The main aims and associated objectives of sales promotions are usually:

- To increase brand and product awareness – attracting new customers
- To increase trial and adoption of new and existing products
- To attract customers to switch brands and products from competing organizations
- To level out fluctuations in supply and demand
- To increase brand usage
- To increase customer loyalty
- To disseminate information
- To encourage trading up to the next size or the next range – particularly pertinent to the car market.

If you were to align this in respect of the hierarchy of objectives it might look like this:

Marketing objective	To increase market penetration by 20 per cent
Advertising objective	To reinforce product and brand to existing customers
Sales promotion objective	To encourage repeat purchase of products and brand loyalty

To achieve sales promotion objectives a number of promotional techniques must therefore be considered.

Sales promotions techniques

There are a range of sales promotion techniques that can be used to achieve each of the above aims and objectives. Typical techniques in both sectors will include:

- Money-off vouchers/coupons
- Buy one get one free
- Customer loyalty bonus schemes
- Twin packs
- Bulk buying
- Discounts
- Try before you buy
- Cash rebates
- Trial-sized products
- Prize draws
- Competition codes
- Point of sale displays.

Trade promotions

Earlier on we looked at the nature of the 'push and pull' promotional strategies, whereby manufacturers are looking to encourage their wholesalers and retailers to take their products and effectively 'take them to market'.

As a result of this process, trade promotions are often based around ensuring that product penetration is achieved. However, in order to achieve product penetration the incentive levels often have to be quite high, as product penetration is likely to be contrary to the typical 'volume stock traffic' aims of the wholesalers.

It is likely that manufacturers will encourage organizations to *increase their stock levels* in order to gain some level of commitment to increase sales potential in the marketplace, but also perhaps with the view of gaining some kind of supply chain relationship, with priority given to one particular supplier.

Alternatively, there is intensive competition for *increased shelf space* within retail outlets. The greater the incentive provided by the manufacturer, the more potential there is for greater shelf-space in the retail outlet. 'White Goods' products are often at the heart of this scheme, with particular brands securing more floor space or shelf space than some of the lesser brands. There is the potential in this situation for a joint promotional activity between the manufacturer and perhaps the retailer to give incentives for a greater number of sales, from which both organizations will clearly benefit.

Good trade promotions, i.e. a good 'push strategy' highly incentivized, backed up by appropriate merchandising and appropriate advertising, may be advantageous. Alternatively, policies such as sale or return are also a good incentive and ultimately reduce the financial risk involved.

Seasonal fluctuations are often problematic to both manufacturers and suppliers, and therefore it might be that through a range of sales promotion activities incentives to buy the products outside the typical season could be achieved. The likely nature of these would be to involve the manufacturer in both the push and pull strategy context, in line with both consumer and trade promotions.

Competitor response sees sales promotion being used very much as a tactical weapon to dilute the impact of competitor activities. Therefore during the launch of a new competitor product, it might be that the focus of trade activity relates to creating high barriers to entry for the trade in order to sustain your market share in the wholesale community.

Specific methods might include:
- Allowances and discounts
- Volume allowances
- Discount overriders – based upon retrospective performance, e.g. on a quarterly or annual basis
- Free merchandise
- Selling and marketing assistance – cooperative advertising, merchandising allowances, market information, product training
- Sales contests
- Bonus payments.

Retailer to consumer sales promotions

The key aims and objectives of this process will be to increase sales through a range of promotional techniques, as you can see below:
- Increase in-store trade and customer traffic – the use of coupons and money-off vouchers
- Increase frequency of purchase – discounted promotions for next purchase
- Increase in-store loyalty – through the use of storecards and rewards systems
- Increase own brand sales – encourage customers to purchase own brand products through a range of sale promotion incentive such as trial packs, in-store demonstrations etc.
- Achieve consistent demand – reduce fluctuations, provide sales promotions in particular time bands to encourage a more consistent approach to shopping

Manufacturer to consumer sales promotions

This relates very much to the 'pull' strategy, whereby the manufacturers take responsibility for creating awareness and demand in order to pull products up through the supply chain to the customers.

Typical sales promotion activities might include:
- Encouraging trial – samples, gifts, trial drives of vehicles – allow customers to decide for themselves
- Disseminating information – information packs on a door-to-door basis, perhaps closely linked with a direct marketing campaign (again utilizing the integrated marketing communications approach)
- Trading up – encouraging customers to trade up from their existing models – a typical activity of car manufacturers and white goods manufacturers.

The list of promotional activities is endless, but the important issue from a promotional operations point of view is to ensure that demand for the products is continuously stimulated and is consistent with the marketing plan.

We will look at the impact of sales promotions on a business-to-business basis later in the text.

Customer loyalty schemes

Ensuring that customer loyalty is achieved, is a major focus of promotional activity.

Table 5.1 11Ps of loyalty marketing

1. Pricing	Be customer specific
2. Purchases	Make product specific offers
3. Point flexibility	Occasionally offer double points
4. Partners	Develop alliances with retailers
5. Prizes	Weekly draw for cardholders
6. Pro-bono	Allow customers to convert points to charity donations
7. Personalization	Direct mail, specifically targeted at the customer
8. Privileges	Invite cardholders to special events
9. Participation	Invite best customers to take part in new schemes
10. Pronto	Generate offers at point of sale
11. Proactive	Use information to predict/pre-empt customer behaviour

As with advertising, a planned approach must be undertaken and programmes tightly managed. Therefore the typical planning process will include:

- Identification of the target market
- Sales promotion objectives versus budget appropriation
- Identification of both cost of communication for the sales promotion campaign, but also the actual cost of the campaign, i.e. the 'fulfilment cost' – the cost of actually hosting the campaign in terms of postage, free gifts, etc. – effectively the cost of the promotion to the organization. Obviously this should be looked at in association with the ultimate benefits in the longer term.
- Implementation – the same applies here as to the advertising programme, but clearly the promotion will probably run in parallel with the advertising programme, therefore issues relating to timescales, drip and burst style promotions, etc. will apply.

It is essential that whatever your promotional objectives are, the appropriate sales promotional activity is applied in the right context. Figure 5.3 highlights possible solutions to meeting PR objectives that might enable you to select the most appropriate method to meet your organizational needs.

Objectives	Immediate free offers	Delayed free offers	Immediate price offers	Delayed price offers	Finance offers	Competitions	Games and draws	Charitable offers	Self-liquidators	Profit-making promotions
Increasing volume	9	7	9	7	5	1	3	5	2	1
Increasing trial	9	7	9	2	9	2	7	7	2	1
Increasing repeat purchase	2	9	2	9	5	3	2	7	3	3
Increasing loyalty	1	9	0	7	3	3	1	7	3	3
Widening usage	9	5	5	2	3	1	5	5	1	1
Creating interest	3	3	3	2	2	5	9	8	8	8
Creating awareness	3	3	3	1	1	5	9	8	8	8
Deflecting attention from price	9	7	0	7	7	3	5	5	2	2
Gaining intermediary support	9	5	9	5	9	3	7	5	1	1
Gaining display	9	5	9	5	9	3	7	5	1	1

Each square is filled with a rating from 0 (not well matched) to 10 (very well matched). Use it as a ready reckoner for linking your objective to the mechanics available.

Figure 5.3 Adapted from Cummins H., 1990 in Worsam, 2000

Question 5.6
What are the most likely sales promotion alternatives open to a manufacturer when trying to attract consumer attention?

Evaluation of sales promotions

It is essential, as with any promotional technique, to evaluate the effectiveness of the promotional campaign. Sales promotions, like advertising, is a very expensive activity and therefore it is of primary importance that as a marketer you understand the propensity for the campaign to succeed or fail.

Typical evaluation methods will include:

- *Consumer audits* – This will indicate if there has been a change in consumer behaviour as a result of the sales promotion campaign and will be especially interested in the success of trials and repeat purchase promotions.
- *Sales information* – Should the objective of the sales promotion be to assist the marketing objective of market penetration, then the measure of increase in sales will be a vital performance indicator.
- *Retail audits* – Specialist organizations such as AC Nielson will track changes in stock levels, distribution, market share immediately after the promotional campaign. This will provide an insight into the basis of an increase or decrease in sales.
- *Sales force feedback* – this is a qualitative approach, and will be based upon sales force experience of the uptake of the sales promotion opportunities in their region.
- *Voucher/coupon redemption* – it is likely that the vouchers and coupons will be coded in order to ascertain the most successful response rate to sales promotion activities – this will endorse the right selection of media, the right kind of sales promotion activity and potentially the most frequently used distribution outlet.

While evaluating sales promotion is essential, the evaluation of the whole promotional mix programme should be undertaken in order to measure the success or failure of the integrated programme of promotional and communications activities.

> **Question 5.7**
>
> How do you perceive that sales promotions adds value to the process of advertising?

Public relations

Publicity and public relations are often interrelated and seen as companions within the promotional mix. Indeed publicity is often deemed to be part of public relations activities and certainly seems to happen as a result of PR. However, let us be clear on the differences:

- *Publicity* – is information, news, communications in relation to the organization – transmitted through a range of different media.
- *Public relations* – is a planned and sustained effort to establish and maintain goodwill and mutual understanding between an organization and its target – publics.

The role of public relations is to look after the nature and basis of the external relationships between the organization and all stakeholder groups. It is aimed at creating a sustainable corporate brand and an overall company image within the marketplace.

The definition of public is:

Any group with some common characteristics, with which an organization needs to communicate. Each public poses a different communication problem, as each has different information needs and requires a different kind of relationship with the organization, and may start with perceptions of what the organization stands for.

Sourece: Marston, 1979 as quoted in Brassington and Pettitt, 2000.

Publics in the main consist of:

- Customer groups
- Local and central government
- The general public

- Financial institution – investors/shareholders/borrowers
- The media – TV, press, radio (locally and nationally)
- Opinion leaders/formers
- Internal marketplace – employees, trade unions, employee relations bodies
- Potential employees.

Target audiences and publics

Target audiences and target publics are defined segments that are selected to receive promotional activity. 'Audience' has traditionally been used in advertising; 'public' in public relations. Both terms have exactly the same meaning, and target audience is gradually replacing the PR term.

A target audience must automatically be a segment. Just as segments must be specifically identified, so must target audiences. Each of these is a specific target audience:

- The individuals within MOSAIC Type 14
- Adult males within MOSAIC Type 14
- Adult males within MOSAIC Type 14 within the Carlton TV region.

It is of primary importance that the organization specifies precisely the use of public relations in respect of both the promotional and marketing mix, and PR objectives must be expressed in SMART terms. Failure to target the PR campaign precisely will potentially mean that the campaign could be wrongly directed and, at the worst, be a complete failure.

Aims and objectives of public relations

Typically PR aims and objectives will closely link to the following:

- To create and maintain the corporate and indeed brand image
- To enhance the position and standing of the organization in the eyes of the public
- To communicate the organization's ethos and philosophy, and corporate values
- To disseminate information to the public
- To undertake damage limitation activities to overcome poor publicity for the organization
- To raise the company profile and forge stronger, lasting, customer and supply chain relationships.

Public relations, as with all other elements of the marketing mix, requires a planned approach and plays an important role at a strategic level. It is also subject to strategic level objectives. For example, the launch of a new model by Mercedes Benz will be subject to a significant PR campaign running in parallel with significant advertising and direct marketing, perhaps on a local level by the local dealerships. Therefore PR becomes a high-level communications objective and it is critical that it is subject to the same intensity in respect of targeting specific groups of the public.

Marketing versus corporate public relations

While publicity is a sub-set of PR, public relations is not a sub-set of marketing – although that is how it is often portrayed. Public relations is very important to marketing, but its role is far broader and of primary importance to corporate level activities in terms of marketing communications.

The public relations practitioner will often report directly to the board, probably to the chief executive officer and/or the chairman. He or she will be very concerned with corporate identity and will be establishing a corporate communications policy, which will include the equivalent of a positioning statement.

If this is the case, it must follow that marketing communications strategy is determined to a great degree by the public relations strategy. Here again is the influence of integrated marketing communications. PR is a companion to virtually all elements of the marketing mix, and without the level of publicity raised through PR activities, many of the other promotional mix strategies may not be as successful.

From a marketing perspective, it will be used to meet marketing objectives and will support them by continually raising awareness, raising the profile and enhancing other marketing activities.

At a corporate level, PR is part of the long-term relationship-building strategy implemented by the organization to remain close to all components of the public. However, it does have a contingency use, with a short-term tactical benefit, in that it is used to respond to certain unpredictable or unexpected events, such as fatal accidents, disasters, etc. We will look at this a little later in the unit under 'crisis management'.

Marketing information to underpin public relations activities

As explained in the previous section, marketing is more likely to provide an underpinning role in relation to public relations and will on many occasions be the think tank behind a lot of the planning and development of PR strategies.

However, marketing also supports the PR process by providing a range of relevant information, both in respect of primary and secondary data. Therefore the following activities are undertaken:

- Consumer and trade press scanning
- Competitive comparisons
- Production of publicity materials
- Promotional videos
- Management and publicity of special events
- Development of corporate logos/symbols and identity
- Internal marketing tools
- Preparation of literature to support corporate activity.

Public relations and attitude change?

The whole basis of public relations is to continually reinforce a positive attitude towards the organization in the minds of the public, therefore for PR to be successful it has to change a range of negative attitudes into positive attitudes (see Figure 5.4).

From...		to	
Negative		to	Positive
Hostility		to	Sympathy
Prejudice		to	Acceptance
Apathy		to	Interest
Ignorance		to	Knowledge

Figure 5.4 Attitudinal change (Worsam, 2000)

In order to undertake this level of attitudinal change you will require a clear and specific understanding of the nature and breakdown of the market in which you operate, both from a customer perspective but also from a media perspective.

Public relations techniques

It has already been identified that PR has two roles, one which is a long-term developmental role, and one that reflects the need to have contingency activities in place. From a marketing operations perspective, you need to understand when to use which particular public relations technique to optimize the level of 'positive publicity' the organization can deliver.

Typical techniques include:

- Press releases
- Press conferences
- Publications
- Advertising
- Media relations
- Events
- Annual reports
- Lobbying
- Internal PR.

You should be more or less familiar with the basis of each of the above techniques; therefore, the focus of this unit will be on the use of them, from a marketing operations perspective.

Press releases – are used in the main as a channel through to various media to highlight specific information or events in the life of the organization. The most common use from a marketing perspective will perhaps relate to either product launches, new initiatives, global growth, etc.

Press conferences – are particularly pertinent at a corporate level, whereby press conferences are usually the channel for announcing a major story or indeed having to respond to a crisis that is in the public domain and the media spotlight.

Publications – are in general the work of the marketing department, and they will provide a range of information, through a range of different media, that can be sent to current and potential clients. This approach would be helpful when organizations are looking at a marketing development programme, and therefore raising corporate awareness is vital.

Media relations – both at corporate and marketing level, it is helpful to have good media relationships with both the general press and also the specialist press. Having close media contacts and good relations may gain both favour and greater access to the potential media spotlight when required. Quite often inviting the media to undertake a particular role in the public relations exercise may gain favour with them.

Events – covers a whole range of both corporate and marketing activities, and highlights yet again close links with other elements of the promotional and marketing mix, with areas such as sponsorship or events linked very closely to a product launch. It is likely that a wide range of publics will be invited to such events in order that the organization's corporate image is enhanced.

Annual reports – are an extremely important publication. They are usually widely distributed, but are especially important for providing shareholders and the financial media with organizational performance levels for the previous year. They provide an opportunity to present the organization in a positive light, reflecting upon past achievements and defining its future direction.

Lobbying – is a very specialist area, which is designed to develop and influence a number of high-level relationships in order to influence organizations such as local, national, and where appropriate, international governments. Lobbying, therefore, is seeking to influence people in authority in order to secure their support to achieve a desired action. All who have an interest, for and against, any piece of legislation will set out to lobby support. Public relations, of course, has a major and highly specialized part to play in this process.

When considering lobbying, remember that it is likely to be a long-term process, which will involve highly targeted contacts with individuals and groups.

You are, of course, selling an idea, persuading others to take a certain course of action. Therefore a decision-making process is operating and there is a DMU to be identified. The likely contacts that need to be lobbied in a parliamentary context are:

- Cabinet Ministers
- Members of the Government
- Members of the Opposition – all parties
- Backbenchers from all parties
- The researchers and other staff reporting to individual MPs
- Staff, at a variety of levels, within each party machine
- Members of an MP's constituency party – especially the selection committee
- Civil servants who advise the Government – at all levels from Executive Officer to Permanent Secretary.

Lobbying is not exclusive to the legislature. Its principles, adapted as needed, are used wherever there is a need to persuade a person in authority to take a certain line of action. There are of course, usually pro- and anti-lobbyists. It is likely that lobbying of this nature will be handled at a corporate level, the materials and information for the lobbying exercise will be provided by the marketing function.

Internal PR

We looked at the importance of internal marketing in Unit 3, which highlighted the importance of developing a structured and meaningful communications process in order to win over the confidence of the workforce and gain support for strategy implementation and the associated change. Internal PR play a vital role in respect of this communication and while they are part and parcel of the overall publics, the workforce requires a more tailored and organizational approach.

The likely emphasis of internal PR will be based around keeping people informed, avoiding cloak and dagger style internal politics. Should a successful PR campaign be implemented internally, then motivation and attitude levels might appear to be more positive within the organization.

Particular techniques included in this area will relate to journals, newsletters and internal briefings.

It is likely that on some occasions internal PR will be based around 'crisis' style PR, perhaps announcing redundancies, changes in management structure, disaster, etc.

When selecting the appropriate public relations technique it is essential to ensure that you undertake an assessment of three criteria:

- *Suitability* – it is vital to ensure that the techniques chosen are targeted and therefore appropriate to the target market, in respect of tone, content and style; that the appropriate medium is chosen, which again meets the profile requirements of the customer base; of primary importance will be the necessity to establish the level of influence and impact the actual technique will achieve.
- *Feasibility* – as with any other promotional activity, PR will be restricted by a budget – therefore any activity or programme of activities will need to come within the required

budget. Particular considerations will relate to resourcing the programme both physically, financially and from a human resource perspective. Ultimately it is important to establish whether the programme is considered achievable and realistic.
- *Acceptability* – are the activities chosen acceptable to the organization as a whole, are they appropriate and in keeping with the corporate identity? An assessment of alternative sources of PR should also be undertaken to ascertain which is the most acceptable approach to achieving the desired level of publicity.

Crisis management

One of the key functions of any PR role will be to handle 'crisis' situations. These can range from management fallouts to serious incidents, accidents and disasters that might need reporting on.

At some stage in the life cycle of an organization it is almost inevitable that they will be hit by some form of crisis that will invoke a whole range of contingency plans, or even the immediate development of an emergency PR plan. For example, British Airways suffered a devastating blow when one of the Concorde airliners crashed on take off from Paris during 2000. This invoked a range of public relations exercises, informing the public of the basis of the incident and providing regular updates as the situation unfolded.

As a marketer you should be alert to potential situations that might emerge as a result of the use of your products or services, in order that you are prepared to deal with the unknown or perhaps unexpected event. It is therefore your role to ensure that, on behalf of the organization, you:

- Are aware of what could happen
- Know how to manage PR should this particular situation emerge
- Develop a number of contingency plans based on the possible situations in readiness for the event.

Organizations such as British Airways and the British Airports Authority (BAA) among others are likely to have contingency plans in place for such events happening.

Evaluation of public relations activities

Public relations are no exception to the rule when it comes to the necessity for undertaking an evaluation of the successes or failure of particular strategies and the associated objectives.

Haywood (1990) suggested that there are eight commonly used measures of results:

- *Budget* – an assessment of whether the planned PR activity has been achieved within the budget defined and also within the timescales set.
- *Awareness* – the measure of awareness can be quite complex and is most likely to be established through a range of marketing research activities to establish the level of brand awareness in the marketplace.
- *Attitude* – combined with research on brand awareness can be research on brand attitudes, whether they are positive or negative, and whether they have resulted in any change in consumer behaviour
- *Media coverage and tone* – first, it will be essential to establish the level of media coverage achieved as a result of planned PR activities. Typical measures might include the number of different media which covered the case, the number of columns taken, key headings and perceived importance of the PR information. Second, the nature and tone in which the PR activities have been covered. Clearly this is far more qualitative in nature and will perhaps be subject to a twofold approach of looking closely at the perceived nature and tone, against the measure of attitude towards the organization. For example, in what could have been perceived as 'negative' publicity, what is the attitude towards the

organization, it is sympathy or empathy? What was it originally and what appears to be the driving force of change?
- *Positioning* – measuring the perception of the position of the organization versus that of the competition. The research undertaken to provide an insight into awareness and attitude will also provide the basis for understanding perceived positioning.
- *Response generation* – this is a very quantitative mechanism and quite easy to generate. It is likely that as with sales promotions, many of the enquiries or leads generated may be subject to some degree of code referencing, or sources of the enquiry will be recorded.
- *Share price* – for large public companies, this is a particularly good indicator of public confidence in the organization. For example, while Marks and Spencer were subject to a high degree of publicity due to rationalization and streamlining of their operations, their share prices were somewhat reduced, which is representative of the level of shareholder and public confidence in the organization.
- *Sales* – this is probably the ultimate measure in the successful implementation of a sound and robust PR strategy. However, bearing in mind that PR is often not designed purely with increased sales in mind, this is not always an objective measure of organizational performance. However, it is a known fact that when a negative perspective of the organization is presented, then sales do drop. The PR challenge then of course is to retrieve the situation in order to get sales back on track.

PR is quite an exciting business to be in, and often it does come under the arm of the marketing department. However, in a number of large corporate bodies, PR officers are part of the corporate arm of the organization, whose role is then likely to be underpinned by the provision of appropriate management information by the marketing department.

> **Question 5.8**
> In what ways do public relations complement other elements of the promotional mix?

Direct and interactive marketing

Direct and interactive marketing must be one of the most rapidly evolving and changing areas of marketing communications and promotional activities. Key driving forces of change relate to:
- Changing dynamics in demographics and lifestyles
- Increasing competition
- Customer power
- Fragmentation of the media
- Increasing costs of media
- Emerging distribution channels
- Changes in market information (EPOS, smart cards, etc.)
- New technologies.

One of the key drivers of growth is the massive movement in technologies, including the rise of databases, improving analytical systems, developments in phone technologies and the information superhighway.

Added to these, it would appear that in today's marketing environment organizations know more and more about their customers. Their profiling and research techniques are far more sophisticated, making direct marketing an excellent tool for very specifically targeted communication campaigns.

These drivers are the common denominator in almost all change strategies; therefore direct marketing is not an exception to the rule.

The use of direct marketing by an organization effectively demonstrates that the organization has taken a decision to avoid dependence on marketing channel intermediaries and has also decided to deal with customers in a highly targeted way. This of course has implications for the level of marketing and management information that a company may need to obtain and retain in the future.

Direct marketing has in the past been viewed as a very tactical approach to meeting marketing objectives, and like sales promotions and PR has been used as part of both an ongoing programme of marketing communications and promotional activities. However, in cases of emergency, i.e. in crisis or indeed in competitive response, direct marketing has proved to be a useful tool.

As a marketing tool, direct marketing evolved from the mail order business and now it is seen as another compatible element of the promotional mix that supports and underpins the marketing communications activity and can often be found conveying the good news of sales promotions.

However, over the years direct marketing has come under fire as 'junk mail' and has also been found to be the source of 'confusion marketing'. In addition to this, direct marketing has been subject to considerable change due to the Data Protection Act and therefore the introduction of issues such as permission-based marketing have had a tremendous impact upon the future shape of direct marketing.

> **Definition**
>
> **Direct marketing**
>
> An interactive system of marketing which uses one or more advertising media to effect a measurable response at any location.
>
> Source: Institute of Direct Marketing

While this is quite a broad definition, it does however, identify some of the key component characteristics of direct marketing. For example, it provides the basis of the relationship, which is defined as interactive, being a two-way relationship between the organization and the customer. At the customer's location this could be via phone, fax, e-mail, Internet, post, to name but a few. However, whatever the nature of the communications and wherever and whoever they go to, it is essential that as with every other form of the promotional mix, there is an underpinning and SMART set of quantifiable objectives.

Objectives of direct marketing

Direct marketing performs a number of tasks, depending upon which element of the promotional mix it might work in parallel with and support.

The aims and objectives of direct marketing might include:

- Increasing direct mail order levels from new and existing customers
- Dissemination of information – provision of information to aid customer enquiries and support the adoption process
- Generation of sales leads – to increase the number of sales leads and ultimately influence a rise in sales income
- Generation of trial leads – to increase the number of customers willing to trial the product, to influence the process of adoption and influence a rise in sales income.

The aims and objectives of direct marketing can be achieved in a number of ways, and can often play a pivotal role in enhancing the selling process, by way of providing sales leads, that might directly result in a sale.

Furthermore, direct marketing objectives can be achieved through techniques such as direct mail, direct response advertising, telemarketing and the Internet, all of which are aimed at increasing sales leads and increasing sales turnover.

Database marketing

For an organization to really optimize its effectiveness in relation to building and developing long-term customer relationships, it is essential that they secure as much relevant information as possible about their customers and retain it in a database system. This in turn provides an opportunity to create closely defined profiles in order that a tightly defined targeting exercise can take place.

> *Database marketing is the application of digital information collected about current and/or potential customers and their buying behaviour to improve marketing performance by formulating a strategy and building personalized relationships with customers.*
> Source: Chaffey, Mayer, Johnston and Ellis-Chadwick, 2000

As information technology plays such a tremendous role in day-to-day business operations, it is increasingly likely that databases will be built to collect information from customers accessing websites. Databases are essentially known as the 'brains' behind the website, which enables a high level of customer profiling and personalization to take place.

Typical consumer information for database building might include:

- Name
- Address
- Occupation
- Geo-demographic profile
- Psychographics profile
- Previous contacts
- Previous responses
- Frequency of purchase
- Purchases made
- Value of purchases
- Type of purchases
- Media responsiveness
- Promotional responsiveness.

    Source: Dibb, Simkin, Pride and Ferrell, 2001

However, many underpinning database systems have failed as yet to achieve the level of sophistication required in developing appropriate data-mining opportunities. In addition to this, unless the site is a transaction-based website, i.e. where customers actually carry out a transaction on-line, it can be difficult to glean sufficient information about the customers to develop the typical profile basis you might prefer.

A further consideration in database marketing currently is that where databases are highly sophisticated, organizations do not understand how to use the information and put it through the data-mining process.

One of the key benefits of a good database, whether it be based on information gleaned from websites or through other sources, is that it forms the basis of the relationship and how it might be maintained in the future. While databases aid relationship management, database marketing does not constitute relationship marketing, in fact it only provides the means by which the relationship might be maintained.

Direct marketing techniques

Direct marketing provides significant scope for communicating directly with customers, and can cut across just about any promotional activity as part of the integrated marketing communications activity, and is not used exclusively for the consumer B2C market. It is also used very much in the B2B market, however, it has always been a central component of marketing strategies in the consumer market for years.

Direct mail

Direct mail has probably been the most used form of direct marketing over the years, but probably the one subject to the most abuse.

Direct mail is widely used in both consumer and business/organizational markets to target their customer groups directly. The financial services sector is a classic example of the use of direct mail. Even with the Data Protection Act, it is likely that some households receive as much as one piece of direct mail per day, in relation to mortgages, pensions, insurance, offers of credit cards, to name but a few.

Organizations such as MBNA sent out over 46,848,000 pieces of direct mail in 1998 and British Airways sent out in comparison 757,000 in the same period. You can see from this how essential direct mailing is to MBNA, but in the case of British Airways is plays a more peripheral role in their promotional mix.

There are many advantages associated with using direct mail, such as targeting. Targeted campaigns can include working on a basis of either geographic segmentation or geodemographic segmentation. This level of segmentation combined with the level of knowledge that exists in relation to market segments means that targeting can become a very exact science.

Other advantages include:

Personalization	Being able to personalize direct mail where appropriate
Response rates	If targeting is exact and appropriate to customer needs, response rates can be quite high. However, if they are not tightly targeted, these can be as little as 5 per cent response
Flexibility	Levels of flexibility available in direct marketing can provide much scope for an interesting and creative campaign. It allows for phased postage, delayed mailing, inserts, different size and frequency, to name but a few benefits associated with flexibility

However, when developing a direct mailing, you must ensure that the information you have is accurate, that customer groups are profiled and then targeted specifically and that the content matches the needs, wants and expectations of the group. This process will be assisted through the database marketing process, and ultimately the information collected will provide a greater insight into the customers and their buying behaviour. At the end of the day, the mailing will only be as good as the marketing research information that underpins it.

When purchasing a list externally, it is essential that you ensure the list provides you with relevant and up-to-date information, and is inside the data protection limits, defined in the Data Protection Act.

There are a number of organizations now that specialize in the development of appropriate automated mailing lists:

- Dun and Bradstreet – they offer 48 list options
- Wyvern Direct Response – based around occupational groups such as accountancy, medical practitioners, hospital contacts
- Wise and Lovey – web site address – http://www.mailing-labels.com

It is expected that more and more on-line automated mailing lists will become available to keep abreast of the changes in technology and the direct marketing sector.

On a less positive note, when looking at the effectiveness of direct mail, consider these facts. In 1997 over 3.7 billion pieces of mail were sent out, and over 100 million were marked 'return to sender', with another 80 million so badly addressed that they were unable to be delivered.

It is essential that if you are purchasing a list, very clear criteria have been developed in relation to:

- Relevance of the list in relation to the target market
- The source and ownership of the list
- The level of detail in the list
- Frequency of updates
- Whether the list is of enquirers, purchasers or respondents
- Frequency of purchase
- Level of accuracy.

Direct response advertising

This is another form of direct marketing and appears in the standard broadcast and standard print media.

Principally it is different from other forms of advertising, as it actually demands a response, by giving a website address, telephone number, or a coupon for a personal visit. This is becoming a popular approach in direct marketing and is growing continually as advertisers try to gain greater value from their advertising experience.

The targeting for direct response advertising is probably a little less scientific than direct mail, and relies much more on an assessment of the average reader or viewer profile than a prepared mailing list. However, the information collected can be used as a database for other forms of direct marketing in the future.

More and more organizations are involving themselves in direct response advertising in order to optimize their expenditure in advertising.

Telemarketing

We have touched upon the issue of personalization, and how through the use of database marketing we can glean enough information to personalize organizational approaches to customers. However, the difference between telemarketing and other methods of direct marketing, is that it is truly a personal approach, whereby there is a direct personal contact, which provides the basis for an interactive relationship between the organization and the customer.

While the personal approach is preferred and is seen as a way of getting closer to the customer, customers can find this approach rather intrusive and are somewhat resistant to embracing deeper and more meaningful relationships with organizations that they might purchase from.

Telemarketing, like other components of direct marketing, should be a planned, highly targeted and controlled activity that will both create and exploit a direct relationship between customer and seller using the telephone.

Telemarketing provides the organization with significant scope as telephone rental and ownership is very high, with over 80 per cent of household possessing them across the Europe Union. The telephone is a particularly powerful communications tool, which gives you direct access to new and existing customers, in a flexible environment, i.e. wherever they are.

Telemarketing also provides the scope to be used for customer service initiatives and customer satisfaction surveys, as well as the basis for developing the existing customer relationship overall.

The scope of telemarketing

- To generate sales leads
- To screen leads prior to following-up
- To arrange appointments for sales representatives
- To direct sales
- To encourage cross/upward selling
- To provide dealer support
- To manage and service accounts
- To undertake market research
- To undertake test marketing.

(Brassington and Pettitt, 2000)

As regards promotional and marketing operations, it is clear that telemarketing plays a pivotal role in:

- Increasing sales levels
- Supporting customers
- Increasing levels of customer service
- Providing technical support
- Information gathering
- Credit control.

One of the key disadvantages of telemarketing is the cost. It is a costly exercise, where few economies of scale can be charged. However, many financial services organizations are given very tough limits in terms of varying sorts of telemarketing in order that economies are achieved, but unfortunately this can be to the detriment of the long-term relationship with the customer.

A key factor of telemarketing as a direct marketing tool is that volume is rather limited in comparison with other direct marketing techniques. While a typical telemarketing representative might make between 30–60 calls per day, an equivalent piece of direct mail could actually achieve a significantly greater proportion of contacts.

Telemarketing, while having many qualities, is probably one of the least effective direct marketing mechanisms. It is certainly one of the least cost-effective, personally intrusive and does not achieve the necessary volume of hits on a day-to-day basis.

> **Case history**
>
> **46,000 Oregonians subscribe to no call list to stop unwanted telemarketing calls**
>
> The Oregon No Call List makes it easier for consumers to prevent unwanted telephone call solicitations to their homes. After consumers add their telephone number to the list, their privacy is protected and the responsibility rests with telemarketers to leave them alone.
>
> The No Call list was created as a response to the Senate Bill 915, passed in the USA in 1999. The list is also designed to address the growing problem of telemarketing fraud, which costs the US consumers some $40 billion annually.
>
> No phone call – no fraud! – The list gives consumers a way to fight back and regain control of their telephone privacy.
>
> For more information see www.ornocall.com
>
> Source: Lexis-Nexis

> **Question 5.9**
>
> How can direct marketing complement advertising and sales promotions?

Internet marketing

The evolution of Internet marketing has moved at a rapid pace. Key underlying trends behind the move towards Internet marketing are:

- Consumer time poverty
- Consumers looking to take control
- Convergence of technologies
- Shift from physical to digital technologies
- Shift from assets to knowledge.

There has been a massive growth in on-line households over the past four years, and between 1998 and 2002 there is a forecasted growth of an average of 40 per cent in ownership of PCs with on-line access within Europe.

Countries such as Asia, Australia, Japan and Scandinavia predict a more modest growth of on average less than 10 per cent.

The number of host computers on the Net has grown from 100,000 in 1990 to more than 40 million by the end of 1998 and was expected to reach more than 100 million by the end of 2000.

By 2000 it was anticipated that Internet revenues would reach some 18 billion dollars.

The average age of Internet shoppers is suggested to be around 34, with some 39 per cent of 15–25 year-olds involved in on-line shopping, 34 per cent of 25–34 year-olds and 29 per cent of 35–44 years-olds, shopping on-line and being continually exposed to Internet marketing.

After grasping some of these facts and figures you will no doubt realize that the Internet is a vital ingredient of the promotional mix, but also a vital component within the realms of direct marketing.

The whole basis of Internet marketing is that it will facilitate an interactive customer relationship on-line. It will enable frequent, customized and targeted messages to specific customers or customer groups.

What are the business benefits of Internet marketing?

The Internet provides a number of significant business benefits to organizations and they can be broken down to four key areas as follows:

- *Market penetration* – because of the nature of the Internet and its global communications ability, organizations can now sell more products to more markets, markets not necessarily accessible previously because of cost. The Internet can also be used to create a more broad awareness of the organization, its products and services and give an overall profile of the organization to potential customers.
- *Market development* – in this situation, the Internet can be used to sell products into completely new markets, taking advantage of low-cost advertising internationally without the necessity of supporting sales physically, in the customer's country.
- *Product development* – the Internet is excellent for supporting the development of new products and services and testing them out in the electronic world.
- *Diversification* – in this sector, new products are developed which are sold into new markets. Good examples of this are Dell and Hewlett-Packard, who extended their market considerably. Dell suggests that the Internet supports $6 million worth of sales every day.

The Internet can be used in many ways to support marketing activities:

- *Sales* – achieved through increasing awareness of brands and products, supporting buying decisions and enabling on-line purchase.
- *Marketing communications* – the use of the website for marketing communications is very powerful, particularly as surfing the Net is an increasing activity.
- *Customer service* – supplementing telephone operators with on-line information. First Direct Bank, Egg are examples of organizations moving in this direction.
- *Public relations* – the Internet can be used as a new channel for public relations and provides the opportunity to publish the latest news on products. For example when you log on to AOL.com, a news page and a number of advertisements and banners appear.
- *Marketing research* – earlier in this section we discussed how the research collected from websites in addition to the databases available enabled organizations to acquire a very clearly defined profile of their customers and their customer characteristics.

The advantages of Internet marketing

So far a picture is evolving of a dynamic electronic world that has increased access on a global basis, that is fast moving, effective and informative. In terms of marketing the key benefits of an Internet presence can be summarized as follows:

- *Cost reduction* – achieved through the need for less resources, less need for actual physical presence, less paper-based activity, particularly relevant to promotional activities and day-to-day business trading.
- *Competitive advantage* – who wants to be a dinosaur? Organizations need to stay ahead of the Internet game and aim to add value through the Internet and introduce new initiatives that will add overall competitive advantage.
- *Capability* – the Internet provides new opportunities for the development of new products and services.

- *Communication improvements* – the Internet, as we keep saying, is a powerful communications tool, with global coverage and can improve communications for both external and internal marketing.
- *Control* – the Internet may provide better quality of market research information through a range of Internet tracking devices.
- *Customer service improvements* – the Internet contains a number of interactive databases that can provide varying levels of information, at speed, improving customer response times. For the Internet banks, banking can take place 24 hours a day, every day.

The disadvantages of Internet marketing

- *The Internet replaces people* – as we have seen in the financial services sector over the last two to three years, there has been a vast reduction in the number of personnel required as a result of the automation of on-line banking.
- *The possible demise of High Street shops* – it has been suggested that within 30 years retail outlets will be a novelty and will be completely taken over by the Internet.
- *The loss of the personal touch* – there is the issue of de-personalizing business activity. The electronic world now works on a virtual rather than physical basis. Organizations must ask themselves about the loss of physical control. Is physical control an added value element of the business, or are speed and efficiency more important?
- *Security and privacy* – there are still issues of security and privacy, in addition to general regulation and control of information on the Internet. Under general regulation, there will of course be the issue of data protection. How do organizations ensure that this can be managed satisfactorily? This presents a significant challenge. Currently many organizations are seeking to ensure that they are not caught out with the various Data Protection laws currently in place.
- *Accessibility* – another issue relating to the Internet is that of accessibility by the majority. While there is a significant increase in the number of homes having a personal computer and growing Internet access across different elements of the world, and it is still anticipated that it will grow significantly, will it continue to grow to meet the expectations of industry?
- *Technological defects* – it has been suggested that there is still a long way to go to iron out some of the technical difficulties to overcome customer dissatisfaction with the process.
- *Information overload* – massive amounts of information make the Internet difficult to work around and hence people spend significantly longer on line searching for their information needs. Therefore, the Internet could be perceived as being expensive and time-consuming.

It is suggested that in the future only the most reluctant electronic shopper may still be concerned with these technicalities, but the majority will actually want the new forms of service on offer to them.

From the organization perspective the initial financial investment must be considered. However, many organizations will surmise that they have to invest early on to get long-term profitability and competitive advantage in the future.

Evaluation of direct marketing techniques

Evaluation of direct marketing activities relates to measuring the level of response any one campaign might have achieved. The evaluation of success will be based upon the pre-determined objectives of the campaign.

Typical measures for successful implementation of the direct marketing campaign will include:
- Response rate
- Conversion rate
- Order value
- Repeat orders.

This information will be gathered through a range of voucher and campaign response codes that will be able to distinguish the source of the direct mail or promotion. This may establish the most popular direct marketing technique for the organization to pursue in the future.

However, it is also essential that from a budgeting perspective the organization not only measures the effectiveness of the campaign, but tries to establish the cost per enquiry and cost per order element of the campaign.

The two components combined will enable an evaluation of campaign effectiveness to be achieved, in order that future campaigns will become more effective in terms of their actual output.

This form of measurement and evaluation will be typical across the full range of direct marketing tools that have been covered in this unit. However, as regards Internet marketing, the database underpinning the website will provide this particular information and will act as a mechanism for evaluating website effectiveness.

Sponsorship

Sponsorship is the provision of financial or material support by a company for some independent activity...not usually directly linked to the company's normal business, but support from which the sponsoring company would hope to benefit.
Source Wilmhurst, 1993

Therefore sponsorship is a two-way mutually beneficial partnership between an organization being sponsored and the sponsor. Sponsorship works on the premise that association largely affects image and that the sponsor may exchange money and/or goods or services in kind in return for the association that sponsorship provides.

Sponsorship objectives

Typical sponsorship objectives may include:
- Increasing brand awareness
- Building and enhancing corporate image
- Raising awareness of brands related to products restricted in advertising through various legislation, such as alcohol and cigarettes.

There are two perspectives to consider in sponsorship, the perspective of the organization being sponsored and that of the sponsor. Both parties will need to consider if the alliance created as a sponsorship arrangement is one that is required by the existing image of the organization and will enhance overall organizational credibility. They will also need to consider how relevant the association would be between the two organizations and how both parties will benefit. The sponsor will need to consider what exposure will be gained as a result of the sponsorship and how similar or dissimilar the target audiences are to their own.

Types of sponsorship

The main types of sponsorship include the following:
- *Programme sponsorship* – for example, *Inspector Morse*, Beamish Stout – typically this is used at the start of a TV programme, during the interval and at the end. The cinema and major films often form the basis of sponsorship alliances. There has been a massive

boom in TV sponsorship and the opportunity is providing broadcasters with a valuable new revenue stream as money from spot advertisers is no longer as plentiful.

A decade ago broadcast sponsorship was worth £1 million in the UK. In 2001 it will be worth in the region of £85 million. In the first quarter of 2001, TV sponsorship was due to increase by as much as 25 per cent (Source: lexis.nexis.com)

- *Arts/sports sponsorship* – e.g. the Carling Premiership. Carling sponsor the Premier Football League in England. Events sponsorship is expensive but can be very high profile and potentially the most cost-effective way of getting increased brand awareness.
- *Sponsorship of other events* – exhibitions, festivals, and opening ceremonies. These are again high profile, and are sometimes very useful forms of sponsorship for smaller businesses that wish to raise their profile locally.
- *Sponsorship of individuals or teams* – Mercedes Benz sponsor the British tennis player Tim Henman, and earlier we had the example of Siemens who provided a £3 million sponsorship deal with the FA Premier League as well as sponsoring Formula One motor racing.

Role of sponsorship

Sponsorship can provide a more cost-effective means of reaching your target audience, but the design, content and message are much more controlled. From a corporate perspective and PR perspective, sponsorship raises the profile of the organization and its corporate values, and in some instances can really bring the brand name and corporate image to centre stage.

Advertisers are being drawn in by the opportunity to convey their brand values by clever association with programming that is in keeping with their product and the desired company image.

Many organizations succeed in ensuring that as part of the sponsorship deal their name is an integral part of the overall event, for example the 'Benson and Hedges Cup'.

However, while sponsorship may appear to be a good idea, it is essential that, like all other elements of the promotional mix, it clearly fits a need and will enhance the possibilities of directly achieving predetermined marketing objectives.

Sponsorship offers vast opportunities for the organization in terms of the value added perspective of merchandising, public relations activities, improved stakeholder relationships, and highlighted ethical and social values. The benefits are quite considerable.

However, a number of key factors should be considered prior to taking the decision to proceed with sponsorship arrangements:

- What relevance does the particular sponsorship arrangement have in terms of the match between the two organizations and the potential target audience? For example it is clear that for Benson and Hedges and Carling Black Label sponsoring sports events will bring in additional sales of both drinks and cigarettes, both during and after the event, as sport effectively is linked to both of these habits.
- *The period of impact* – how long before and after the event will the sponsorship profile last for? Is the event a one-off or a sequence of events?
- *The uniqueness of the sponsorship agreement* – from a competitive perspective it will be essential that the agreement you hold with the sponsored organization allows you to differentiate your brand, market and competitive positioning in a unique way. In some situations this level of expectation is not achievable, but if the potential fit of the organization and the sponsorship deal is good, then high profile sponsorship might be achieved.
- *The level of spin-off promotions is also essential* – for example, the importance of an integrated approach between other elements of the promotional mix will be essential to maximize and optimize cost-effectiveness of particular high profile events. Here

advertising, merchandising and promotional incentives may be a particular match for the promotional mix.

Therefore, for successful implementation of a sponsorship strategy, it is necessary to clearly define the position of sponsorship and ensure that it is fully representative of corporate and marketing communications goals and effectively integrates sponsorship with other elements of the promotional and marketing mix.

Regulations governing sponsorship

The ITC (Independent Television Commission) Code of Programme Sponsorship regulates television sponsorship and the Radio Authority Code of Sponsorship Practice regulates radio sponsorship. Regulations for sponsorship are also covered by BCASP, the British Corporation for Advertising and Sales Promotion. You may wish to look at the website www.prsource.co.uk for further information on this area.

Evaluation of sponsorship

At each stage of the promotional mix, the importance of evaluation has been highlighted. Sponsorship is no exception and therefore the following methods of evaluation should be undertaken:

- *Media exposure measurement* – how much media coverage did the sponsorship activity actually achieve (a similar process of measurement to PR applies)?
- *Assessment of the sponsorship communication results* – pre-testing and post-testing of awareness, corporate image perception and improvements in general attitudes and opinions about the sponsor.
- *Feedback from all participants in the sponsorship process* – obtaining qualitative feedback from all participants as to the success or failure of the sponsorship agreement and ascertaining the position of mutual benefits between the sponsor and the sponsored party.

Personal selling

In the context of promotional operations it is important that you have a clear overview of how the personal selling process can both be compatible with other elements of the marketing mix and also enhance the effectiveness of the marketing mix.

> **Definition**
>
> **Personal selling**
>
> An interpersonal communication tool which involves face-to-face activities undertaken by individuals, often representing an organization, in order to inform, persuade or remind an individual or group to take appropriate action, as required by the sponsor's representative.

When preparing a marketing communications plan, the role of the sales department will usually include some form of personal selling objectives. Particular emphasis will include an analysis of the specific responsibilities associated with personal selling, the role of personal selling overall and how it will influence and enhance other elements of the marketing mix.

It is a known fact that personal selling is the most expensive element of the marketing mix. It is resource intensive, time ineffective, contributing little or no economies of scale, with high contact costs and customer maintenance costs. However, it is probably one of the most effective methods of influencing decision-makers to the stage of adoption. At a strategic level the balance of personal selling versus other more cost-effective methods of the marketing mix must be considered in order that the target market receives the most relevant approach to meet its information-based needs.

Sales force activity will be subject to a number of associated sales objectives that will directly relate back to the marketing objectives, and will be predetermined in order that the organization can optimize and maximize the potential impact of the personal selling team in association with other promotional activities.

Sales force objectives

Sales force objectives will not all relate directly to increasing income. They may also relate to cost saving, customer relationship management and developing new leads.

Therefore typical sales objectives could be:

- To increase sales turnover by 20 per cent within a 12-month period
- To reduce the number of clients with minimum viable order levels at the end of a 12-month period
- To reduce the cost of sales by 10 per cent within a six-month period
- To increase the number of distribution outlets by 15 per cent in a 12-month period.

Often personal selling goals are misunderstood and are assumed to be about an increase in sales, where actually personal selling goals will be about increases in overall revenue and profitability. Profitability might be improved by an increase in minimum order levels in order to achieve economies of scale.

The task of personal selling

There are four key tasks associated with personal selling:

- *Order takers* are effectively personnel who take orders from customers at the place of supply – e.g. holiday bookings, train tickets, retail outlets.
- *Order getters* are sales personnel who effectively visit organizations/customers in order to try to gain orders and future business from them.
- *Order collectors* are personnel whose role it is to gather orders – this is very much a telemarketing role.
- *Order supporters* – these are back-office personnel who underpin the personal selling process by providing information, customer service and support.

While this is one perspective, the role and task of personal selling is far more extensive than this and includes activities such as:

- *Prospecting* – gathering information in order to gain sales leads and prospective clients.
- *Communicating* – being the provider of information about the organization, its products, services and after-sales care.
- *Selling* – the actual role of convincing a potential customer to adopt the product; overcoming resistance and handling objections relating to, e.g. the company, the product, the service, the pricing strategy, the individual, competitive comparisons, need or want related issues.
- *Market research/information gathering* – environmental scanning, competitor intelligence, customer intelligence.
- *Servicing of accounts* – maintaining and providing ongoing customer service, including technical support, financial contractual arrangements and logistical arrangements.
- *Allocating* – ensuring that the allocation of products to customers is undertaken at all times, in particular in times of production shortages.

- *Customer relationship building* – building and sustaining long-term customer relationships.

Personal selling is a vital role within the organization, but it underpins a range of other promotional activities that it can only achieve through the appropriate level of sales and marketing support and with the appropriate tools of the trade.

It is essential from a marketing and promotional operations perspective that the sales team is kept briefed of any changes to the product portfolio, services mix or any essential information that might either enhance or inhibit sales team performance. As a marketer you therefore have a responsibility to support the sales team in a range of ways in order that they can open and close a sale effectively and efficiently.

- Provision of market information to support the selling process – customer and competitor intelligence
- Provision of potential leads from the market scanning process
- Client history – database information about purchasing behaviour, purchasing trends, frequency and value of orders
- Financial reports – Dun and Bradstreet reports, annual reports, etc.
- Provision of a range of appropriate promotional materials that include company history, product portfolio, services mix, financial package, support packages, etc.
- Sales aids – product samples, service packages, demonstration equipment
- Provision of promotional plans in order that sales staff can co-ordinate their call plans in line with particular promotional initiatives
- The provision of promotional incentives, merchandising, etc.

Opening and closing a sale

As advertisements raise awareness and desire a response, as sales promotions provide an incentive to purchase, personal sales staff provide the opportunity to actually close the sale.

The role of the sales person will be to effectively take the buyer through from the opening of the sale to the closing of a sale and the signing of the purchase order and contract.

Evaluating sales performance

Evaluating and measuring sales performance will be very much based upon the sales objectives set for the organization. But the objectives set will be SMART and therefore clearly defined and clearly linked with marketing objectives and overall corporate performance goals.

It is likely that sales performance will be measured against objectives on a regular basis, anything from weekly to quarterly. However, in most organizations sales performance against actual planned achievement is measured on a monthly basis.

It is also likely that other factors relating to sales performance will be measured, such as:

- Productivity – calls per day, calls per account, total number of orders versus calls
- Account development – total of new accounts, total of existing accounts, growth of sales from existing accounts
- Expenses – expenses versus number of calls made, cost per call.

With the evolution of IT, sales measurement techniques are becoming more sophisticated and more effective and the speed at which information becomes available is of the essence. A drastic reduction in sales performance can mean that other elements of the promotional mix might be subject to increased activity to compensate for the drop in sales. However, the drop in income often inhibits too much marketing expenditure of a contingency nature to be undertaken.

```
┌─────────────────┐
│ Prospecting for │
│   customers     │
└────────┬────────┘
         ▼
┌─────────────────┐
│    Qualifying   │
│     prospects   │
└────────┬────────┘
         ▼
┌─────────────────┐
│  Developing the │
│   relationship  │
└────────┬────────┘
         ▼
┌─────────────────┐
│  Presenting the │
│  sales message  │
└────────┬────────┘
         ▼
┌─────────────────┐
│ Handling queries│
│  and objections │
└────────┬────────┘
         ▼
┌─────────────────┐
│ Closing the sale│
└────────┬────────┘
         ▼
┌─────────────────┐
│Providing service│
│   and support   │
└────────┬────────┘
         ▼
┌─────────────────┐
│  Developing the │
│  relationship and│
│maintaining commitment│
└─────────────────┘
```

Figure 5.5 *The personal selling process*

Summary

This unit has been particularly extensive as it seeks to provide an overview of the key components of the promotional mix.

One of the critical success factors of implementing the promotional operations plan will be the degree of synergy and integration that exists between each of the promotional mix elements.

It is clear that the mix elements are indeed complementary to each other. Some of them are more effective and efficient in terms of targeting volumes, while other elements have a key strength in developing customer relationships in the long term.

Ultimately, the key success factor for any promotional mix will be its ability to meet the marketing objectives and bridge the successful implementation of the marketing strategy.

Promotional planning in complete isolation of the marketing plan could be untargeted and a complete waste of valuable resources.

At an operational level you are likely to be involved in the development and implementation of promotional plans. Therefore you will need to clearly identify the direct objectives, relate them back at all times to the marketing plan, undertake an integrated approach of promotional mix tools to optimize the effectiveness of a combined campaign and, of course, evaluate the implementation for measurement of success.

Further study and examination preparation

Extending knowledge
Recommended reading

The basis of this text is to provide you with an overview of the key components of marketing operations. However, you are advised to read more widely from other recommended texts. For this unit a more in-depth approach is found in Chapters 15–17 of *Marketing Concepts and Strategies*, 4th European edn, Dibb, Simkin, Pride and Ferrell, 2001.

In addition to this, you should be looking at Mad.com or purchasing *Marketing* and *Marketing Week* in order to keep abreast of various promotional mix activities undertaken by large corporations.

Study tip

Questions on various elements of the promotional mix are very popular and therefore you should ensure that you are familiar with the elements and how they can provide the basis for successful adoption of products or services.

In the June 2000 paper, you will see that there were three questions with a direct reference to elements of the promotional mix: Questions 2, 3a and 3b.

It is a significant area of the syllabus and equates to almost half of the syllabus weighting in respect of the marketing mix, therefore never underestimate it as a subject area.

Question 5.10
June 2000, Question 2

Go to www.marketingonline.co.uk or www.bh.com/marketing to access Specimen Answers and Senior Examiner's advice for this exam question.

Unit 6
Product operations

Objectives

This unit will be focusing on the role of the product in implementing the marketing plan and will therefore focus on product operations.

The following learning outcomes will be addressed within this unit:

- Understand the needs to integrate marketing mix tools to achieve effective implementation
- Select an appropriate integrated mix (4Ps) for a particular market.

The indicative content underpinning the learning outcomes for product operations is:

- The nature of products, components and life cycles
- Brand management: brand values, brand planning and threats to the brand
- Product portfolio, product mix
- New product development.
(Syllabus reference 1.2.3)

Product operations

While the basis of this unit will reflect product operations, it is in line with the syllabus that you are reminded of the nature and purpose of the product, its components and the product life cycle. You may have already studied for Marketing Fundamentals, where you will have covered some of the basics of the product; however, this is a useful form of revision and will also look at some additional elements of the product.

The product is the core of the marketing mix and is the basis of meeting customer needs and wants with the benefits and features that the product might offer them. From an operational perspective, should the product fail to live up to expectations then ultimately its failure will impact upon the achievement of the marketing objectives and will likely weaken any competitive strength that the organization might possess.

The product poses enormous challenges to many organizations and in turn the marketing function. The product is at the centre of the decision-making process and ultimately the adoption and exchange process that essentially links the organization and its customers together. The product is the component that gives the customer the benefits and possibly experience they have been looking for.

A product is a tangible item purchased by a customer and designed to meet their needs and wants. However, while the customer does purchase a product, what they are actually purchasing is the *benefits* that the product has on offer.

Primarily, the product is the acid test of whether or not the organization fully understands the nature and disposition of the customer and their actual needs and wants.

At this point it is advisable to ensure that the differences between products and services are clearly understood, as services will form the subject of another unit in this book.

Definition

Product

A product is a physical good, service, idea, person or place that is capable of offering tangible and intangible attributes that individuals or organizations regard as so necessary, worthwhile or satisfying that they are prepared to exchange money, patronage or some other unit of value in order to acquire it.

A service is an intangible item. When you buy a service, it differs from a product in that it does not result in the physical possession of anything. Essentially you purchase an experience, something that is not consistent and cannot be reused or taken away.

As marketers, what we need to do is to market these benefits to the customer, as the purchase of benefits is critical to the customer experience. Products are described as having three characteristics:

- Physical
- Functional
- Psychological.

Physical characteristics such as shape, size, colour, etc. can change according to the function of the product. For example a hairdryer could be black with a curved handle, difficult to hold. A functional characteristic could be the speed at which the dryer works and the number of varying heat settings it has.

The psychological characteristics are unique. This is concerned with the customers' values and expectations relating to the product or service. If the hairdryer provides a professional finish to your hair and you feel good about yourself then you are likely to be pleased with all of the three key features. If it gives you a good style from drying, but it is difficult to hold then it might have a psychological effect, in that you may not wish to purchase another one.

Benefits are key to the success or failure of a product and to assist you in understanding how the product evolves, you need to realize that the product can be broken down into smaller elements (see Figure 6.1).

Figure 6.1 The anatomy of the product

The *core* is as it sounds the centre or heart of the product. The core product provides a very basic function. It is usually seen as the no-frills version of the product; it should deliver the desired benefits effectively. The core product then provides the basis for the next level.

The *tangible/actual* product relates to making the product a reality. The product becomes a real product, with real characteristics and benefits that can then be communicated to the customer to encourage purchase.

The *augmented* product is the core/tangible product, with a number of add-on extras which makes the product more marketable and enables organizations to be competitive. These extras do not directly affect the workings of the product as it can exist without them, but they add value to the product in the long term. For example, a car with leather seats: it does not matter whether or not the seats are fabric or leather, what is important is that you can sit on them to drive. The third level is the *potential* product. This means that the company must be responsive to the marketplace and to the change that continues to take place within it, and therefore the organization and the marketer will need to consider what the potential product will be like in the future. The car market is a classic example of this. No sooner have they launched a new model than they are working on the launch of the replacement product. The continuing future development of the product is a strategic issue and will be reflected in the overall strategic direction of the organization.

> **Question 6.1**
>
> Using the concept of the model in Figure 6.1, explain how BMW might build from the core product through to the augmented products.

Product classifications

Part of your role as a marketing manager at an operational level will be to categorize the products manufactured by your organization so that you can ascertain issues relating to features, benefits and functions. Then you can contribute to the development of an appropriate integrated promotional mix.

There are three categories:

1. Durable
2. Non-durable
3. Service product.

Durable

Products that are durable last for a period of time, e.g. a car, stereo system, washing machine, etc. Eventually they will have to be replaced, but they do have a steady life cycle appropriate to the product.

Non-durable

Non-durable products are different in that they can only be used a small number of times, or even only once. They do not have a durable lifespan, e.g. food, drinks, printing paper, disposable contact lenses or disposable nappies. Many of these products are known as FMCGs – fast moving consumer goods.

Service products

Services are intangible – you have nothing physical at the end of the service experience, e.g. holidays, hairdressing, personal banking/financial services.

These three classifications then break down into smaller groups as follows:

- **Convenience products** – These are frequently purchased products, such as food, drinks, petrol.
- **Shopping goods** – These goods are those that customers will shop around for, comparing and contrasting value in terms of benefits versus brand and price.
- **Specialty products** – These possess unique characteristics that customer/consumers will look for. The likelihood is that they will have very specific ideas and expectations of the products and alternatives would not be considered as appropriate. There will also be much emphasis on the brand, e.g. cars – Porsche, clothes – Calvin Klein.
- **Unsought goods** – This area is particularly interesting and relates to customers not really wanting this product, but ultimately could be persuaded to purchase through strong marketing and effective promotions and communications. For example, air circulation systems in the home, air conditioning units.
- **Business products** – This is quite a substantial area as it really relates to any products that support and enable the business function to take place.
- **Process products** – These goods ultimately become part of the producer's own products.
- **Plant and equipment** – These products are exactly as they sound: they are the fabric of the organization, the equipment and machinery that are needed to enable manufacturing and productivity to take place. Clearly in today's technical age there will be a huge amount of computer-aided technology that will enable a higher level of competitive design with more technical detail and capability than ever before.
- **Supplies and services** – Here you are looking at the things that make the world go round and make business happen. All of the supplies and support service organizations need, come under this heading – maintenance and repair, financial services, cleaning services, etc.

Being a product manager in a marketing context will be a very challenging and complex role. Your aim will be to develop a product that is compatible with the existing product portfolio, meets customer needs and wants and forms part of the overall strategy in line with both corporate and marketing objectives.

Branding

A successful brand is an identifiable product, service, person or place, augmented in such a way that the buyer or user perceive relevant, unique, sustainable added values, which match their needs most closely. (De Chernatony and McDonald, 1998)

A brand is a highly powerful tool, because it provides a balance of functional benefits and performance values. The term 'brand' is used to describe the 'personality' of a particular company's products. The brand concerns use of design, colour, typography, the quality that brand portrays and the actual identity of a product or service as the customer sees it. The brand is not just a name, the brand is a multi-functional concept.

There are many well-known brands throughout the various segments that have built up reputations as providers of good quality produce or services. For example, Nokia, Coca-Cola, Nike, Reebok, BMW are all well-known brands of reputable quality.

Branding is of primary importance to the organization, as it provides the organization and its product portfolio with an identity, something that people can associate with. It is essentially the key to successfully differentiating the organization and its products from the competition. However, to develop a successful brand will require a considerable investment in both time and money, and investment, which if properly planned and managed should reap significant rewards.

The brand plays a number of roles from an input perspective, output perspective and time perspective.

Brands are complex, but ultimately they rest in the minds of customers as a basis on which to identify with a product, quality and image that is portrayed (Table 6.1).

Table 6.1 Different brand interpretations (Adapted from De Chernatony, 2001)

Input Perspective	Output Perspective	Time Perspective
Logo	Image	Evolving entity
Legal instrument	Relationship	
Company		
Risk reducer		
Positioning		
Personality		
Cluster of values		
Vision		
Value added		
Identity		

These points realistically need little explanation, however, it is essential that you are aware that the input perspective relates to everything that is put into the brand to actually make it a brand and, from the perspective of the organization, what are the inputs that make the brand successful. This means the way in which the brand is managed, i.e. the resources required to ensure that the brand is of significant value, both rationally and emotionally, to the customer.

From an external perspective, the brand will be perceived and interpreted by the customer: how it impacts upon the customer, motivates them, fulfils them and actually achieves some purpose for them.

'Time-based' is something of a radical component in branding. How long is a piece of string, some might say, but it is indeed an important factor. It may appear that some brands, such as Ford for example, might go on into perpetuity, forever. However, this would be a complacent and dangerous strategy to follow; one with likely catastrophic results.

Brand values

Brand values are often difficult to define. However, they represent key success factors of the organization and its products. Rokeach (1973) suggested that:

> *A value is an enduring belief that a specific mode of conduct or end-state of existence is personally or socially preferable to an opposite or converse mode of conduct or end-state existence.*

Values are essential in any organization, both from the internal perspective, where values will define the basis on which the organization does business, but also from the external perspective, where values essentially become meaningful and often the source of 'added value'. For example where quality is a value, quality is a perceived benefit to the customer.

Brand values, therefore, become the basis of an organization being perceived as different. However, while they might form the basis of differentiation, the organization must be clear as to why they arrived at these values in the first place, and what they might mean to the future vision of the business.

As a customer it is likely that you will be drawn to brands that hold values compatible to your own personal ones, and by the same token employees are often drawn to organizations who associate core principle values very much in line with their own.

Where are values formed? Values are formed as a result of a range of influences on each individual from childhood through to adulthood. Key influencers in our lives, parents, peers, and colleagues form them. A value is a belief, something we believe in, see as important, and allow to shape and form our behaviour.

As a result of the key components that define values, organizations therefore are challenged to specifically develop values that are akin to their customer groups, their target markets, which makes the segmentation process all the more complex. However, not only is the segmentation process complex, but the expectations of the organization in the minds of the customers as a result of their brand values are highly demanding and need careful planning.

An excellent example of brand values is that of the Virgin Brand. Richard Branson declared that the qualities associated with Virgin are:

- Quality
- Innovation
- Value for money
- Fun
- A sense of challenge.

These are more formally known as a cluster of values. These core values will, therefore, be at the core or heart of whatever Virgin do in the future. If they continue to extend the brand, as they have done on many occasions before, these values should continue to be the core of all of the businesses, not just exclusively one.

Branson used five values to demonstrate the ethos of his organization, five being an appropriate number and sufficiently challenging to deliver.

Many organizations develop brands for an external perspective and with the 'external' customer in mind. However, more and more organizations are moving towards making the brand values the focus point of the whole business, both for internal customers and external customers; actually making them a core rather than peripheral activity.

Core and peripheral values

While developing and defining corporate values is an essential activity, there are two levels of values which a company can focus on.

Core values are those values which the brand will always uphold, regardless of the external drivers of change, which are here to stay. On the other hand *peripheral values* are those that are of secondary importance to the brand, and those that might change with market forces and conditions. Therefore, while quality might always be a core value, a peripheral value might be related to an activity or service level that the organization changes in line with market forces.

In essence, establishing brand values provides a robust basis for ascertaining appropriate behaviour on the part of the organization. Values contribute in part to the vision and mission of the organization and ultimately establish a culture based upon which the organization can do business, meet customer needs and actually make a difference to customer experiences and customer achievements.

Brand loyalty

One of the benefits of defining corporate values is that there can be a brand association between the customer and the organization. This brand association can often be the basis of a long and loyal relationship. Brand loyalty is a hot topic in today's competitive environment, with significant pressure on brand switching to gain market share from competing organizations.

In achieving brand association the brand should be tightly targeted and assist customer achievement, so that brand loyalty and customer retention can be achieved.

Brand loyalty, brand preference and brand recognition are objectives of branding and form the structure and basis upon which brands are developed. However, in this context there is a significant difference between brand recognition and brand preference. Brand recognition is a measurement of customer awareness: the case study on Egg in Unit 1 or easyJet both make reference to the level of brand recognition.

The more important measures of success will indeed be brand loyalty and brand preference; they will form a very vital part of the brand planning process.

> **Question 6.2**
> What are the long-term benefits of building brand loyalty?

Brand planning

Planning in relation to brands is an essential activity, as it determines the future behaviour of the organization and provides a SMART basis on which the organization is to operate. Planning ensures delivery of brand values and the whole brand experience to the marketplace.

Typically there are long-term and short-term objectives relating to the brand, as with any other marketing activity. Long-term objectives are often perceived as being particularly stretching on the part of the organization, where they form part of the greater vision for the future. For example, back in the 1960s, IBM set themselves a brand objective of 'reshaping the computer industry' while Boeing set a long-term brand objective of launching a commercial jet aircraft, which they ultimately achieved through the launch of the Boeing 707, bringing jet travel to the commercial market.

Short-term objectives, however, relate to the more immediate future, whereby sub-sets of objectives need to be defined to underpin the longer-term vision. Therefore, they will relate to ways of achieving the long-term goals. For example, Boeing determined that they would:

- Be the airlines' first choice
- Show strong profitability and meet investors' expectations
- Have a global network and a global outlook
- Delight customers.

In many ways, brand planning will be quite a strategic role. However, it is useful for you to be aware of the implications of brand planning, as in a product management role or marketing management role, responsibility will lie with you in terms of the overall implementation of the plan and the tactical activities involved.

Brand strategies

Detailed below are three strategies that companies engage in at different times and for a variety of reasons:

- *Family branding* – Here the power of the family name, such as Nestlé (see Figure 6.2), Heinz, Cadbury's and Kellogg's is used to promote the family of brands. The name of Heinz is used to promote the diversity of the product range. Cadbury's achieves a similar effect in its sponsorship of *Coronation Street*, where it is able to use its brands to suit the season. Beamish also achieved publicity through its sponsorship of *Inspector Morse*.

- *Brand extension* – Here a brand can be extended using the name of the original. A good example of this would be Mars ice cream bars. The attraction of brand extension is that launch costs are not as great because the family name is already well known. It also represents less of a risk to consumers, who might be worried about trying something new.

- *Multi-branding* – Manufacturers introduce a number of brands that all satisfy very similar product characteristics. For example, in the detergents market, Lever Brothers and Procter and Gamble have several brands all fulfilling the same purpose. It also means that anyone trying to enter the market for the first time would have to launch several brands at once to compete.

- *Own branding* – Many food manufacturers supply large retailers with goods under their own brand names. For example, Northern Foods supplies cakes to Marks and Spencer from its Park Cakes bakery, as well as producing its own brand products. This practice allows the manufacturer to maintain high levels of production. Some manufacturers concentrate on production only, leaving the problems of distribution, design, quality and marketing to a multiple retailer.

Figure 6.2 Brand family

Advantages and disadvantages of brand strategies

There is an obvious benefit for a new product if it can have a well-respected name in its brand, but the policy can be harmful to a whole range if one product gets a bad name.

When using a brand you can send out a message of quality, reliability, style, effectiveness and luxury. Effectively a brand should be meaningful; it should stand for something customers can relate to.

Brand threats

Brands are no exception when it comes to threats from external forces, as attacking a brand, particularly a well-known brand, can reap rewards in terms of high levels of publicity, as in the case of British Airways and Virgin and indeed Camelot and Virgin. But it can also actually impact upon marketing share.

Typical threats therefore include:

- *Competition* – this component has just been covered. Brands do need to protect themselves against high levels of competitor threat. The key to success in overcoming brand threats is to ensure that the branding strategy relates to uniqueness, differentiation, robust corporate identity and strong core brand values.
- *Brand names* – the key threat here is the potential misuse or copying of brand names. Some organizations use brand names in order to heighten awareness of their brand, or to give it a comparable position with another brand. For example, Kleenex is a brand of paper handkerchiefs (i.e. paper tissues) in the UK, while in Iran, if you wish to purchase a box of tissues, it does not matter what the brand name is, tissues are known synonymously as 'Kleenex'. Therefore, in Iran, this has diluted the power of the actual Kleenex brand and its associated product.
- *Copyright* – a major infringement of intellectual property rights is the use of trademarks, designs and logos that have been legally protected against misuse and copy. If they are not legally protected, then other organizations can use them and benefit from them.

Managing the brand

Branding is an absolute minefield; and is a subject in its own right. We have only touched upon some of the generic issues associated with branding. Branding is a core activity, a differentiating activity and one that enables the organization to establish a corporate identity and a vision based around clearly defined brand values.

To ensure that the brand is successful and there is synergy between the branding strategy and the remainder of the product, and the marketing mix, it is essential that the brand be carefully managed.

Successful brands

> **Key points**
>
> To create a successful brand a company must:
> - Make quality a priority
> - Offer superior service
> - Get there first
> - Differentiate its brands
> - Develop a unique positioning concept
> - Support the brand
> - Deliver consistency
>
> Adapted from Dibb, Simkin, Pride and Ferrell 2001

These key points set the tone of the role of brand management, which is essentially based around building an effective brand that will ultimately support the corporate goals and marketing objectives.

The focus of any marketer's role is based upon creating an awarness of the brand and its associated values to the customer, monitoring consumer reactions, and meeting their needs.

Packaging

Packaging plays a hybrid role in terms of its overall function within marketing and its contribution to the successful implementation of the marketing strategy. It has many facets and plays a significant part in:

- Protecting the product
- Providing economy and convenience
- Promoting the brand
- Advertising a brand and products
- Providing important and essential information in relation to the products
- Legal/ethical associations.

The design of packaging is extremely important, as it provides a way of achieving the above elements while also providing the basis of developing competitive advantage. At the end of the day, packaging could influence a customer's purchase decision, through promoting its features, benefits, uses and image all in one go.

Packaging considerations

There are many issues associated with packaging that do confirm its hybrid function within marketing, overlapping considerably with the promotional and product mix, with an influence on and implication of 'price'. Therefore, developing an appropriate packaging solution is a challenge. Principally a package will have to protect, communicate and provide convenience to user, distributor and retailer. Therefore, the following points are key packaging considerations:

- Cost
- Logo/image design
- Safety/tamper resistance packaging
- Packaging design
- Packaging with promotional value
- Environmental responsibility
- Multiple channel users
- Meeting legal requirements based on weights, measures, contents.

From the marketing perspective, it will be vital to the successful design of the packaging that a research programme is undertaken to establish how the target market reacts to particular packages, what they expect from packaging, how they perceive packaging as a value added component of their overall product experience.

Therefore, as a marketer you will need to establish the relative costs of packaging in order to achieve a balance in the supply chain needs so that the right combination of functionality, value and cost of packaging can be achieved.

Question 6.3

Explain the concept that packaging has a hybrid function in marketing.

Product management

Creating a product range

One of the key functions that you will undertake in a marketing role is assisting in the creation of an appropriate portfolio of products, i.e. a product range. This means that an organization will have a range of products that they sell, either similar or even diverse products. The better and more appropriate the range of products the more likely they are to sell them. Take, for example, many 'white goods' organizations, which sell a range of products from TV and washing machines to kettles.

Within the product range there is a *product mix*, which is the portfolio of products an organization sells. This can be broken down into three areas. This really relates back to the circular diagram, the anatomy of the product, earlier in this unit. In simple terms it means that a manufacturer will start off with a core product and will then build on that product, or the idea of it, to build a product range.

The *product line* is a group of closely related products, e.g. Colgate offer a number of various toothpastes, but they are all marketed as Colgate–Palmolive in terms of TV advertising and overall marketing.

The *product mix* is the total portfolio of products that a company has on offer. For example, Cannon manufacture a variety of photographic products, this would then be their total product mix. Procter & Gamble also have a very broad range of products from medically related products through to soaps, soap powers, etc., this would be their product mix also.

When considering the product mix, organizations must establish the breadth and depth of the product mix. The depth being how many products are within a product line, e.g. how many different types of toothpaste are under the Colgate–Palmolive brand as opposed to the breadth of the product, relating to how many product lines Colgate–Palmolive make, e.g. toothpaste, soaps, etc.

As part of the strategic planning process, the organization should reflect on their existing product range to ensure that their products fit with one another, are compatible and continue to meet the needs of increasingly powerful and vocal customers. Therefore, a decision will be made at a strategic level whether or not to launch new products, withdraw existing products and to extend or decrease the life cycle of a product.

As the product is at the heart of the organization and the reason for its overall existence, this is a serious decision that must be undertaken in an informed way, with a structured analytical approach, understanding customers, market forces, key drivers and factors influencing change. Much of this information will be provided through the marketing audit process, where both the macro and micro audit will likely identify critical issues associated with the product mix.

The product life cycle

The product life cycle (see Figure 6.3) is probably one of the best known concepts in the whole theory and practice of marketing as a business function.

It is not rocket science to understand that every product does actually have a life cycle. It doesn't matter what it is, it has an existence, sometimes a planned existence – sometimes even planned obsolescence.

The product life cycle is an invaluable tool in providing an insight into a common pattern of industry sales, one that might be helpful in ascertaining the expected life of products within your product portfolio. One of the big failures of many businesses has been the failure to recognize a product's ability to exist and to operate at a competitive level.

The marketing mix will vary at each stage of the product life cycle. As you saw in Unit 5, different types of promotional activities are required to underpin particular points in the cycle. A product life cycle can effectively be extended or decreased according to particular marketing activities that are undertaken. This could be achieved by product modifications, product repositioning, re-branding, and market development, to name but a few possibilities.

New markets can often mean that new uses for the product have been identified. This can extend the product for a considerable period of time.

One common factor across all industries in relation to the product life cycle is that different products have different time horizons; some extend forever, and others will decline and become obsolete very quickly.

Figure 6.3 The product life cycle

Development

Figure 6.3 illustrates the various stages involved in a product's life cycle existence. A product is in the development stage when market research, product development and marketing testing activities are undertaken. Development costs are high and sales volume will be low, income levels will be non-existent.

Growth

The product then passes through a growth stage when it is received positively and sales volume increase rapidly. Development costs start to be recovered and costs per unit decrease as production quantities improve. Some profit may appear to be emerging; this will of course vary between organizations based upon the nature of the products and the level of investment required.

Maturity/saturation

The product becomes fully developed and the initial needs are satisfied. Its success will be dependent on repeat purchase. It is likely that competitors will appear in the market. As the market becomes saturated, sales will slow down and profits will start to decrease.

Decline

It is very likely that during the decline stage of the life cycle sales will eventually decline and it will be too expensive to maintain the product.

Figure 6.3 illustrates a typical product life cycle curve. However, in practice, product life cycles can be short, long and of various shapes, depending on various curves. For example, fashion products come into play very quickly and also drop out of the market very quickly as the next fashion comes on board.

At each stage of the product life cycle the marketing activities and communication activities will change. For a new product launch, the message will be creating awareness, introducing the product to the market. The saturation stage will probably include incentives and promotional activities to encourage customers/consumers to keep purchasing the product.

By the time you get to decline the organization should be ready to launch a new product and therefore the message will be to complete the cycle of the existing product in preparation for the new product. A good example of this would be the car market. Often car prices are decreased significantly to clear existing stock, to make way for the latest model.

However, the product life cycle does have some limitations. There is a significant danger that organizations might have an over-dependence on the life cycle, meaning that a temporary drop in sales might actually indicate the need for early withdrawal from the market, and be wrongly interpreted as an early decline.

One of the most inhibiting factors of the product life cycle is that in the real world the product life cycle is flexible and will change rapidly depending on demand and the activity within the external marketing environment. The change in demand could be based around government policy, competitive activity, technological advances, etc. The changes can be quite sudden and then misunderstood.

The product life cycle is a very difficult area to manage but organizations understand that:
- It is dangerous to rely too heavily on one product for too long
- Product life cycles must be tightly managed and continually monitored
- While there might be a predetermined cycle that defines the direction that a product might follow, it does not always take into account the unexpected and the unforeseen external driving forces, technological changes or competitor activity, and can therefore be seen as a little inflexible.
- A product portfolio should undergo ongoing review and identify products that should be discontinued or products that should be modified.

On a more positive note, it does aid planning and enables organizations to set key objectives relating to new product development, to when to launch products and to when it may re-design products or even make them obsolete. The advantages of the product life cycle when used as a planning tool are:
- It is a very valuable tool as it helps demonstrate the various stages in the product's development
- It helps forecast potential future demand
- It reminds us of the fact that all products have a limited life
- Profit levels are not constant but change throughout a product's life in a way that is, to some extent, predictable
- Products require different marketing programmes at different stages of their life cycle.

It is important to understand that not all products go through the stages as described above. For example, a product may be developed and launched and may not be successful and therefore declines before it has the opportunity to grow or mature.

Later in the unit you will be spending some time looking at the management of the product life cycle to provide you with an insight into some to the marketing challenges, both at strategic and operational level. It is essential that the product life cycle is examined in this context in order to highlight potential tactical level activities that a product or marketing manager might be involved in.

Managing the product life cycle

Product operational planning in the context of marketing operations is concerned with the tactical activities that underpin any particular product-based objectives, such as product development, product line extension, product differentiation and product positioning.

This level of operational planning should without exception underpin the strategic marketing process, exploiting marketing opportunities and growth strategies in an ever-changing environment.

One of the challenges of product management is that a massive growth in innovative products, competitive activity and market saturation will find organizations presented with fewer and fewer opportunities. Therefore, the management of the product life cycle is an essential activity, in order that every opportunity available can be exploited and the life cycle is extended. Sales will thus be optimized and profit potential maximized.

Marketing strategy for growth

With new and innovative products it is very likely that product sales could grow at an unprecedented rate. At this stage in the product life cycle the competition may see and anticipate the rapid rate of growth and enter the market with their version of the product. It is likely that the competition will be highly aggressive, with high levels of advertising and sales promotion activity as they strive to gain their market share by incentivizing customers to switch brands.

As a product or marketing manager, it will be necessary for you to monitor these reactions very carefully and feed back into the strategic marketing process, in order that remedial action can be taken. It is more likely that the actions taken will be of a more tactical nature, principally striking back at the competition. However, in many instances, a strategic decision may have been made much earlier on the product offering, either by extending the product line or by differentiating the product offering.

Targeting of customers may need to be much more tightly defined as each of the competitors strives for market share. Increasing variations on a theme may be required in order to fully differentiate the product offering from that of the competitors.

Typical strategies at this stage will include an increase in push strategy activities by the manufacturer in order to gain preference with suppliers and retailers and command a higher proportion of supplier preference, and pull strategies, targeting more and more distributors, effectively saturating the market where appropriate with your own products.

As indicated in Unit 4, advertising activities will change to include brand awareness and brand benefits, aiming to position the products suitably in the minds of the customer.

In respect of the pricing element of the marketing mix, if growth is rapid then it might be expected that return on investments will also be achieved at an early stage, or that there is significant payback to reduce the price of the products. However, it might be that an increase in sales and volume might also generate economies of scale that could also enhance the possibilities of price reduction.

Price sensitivity may be an issue at this stage depending upon the products, but with more and more substitute products entering the market, it is likely that price will be a critical issue that will need careful management. Pricing will be positioned to sustain market share, and continue the life cycle as long as appropriate.

Marketing strategy for maturity

Managing the product life cycle through maturity throws up some interesting dynamics. It is likely that once a product has reached maturity new products, and modified products, are running closely behind. It is probable that in this instance enough modifications will be made in order to differentiate the product suitably in order to reverse its position in the cycle, back towards a growth trend. This is a common policy of car manufacturers who are known historically for changing the light settings, bumper shapes and perhaps superficial features to enhance the look of the car, in line with customer expectations. In doing this, it is likely that the life cycle of the car will be extended. Modifications will reflect three particular categories, quality, functional and style modifications.

A typical example of this is the Ford Mondeo. This particular vehicle, along with the Ford Escort, has underdone a number of modifications, and their life cycle appears to have been endless. Mercedes Benz are currently involved in this very modification process, as they launched the modified A Class at the same time as extending the product line to include a new A Class model. They have modified all three categories.

Segmentation and positioning become an issue, as customers' expectations change and become more diverse. It is a possibility that marketing development and market penetration strategies could be pursued simultaneously, maximizing profit potential.

Other typical activities might include cost cutting, intensive promotional opportunities and repositioning or even re-branding.

Marketing strategy for declining products

It is likely that the product has declined to such a stage that profitability has been significantly reduced and is probably non-existent. More innovative products and more up-to-date versions of the same will have replaced the product. The fall may have been predicted, or it might have been forced. However, where possible the decline of the product in the life cycle should be carefully managed.

The organization has a number of potential choices available to them at this stage:

- Obsolescence – remove it from the product portfolio altogether and replace it
- Repositioning – identify new uses for the product and new markets, position it differently in the minds of the existing and potential customers.

Obsolescence is increasingly common as a result of new technologies. In the last 20 years we have seen the demise of the record player for the CD player and the video player will ultimately decline to be replaced by the DVD player.

In respect of distribution, high levels of promotional activity might encourage customers to continue to purchase and assist distribution channels in moving the stock over for replacements or new products. It is likely that a number of distributors will remove themselves from the channel for a period, or even be removed, in order to maintain profitability.

Depending upon the product again, price sensitivity may be an issue. In the car market it is usual that the price of cars that are in decline is ultimately reduced to clear them once the new replacement models are launched.

Advertising at this stage will be limited, but as already indicated, some level of promotional incentive may still be offered to speed up the decline and obsolescence process in order to release the stock.

Making a product obsolete and actually deleting it from the portfolio also requires some careful management. It is suggested that there are three key ways of deleting a product from the market:

- *Phase it out* – a natural process, whereby the product strategy does not change until the product has sold out. It is expected that no attempt will be made to revive the product or change it. The Ford Escort was phased out in favour of the Ford Focus.
- *Run it out* – increase and intensify the marketing effort in order to effectively clear out stock.
- *Drop it* – if retaining the product is eating into company profits, and it is being retained at a cost, it is likely that the organization will drop the product immediately and end its product life cycle.

As already suggested, a lot will depend on the product itself, the circumstances, i.e. is it a natural deletion, a forced deletion, is there loss of face and an effect on competitive positioning? These factors will all impact upon the approach to production deletion. If retaining the product is eating into company profits, and it is being retained at a cost, it is likely that the organization will drop the product immediately and end its product life cycle.

> **Question 6.4**
>
> You are one of a team of product managers for a large motor vehicle manufacturer. You have been asked to prepare a briefing paper on the possible marketing activities that might be involved in sustaining a mid-range vehicle at the maturity stage of the product life cycle for a further three years.

Product portfolio planning tools

You should now understand that while the product life cycle has its own set of limitations, it is still a critical planning tool which helps focus the organization on the future of its product portfolio.

It is of primary importance that organizations continually monitor and control how their products are doing in the marketplace, what products are in growth and what products are then in decline.

To assist with this process many organizations use what is formally known as portfolio matrices.

Probably the best known and most established matrix, is the Boston Consulting Group matrix, known as the BCG (see Figure 6.4).

Figure 6.4 The BCG matrix (Adapted from the Boston Consulting Group, 'The Product Porfolio', Perspectives, August 1970)

158

The BCG matrix

The BCG matrix has two key dimensions associated with it, namely relative marketing share, i.e. the level of growth in the product's market, and second, the product's market share in comparison to that of its competitors.

Market growth is an imperative to many organizations, as it presents an opportunity in the marketplace for extension, expansion and innovation. However, in low growth markets, it is more about survival of the fittest, as competition is highly intensive as each competitor strives for their portion of a much smaller market potential.

Each of the four quartiles of the BCG offers an indication of potential opportunities or even potential decline in market share.

Stars

Principally stars are products that command high levels of market share, with good potential for growth in the future. Key components are:

- The product has moved to a position of leadership in a high growth market
- Income needs are high in order to maintain market growth and keep competitors at bay
- The product generates a large amount of income
- As long as the market share is maintained, the product should become a cash cow.

Cash cows

Cash cows are essentially products that have a dominant share of the market, but with little potential for growth, effectively reaching a level of maturity. Key components are:

- Products have a high market share and a low level of market growth. Stars become cash cows when the market rate begins to fall
- The term 'cash cow' comes from the principle that products generate considerable money but use little cash
- Economies of scale are strong.

Question marks

Question marks, alternatively known as problem children, are very much as they sound. They are principally products that have a small market share of a growing market. However, they are often subject to high levels of investment in order for them to succeed in any significant growth in market share overall. Key components are:

- High growth markets, with low market share
- Considerable investment is required in order to keep up with market developments
- If trying to improve competitive position, levels of investment required are high
- The term 'question mark' arises when one needs to decide whether to invest or divest in a market.

Dogs

The position of 'dogs' in the BCG is one typically of low market share, with no real potential for growth. This can often be an indication that the product is nearing the end of its current life, and should be potentially considered for repositioning or deletion from the product line. Key components of dogs are:

- A weak market share in a low growth market
- A low level of profit or a loss would be typical in return

- Very often dogs take up more time in terms of management than can be justified, so phasing out of the product is likely
- Strategically, the issue is whether or not to hold on to the business.

The Boston Consulting Group matrix is one of many matrices now in use, but overall, its main purpose is to provide a framework for considering future market growth for both products and services.

From a marketing perspective, the BCG enables the organization to actually classify the company's products into four clear categories that will, in the main, shape their place in the future marketing strategy. While principally this is a planning tool, which should be used in the strategy development stages, it is important that it is clearly linked with the product in the context of product operations. This is because it will be part of the marketing manager's role to continually evaluate the performance of the product within the marketplace, and to contribute to inform the planning process of the potential growth and market share of the existing product portfolio.

There are a range of alternative models such as the GE matrix, or marketing attractiveness business position model (Figure 6.5); however, this is more of a strategic level model. This model indicates levels of market share on the same basis and will ultimately be able to indicate high, medium or low levels of marketing attractiveness. In using this, organizations will be able to potentially establish market attractiveness and different levels of growth, which will indicate the need to either invest and grow or divest and harvest.

Figure 6.5 The GE (General Electric) matrix

Both the product life cycle and the BCG matrix have a number of attributes (see Figure 6.6) that will be tremendously helpful in planning for product involvement in the marketing strategy.

Typical outcomes from analysis undertaken through the BCG matrix, will be the identification of new opportunities for product development potential, the need for repositioning of products or the need for deletion of products. In terms of potential marketing strategy, the BCG will assist in defining how growth objectives might be achieved through product-based activities.

	PLC	*BCG*
Planning strengths	Five-stage view Easy to understand	Focus on SBU or products Allows variety of planning approaches Can be quantified Allows prediction
Planning weaknesses	Historical only No predictive capability Not quantifiable	Circle sizes may not reflect true benefits Likely to distort true picture as visuals are simplistic Quadrant position dependent on management decision, not objective data
Control strengths	Can suggest possibility of need for action Provides a useful visual shorthand	Relative markets share shown Accurately reflects position Can be current or future based Encourage forward planning
Control weaknesses	Totally useless Imprecise and inaccurate Not quantifiable	Little value in stable markets, but has been developed into models which are useful

Figure 6.6 Strengths and weaknesses of the PLC and BCG

Question 6.5

As a marketing manager using the BCG matrix, what information would you expect it to provide you with, and how might you use it?

New product development

Product development is one of the possible outcomes of the marketing strategy development process, determined by the outcomes of the marketing audit and the use of the BCG and the Ansoff matrix.

It is a known fact that new products and new ideas are far more appealing to some customers than others.

New product development is a highly expensive process that requires massive amounts of time and investment and therefore a clear understanding of the rationale for production development is needed. Therefore a number of critical questions should be answered.

- Has a customer need been identified?
- Has the analysis from the BCG shown that the potential market is large enough to generate sufficient revenue, return on investment and profitability.
- What is the level of resource required – does the company have the R&D expertise, technological ability and innovation required for new product development in the 21st century?

The basis of the answers to these questions will come from producing a formal method for assessing new product ideas – the 'new product development process' – where the feasibility and viability of future development is likely to take place.

Number of new product ideas

- Idea generation
- Screening new ideas
- Business analysis
- Product development
- Test marketing

Figure 6.7 The new product development process (Withey, Lancaster and Ashford, 2001)

The new product development process

Idea generation

The formal process begins with the generation of new ideas. These can come from a variety of sources. A company's own R&D department will be working on new ideas all the time. Innovations can also come from the customer service department, where staff and customers can be encouraged to come forward with ideas. The sales and production departments are another important source. All ideas are listed and submitted to the new product team, where they will be considered. Effectively, a number of people can be involved in this process, both internally and externally to the organization.

Screening new ideas

Once the ideas have been assessed for their initial viability, it is necessary to devise a method of screening these so as to reduce them to a manageable number that are considered to have real prospects. A series of potential key success factors, which research has shown are desirable to the consumer and to the company, will have been identified. In the 21st century, with the continuing rapid growth of information communication technology, and substantial databases, it is possible to closely match the characteristics of your products to consumer needs.

By clearly identifying the characteristics of your customers, it is possible to identify relevant market segments and niches to which marketing activities can be targeted.

Having identified the different segments, it is likely that they will have different needs. As a marketer, you need to establish the difference or differential between your products and services and those provided by your competitors.

The new ideas can then be compared so as to establish a short list of those that fit most closely to these criteria. Some of the factors that will come under consideration are raw material availability, production, distribution and the effect on sales of other products. Robust research programmes should inform the product design and development process. The characteristics identified against the potential benefits on offer should provide a basis of designing the perfect product solution.

Product development

At this stage in the process it is likely that the first prototype will be developed in order that the product is taken from conception to reality. The costs involved in this particular element are phenomenal. One of the key issues of product development will be to ensure that the investment in product design will create a new, innovative product that will achieve sustainable competitive advantage in the future. Therefore good sound design principles will provide the basis for competitive advantage in the marketplace.

From a technical perspective, it is likely that the key activities will relate to fine tuning both from a performance point of view, but also in relation to ensuring that customer expectations will be delivered.

The product will have been technically designed and specifications drawn up in preparation for the manufacturer in advance of any full-scale production. However, the decision to launch is a critical factor and will require high levels of business and analytical skills, in order that full-scale production can be implemented.

Concept testing

The next stage, known as concept testing, is to determine whether the new product is likely to appeal to customers. A sample is often made up with varying forms of packaging and often company employees are asked for their opinions. Focus groups are frequently recruited at this stage. The beauty of concept testing is that it makes it possible to gauge consumers' reactions before the company has incurred heavy costs in production runs.

Packaging is also part of the concept testing and with revolutionary technology a range of packaging options can be designed and form part of a virtual concept test. This is an evolving process.

Packaging, like the product, will provide a basis for differentiation and competitive advantage, therefore it is equally important to concept-test the packaging in line with the product.

Business analysis

At this stage, the company has to consider the financial viability of the new idea. Research and forecasting techniques are used to determine the likely level of demand. A cost analysis will examine not only direct production costs but also capital investment and marketing costs and even new personnel. Profitability can then be established in terms of 'breakeven' and rate of return analysis.

Test marketing

The purpose of test marketing is to gain consumers' reactions in an area that has been selected for the test. These are often television areas, such as Tyne Tees, which are considered to be representative of the total market. The test allows the company to evaluate sales and distribution prior to a full-blown launch. Any problems or flaws in the product or its promotion can be identified and made good before the continued rollout.

Launch

Assuming the test-market operation has proved successful, then the product can be launched nationally. Production capacity will have to be increased to cope with the anticipated demand. The promotional campaign can be extended to national media and further distribution channels enlisted. Having an existing distribution network will improve the chances of success.

Case history

EarthShell debuts biodegradable hot beverage cups

EarthShell Corporation, USA, innovator of disposable food service packaging, designed with the environment in mind, plans to begin in-service test of hot beverage cups as part of the company's intention to enter the growing hot-cup market.

Designed for use with hot beverages such as coffee, tea and speciality hot drinks, the test for the cups is scheduled to begin with a US restaurant chain during the next 60 days. In the USA alone the hot-cup market is valued at just over $1billion annually.

The new EarthShell cups are designed to meet or exceed the performance of other disposable hot-cup products currently available while offering the unique environmental attributes associate with other EarthShell products.

EarthShell's initial product development focused on plates, bowls, hinged containers, the recently-announced new sandwich wraps and now, cups for hot beverages. Following product testing being announced during May 2001, the company will provide more details regarding product availability and other significant characteristics of its first entry into the cup market.

In keeping with the company's mission, hot cups from EarthShell are designed to have unique environmental advantages when compared to traditional hot cups made from polystyrene foam and paper.

EarthShell Packaging, made from a composite material consisting primarily of natural limestone and renewable starch, is environmentally preferable from start to finish. When compared to traditional packaging, it uses less total energy and results in low greenhouse gas emissions.

> EarthShell Packaging is strong and provides good insulation, biodegrades when exposed to moisture in nature and is recyclable through composting.
>
> EarthShell packaging is designed to be cost and performance competitive, compared to other foodservice packaging materials, and also to provide environmental advantages.
>
> www.EarthShell.com
>
> Source: Lexis-Nexis.

The product adoption process

In Unit 4, 'Theories of communication', we looked at the theory relating to the adoption process, examining the communication problems that might exist in encouraging customers to adopt or indeed switch their brand and product.

However, while many promotional activities and communication processes may draw attention to the product and in fact provide an incentive to buy, in the long term if the product is not acceptable in terms of customer needs and expectation then the process of adoption will fail.

For a new product to be successful, it must first be bought or adopted by individual customers, households and organizations. Diffusion occurs only once acceptance of the product spreads in the marketplace. The diffusion process follows a similar shape to the product life cycle curve. Despite all this effort, it is reckoned that only 10 per cent of new products are successful.

The key to successful diffusion of innovators will be to target them precisely for their characteristics as innovators. From there it is likely that you will continue to target each of the groups, until ultimately you have targeted them all. Each group will require a different approach, a different communication, as they have different lifestyles, different habits, differing attitudes and be subject to entirely different influences.

Everett Rogers identified several different categories of people, based on the ease with which they adopted new products.

Innovators

These are people who will buy simply because the product is new. This is not a good indicator of a product's future potential.

Early adopters

This group are those who are willing to try new products before they have achieved widespread acceptance. They are often regarded as opinion leaders in their own circle. Acceptance by this group is essential for any new product.

Early majority

The early majority are a cautious group and will only adopt the new product once it becomes socially acceptable. Acceptance by this group will determine whether the product will gain widespread acceptance and succeed as a mass-market product.

Late majority

This group are even more risk-averse than the early majority. They will only consider adopting the product after they are sure that they are going to like it. At this stage, the product is well established.

Laggards

The laggards are those who resist the new product and may never adopt it. They are generally timid and cautious by nature.

The categories of adopters will vary according to the product. For instance, innovators are not always the same people in each market. Some people may be early adopters in the telecommunications market but laggards in new organic food. Having knowledge of adopters is very important and careful targeting of this group with launch promotional material such as direct mail will help the launch to be a greater success.

Summary

The product is the very core of what the organization is about; the product is the purpose. The product on its own is worthless, but carefully managed, branded and packaged, the benefits it provides and the satisfaction it will achieve are the key factors to its overall success.

The main aim of any organization should be to create products that customers need, want and expect, always ensuring quality, innovation, customer delight and value is at the core of their strategy development and business activity.

It is of primary importance that the organizations create a differential between themselves and their competitors, through the successful planning implementation of a brand and product strategy, that places them in a uniquely differentiated and competitive position.

However, the critical success factor in establishing product and brand success is ensuring that an integrated approach is taken toward the utilization of the marketing mix. This will be a marketing imperative.

Marketers, are becoming increasingly aware of the speed of change, resulting in shorter life cycles, faster levels of innovation, rapid speed of products to market, accelerated diffusion and excessive competition.

With the added impetus of global marketing and new technologies, product development, product innovation and robust product planning are providing the most significant challenge of the 21st century – where do we go from here?

Further study and examination preparation

> **Study tip**
>
> Product-based questions are highly likely within every exam. Questions will be framed on the basis of being part of the overall marketing mix, or on an individual basis. You will be expected to take an integrated approach to the managing of the marketing mix, and while being able to understand key marketing elements in isolation, it is essential to look at them as integrated also.
>
> You will be expected to have some understanding of branding applications, product development, product portfolio matrix models and of course the planning life cycle. The questions will put you in the position of a marketing manager, product manager, or even brand manager, therefore you will need to look at these subjects in an applied way.
>
> In the June 2000 paper alone, there are four questions that have some bearing on this particular unit, emphasizing its significance.

Extending knowledge

Recommended reading

As with all other units, the purpose of this text is to consolidate your more extensive learning, providing you with an overview of the key elements. Therefore additional reading is recommended in order that you supplement your learning significantly.

Chapters 8, 9 and 10 of Dibb, Simkin, Pride and Ferrell, *Marketing Concepts and Strategies*, 4th European edn.

Chapters 1, 2, 4 and 6 of Leslie de Chernatony, *Brand Vision to Brand Evaluation* provides you with an overview of the necessary level of branding knowledge and understanding at this time.

Question 6.6

June 2000, Question 4b

Go to www.marketingonline.co.uk or www.bh.com/marketing to access Specimen Answers and Senior Examiner's advice for this exam question.

Question 6.7

June 2000, Question 3b

Go to www.marketingonline.co.uk or www.bh.com/marketing to access Specimen Answers and Senior Examiner's advice for this exam question.

June 2001, Question 4

Go to www.marketingonline.co.uk or www.bh.com/marketing to access Specimen Answers and Senior Examiner's advice for this exam question.

Unit 7
Price operations

Objectives

In this unit you will be focusing on the importance of pricing operations, and the implications and impact of pricing upon other activities within the marketing mix.

The learning outcomes associated with price are in line with the other units relating directly to the marketing mix and include:

- Understanding the need to integrate marketing mix tools to achieve effective implementation of plans
- Selecting an appropriate integrated marketing mix.

The indicative content of the syllabus underpinning those learning outcomes in the context of price is:

- The importance of price and its determinants
- Pricing models for decisions based on cost competition and demand
- Pricing objectives and method
- Adapting the price for the marketing mix.

  (Syllabus reference 1.2.2)

Introduction

The focus of this unit on pricing operations is to allow you to consider the role of pricing within the marketing mix, the importance of price and its overall influence, and the considerations when setting pricing objectives. Furthermore, it is essential that you consider how flexibility in the role of pricing must be delivered in order to develop a marketing mix designed for sustained competitive advantage.

One of the key differences about price is that it is the only element as such that generates income rather than having a cost base to it. It is the determinant that focuses on maximizing revenue in order to meet profitability objectives and goals determined by the organization. Price is not just about generating revenue for the organization, it is about creating a better environment and a more effective long-term relationship with the customer. It is about placing a value on something, be it a product or service.

Value has to be perceived by the customer in order that the required revenue is generated. Customers do not just want products to be cheap or reasonably priced, they expect a certain level of value for money. That means that the product needs to be a certain level of quality, demonstrating that value in a clear and transparent way.

When a marketer becomes involved in pricing it is necessary that price does reflect the product offering, i.e. the quality, the benefits and the functionality. Furthermore, the pricing strategy being implemented must match the expectations of the customer. Setting a high price is only acceptable if offering high value.

While price is seen to be possibly the most flexible element of the marketing mix, it is possibly the most difficult to manage and it has to reflect the state of the market on a continuous basis. Due to the intensively competitive nature of the marketplace today, price is the most changeable element of the mix. It has to respond to economic changes, competitive activity, customer demand and cost of materials, costs of distribution and a number of other key market drivers.

The role of the marketing manager in relation to pricing is sometimes rather ambiguous in many organizations and the waters become muddied between the accounting/financial arm of the organization in trying to maximize profitability. Sadly, in a less market-oriented organization, price setting will often be undertaken in a vacuum without considering the influences and implications of pricing and without realizing that considering price alone is not enough.

In many instances setting prices is a thankless task. As the customer, if it is too cheap, we think it is too good to be true and ask the question 'What's wrong with it?' If it is too high, customers may not want to buy it. If organizations do not get the price right the rest of the marketing mix could potentially be wasted; therefore the mix depends on the right product at the right price!

It doesn't matter who the organization is, or what they do, what matters is to understand that price does not stand alone, it interacts with the whole organization and the other 6Ps. Price is very visible; therefore it has to present 'value' to the customer.

Price perception and the customer

In the introduction, it was stated that price is the value placed upon either a product or service. As a marketer, developing a marketing mix that is appropriate to customer needs and understanding the implications of it, will be critical.

Having developed and communicated the nature of the marketing strategy, the organization is effectively signalling a whole range of information, perceptions and values about the product, its characteristics, benefits and performance. Ultimately, putting a price on a product raises expectations. It is then up to the customer to decide if it meets their needs or matches their perception.

Understanding the implications of price means understanding customer behaviour, motivations, culture, attitudes, values and perception. Of course, market segmentation does offer some answers to these questions, but it does, needless to say, leave price as the hot potato of the marketing mix.

Price is often perceived as being constant, but unfortunately it will change, both in reality and in the minds of buyers depending upon how their circumstances change. Constancy is one thing that price does not necessarily present. With supply and demand indicators changing, as demands of raw materials and components vary, competitive intensity and product rarity, price can change drastically.

Perspective of price and the organization

Price is the only element of the marketing mix that generates revenue for the organization. Everything else about the organization relates to a cost. Therefore pricing is the opportunity to gain some return on investment (ROI) or return on capital employed, meeting profit objectives and looking at growth opportunities from profits year on year.

It is, however, essential that the organization always considers the price from the perspective of the customer and then relates it to demand. The price that is charged is very much based upon the supply and demand factor of the market, the supply being the availability of the product and the demand based around how many people in the market actually want it. This is often a good starting point for the organization in establishing its potential pricing strategy.

Pricing in relation to demand

You should now be aware of the link between product quality and price and how price can be sensitive to the perception of the customer and how they see value for money. However, pricing is more complex than this. Pricing has to reflect a number of influences, demands and key drivers, and therefore pricing is subject to the following:

- The subjective beliefs of customers with regards to different pricing

- Competitors
- Quality.

It is necessary to predict the impact of price changes on consumers, distribution and on your competitors. Prices need to mirror the degree of demand for a product in a given market.

Different pricing strategies are relevant at different stages of the product life cycle in line with the relative costs involved. Generally speaking, price decreases in time in line with the decrease in costs involved.

This concept is known as price elasticity. This is a term used to explain that, generally speaking, demand will decrease as prices increase and that supply will increase as prices go up. Elasticity in demand is the term used to explain that price changes in line with the volume sold.

Influences on price

One key activity of the marketer through both marketing research and the audit process, is to understand the key influences upon pricing.

Pricing is a complex area to manage, with just taking on board the internal considerations such as the running costs of the organization, development costs, overhead costs, the organization's objectives and its corporate mission. To add to the internal complexities, there are a significant number of external considerations an organization must be aware of.

Organizations have to be very responsive to the state of the market environment, and responsive to the range of factors already discussed, such as competition and demand.

While an organization has to be responsive, it also needs to manage the uncertainty. The 21st century seems to have given the market higher levels of uncertainty than previously experienced. To this end organizations need to endeavour to understand a range of factors relating to the external environment. Figure 7.1 highlights the factors affecting the pricing decisions of the organization.

Figure 7.1 Influences on price

> **Question 7.1**
>
> On what basis do external market forces influence the price charged for a hotel room?

One of the most prominent headlines from autumn 2000, and an issue still going strong has been the significantly high fuel prices and vehicle taxation in the UK and indeed some parts of Europe. Consumers, it would appear, have been subject to ever-increasing fuel prices and are continually threatened with the £4 gallon of petrol and the 90p litre. However, during 2001, this threat eased considerably and the price of petrol has reduced significantly.

However, there is still much concern in relation to fuel prices and consumers are continually angered by the threat of high fuel prices, particularly as some of the big oil producers such as Shell, BP and ESSO have been announcing considerable annual profits. However, while profits are being made on a global scale through other business opportunities, the influence of supply and demand factors in the oil production markets, is eroding profits made in the UK. This coupled with the high levels of taxation invoked by government finds the UK oil market subject to high costs and high demands, a balance that appears very difficult to manage.

Recently, legislation in respect of transportation has also had a significant impact upon costs, not least because of the vehicle emissions ruling. The higher the emissions, the higher the tax burden. The higher the tax burden the higher the cost of distribution is to the consumer. In many instances, the cost of distribution is over 50 per cent of the total cost of the product. In the UK and much of Europe, the customer has been subjected to a number of disputes as they try to gain the upper hand in achieving price reduction.

In the UK there has been much discussion about new types of transportation taxes, such as tolls on UK motorways during peak travel times.

The issue of high priced fuel is continually pertinent to many organizations, external influences, customer dissatisfaction, government intervention, and varying world trade organizations.

Marketers should continually be alert to the power of the various driving forces in the marketplace and how they can ultimately command through asserting their power, changes in pricing structures and overall prices charged.

The process of globalization is also having an affect on price, and later in the text we will look at the implications of price from an international and global perspective.

Correlating price with value

Having looked at a number of influential factors in relation to pricing, it is clear that perceived value has a major impact upon the customer's decision to adopt.

Some of the typical factors that affect perceived value are:

- Life cycle of the product
- Product benefits and functionality
- Quality
- Prestige and status of the brand
- Ease of use
- Value added measures
- Differentiation
- Packaging

- Service and technical support
- Competitive alternatives (substitutes).

While these are just some of the factors affecting value, clearly it is a prominent issue. Principally the customer will be paying a price in exchange for 'perceived value and benefits' and therefore the price has to be representative of the overall deal. Essentially these factors start to form the basis of strategic price determinants.

There is a basic rule in pricing, which means that you price your product or service at the level that your customers expect to pay for the quality you are delivering. This does not just mean that high quality justifies high price, nor does it mean that high price means high quality. What it does mean, however, its that the organization has to effectively justify the price that they charge.

> **Question 7.2**
>
> The value proposition, i.e. perceived value, is of vital importance when determining a price. How might you use other tools within the marketing mix, such as product and promotion, to justify the value proposition?

Strategic pricing determinants

Before setting pricing objectives, it is important to consider the determining factor of pricing, i.e. the key influences in relation to ascertaining the correct pricing positioning and pricing objectives for the organization.

Demand as a determinant

As a marketing manager, you will most likely be responsible for collecting various data that through analysis will identify the forecast levels of demand for products within the marketplace.

Demand relates to customers actually wanting to purchase or even needing to purchase particular goods or services. The likely scenario is that the higher the demand for the product, the lower the price and the lower the demand for the product, the higher the price.

The basis of this scenario is that the higher the demand, the more likely the organization are to invoke economies of scale, and from there they pass on their cost savings to the customer, thus lowering the price.

The lower the demand, the less likely it is that economies of scale will be achieved, therefore likely costs of raw materials and related products will be higher, therefore the cost of the product will be higher.

Forecasting demand can be quite a difficult process, but once potential demand has been established, the price can be set accordingly. Forecasting demand will provide an insight into potential for growth; high levels of growth would potentially mean high levels of demand.

While demand is important, issues relating to elasticity in demand, need to be answered. As a marketer it will be part of your role to undertake a range of exercises relating to ascertaining the level of demand and how fluctuations in price might increase or decrease the demand.

The likely findings of this exercise will probably highlight that marginal increases in price are unlikely to affect demand and therefore if they do not affect demand, demand is inelastic. However, if a significant increase in price is implemented, demand could potentially drop dramatically, therefore highlighting elasticity in demand and probably a fickle market.

As an example, if your organization reduced prices by 25 per cent, but as a result only saw a 5 per cent increase in sales, demand is deemed inelastic. On the other hand, should the 25 per cent price reduction invoke a 50 per cent increase in sales, then price would be elastic. This highlights a degree of market sensitivity at a certain level in respect of price (see Figure 7.2).

Figure 7.2 Price inelasticity

Figure 7.3 Price elasticity

Price sensitive markets as a determinant

One of the most frequently asked questions in marketing today is 'Is the market price sensitive?' or 'How price sensitive is the market?' The volatility of the marketing environment currently dictates that organizations should maintain an awareness of the price sensitivity issues within the market.

In order to be able to balance price sensitive issues and address them fully, it is essential that the organization defines some key indicators that will ultimately signal to them the level of sensitivity that exists.

Some of the key indicators to observe are:

- Frequency of purchase
- Necessity of purchase
- How much is the product needed
- How much does it cost
- What are the competitor alternatives within the market
- What else can the customer's money be spent on
- The effect of quality on price
- Stock/inventory.

Drawing anything conclusive from an analysis of the above points may prove to be rather difficult and will be the result of some quite complex analysis. However, the flexibility that surrounds pricing strategies will ultimately provide a basis for a well-balanced pricing strategy that will possibly provide perceived value, a robust competitive response and the level of profitability required.

A word of caution however: while price sensitivity is an issue, customers do not always make their purchasing decision based upon price, and on occasions it will be quite the contrary.

Understanding levels of price sensitivity in association with demand will help the organization ascertain the most appropriate pricing strategy in order to retain some form of consistency in demand, to avoid significant fluctuations.

Competitors as a determinant

On a number of occasions, the significance of the levels of intense competition has been mentioned. Competitive response profiles for each competitor are essential in managing price competition.

It has already been established that competitor activity also plays a leading role in the price of products for the customer. In the 21st century, price wars are commonplace. Price cutting is used to increase demand, improve market share and beat off the competition. Supermarket wars are a prime example of this. Cost cutting, special offers and reward cards are all part of the war to gain market share. However, Nigel Piercy (1997) suggests in his book *Market Led Strategic Change* that price wars are both dangerous and contagious.

Customers are responsive to pricing cutting, as long as the perception of brand and product value remains unchanged. However, all organizations are forced to consider feasibility and viability of their marketing activities and corporate goals. Should the competition continue to intensify and profit margins continue to narrow, the infrastructure of the organization may have to change radically to remain competitive.

The pressure on organizations to be involved in competitor price is significant. Some of the key influences on price wars are:

- Customers no longer equate low price with low quality
- Saturation of some markets

- Price is a good tool to attack competitor weaknesses
- Undercutting the competition is the only way to compete successfully and make an impact
- The perception of reduced price and increased value is attractive to customers
- Part of the retail sector culture is to implement ongoing sales promotions.

Price wars create a vicious circle. For example, over the past two years or so there have been significant supermarket wars. As ASDA (Wal-Mart) have reduced their prices on the 'roll-back system', Sainsbury and Tesco have followed suit with alternative promotions and have come up with appropriate strategies to detract from the cost cutting in the competitor organization. The mobile communications and personal computer market is another very visible example of this type of behaviour.

In order to manage the demands of competitive intensity and its impact upon price, there are a number of options open to organizations to pursue, they include:

- Matching the price of the competitor
- Reducing the price below that of the competitor
- Implementation of further price changes. This may include additional reductions in a further product lines
- Introduce new promotional incentives – 2 for the price of 1, get 25 per cent free, free delivery, etc. However, you must be aware that promotional incentives are often only a quick fix to what is a long-term problem.

Price affects market share; therefore organizations must take action to avoid losing volume of market share. This then comes back again to elasticity in demand and price sensitivity issues. Issues relating to market share will of course be detected through the use of portfolio planning tools.

Case history

Pharmacies price war

The Restrictive Practices Court has ruled in favour of lifting price controls on over-the-counter drugs. In response, the UK's leading supermarkets quickly moved to slash prices on a range of branded medicines like headache tablets, vitamins and flu remedies by up to 50 per cent. The ruling will have a knock-on effect on independent pharmacies and it is widely believed that many will go out of business.

Even some of the larger operations say they will pinch. Shares in Boots fell 6 per cent on the news and the company said the decision would knock of £15 million of profits within a year.

Because many of the independents rely on the margin gained from over-the-counter drugs, it was estimated around 15 per cent will go out of business because of the decision.

Source: Lexis-Nexis

Question 7.3

What appears to be the overall impact of competitive pricing in the 21st century?

Product positioning and product life cycle as a determinant

Pricing will affect demand in many situations, and therefore issues in relation to product perception, product position and the stage in the product life cycle will be of the essence when designing appropriate pricing strategies. If you refer back to Unit 6 on 'Product operations', issues relating to price and profitability in the product life cycle are addressed.

Debtors and creditors as a determinant

Issues relating to liquidity, credibility, payment terms and cash flow will all influence the basis of pricing strategies. Pricing strategies will reflect largely the financial management of the company and will need to link closely to their key performance indicators.

The break-even analysis

The point at which an organization will become profitable will be one of the single most important components of the decision-making process. Feasibility, viability, return on capital employed, will all be linked to ascertaining the break-even point. Break-even charts can be extremely useful in evaluating proposals for new products or projects designed to improve profitability. They are based on the marginal approach and, being visual, produce an impact which figures alone rarely achieve.

This can be illustrated in a simple graph – see Figure 7.4.

Figure 7.4 Break-even analysis

Break-even analysis involves looking at the break-even point of different price levels.

The break-even costs can be calculated simply as follows:

Break-even point = Fixed costs/(Price per unit − variable costs per unit)

Fixed costs are those costs that are constant, for example, property rental, permanent fixed salaries, car fleets etc.

Variable costs are those costs that change based upon the amount of products manufactured, the cost of raw materials, temporary labour.

Add the two together and you get the total cost of production.

This is the starting point for actually setting the price for many organizations. They would then go on to consider how their price should sit within the marketplace, taking into consideration the factors we have already discussed, i.e. the key influences on price both internally and externally.

To obtain an accurate price, it is essential that the organization establish an accurate cost.

As part of your studies within Management Information for Marketing Decisions, you will undertake the physical working out of break-even analysis.

While break-even analysis is an essential component of determining price and future approaches to pricing strategies, you should be aware that in essence, break-even will be a strategic decision. You as the marketer will be responsible for implementing the break-even objectives. However, it is essential that you understand the basic principles of using such models, in order that you clearly understand the basis of how the organization establishes pricing objectives.

Marginal costing and pricing

It is given in pricing that sales revenue must at least cover the overhead costs before profit can be achieved. Therefore revenue should cover production, distribution and marketing costs and most likely make a contribution to the overall fixed costs of the organization.

Should a price be determined to recover the variable costs only, then the recovery is at the margin.

As a marketer you will need to establish what the marginal cost is of producing one or more additional units, in order that you ascertain the most cost-effective number of units to manufacture to achieve profit.

Pricing objectives and strategies

Primarily, pricing objectives are set by companies in order to maximize sales revenue over and above costs in order to achieve profit.

Pricing objectives therefore reflect the basis of achieving profitability:

- *To achieve return on investment* – to ensure sufficient sales revenue to cover all associated cost bases and to pay back initial investment costs.
- *To maximize profits* – companies who struggle to compete and have low market share may need to charge high prices to maximize profits.
- *To maximize sales revenue* – this will relate to setting prices at a level that will maximize sales turnover – more formally known as penetration pricing.
- *To achieve product quality leadership* – the basis of this objective will relate to providing the best quality product in the market in order to differentiate itself against its competitors, but will charge more than the competitors.
- *Market skimming* – is where a company sets a high price to capture those customers who are willing to pay more for a product. Essentially this is more crudely defined as skimming the cream off, or targeting the top tier of the market. These people are likely to be the innovators, first in line in the adoption and diffusion process.
- *Survival* – is as it sounds, generally setting objectives that ensure survival in a highly competitive market. Therefore the aim is to generate enough income to cover all costs, potentially working on a break-even basis in order to stay in business.

One of the greatest challenges of pricing and the marketing mix is to define pricing objectives that allow for the achievement of gaining market share, achieving profitability, providing technical leadership, innovation and quality leadership. Balancing this ship can be very tricky.

As with all other components of the marketing mix, pricing objectives must be clearly defined in line with meeting the overall marketing objectives and corporate goals. The role of pricing will be to integrate fully and support all the other elements of the marketing mix.

> **Question 7.4**
>
> Explain why it is vitally important that pricing objectives reflect the marketing objectives and marketing strategy.

Strategic pricing

Two of the pricing objectives are highly strategic and will closely reflect the basis of the marketing objectives. It is therefore essential to understand the key characteristics of price skimming and market penetration.

When a new product enters into the market, it is likely that either one of these strategies will be adopted in order to aid market entry but, at the same time, gain early return on investment.

Price skimming has the following features:
- There is a relatively high price per unit
- It is a good strategy to apply to new products and services with little price sensitivity (the development stage of the product life cycle)
- The price can be dropped when a market comes into existence
- The market can be segmented easily
- Profit is made on a per unit basis.

Price penetration has the following features:
- It offers a low price per unit
- Price penetration is used when a large volume of the market share is involved
- Profit is made through volume sales
- Price penetration applies to 'me too' type product (copies of other market leading brands)
- Low price is aided by high promotions.

The two strategies above are key to ensuring supply and demand at a strategic level. But there is a tactical level of pricing that also needs to be considered.

Tactical pricing strategies

Whatever pricing objectives the organization adopts, it will be important to define the appropriate strategy in order that they are achieved.

The development of appropriate pricing strategies will not only focus on the methods of costing, but also on the integration of pricing within the marketing mix. It will take into consideration external and internal influences as they have been described earlier in the unit.

Tactical pricing provides the basis for the implementation of the marketing plan and its price-based objectives.

There are three options to consider here:
- Marginal pricing
- Quantity discounts
- Differential pricing

- Cost-plus pricing
- Demand-based pricing.

Marginal pricing

This involves:

- Offering a special price
- For a limited time period only
- Profit is still made.

For an example the introduction of a new consumer product to the market, e.g. a new drink at a special price for an introductory period of time that is limited. The customer might be motivated to trial the product at the cheaper price and may at least temporarily move from the brand they use currently. In saying this, there is research to prove that more often than not the majority of customers return to their own existing brand preference once the promotion has ended.

Quantity discounting

This involves:

- The principle that manufacturer prices are at their cheapest when large quantities are produced (economies of scale)
- Money is received quickly
- Removing chances for the competition (in encouraging bulk purchase)
- Adding benefits for the customer.

A good example of this would be the purchase of print cartridges from the stationers. If a high usage or minimum purchase for a set period can be guaranteed then the customer may consider bulk purchase to obtain additional discounts. As the stationer does not have to store the materials for as long, it makes storage easier to manage for them and potentially cheaper.

Differential pricing

This involves:

- High fixed costs
- The relevant application of seasons and timings
- Benefit to both the producer and the consumer.

Differential pricing strategies set different prices for different markets, a point picked up earlier in this unit, and also within 'Product operations'.

The leisure industry is an example here. During the week many hotels charge very high corporate rates, e.g. £150.00 per night, room only. At the weekend many of the same hotels have weekend special offers of £150.00 per weekend, per person, for dinner, bed and breakfast. Therefore differential rates are charged for corporate booking than for leisure booking. This strategy underpins the continuous use of hotel rooms throughout the season, but uses different pricing strategies for different target markets.

Other factors involved are:

- Geodemographics (i.e. geography and demographics) – where perhaps because of remoteness of a town, the cost of distribution is higher, as already illustrated in this section
- The same products or services being sold in the same position at different prices geographically.

A good example is possibly the price of eating out. Within the UK there is a considerable price differential based upon geographical location. A further example related to earlier discussion is the price of petrol, which is considerably higher in more remote locations than in the main towns and cities.

Cost-plus pricing

This involves:

- Covering the overhead costs, plus a percentage on top, to meet marketing/profit objectives
- Usually used for projects that are more difficult to cost out, or actually take a long time for completion
- Cost-plus pricing is a useful pricing tool while markets are volatile, because you can always change the percentage on top of costs, and adjust it to meet market demands.

Cost plus pricing is a simplistic approach which determines the cost of manufacture, plus a specified percentage above the price in line with the organization's requirements, which will ultimately achieve the selling price.

Eight stages to establishing a price

To summarize the key principles of pricing and to put your learning into a more practical context, Dibb, Simkin, Pride and Ferrell (2001) suggest that there are eight key stages to determining or establishing a chargeable price (see Figure 7.5).

Figure 7.5 Stages for establishing price, adapted from Dibb, Simkin, Pride and Ferrell 2001

The route to setting higher prices

As a marketer you will always be challenged to identify a potential route for charging higher prices, as it is unlikely that profit goals will allow for the sustainable continuance of low prices. Some of the points to consider in doing this are as follows:

- The strength of the customer relationship built by the salesforce – how does this impact upon the ability of the organization to negotiate higher prices?
- Is the perceived value, i.e. the value proposition, enough to give the organization competitive advantage?
- Does the marketing segmentation strategy highlight where some target groups are more or less price-sensitive than others?
- How might the branding strategy allow for several price positions to be upheld in the market?
- Are there any opportunities for skimming the market – price skimming?

Summary

The price element of the marketing mix leaves marketers aiming to balance all of the eggs in the basket, to achieve the ultimate blend of price, quality and perceived value. A balanced marketing mix will ensure the customer is getting the right product in the right place, at the right time, for the right price.

Customers are very fickle today and clearly understand that they have significant choice, and indeed power, in the marketplace and that they have significant influence upon supply and demand.

Prices will vary according to what people are prepared to pay in different situations. Different prices might also reflect what customers can pay or are prepared to pay. However, from a management perspective, you are challenged to consider whether price is simply what the customer will pay, or a more flexible marketing tool than just that.

In order to understand the influence of price on the customers and competitors, a marketer must understand the need for significant ongoing research into the state of the external environment and the activities of competitors and gain a key understanding of buyer behaviour and expectations.

The critical success factors in relation to price are to maintain the organizational objectives, yet endeavour to remain sensitive to the needs of the customers, ensuring that you can address their long-term needs, including the further development of new and innovative additions to the product range and lines. The key to price is to link the product quality with clear indication of value for money from the organization to the customer.

Pitching the price at the right level may be the difference between profit and loss or survival and failure, as pricing will reflect the long-term profitability and market share. Therefore, in order to achieve a marketing oriented approach to pricing, the organization should take into account a broad range of factors:

- Marketing strategy
- Value proposition
- Price-quality relationships
- Competitive pricing
- Costs
- Ability to negotiate higher prices
- External market forces
- The effects of globalization
- Product line pricing.

Further study and examination preparation

> **Study tip**
>
> The basis of pricing in the context of marketing operations relates to understanding the concepts of pricing, the implications of pricing and possible approaches to implementation of pricing strategies in line with the corporate goals and marketing objective. The technicalities of pricing are covered in Management Information for Marketing Decisions, which is where you will learn the actual basis of calculation. Therefore from an exam perspective it is likely that you will discuss potential pricing strategies, discuss influences on price and some of the strategic determinants.

In the exam, pricing is invariably included as an integral part of the marketing mix, with some individual pricing questions appearing on some, but not all, papers.

Question spotting and question prediction is a dangerous game, therefore always be well prepared, ensuring that you have a full knowledge and understanding of the subject in preparation for providing good robust answers.

Extending knowledge

Recommended reading

Recommended reading for this unit again comes from Dibb, Simkin, Pride and Ferrell (2001), Chapters 18 and 19. This will provide you with a very broad perspective of pricing. You will find these chapters very useful again when you study for Management Information for Marketing Decisions, as they explain some of the basis of the calculations required.

Question 7.5

December 2000, Question 5

Go to www.marketingonline.co.uk or www.bh.com/marketing to access Specimen Answers and Senior Examiner's advice for this exam question.

Unit 8
Place operations

Objectives

Place operations highlights the importance of distribution as a key factor in achieving the ultimate marketing mix. It is the final component and relates to ensuring that customers are able to gain access to and purchase their chosen product.

This unit reflects the same principal learning outcomes as the other marketing mix units, in terms of understanding the need to integrate the marketing mix tools and achieve effective implementation of plans.

From a place perspective, the indicative content reflects the following:

- Distribution channels
- Consumer and business-to-business (business-to-business will appear later in the text)
- Criteria to select and evaluate alternative channels of distribution.

(Syllabus reference 1.2.4)

Introduction

It is a known fact that without distribution – 'place' – the best product or service will not be delivered and the marketing mix will break down and fail. It was once said that the 'place' was one of the most powerful elements of the marketing mix, as it is the one way that we can both reach and actually service the customer.

Distribution is seen as a component part of the product. Therefore, in order to achieve total satisfaction, customer service will play an essential part in the overall achievement of customer satisfaction, retention and a sustainable competitive advantage.

Distribution works on two key principles:

- It organizes the exchange process through distribution
- It organizes communication.

Place plays a pivotal role within the marketing mix, and the key to success will be its successful integration within it, ensuring that customers get their products at the right place and at the right time. This will involve a range of alternative marketing activities based around promotion, price and the actual product design and packaging.

Distribution plays an important role, primarily because it ultimately affects the sales turnover and profit margins of the organization. If the product cannot reach its chosen destination at the appropriate time, then it can erode competitive advantage and customer retention.

An additional factor now facing distribution is the power of the buyers. As buyers we are becoming increasingly impatient, not wishing to wait for our products for any period of time. Therefore, if distribution is a significant player in the decision-making process the consequences of an inadequate distribution strategy may be catastrophic. There is an expectation in relation to delivery, in the same way there is with product and price. The combined package provides an expectation in the mind of customers and it also influences their overall perception of the value proposition.

Distribution provides many extensive new business opportunities and is currently at the centre of a range of strategic alliances, mergers, acquisitions, joint ventures and licensing agreements. In addition to this, the emergence and explosion of the Internet and other information communication technologies has put distribution on track to be one of the most lucrative business propositions of recent years.

Distribution requires a high degree of management skill, synchronization and integration with the overall organization, as it will be one of the major components in achieving a sustainable competitive advantage. Controlling the flow of products between the manufacturer or producer is no easy task, and as pointed out above, failure to control the flow effectively could decide the level of success you might enjoy in the marketplace.

Influences on distribution

Distribution is subject to a key set of influences in the same way as the other elements of the marketing mix. It is subject to external driving forces, internal forces and of course the forever-increasing power of the customer. Influences on place operations will therefore include:

- Fuel prices
- Environmental legislation
- Taxation
- Transportation choices
- National/global transportation infrastructure
- Nature of product and product characteristics – perishability, etc.
- Packaging
- Product life cycle
- Changing lifestyles
- The emergence of information communication technology
- Customer expectations
- Level of complexity in customer buying behaviour
- Competitive strategies
- Production targets
- Demand
- Market size
- Contribution towards costs
- Marketing mix components
- Customer services
- Technical support.

The list is tremendous and some of the factors have significant influence on the cost of distribution. Already in many organizations distribution claims up to 50 per cent of the product costs, which is a considerable amount to absorb when designing appropriate competitive pricing strategies.

Logistics management plays a significant role in dealing with some of these influences and managing through them, in taking decisions such as appropriate order quantities, delivery methods, channel lengths, frequency of delivery, stock and inventory considerations, customer care and customer satisfaction. Each of these elements of logistics management will have a huge influence in achieving a balance between price and profitability.

> ### Question 8.1
> In what way do you think changing lifestyles have impacted on and influenced distribution strategies?

Marketing issues for distribution

Marketers need to be aware of the implications of distribution in respect of marketing. At the end of the day, distribution is about providing a service, a service of delivery to the customer, essentially getting the product from A to B. Therefore, there are some principal marketing issues that should be addressed.

The main marketing issue relates to channels. It is essential that you understand that the successful management of the supply chain will be achieved through selecting, motivating and controlling distributors and distribution outlets. However, if you reflect back on Porter's Five Forces, you will see the difficulty that faces any marketer in achieving that, as the power of the supplier can be quite significant.

The other key component of successful distribution is meeting customer expectations in respect of delivery and service promises the organization might make. Think back to the importance of the value proposition. How does it position your business in respect of meeting delivery promises throughout the length and breadth of the distribution channel? The implications of achieving this will be a logistical challenge.

In order to achieve this wish list, a closely designed integrated marketing mix will need to exist. It will be essential that the underpinning support required by the distribution channel be in place in order to adopt both push and pull strategies in the marketplace.

Distribution channels

The distribution channel consists of a group of individuals or organizations that assist in getting the product to the right place at the right time. They enable the manufactured products to flow from the manufacturer to the end-user in many different ways.

Because of the nature of the marketing environment and the growth in international trade in what is termed the 'global marketplace', distribution can often be very involved, with a number of varying groups playing a key role in moving the products around.

Those groups are known as marketing intermediaries; they are really the middlemen. Intermediaries play a key role in ensuring that the manufacturer's target market is a group of very satisfied customers. Their role is to make sure that the product is available just when the customer wants it and from the place in which they want to purchase it.

Within each distribution channel there are a number of different levels and different links, which will of course vary from channel to channel. However, as everything changes over time, the channels are predictably becoming shorter and shorter, with more and more people choosing to cut out the middleman in order to reduce costs and become more competitive.

The choice of channel is a strategic decision in the main and will have implications across the corporate organization in the way in which they do business. It most definitely impacts upon their quality programmes, corporate development processes and, very importantly, resources.

Channel members

Intermediaries play a very important role within the distribution channel and the supply chain. In the main there are organizations such as transportation companies, merchants, agents, wholesaler, warehouses, retail outlets, to name but a few. Let us look at a brief overview of the function of each of them.

Wholesalers

Wholesalers are the middlemen at the early end of the distribution channel. It is very rare that they will sell directly to the end-user. They will buy products from the manufacturer, store them within their warehouses and sell the products on to the trade. This means that the wholesaler takes financial responsibility for the products, in fact they take legal title and physical possession of them. Producers will likely support the marketing activity through various push and pull strategies in order to ensure market demand increases.

Retailers

As a result of the technology revolution, the retailer is now not just on the high street but on the superhighway, the Internet. This is having a significant impact upon distribution, as you will see later in this unit.

The role of retailers is essentially the final stopping point for the product prior to its sale. Their role is to manage the transaction in which the buyer resolves to make their purchase decision and then the actual purchase. They will often act as the broker of information, the link between the customer and the producer, and the source of the customer relationship management.

Retailers have a highly prominent position in the channel and therefore potentially have the most challenging role in actually securing the transaction.

They may require considerable technical support, customer services backup, stock ordering facilities, technological systems underpinning the sales process, information and merchandise.

Distributors/dealers

Distributors and dealers are groups of intermediaries who are associated with stocking products for manufacturers and selling them on, including after-sales service and credit facilities. For example, when you purchase a Hotpoint washing machine, you may buy it from one of the big retailer outlets such as Comet or Scottish Power; you may also buy an extended service warranty. The warranty does not come directly from Hotpoint or Scottish Power, but from a third-party distributor.

Dealers are slightly different in that quite often they will specialize in selling one particular brand; for example, car dealerships are often associated with the manufacturer and therefore they sometimes sell on to the end-user, and the channel is somewhat shorter.

Agents/brokers/facilitators

Agents and brokers, as a general rule, do not take physical possession of the goods, but act on behalf of the manufacturer to sell their goods. Their main purpose is to bring buyers and sellers together. This is particularly common within international trade, where organizations do not necessarily have a physical presence.

Franchisee

Franchising is quite a common form of making a product available in the marketplace. The Body Shop was well known at one stage for franchising activities, as are Kentucky Fried Chicken and McDonalds. Franchising means that the franchisee holds a contract to market and supply a product or service that has been very strictly designed and developed by the franchiser. The franchiser will most likely have strict terms and conditions on store design, store layout and contents sold within the retail outlet.

Licensee

This is very similar to franchisee. The licensee pays royalties on sales or supplies to the licensor. The licensor is more often than not the manufacturer of the product.

Merchandiser

Merchandising relates very closely to retailing. Merchandisers are responsible for store displays relating to different products. For example, most supermarkets now sell CDs in store. Many of the suppliers of the CDs employ merchandisers to go into the store to check supplies and set up promotional displays.

Why use intermediaries?

Due to the intensity of competition currently being experienced, many organizations are faced with cost reductions, resource reductions and often as a result, restructuring. So why, in the circumstances, should we continue to use intermediaries. What is the rationale that lies behind it?

Whilst distribution is highly expensive, naturally, there are a lot of add-on costs, such as those associated with marketing, administration, packaging, order processing and receiving and making payments. For an organization to undertake all of these activities will be quite costly.

Take the example of a producer with a network of links, a combination of retailers, wholesalers, agents and merchandisers. The network consists of 10 key buyers, who then distribute out to another 10 buyers; there are then 100 links in the network. The physical and logistical management involved might be horrendous. The costs will also be inextricably linked to the size of the network and the management exercise.

Therefore, the rationale behind the use of intermediaries in circumstances such as this is to invest in them and their activities in order that they take on the responsibility for marketing and administration within their network, further pushing the products out into the market. This may be a good value proposition to the suppliers, if the intermediaries are provided with some form of incentive such as heavy discounts or even profit related returns.

Of course, while the financial benefits are significant, there are other benefits also, and other ways of adding value in the range of the customer-supplier relationship. The basis of these benefits can be segmented into three different groups (Figure 8.1).

Figure 8.1 Valued-added services (Adapted from Brassington and Pettitt, 2000)

It is likely that in a large distribution network, channel members may have to perform a number of these value-added business functions in order to support their own organizational objectives. Should a manufacturer agree to supply an intermediary with their products, it may include securing a commitment from them to market their products appropriately to the target markets. Table 8.1 provides a more detailed basis of how the above value-added services might be undertaken.

Table 8.1 The role of the intermediary. Adapted from Dibb, Simkin, Pride and Ferrel (2001)

Category of Marketing Activities	Possible Activities Required
Marketing information	Analyse information such as sales data. Carrying out research studies
Marketing management	Establish objectives, plan activities and manage. Co-ordinate financing, risk taking. Evaluate channel activities
Facilitating exchange	Choose and stock products that match buyers' needs
Promotion	Set promotional objectives, co-ordinate advertising, personal selling, promotions etc.
Price	Establish pricing policies, terms and sales
Physical distribution	Manage transport, warehousing, materials handling, stock control and communication
Customer service	Provide channels for advice, technical support, after-sales service and warranties
Relationships	Facilitate communication, products, parts. Credit control etc. Maintain relationships between manufacturer and retail outlets, and customer/consumer

Question 8.2

Explain with examples how the use of intermediaries can prove cost-effective in an organization.

The distribution channel and the customer

There are many variations in respect of the distribution channel structure (see Figure 8.2), however, should intermediaries be deemed as appropriate in the business environment, the following channel structures would be available to you:

1. Passing of goods and services direct from the manufacturer to the consumer
2. Passing of goods and services via a retailer and then on to a consumer
3. From the manufacturer via a wholesaler and then directly on to the consumer
4. The passing of goods and services from manufacturer via a wholesaler, then on to a retailer and subsequently on to the consumer
5. Additionally, the manufacturer can distribute the products and services via an agent to a wholesaler and then follow the routes show in points 3 and 4.

Quite often the types of channels of distribution used by organizations will depend upon the structure of the market, the size of the market, the complexity of the market and the geographical dispersion of the market, among other factors.

Figure 8.2 A typical range of channels of distribution

Selecting the channels of distribution

For a manufacturer to select a channel, they must consider the most appropriate one to meet their customer needs. They must consider the following:

- What are the product characteristics and how do they affect methods of distribution?
- Who are their customers?
- Where are their customers?
- What are their customer requirements?
- How, when and where do they want to buy their products?
- What are their competitors doing by way of distribution?
- What is the cost of distribution?
- What are the legal and regulatory constraints of distribution?

These are important issues and require significant levels of analysis in order to gain an understanding of the situation. Clearly some of these questions will form the basis of the marketing audit. Ideally the marketing mix has a clear focus on achieving customer satisfaction and achieving the profit objectives of the organization.

As competition is so aggressive in the marketplace, organizations will always look for new and improved ways of distributing their products. At the same time, retail outlets seem to be concerning themselves with providing as much as possible for the customer to save them going elsewhere, and obviously with the ultimate aim of securing a significant market share and increased profitability.

Supermarkets have moved away from just supplying food-based products to include fashions, music, electrical goods, cosmetics, etc. All of this is focused on meeting all of the above distribution factors. With the recent take-over of ASDA by the American owned Wal-Mart, this kind of service provision is likely to grow and include an even broader range of products.

Intermediary selection criteria

There are two perspectives of intermediary selection, the strategic perspective and the operational perspective: strategic in relation to looking at the 'bigger picture' and 'operational' looking at the ability to implement the strategic marketing plan and distribution strategy.

Operational criteria

- Knowledge of local markets
- Appropriate premises and equipment
- Technological systems and processes
- Customer convenience
- Product knowledge and expertise
- Payment facilities
- Salesforce structure, size and effectiveness
- Efficient customer service infrastructure.

Strategic criteria

- Plans for growth and expansion
- Resource capacity and future development
- Quality assurance processes
- Management ability
- Innovative
- Willing partnership
- Levels of loyalty and co-operation.

The balance of power within the distribution channel

The balance of power within the distribution channel is an interesting concept to consider. As each party has its own set of objectives to pursue and its own agenda, fitting in with a partner organization can potentially cause conflict. Who then holds the balance of power? Is it the manufacturer because they have the products available for market? Or the intermediary, who may decide they do not want to sell on the product to retail outlets? Or is it the retailers themselves, who will decide on the most appropriate brand to sell to their customers?

Channel co-operation is critical and channel members need to be united in their destiny. They should share information, agree to be directed to the same target markets and together maximize efficiency.

Often a channel leader will be identified to enable a co-ordinated effort of all parties in the marketing channel. Without co-operation the member objectives or the channel's objectives will not be achieved.

To become a leader within the channel, the channel member must want to direct and influence the channel's overall performance. To do this the channel leader must have significant power and driving force in order to succeed. To gain power in the relationship, the organization will likely be a significant size, with major resources. They must be experts in their field, and have the respect of the other channel members. They must be able to punish or reward other channel members effectively to get what they want.

The channels will perform most effectively when they co-operate, co-ordinate and integrate their activities. Should they divert their gaze from the ultimate goal at any stage the channel will go into conflict and their effectiveness could be challenged and competitors could seize their opportunity to deflect customers to their products and markets.

Channel strategy

There are three types of market coverage:

- Intensive
- Selective
- Exclusive.

Intensive distribution means that as many available outlets as possible hold this product, e.g. chocolate, newspapers, bread, etc. Intensive distribution will mean convenience to the customer and increased customer satisfaction. The sale of groceries in petrol and service stations is an example of how intensive distribution has grown.

Key characteristics include:

- Maximum number of outlets covered to maximize availability
- Target outlets in as many geographical regions as possible
- Consumer convenience products
- High number of purchasers
- High purchase frequency
- Impulsive purchase
- Low price

Selective distribution is different in that some products are only available from some outlets, e.g. electrical appliances, certain brands of clothes and fashion products.

Key characteristics include:

- Medium level of customers – but likely to be significant
- Less intensive distribution of outlets
- Retailers may require specialist knowledge
- Shopping based products
- Medium number of shoppers
- Purchase is occasional
- Purchase is more likely to be planned
- Medium price

Exclusive distribution is where possibly only one outlet in a certain geographic area supplies a product. This method of distribution usually relates to speciality products, e.g. special cars, specialist clothing, etc. Often exclusive distribution is relevant to niche products.

Key characteristics include:

- Relatively few customers
- Limited retail outlets
- Close retailer/customer relationship

- Speciality products
- Infrequent purchase
- High involvement and planned purchase
- High price

> **Question 8.3**
>
> You have been asked by your manager to recommend and justify the most appropriate distribution strategy for a new palm-top product, which is a portable keyboard that can be plugged into the palm-top enabling it to be used as a mini-PC.

Vertical channel integration

An easy definition of Vertical channel management, as quoted by Hill and O'Sullivan (1999) is:

A distribution system where two or more channel members are connected by ownership or legal obligation.

A further definition is:

A marketing channel in which a single channel member will co-ordinate or manage channel activities to achieve efficient, low-cost distribution, aimed at satisfying target market customers.

When you look at the varying distribution channels illustrated earlier in the unit, and you see the varying organizations involved, it is very likely in today's environment that organizations, for reasons of economies and profit objectives, are becoming very interrelated.

A prime example of this would be a supermarket such as Wal-Mart, which is likely to service its own supermarket stores from its own network of central warehouses. This means that they own their own warehouses and their own logistics company.

This method of distribution ensures profit maximization is achieved across all areas of the business, with utilization of resources across the board. In doing this, the organization benefits from income vertically up and down the supplier/manufacturer chain. This particular strategy would invoke the demise of the middleman as the manufacturers endeavour to buy them out to service their own functions in-house wherever possible.

However, the vertical marketing system then undertakes the complex task of managing all associated management functions and all of the marketing mix activities in-house, which means that the marketing activities are much more closely related and integrated, and often therefore much more effective. These areas include:

- Product design and development
- Branding
- Pricing
- Promoting
- Stock control and storage
- Merchandising
- Transportation
- Retailing
- Customer services
- Finance/credit
- Warranties and guarantees.

Horizontal channel integration

Horizontal channel integration is easily defined:

The combination of institutions at the same level of channel operation under one management.

This means that organizations that exist at the same level in the channel, e.g. the retailer level of the channel, may integrate with another organization by actually purchasing it. For example, there have been a number of significant mergers and takeovers within the mobile communications network, supermarkets (e.g. ASDA and Wal-Mart, Kwik Save and Somerfield) and the financial services sectors.

In this situation one business will purchase another business, either in the same field or similar, they will re-brand it, but pool resources such as marketing activities, marketing research, advertising, databases, personnel, distribution and warehousing. The net effect is that organizations can extend their market share both nationally and globally, while reducing their overhead costs significantly, but increasing their effectiveness, making them more competitive overall.

Physical distribution management (PDM)

Physical distribution mangement (PDM) is the term used to describe the management of every part of the distribution process. PDM can be contracted out to specialist or is best developed as a specialist function within the organization. It is the process which ensures that the correct product gets to the correct customer within a given timescale, as cost-effectively as possible.

Part of PDM would include being aware of what your competitors are offering, as suggested above. Elements for consideration would include:

- Costs involved
- Methods of transport – road, rail, plane, shipping, etc.
- Routes used
- Stock, storage and stock control
- Protection and delivery of stock
- Timing – a key element
- Evaluating the effectiveness of methods of distribution and being aware of other alternatives.

Distribution is an integral part of the marketing mix. With the right distribution strategy in place, that is with the right mode of delivery, the right speed of delivery to the appropriate place of purchase, customer satisfaction can be significantly increased. Failure to deliver these practical points will result in the loss of orders and income to the company and long-term customer loyalty will decline.

The key objective of physical distribution management is to find the most cost-effective way of meeting customer needs in relation to purchasing their product, whoever they are and wherever they are.

Physical distribution management includes the following functions:

- Customer services
- Order processing
- Materials handling
- Warehousing
- Stock/inventory management
- Transportation.

The key success factors of physical distribution management include all elements of the marketing mix:

- Product characteristics – how do they affect delivery requirements?
- Packaging – can it be transported?
- Pricing – how much does distribution add to the cost of the product?
- Promotional campaigns – creating an awareness of the product and where and how it can be purchased.

Timing is a critical element of PDM, as many companies work on the delivery of materials and components on a *'Just in Time'* basis (JIT).

JIT is just as it sounds, it means that the manufacturer of products, or the supplier of raw materials, must deliver the necessary materials or components as and when required. For example, a window manufacturer, who makes windows for office buildings, will be making windows to order and will be required to deliver them at certain periodic times in the construction of the building. Because storing glass and the metal or plastic structures is difficult, the organization will deliver as and when the office block construction company needs it.

The concept of JIT was developed to encourage maximized efficiency of manufacturing. The process will reduce the storage space requirements, which is a direct cost saving to the organization, but it also means that the organization will only pay for the materials when they have taken delivery of them, rather than in a bulk order at the beginning of the contract. Both save significant amounts of money, which means that the cost savings can be passed on to the customer, making products cheaper to purchase.

JIT is very much linked to quality applications and improvements. Should the organization take a mass delivery of a component, and leave stock standing around, it could be damaged or problems with the delivery may not be discovered until it is too late. Therefore, quality assurance controls and measures can be implemented as the components are dispatched which then aids the quality improvement process. This then enables organizations to work towards zero defects, which means zero wastage of time and materials, which means cost effectiveness and quality improvement and ultimately a higher level of customer satisfaction.

Within the retail sector, JIT plays the same sort of role. You will note that retail outlets very rarely run out of standard stock products, because they have good stock control processes and systems that enable JIT delivery of those stock items.

Most retailers now work with electronic point of sale systems (EPOS). EPOS registers your purchase at the point of sale, i.e. the payment checkout. The product is scanned into the computer as sold and the computer automatically registers this as a stock reduction. When the stock reduction reaches a certain minimum level, the computer automatically generates a message to place a stock order for that particular product to be in store by a certain delivery date.

The EPOS system allows retailers to monitor frequency of purchase of certain products, which then enables them to forecast demand of their stock products. This in turn helps them plan for their stock requirement and come to appropriate agreements with their suppliers on delivery and storage requirements.

Push and pull strategies

The way in which products make their way to customers is a critical consideration to marketers. The push element relates to distribution and how personal selling links the supplier to the customer, pushing the product out to the market.

On the other hand the pull strategy is very heavily reliant on advertising, packaging and sales promotions directly aimed at the consumer, effectively pulling them or attracting them to the product, encouraging them to purchase and forge a lasting relationship.

The huge growth in Internet marketing and direct marketing has really speeded this process up, with promotional incentives. For example, Marks and Spencer are now giving discount vouchers to M&S storecard holders to encourage them to make additional purchases. Next Directory offers free delivery or 20 per cent off orders over £100.00. These are pull strategies. There has been a significant rise in pull strategies as a result of the surge in Internet-based shopping. It shortens the distribution channel and makes the response times quicker.

Key factors influencing push strategies might include:

- Levels of economic and financial stability
- Need for economies of scale
- Mature or saturated markets
- Consumer credit restrictions
- Political instability
- Intense competition
- High operating costs
- Indications of low market growth.

Key factors influencing pull strategies might include:

- Levels of economic and financial stability
- Innovative culture
- Underdeveloped retail infrastructure for the products
- High investment potential
- High levels of market growth
- Social stability
- Political stability.

Question 8.4

Push and pull strategies are a concept with which you are becoming increasingly familiar. Explain what promotional activities might be undertaken to aid the distribution process for both push and pull.

As a marketing manager you will need to understand the importance of supporting onward suppliers in order to maximize economies of scale, associated profitability and benefits of a robust channel strategy.

The impact of the Internet on channel decisions

Distribution is currently subject to a fast pace of change as a result of huge growth in information communication technology, and the majority of manufacturers and distributors have clearly been considering the above points in association with the new channel alternative of the Internet. Manufacturers and suppliers are being forced to reconsider the traditional routes to market that are in favour of the Internet.

In February 2001, e-commerce revenue as a percentage of GDP was 0.062 per cent; business-to-business (B2B) revenue was equivalent to $2.03 billion, business-to-consumer (B2C) $0.34 billion. The potential growth for Internet marketing is phenomenal.

This evolution of change might appear to be slow, but customer demand is growing and customers are becoming impatient with many organizations and their inability to change. Companies such as Procter and Gamble are selling colognes like Hugo Boss on a website. Dell and Hewlett-Packard are now established traders on the Internet.

The most visited e-commerce sites in November 2000 were:

- Amazon.co.uk
- Amazon.com
- Egg.com
- Argos.co.uk
- Lloydstsb.com
- Tesco.com
- Barclays.co.uk
- Lastminute.com
- Railtrack.co.uk
- Beeb.com

In the US the most visited in the same period were:

- Amazon.com
- Ebay.com (on-line auctions)
- Americangreeting.com
- Bizrate.com
- Mypoints.com
- Mapquest.com
- Half.com
- Travelocity.com
- Toysrus.com
- Expedia.com

Case history

Amazon.com

www.amazon.com is one of the world's most popular online bookshops. Amazon.com was launched by Jeffrey P. Bezos, in a small art gallery in Seattle.

Amazon used an Internet site to sell books from 3.1 million available titles. They very quickly became a leading online music provider as well as videos. They offered a wide range of other products, including toys.

As a result of their Internet strategy, Amazon have been able to discount books by as much as 40 per cent. Books are mostly ordered directly from the distributors and delivered within 2 to 3 working days subsequent to customer selection. The performance and case history of amazon.com has been amazing. By the end of 1998 they had over 4.5 million customers worldwide with sales of over $500 million.

Amazon has forced traditional book retailers to rethink their traditional distribution and retailing strategies in order to refocus their business and actually survive.

> Amazon have to be credited with their ability to make shopping simple for the customer to buy books and have established communications between customers on a regular basis by successfully managing customer relationships. By the end of 1998 they were gaining an average of 9000 new customers per day and while traditional booksellers were discounting perhaps the top 100 books, Amazon were discounting over 400,000 titles.
>
> The strength of their business is the Internet model over the traditional models of distribution. Amazon offers the ability to browse on-line instead of in-store, they have limited staff overheads, and little need for massive physical facilities. Everything is going for them rather than against them.
>
> Out of six European countries, Amazon was the top website, continually used by over 50 per cent of all Internet shoppers.

Direct mail order and the Internet are rapidly changing the structure and the process of distribution. For example, in the summer of 1998, the AA (the Automobile Association) announced the closure of all 140 of its high street stores in favour of the Internet. They were quoted as saying 'It seems our customers prefer to deal with us by phone, fax or on the Internet. Our high street stores were becoming economically unviable'.

The impact of the Internet on the financial services sector has been significant, with many customers now banking on-line. This has seen a significant reduction in the number of personnel working for financial services and in the future it will have an incredible impact on the role of the very popular call-centres.

The last few years have seen a complete change in distribution trends, often leading to the demise of many middlemen. A good example of this is the leisure industry, which now trades products and services directly to the end-user through the Internet and TV's CEEFAX and FASTEXT, in particular the sale of holidays, flights, rail travel and hire cars on the Internet. In addition to this, the evolution of response-based advertising, influenced by the increasing growth of digital TV, will take on a new dimension with the growing harmonization between the Internet and digital technologies.

> ## Case history
>
> ### Airlines off to flying start
>
> The chairman of Lufthansa, Jurgen Weber, is a huge fan of e-commerce. He points out at every opportunity that a global airline that knows about developing transport networks should also be perfectly at home in the world of virtual networks.
>
> The enthusiasm for e-commerce, however, is quite transparent and essentially to do with hard cash. At the end of the day, the more tickets Lufthansa can sell over the Internet, the lower the company's marketing costs will be, since every ticket sold through a travel agency is subject to a commission of at least 5 per cent.
>
> When clients book their tickets on line the costs of travel agents, expensive call centres and the infrastructure to resource them can be saved.
>
> The Marketing Manager of Lufthansa has set the target of building up online ticket bookings to 25 per cent of total sales by 2005 compared with 10 per cent for call centres. By 2003 Lufthansa is expecting to save over £63 million/year, some 100 million euros in direct sales.

> Lufthansa's Internet strategy is similar to that of its competitors. It is hoping for particularly high sales from its website, but also through its participation with OPT (a joint travel agency service for a number of European airlines).
>
> The whole purpose of the Internet strategy will be to create the ability to gauge purchasing trends and characteristics through 'electronic footprints'. Doing this will enable Lufthansa, and other online organizations alike, to tailor marketing and control sales more effectively, increasing profits and customer satisfaction.
>
> Source: Connectis, March 2001

The evolution of the Internet as a distribution channel has created many new business opportunities both at home and abroad, and of course on a global scale. The Internet continually offers new sales channels for distributing products through electronic means, providing the opportunities for a vast range of marketing objectives such as market development, market growth or even market penetration to be achieved.

The potential business benefits of the Internet are endless. The following list provides an insight into the views of 300 executives from across Europe (Source: Chaffey, Mayer, Johnston and Ellis Chadwick, 2000).

At a strategic level:

- Improve corporate image
- Improve customer service
- Increase visibility
- Create market growth opportunities
- Lower overall business costs
- Move towards online transactions.

At an operational level:

- Speed of transactions increased
- Management of information improved
- Increased service levels to customers
- Removal of time constraints
- Removal of distance constraints
- Ability to complete transaction electronically
- Access to full competitive arena
- Opportunities for new revenues
- Cost-effectiveness
- More effective/closer relationships with business partners
- Improved understanding of customer requirement.

Almost without exception each of those benefits impacted upon the process of distribution.

In the long term it is clear that the Internet has serious implications for both marketing and channel structures. Intermediaries will no longer be the typical agents, or brokers, but they may be search engines such as Yahoo!, Excite, AltaVista or Infoseek – they will be formally known as cybermediaries.

The market will be full of virtual sellers, financial intermediaries, forums and user groups and evaluators. What we will see is more formally known as disintermediation, which through the Internet will give organizations the opportunity to sell directly to their customers.

Other structural changes might include customer relationships being more short term, as customers become more fickle and are shaped and directed by market forces, and essentially the impact of the Internet on the supply chain can be used to improve the quality of service delivered through to the end customer.

Ultimately, the basis of many business and marketing plans will reflect the nature and scope of the Internet as a distribution channel, reaping both tangible and intangible benefits. While the world of the Internet has suffered a temporary blip, the one thing that is sure, is that it is here to stay.

> ### Question 8.5
> What do you understand by the term disintermediation and what are the overall benefits?

Evaluating channel effectiveness

It is essential that having selected an appropriate distribution channel and intermediaries, their efficiency, effectiveness and performance are continually managed.

Key performance and evaluation measures include:

- Regular reviews
- A forum for problem review and solution
- Monthly, quarterly and year sales data analysis
- Average stock levels
- Lead and delivery times
- Zero defects
- Customer service complaints
- Marketing support – achieving marketing objectives, level of marketing activity, sales promotions, distributor incentives
- Spot-check of distributions further down the supply chain
- Annual performance audit.

From an Internet perspective typical evaluation methods of marketing effectiveness might include:

- Number of leads
- Increased sales
- Customer retention
- Increased market share
- Brand enhancement and loyalty
- Customer service.

These are just some of the performance evaluations that you might implement. However, the tone and commitment to the distribution partnership will determine how much of this information should be provided in management reports, and the timings. Should the relationship be of a different nature, and perhaps the producer has less leverage, then some of the information required for performance evaluation could be significantly harder to come by.

Summary

The process of distribution is costly, complex and logistically challenging and will often involve many different groups of people or organizations. Right through the 1990s and continuing on into the new century, there has been a significant shift in distribution patterns, including the ongoing demise of many traditional middlemen. More and more organizations are merging, developing alliances and utilizing and pooling resources where possible, always looking at ways in which they can be more cost-effective, and expanding into broader geographical, in fact global markets. As the external marketing environment is so competitive organizations have to find ways of increasing their market share and, obviously, increasing profits for shareholders.

Selection of the appropriate channel can give organizations the competitive edge over others by reaching customers in new and more innovative ways, particularly with the increasing use of the Internet.

Developing relationships between suppliers and customers is the essence of long-term customer loyalty. Should the marketing mix break down as a result of poor distribution strategy and management, then customers will go elsewhere.

Physical distribution management is a phenomenal task; it is complex, costly and critical. It has many facets, but its key role is getting the products to the customers, when and where they demand them.

One thing all organizations should bear in mind is that it is highly unlikely that customers will 'beat a path to their door'. The marketplace is vast and so is the amount of choice. Ensuring your product is visible when it should be will be one of the keys to marketing success.

Further study and examination preparation

Study tip

Distribution is raising its profile as a serious business function aided by the rapid evolution of e-commerce. You should be prepared to answer questions about any aspect of place operations. You should already be familiar with the basics of distribution in areas such as types of transportation and the roles of the various intermediaries through either studying for Marketing Fundamentals, undergraduate studies or experience.

The concentration will be on the operation level of the subject, rather than a strategic level. Therefore it is likely that distribution-related questions, will be about tactical implementation of distribution strategies that underpin overall marketing objectives and corporate goals.

Question 8.6

June 2000, Question 3a

Go to www.marketingonline.co.uk or www.bh.com/marketing to access Specimen Answers and Senior Examiner's advice for this exam question.

Unit 9
Managing marketing relationships

Objectives

The key to success within any marketing environment will be the realization that managing marketing relationships is crucial to long-term customer loyalty and customer retention, as is the necessity to manage each market differently in order to optimize customer relationships and the associated benefits.

This unit is broken into four parts, which reflects the structure and content of the indicative content of the syllabus:

- Relationships with customers
- Relationships with outside suppliers
- Internal marketing relationships
- Relationships with the wider public and society.
  (Syllabus reference 1.3.1, 1.3.2, 1.3.3, 1.3.4)

Note: Relationship marketing will also be part of your studies within marketing customer interface, but there is a greater concentration of the scope of relationship marketing within the marketing operations syllabus, from the point of view of covering a broader audience.

Introduction

In the majority of situations the basis of any type of relationship that is established is due to the way in which the supplier creates expectations. In creating expectations, you determine the nature and tone of the relationship and essentially you form and define customer behaviour in response to your organization and its product or service offerings.

The balance of optimizing customer relationships is a difficult one to manage, as quite often concentrating efforts on one customer or group of customers means that another customer might be neglected, ultimately to the detriment of the organization.

Pleasing the customer, creating customer satisfaction, seems to become a greater challenge almost daily, as organizations strive to achieve some form of competitive advantage. Customers become more demanding, assert their buyer power, and their expectations are continually rising, all the time making the value proposition more difficult to achieve.

With the growing influence of a number of key driving forces through SLEPT factors in the market, managing the marketing relationship is becoming a more turbulent affair. Every concept of every relationship now appears to demand more of the organization. The role of stakeholders, the growing influence of social responsibility and ethics, and internal marketing factors are now squeezing organizations from every angle, in order that they please all of the people all of the time.

The emphasis is now on knowing your markets, knowing your individual customers, being able to address them directly. Thus having 'an electronic footprint' of them is essential if you are to establish a robust long-term relationship with them.

Ignoring the issues of managing relationships will ultimately leave organizations and marketers in a very vulnerable position.

One of the main reasons that organizations will, however, start to make positive moves towards managing marketing relationships is in order to maximize their effectiveness by retaining existing customers rather than focusing consistently on new customers. Long-term relationships provide the basis of consistency, synergy and achieving satisfaction. The long-term profitable benefits to the organizations will be considerable. For example, a 5 per cent reduction in customer defections can improve profitability by an excess of 25 per cent.

Relationship marketing

> **Definition**
>
> **Relationship marketing**
>
> Relationship marketing is to establish, maintain and enhance relationships with customers and other parties at a profit so that the objectives of the parties involved are met. This is done by mutual exchange and fulfilment of promises (Gronroos, 1994). Relationship marketing refers to all marketing activities directed towards establishing and maintaining successful and relational exchanges (Morgan and Hunt, 1994).

The fundamental principle upon which relationship marketing is founded, is that the greater the level of customer satisfaction with a relationship – not just the product and service – the greater the likelihood that the customer will stay with and be retained by the organization.

For relationship marketing to succeed in any organization, there will need to be a cultural shift, as discussed in Unit 3 on 'Marketing planning, implementation and control', away from the old transactional style of marketing to the more dynamic and rewarding basis of relationship marketing.

From transactional to relationship marketing

A more conventional approach to marketing has been the old transactional marketing, whereby the functions of marketing, customer services and quality have been separate entities within the organization. However, the disintegrated approach to marketing meant that the potential to optimize marketing relationships was being lost, as the lack of co-ordination between the three functions gave way to a fragmented approach to achieving customer satisfaction. Ultimately and in many instances this started to prove problematic with many organizations, as they found they were suffering lack of market share compared with the more relationship-focused business.

There are therefore, a number of significant differences between the concepts and contexts of transactional and relationship marketing, as illustrated in Table 9.1.

Table 9.1 The shift in relationship marketing – Source: Payne, Christopher, Clark and Peck, 1998

Transactional focus	Relationship focus
Orientation to single sales	Orientation to customer
Discontinuous customer contact	Continuous customer contact
Focus on product features	Focus on customer value
Short timescale	Long timescale
Limited emphasis on customer service	High customer service emphasis

Limited commitment to meeting customer expectations	High commitment to meeting customer expectations
Quality is the concern of production staff	Quality is the concern of all staff

Principally the key difference in the management of the relationship is that the basis of it will be a long-term relationship, a long-term view achieving long-term customer loyalty.

In order to establish and construct a relationship programme, or indeed a relationship chain, there are four factors that the organization will need to concentrate on, each of them we have covered in other units:

- Defining the value proposition ('Product operations' Unit 6)
- Identifying appropriate customer value segments ('Marketing planning, implementation and control' Unit 3)
- Designing value delivery systems ('Place operations' Unit 8)
- Managing and maintaining delivered satisfaction (all units).

For an organization to succeed it is of course essential that the value proposition meets the expectations of the customers, that the expectations in their minds meet those in the mind of the supplier and that there is little scope for customer uncertainties, a concept that you will come across in selling. Therefore, the value proposition needs to fill any gaps in expectations.

Market segmentation has been a continuous thread throughout: the more closely defined the target markets, the more likelihood of success. The more you know and establish in the relationship with your customers, the closer you get to delivering what they really want, again closing the expectations gap.

In the unit on 'Product operations' some time was spent on the definition of value: establishing values, core values and peripheral values. For relationship management to work, defining the method of actually delivering that value will be essential. This will include a range of delivery systems and channels, and these should be appropriately tailored to the customer needs. Of course, with the growing influence of digital marketing and service technologies, it will make it far easier for you to perhaps support a diverse range of customers. However, a word of warning, you should be aware of the fact that while it gives you strength to manage customers, so too does it give a competitor strength. The switching process from one company to another can often be fast and painless.

Because the quality and strength of customer relationships is vital to the survival and profitability of all organizations, it is essential for competitive advantage to be sustained, customer loyalty to be achieved, and the process of delivering customer satisfaction to be clearly defined, to avoid any potential gaps in customer perception of the value proposition and their expectations.

While this seems quite broad, with every group of customers, or each individual customer, these are core issues in sustaining the relationship. This applies to the context of each customer group that will be the focus of this unit. It is, therefore, essential that at this stage you actually have an understanding of how broad that scope can be.

The scope of marketing relationships

Figure 9.1 The scope of relationships (Adapted from Morgan and Hunt, 1994)

The scope of the managing marketing relationships is significant (see Figure 9.1), stretching as it does across four key groups: customers, suppliers, internal markets and stakeholder markets, each defined in terms of relationship marketing partnerships.

In addition to this, the scope broadens once more, as you look at managing marketing relationships in the broader context of business sectors:

- Organizational markets
- Service markets
- Not-for-profit markets.

Each of these particular elements is the focus of other units in this text, where some issues pertaining to relationship management are discussed.

However, in brief, the critical issues relating to each market sector are:

- *Organizational markets* – require high levels of relationship management due to the intensity and time dimensions of the process of purchase. The market is essentially less fickle and more rational, which provides the basis of establishing closer links. Closer links mean working towards gaining preferred supplier status. The basis of achieving this will ultimately mean long-term supplier/buyer relationships, effectively putting a relationship on a strong footing. In the unit 'Industrial/business-to-business and services marketing' (Unit 10) you will see more about the two different approaches to relationship management. They are adversarial and collaborative agreements.

    Essentially relationship marketing is about collaborative relationships, working together optimizing opportunities and maximizing potential.

- *Service markets* – relationship marketing in the context of services is the major imperative, as at the core of any successful services delivery will be the relationship between the service provider and the service consumer. Never before has the power and strength of that relationship become so relevant. The whole basis of its success is upon the key factors of relationship marketing, as defined in Table 9.1:
  - Continuous customer contact
  - Focus on customer value
  - Long timescale
  - High customer service emphasis
  - High commitment to meeting customer expectations
  - Quality as a concern to all staff.
- *Not-for-profit markets* – this relationship is the critical success factor and should be the core of these markets. In order for charities, for example, to succeed they need to establish long-term relationships in order that they can sustain three key factors:
  - Donors – the givers of money and equipment to support their work
  - Volunteers – the people who give time and effort and avoid company overheads
  - Client – the users of the charitable service – the charity need to gain trust, understanding and often long-term relationships in order to undertake the work at the heart of their organizations.

> **Question 9.1**
>
> Think about the scope of your own organization or one you know well, and make a list of groups of individual customers with whom you have relationships – you might be surprised at the balance of the group.

Planning for relationship management

A marketing relationship does not just happen, evolve or emerge, it has to be planned. As with all other aspects of marketing, it requires a structured approach to ensure that relationship marketing does maximize business potential, provide the basis of profitability, and create sustainable competitive advantage, through robust and long-term customer, supplier and stakeholder relationships.

In order to plan for relationship marketing there needs to be an understanding of some key factors: customer loyalty, the dimensions of quality, building trust and the basis of continuous improvement.

Customer loyalty

To achieve customer loyalty is highly challenging, as it looks at the loyalty of all customer groups that are involved in the relationship marketing process. For relationship marketing to be truly implemented and part of the business culture, it has to focus on all customer groups.

We have already established that relationship building is a long-term process, and in order for customer loyalty to be achieved, there are a number of key identifiable stages that the relationship moves through. This is more formally known as the 'Relationship marketing ladder' of customer loyalty (see Figure 9.2).

```
              Advocate
                              ↕
                            Emphasis on
              Supporter     developing
                            and enhancing
                            relationships
                            (customer
              Client         keeping)
                              ↕

              Customer
        ↕
 Emphasis on
 new customers
  (customer   Prospect
  catching)
        ↕
```

Figure 9.2 The relationship ladder (Payne, Christopher, Clark and Peck 1998)

The ladder highlights the process from targeting the customer, to adoption, to developing the relationship from customer to long-term client. From here it is then essential to encourage them to become both a support and advocate of the company, in order that they can become marketing tools, on your behalf. Thus you not only retain them, but also use them to grow your market.

The recent addition to the ladder is that of partnership. In the organizational marketing context, partnership is a very positive stage to move towards, in order to secure optimization of opportunities to be exploited to the benefit of both the supplier and buyer organizations.

Customer loyalty, however, has two dimensions: long-term loyalty, which is the basis of a true relationship marketing scenario and false loyalty. This will essentially be driven by a number of key factors:

- Limited completion of the task
- High switching costs
- Proprietary technology
- The attraction of some loyalty scheme.

The key objective in this context, therefore, will be to actually switch the power base of loyalty to a more long-term relationship and indeed partnership.

Customer loyalty, of course, is very interlinked with brand loyalty, which was discussed in the unit 'Product operations'.

The key dimensions of relationship marketing

In 'Industrial/business-to-business and services marketing' (Unit 10), you will look at the basis of services marketing, that is to ensure that quality is at the core of the business and the relationship with customers.

Therefore, there are some key dimensions upon which an organization must deliver in order to provide a basis for a relationship.

- *Reliability* – ability to perform the promised service dependably and accurately
- *Responsiveness* – willingness to help customers and provide prompt service

- *Assurance* – knowledge and courtesy of employees and their ability to inspire trust and confidence
- *Empathy* – caring, individualism, attention, the firm provides it customers
- *Tangibles* – physical facilities, equipment and appearance of personnel.

In order for the relationship to be established, the basis of the quality gap must be filled, i.e. the difference between the customer expectations and the organizational perception of what is being delivered.

A relationship based upon trust

Morgan and Hunt suggested three dynamics to trust within a relationship (see Figure 9.3).

Figure 9.3 What builds trust? (Source: Morgan and Hunt 1994)

These are three quite simplistic components that would form the basis of any relationship, personal or business. The basis of trust provides the opportunity to develop a relationship that includes co-operation, leading to relationship commitment. While principally they should be the basis of relationship marketing aims and objectives, typically these three components can often be overlooked, perhaps assumed or even ignored. However, in Figure 9.4 you can start to see the benefits of building a relationship on trust, as you can save on relationship termination costs, gain many benefits and look towards a relationship based on shared values. Opportunistic behaviour will be a great benefit of partnerships in a relationship management context.

Communication is an absolute, as the more inward and outward-bound communication that exists, the more you will find out about the customer, their needs, wants and perhaps their competitive experiences, all of which will only serve to strengthen the basis on which you might operate.

Figure 9.4 Relationship model (Adapted from Morgan and Hunt, 1994)

Customer retention management

The most simplistic view that any organization could take of customer retention management is that the way to keep customers is to keep them satisfied. Some organizations think that this means zero defects, others are realizing the increasing importance of this and are really looking at ways in which retention is not just a concept but a reality.

Payne *et al.* (1998) have developed a number of techniques for measuring customer satisfaction and essentially linking them directly to profitability. Principally what they are doing is measuring customer retention, where customer satisfaction is measured at the rate at which customers are kept.

Payne *et al.* suggest that a retention rate of 80 per cent means that, on average, customers remain loyal for five years, whereas a rate of 90 per cent pushes the average loyalty up to 10 years. And as the average life of a customer increases, so does the profitability to the firm.

They go on to suggest that long-term established customers are more profitable for six reasons:

- Regular customers place frequent, consistent orders and, therefore, usually cost less to serve
- Long-established customers tend to buy more
- Satisfied customers may sometimes pay premium price
- Retaining customers makes it difficult for competitors to enter a market or increase their share
- Satisfied customers often refer new customers to the supplier at no extra cost
- The cost of acquiring and serving new customers can be substantial. A higher retention rate implies fewer new customers need to be acquired, and they can be acquired more cheaply.

Here you see some of the benefits alluded to within Figure 9.4, so therefore a relationship based on trust can gain commitment and co-operation, with all of the other add-ons as previously discussed.

Customer retention in consumer markets

In consumer markets, customer retention schemes are in the main focused around loyalty cards. Most people on average will have at least five loyalty cards on the go at any one time. For some consumers the benefits are very worthwhile. For example in ASDA 400 points on your petrol card give you an £8.00 George voucher, or a £5.00 store voucher, while House of Fraser provide you with vouchers once you exceed a certain level of points.

Loyalty cards became highly popular in the mid to late 1990s as the intensity of competition began to rise in the supermarket wars, closely followed behind by banks and credit card companies. For example, the American Express Blue Card gives you a penny back for every pound you spend on their card, at the end of the year. Boots followed suit with their loyalty card, which proved to be very beneficial to the customer. With double points and special offers, the Boots card has been branded as a success by its customers.

Case history

Tesco

In 2000, Tesco, the UK supermarket giant, launched an advertising campaign designed to capitalize on the announcement at the time, that Safeway, a major rival of Tesco, intended withdrawing their ABC loyalty card scheme, claiming that it was no longer providing the benefits it was previously planned to do.

Tesco then launched its own newspaper advertising campaign, stating that 'Safeway has decided that it can no longer afford to say thank-you to its loyal customers. At Tesco we don't think you should have to choose between points, deals or low prices. We think you should have them all'. A further advertisement said 'Safeway's ABC card isn't worthless after all. Bring it to Tesco for £2.50's worth of Club card Points'.

Despite the decision to remove the loyalty card, Safeway have benefited from other schemes that they continuously use, that reward the customers in different ways.

Source: Adapted from 'Loyalty Schemes Have Their Points', *Financial Mail*, May 2000.

Customer retention in organizational markets

We have already touched upon some of the issues relating to this within this unit, and will develop the issues relating to customer retention management in Unit 10. However, there are five basic principles that an organizational market should consider:

- *Technical support* – providing added value to clients in industrial markets.
- *Technical expertise* – providing expertise in design and engineering can be a unique selling point (USP) of the organization and add to the value proposition.
- *Resource support* – ensure that a range of versatile resources are available to support the relationship, that are cost-effective and efficient, and that could ultimately see the development of an alliance when business opportunities are presented (the basis of partnerships).
- *Service levels* – these appear to be of growing importance and will relate in particular to time, delivery and product quality.
- *Reduction of risk* – giving as much insight into the product proposition as possible through exhibitions, trial use, product delivery guarantees.

> **Question 9.2**
>
> Why do you think customer relationship marketing is so important in organizational markets?

Customer retention in not-for-profit markets

The basis of customer retention in not-for-profit organizations is covered in some depth in Unit 11.

Essentially one of the key considerations is that marketing activities in not-for-profit markets need to be very focused at each of their customer groups, as we ascertained earlier, those being donors, volunteers, client/users.

It will be essential that the charity understands their target markets and segments them exactly, as each of them will manifest different customer retention characteristics, particularly as their personal reasons for charitable involvements will be very diverse.

Key relationship marketing issues will include:

- Analysing acquisition and retention costs
- Managing customer retention and customer acquisition activities concurrently
- Recognizing how emphasis needs to be placed on all markets in order to achieve the success the objectives demand
- The need to have adequate information sources about each of the customer groups.

Of course within the not-for-profit sector there are some far broader strategic issues that typical organizations will grapple with, such as the challenges of the functions of management and marketing, developing and understanding the basis of market segmentation strategies and finally the scope of their mission, which in many instances can be huge.

All in all, the challenges of both relationship and retention management in the context of marketing, are quite daunting.

Key account techniques to aid customer retention management

Key account management seems to be growing in importance as a tool to retain customers, particularly in the organizational sector of the marketing environment.

There are a number of symptoms of change that have resulted in the necessity to re-examine how, through our key account management practices, we build and develop the level of relationship demonstrated in Figures 9.3 and 9.4.

Typical symptoms of change, as suggested by McDonald, Rogers and Woodburn (2000) in *Key customers – How to Manage them Profitably* are:

- Compressed time horizons
- Intensity of competition
- Shorter product life cycles
- Shorter technology-based life cycles
- Transient customer preferences
- Increasingly diverse business arenas.

So, based upon the earlier discussion on the key components of customer retention management, how do you continue to satisfy the customer in this changing environment? Table 9.2

provides an insight into the issues driving customers and how perhaps a company can respond to them directly through the relationship marketing strategy.

Table 9.2 Pleasing the customer (Source: McDonald, Rogers and Woodburn, 2000)

Symptoms	Challenge
Customers are more demanding and more knowledgeable	Quality and traceability favour supply chain partnerships
Purchase behaviour strategic rather than tactical	A strategic and sympathetic approach to selling is required
Concentration of buying power	Selling companies need to add more value
Higher expectations	A greater investment and closer relationship to the customer required
Customer identity and role more complex	Need to better manage the complexities of multiple market channels

From a key account perspective, understanding the relationship between the buyer and the seller and the two organizations will be extremely important. While typical marketing mix factors are highly relevant, the relationship goes beyond these dynamics to the need to understand the strategic intent. Strategy development as the basis of the relationship may provide new business opportunities and business development. Therefore, it is essential when pursuing relationships and indeed managing relationships that the organizations have a good understanding of each other, as demonstrated in Figure 9.5.

Figure 9.5 Intercompany relationship (Source: McDonald and Woodburn 1999)

There are risks and implications of key account management that all organizations should always consider in order to plan the relationship sensibly to optimize it and grasp potential opportunities that are affordable and not damaging.

The risks associated with key account relationships include:

- The risk of being vulnerable to opportunism and not obtaining a satisfactory saving or return on investment in the relationship
- The risk of committing to one partner at the exclusion of others
- The risk of misunderstanding the relationship and failing to achieve reciprocal security.

While risk is something that all organizations should be aware of, there are also a group of limitations that can hinder the profitability of a customer relationship:

- Close relationships with key accounts have sustainable cost implications
- The mismanagement of just a few large accounts can be potentially loss making and even catastrophic
- Customer relationships should be carefully selected and prioritized for prudent investment of scarce resources.

Characteristics of key account management

There are a number of different stages of key account management. However, for the purpose of this text, we will look briefly at the characteristics of basic key account management first, and then at the characteristics of interdependent key account management. These different approaches will enable you to focus on the nature of the relationship employed at different levels.

Basic key account management characteristics

- Transactional/operational – an emphasis on efficiency
- Can be stable or trial state
- Buyer is likely to be outsourcing
- Easy to exit
- Driven by price and success measured on price
- Little information sharing
- Single point of contact
- Reactive rather than proactive buying
- Business relationship only
- Reward structure of key amount managers paramount
- Standard organization, which suits selling company
- Small amounts of growing business.

You will notice in Unit 10, 'Industrial/business-to-business and services marketing', that the characteristics displayed by an adversarial relationship are very similar.

However, moving that on a stage further is more akin to the nature of customer relationship management and retention management as we understand it, and is essentially based upon the collaborative approach of relationship management.

Characteristics of interdependent key account management

- Both acknowledge importance to each other
- Principal or sole supplier
- Exit more difficult
- High level of information exchange – some information sensitive
- Wider range of joint and innovative activity
- Larger number of multifunctional contacts

- Streamlined processes
- Prepared to invest in the relationship
- High volume dialogue
- Better understanding of the customer
- Developing social relationships
- Development of trust
- Cost savings
- Proactive rather than reactive
- Joint strategic planning and focus on the future
- Opportunity to grow business.

Source: McDonald and Woodburn, 1999.

In real terms it is highly unlikely that a relationship will move beyond this point, in fact the more likely scenario is a hybrid between the basic key account management concept and the interdependent key account concept. However, in our key account management, the necessity is, within the limitations of the business, to develop an interdependent approach.

> **Question 9.3**
>
> What value does key account management bring to the customer retention and relationship management process?

The marketing mix for customer retention management

As you will be beginning to conclude, the foundation of success in managing marketing relationships and customer retention marketing, is the value proposition. Therefore, it is essential that the use of the marketing mix as a key set of tools be optimized in order to have maximum impact upon the customer base, meeting their expectations and retaining them and your competitive advantage.

Therefore, the following marketing mix suggestions should be considered. They relate back to, and build on, your studies in other units.

Product extras

- Product and service augmentation and innovation – guarantees of standards and service levels, preventive maintenance
- Customizing the offer – relationship building
- Cross-selling other products in the product line or portfolio

Relationship pricing

- Price incentive for increased customer spend and perhaps customer share
- Price sensitivity – what are the issues with price sensitivity – is it a relationship issue?
- Perceived value – the value proposition versus the price

Specialized distribution

- Priority customer handling – e.g. British Airways offer Executive and Standard check ins
- Pre-view evenings – Marks and Spencer's, House of Fraser, Laura Ashley – typical tactics in relationship marketing

- Exclusive or selective distributors
- Multiple accessing options, i.e. the Internet, retail outlets, direct marketing

Reinforcing promotions

- Sales-force responsiveness – think back to Unit 4 'Theories of communication'
- Loyalty schemes – reward cards, membership benefits, sales promotions, magazines
- Tailored direct marketing

Relationships with outside suppliers

In order to both survive and remain competitive more and more organizations are moving towards the use of outsourcing agencies, consultancies, distributors and agents to undertake work for which they do not have the skills and capacity within the organization.

In addition to this, there have been a growing number of franchise, agent and distributor relationships established, as the economic forces place pressure on downsizing, overhead reductions, shared risk and cost savings.

There is little point in an organization investing in high-level skills, high-specification technology and resources, to undertake a one-off project when the work can be outsourced for a fraction of the price, for the same return, i.e. the project/contract outcome.

Typical areas of outsourcing within a marketing context will include:

- Market research
- Promotional activity and advertising
- Research and development
- Management consultancy
- Project management work
- Distribution
- International development.

However, there are a number of potential risks involved in using external agencies and, therefore, caution should be exercized in using outsourced agencies/consultancies if the project is highly important and potentially highly confidential or where there is the threat of conflict, leakages or internally associated problems.

Different types of outsourced relationships

When taking the decision on whether or not to outsource project work, it is essential that the outsource supplier will contribute value to the organization and the achievement of their objectives.

Distributors – will add value to the product through offering special services such as stock handling, credit facilities and after-sales service. On many occasions distributors are able to offer specialist technical services and advice to customers on behalf of the manufacturer. The management of the distributor relationship was covered in Unit 8 'Place promotions'.

Franchisees – hold a licence to supply and market a product or service to the design and specification of the originator. A franchise agreement covers the exact specification of the product, merchandising, store layout and proposed marketing and promotional techniques.

One of the key benefits of franchisees is that the brand name is extended everywhere but the risk of the business is shared. Typical examples of franchised outlets are the Body Shop, McDonalds and Kentucky Fried Chicken. The downside of franchising is that with the best will in the world the standard of service will vary. Therefore, measurement and control of their activities against their contracts will be essential.

Agents – have the legal authority to act on behalf of the manufacturer. As you will see in Unit 12 'International marketing', agents are increasingly used overseas as a form of expanding markets internationally. They do not actually take any legal title of the goods, and they do not handle them, their role is based upon generating business leads, orders and repeat orders through the personal selling process.

They differ from a salesforce in respect of their terms and conditions of employment. They are generally self-employed and will work on a commission basis and are likely to act on behalf of a number of similar companies.

There are many risks associated with the use of agents, as there is the potential for conflict of interest and leaks. However, the benefits of having a native agent in the home company, based upon a relationship of trust, commitment and co-operation, will outweigh the risks.

The advantages and disadvantages of outsourcing

Outsourcing work to suppliers has a number of advantages and disadvantages as can be seen from Table 9.3.

Table 9.3 The advantages and disadvantages of outsourcing to suppliers

Advantages	Disadvantages
Reduced costs	Information leaks
Access to wider skills and technology	Requires trust and commitment
Access to a wider pool of talent and abilities	Lose in-house motivation for innovation
Use only when needed	Time lags
Solves specifically defined problems	Lack of control and motivation
Access to high cost and high tech facilities	Good communications needed

Care should be taken when using external resources to ensure that they are sufficiently briefed, tightly managed and their performance is continually monitored and controlled.

Supplier selection

The task of selecting a supplier should not be underestimated. However, the size and complexity of the task will relate to the nature and context of the outsourced supplier. As you will have seen above and from previous studies, the complexity of appointing a channel member or the appointment of a franchisee are quite complex, contractually binding and subject to frequent review and evaluation, based on the terms and conditions of the contract.

However, while the outsourcing of work to agencies and suppliers is likely to be a little less complex in some respects, their appointment where appropriate should be formally contracted, briefed and the outcome monitored and controlled.

Selecting the right supplier for the task should therefore be criteria-based and objective-based and relate very closely to the organization's objectives and strategy implementation.

In selecting an agency a number of key questions should be addressed, as shown in Table 9.4. These questions at least would allow you to ascertain the level of service and value a supplier might contribute to your organization in the achievement of its overall corporate mission.

Table 9.4 Agency selection questions

- Do the agency/consultancy fully understand the requirements of a brief?
- Do they know and understand the necessity of marketing research and how to use it?
- Is their strategic thinking sound?
- Is their thinking imaginative and creative?
- Are they professional and businesslike?
- Can they work with senior people?
- Are their capabilities high in all key areas, management, strategy, and creative media?
- Do they work well as a team?
- Is their creative work of a high quality?
- Can they work internationally?
- What is their attitude towards costs? Will they work effectively to reduce costs?
- Will they fit with our working practices?
- How important to them will our account be?
- Do they have a proven track record in the project area?
- Do they demonstrate good project management skills?
- Are they trustworthy and reliable?
- Do they work to deadlines and targets?

The agency brief

Briefing the agency or consultancy to which you are preparing to outsource the work provides a face-to-face contact between the management team, key staff and key contacts involved in the delivery of the project outcome. This enables relationships to be established and group dynamics to evolve.

It is essential that the brief is clearly defined in measurable terms, in order that all involved within the project know the exact parameters to which the consultant is working. If a project has clearly defined objectives, i.e. SMART objectives, then you have the basis for a control and evaluation plan.

Typical brief headings might include:

- Current situation
- Task/project objectives and outcomes
- Position of the project in terms of importance to the global project being undertaken
- Guidelines on the management of the relationship – frequency of communication and review meetings
- Proposed presentation guidelines for project
- Preferred approach
- Target deadlines
- Available resources – information, people, physical resources
- Budget
- Lines of responsibility and reporting.

It is always safer for an agency brief to be as tightly defined as possible in order for the objective of the project to be achieved.

Evaluation and control

Based upon the above briefing criteria you now have the basis for measurement and control of the relationship. The following controls could be implemented:

- Regular reviews – project reviews against defined criteria
- Project updates – timings of delivery/target deadlines against actual deadlines
- Budget usage – target against actual
- Timelines
- Requirement for remedial work – project gaps
- Relationships – positive, negative, empowerment
- Appropriate resource allocation.

The list for evaluation and control of a relationship is endless and will need to be tailored to the organization; however, the above headings and bullet points will provide you with a generic starting point, which can then be adapted to the specific agency/consultancy relationship.

Building supplier relationships

The psychology behind supplier relationships reflects very much the components of the inter-related approach illustrated in Table 9.4 and based upon the relationship model in Figure 9.4. However, on this occasion the balance of power is different.

You will recall looking at Porter's Five Forces in the unit on 'The marketing audit', where you looked at the power of the buyer and the power of the supplier. Much of what you have looked at in this unit so far has focused on the relationship from an organizational perspective of the organization pleasing their customers. The same principle applies here, only on this occasion the outsourcing organization is the buyer.

Therefore, the power base in the outsourcing relationship will be the party buying the agency service and, therefore, the drivers of the relationship might be based upon the following:

- The organization is highly likely to be a large proportion to the agency/consultancy order book
- The buyer covers a high proportion of the supplier's costs
- The buyer could switch provider if switching costs are low – this will obviously depend upon the complexity of the programme
- Threat of backward integration – there is a possibility that if the work outsourced is not achieved to a satisfactory standard, it will be taken back in-house.

However, in some situations you will also have the supplier's power driving the relationship, where their supplies are exclusive and concentrated in terms of distribution. This would be particularly relevant in highly specialized services.

The most favourable solution to managing the balance of power between the buyer and supplier at this level is to implement an interrelated approach to the relationship.

The management of the relationship will likely be on a key account approach, which will be a sensible approach to take in order for the buyer/supplier relationship to be mutually beneficial and mutually dependable, with limited conflict, based upon trust, commitment and co-operation.

Managing internal marketing relationships

> **Definition**
> **Internal marketing**
> Marketing by a service firm to train and effectively motivate its customer-contact employees and all the supporting services to work as a team of people to provide customer satisfaction. (Kotler *et al.*, 1999)

The fundamental component of achieving successful relationship marketing is the infrastructure of the organization – the culture, leaderships, skills, resources, synergy, co-ordination and co-operation of the employees within the organization. Without these key factors being addressed by the organization, success in the external market is likely to be limited. The basis of these areas were included within your studies in Unit 3 'Marketing planning, implementation and control'.

The overall aim of internal marketing, therefore, is to ensure that everybody within the organization contributes towards developing a marketing-oriented, customer-focused culture in order to improve levels of services to customers.

It is necessary that an integrated approach towards achieving customer satisfaction, is taken by the whole of the organization to optimize the skills, talents and abilities that employees have on offer to meet the needs of the external market.

In Unit 3, 'Marketing planning, implementation and control' we looked at the importance of internal marketing as part of the implementation process, and saw that indeed, internal components and infrastructure needed to be in place in order for the corporate goals and marketing objectives to be achieved.

Therefore, the key to managing internal relationships is having a rational understanding of the key factors listed below, in order to establish a basis for the relationship between employees to be built in the context of trust, co-operation and commitment.

The same benefits that are highlighted within Figure 9.4 and Table 9.2 operate in the internal context of marketing also, with perhaps the difference being that employee relationship termination may well result in the employee switching to competing organizations. Should an employee move to a competitor, they take with them a lot of inside knowledge of their previous employer, which ultimately will influence them within their new role. This should obviously be avoided.

Internal stakeholders

Internal stakeholders are people who are likely to be involved in internal marketing and those who operate within the boundary of the organization and who have an effect on the organization's overall performance. The stakeholders are likely to include shareholders, directors, management and the workforce.

As stakeholders, they expect to receive some reward for their efforts, either through payment or share options.

The way in which staff are paid can often have a significant bearing upon their overall performance and often the provision of a stake in the organization is a good incentive and motivational factor.

Internal relationship marketing techniques

In the main, most organizations now recognize the pivotal importance of internal marketing in respect of achieving robust customer relationships with their external customers. However, organizations do need to address a number of key issues in relation to successful implementation, all of which have been covered within Unit 3 'Marketing planning, implementation and control'. As a reminder, these are the key components of internal marketing success:

- Create an internal awareness of the corporate aims, objectives and overall mission
- Determine the expectations of the internal customer
- Communicate to internal customers
- Provide appropriate human and financial resources to underpin the implementation of the marketing strategy
- Provide training in order that employees have the appropriate skills and competences to undertake the task at hand
- Implement a change in tasks and activities appropriate to the objectives of the organization
- Provide a structure whereby cross-functional integrated teams across business units can work together, in order to aid communication of business activity relating to the achievement of corporate goals
- Provide the systems and processes that enable successful delivery of services and products, enabling employees to successfully implement them and achieve organizational success
- Maximize the opportunity for customer interaction through effective management of service levels, e.g. response times, reply processes
- Internal monitoring and control.

For internal marketing to be successfully implemented, a planned approach is essential to allow evaluation and measurement of the successful execution of the plan.

The plan could be designed with the following headings:

- Internal vision
- Aims and objectives
- Internal marketing strategy
- Segmentation, targeting and positioning
- Marketing programme (to include all elements of the marketing mix)
- Implementation
- Monitoring and control of the success or failure of execution.

Question 9.4

Why is it important to have highly motivated personnel in order to successfully implement a relationship marketing programme within the organization?

Importantly, in terms of managing customer relationships, internal marketing forms the basis of the 'relationship management chain' (Figure 9.6).

```
                    ┌─────────────────────────────────────────┐
                    │      MANAGING INTERNAL MARKETS          │
                    │      • Market planning – internal       │
                    │      • Culture, climate and employee    │
                    │        retention                        │
                    └─────────────────────────────────────────┘
```

Define the value proposition	Segmentations targeting and positioning	Operations and delivery systems	Measurement and feedback
Understand the customer value	Identify the preferences	Mass customization	Service process monitoring
Where can we add value?	Segment profitably analysis	Partnering	Customer satisfaction studies
Competitive benchmarking	Configure the value package	Process re-engineering	Employee satisfaction studies

```
                    ┌─────────────────────────────────────────┐
                    │      MANAGING EXTERNAL MARKETS          │
                    │      • Market planning – external       │
                    │      • Customer relationship management │
                    └─────────────────────────────────────────┘
```

Figure 9.6 The relationship management chain – (Adapted from Payne, Christopher, Clark and Peck, Relationship Marketing for Competitive Advantage)

Essentially, in order to establish a really effective relationship chain within the organization will require a focus upon a number of critical issues – to which we made reference earlier:

- Defining the value proposition
- Identifying appropriate customer value segments
- Designing value systems
- Managing and maintaining delivered satisfaction.

Exam Question

December 2000, Question 1b

Go to www.marketingonline.co.uk or www.bh.com/marketing to access Specimen Answers and Senior Examiner's advice for this exam question.

Relationship marketing with the wider public and society

The final stage of managing marketing relationships relates to managing marketing in the broader context of the wider public and society, i.e. carry out the marketing activity in a way that is socially acceptable, ethically driven and is proactively incorporated into the organization's vision, mission, ethos, culture and day-to-day business dealings.

At times ethics and business seem to be mutually incompatible, as we saw in the mini-case study on Exxon in Unit 2 'The marketing audit'. However, social and ethical marketing are a very politically correct element of today's society and business at large. A further example of how a social and ethical issue in the context of 'green marketing' has affected a high volume market is McDonalds. McDonalds have been involved in a number of social and ethical responsibility issues, in respect of the construction of their products and packaging, which they have had to address so as to retain favour with the marketplace. This was a costly exercise and one that was carried out under the spotlight of huge publicity.

Today there are a number of dynamic groups and individuals who engage themselves in social issues, such as human rights and, in particular, green issues. With the introduction of the Kyoto Agreement, there has been a significant impact upon how organizations manage their activities to remain within the framework of reference that the agreement has defined. Failing to redress the balance between where the organization is and where it should be in respect of the Kyoto Agreement has been shown to cause high levels of discomfort.

Organizations are becoming increasingly socially aware. For example, BMW and Honda are both involved in recycling elements of their vehicle materials for future uses. This is the kind of social responsibility more and more organizations are now considering. This then results in a change in strategic direction for the future, or becomes a strategic issue when developing corporate, business and marketing plans.

The drinks industry is under constant attack and the particular target is alcoholic soft drinks, which took the market by surprise, indeed by storm, in the summer of 1995. In particular, drinks such as Hooch, Lemonheads and Vodka Sauce are the source of constant contention between consumer movements and the brewing industry with regard to the problem of under-age drinking and distinguishing between an alcoholic drink and a soft drink.

Marketing and social responsibility

Marketers are not blind to criticism. A company knows that if the products it sells are not acceptable to the consumer, then it has problems.

> **Definition**
>
> **Social responsibility**
>
> The obligations and accountability to society of individuals and organizations above and beyond their primary functions and interests.

Manufacturers need to care for consumers in terms of safety. This could involve environmental or health consequences. The social costs and benefits of new products must also be examined. Marketers have to consider their response to, say pharmaceutical products, where the side-effects of new drugs must be researched, and often through contentious methods such as testing on animals.

Marketers must also consider other issues important to social marketing, such as environmentalism, legislation, consumerism and consumer pressure.

Environmentalism – green marketing

Wastage, effluent, emissions of fumes and acid rain have to be taken seriously by manufacturers. Due to the high level of industrialization in the modern world, the environment is under constant threat from global warming. In recent times we have experienced severe weather effects, such as heavy rain, gales and significant flooding. All of this relates to environmentalism and as such means that organizations must in the future consider their strategy in relation to these issues.

Organizations such as NIREX, who dispose off atomic waste, are subject to heavy criticism by environmental groups such as the Green Party and also by the press. Their contact with the consumer is minimal; they deal with industry, hence they are little influenced by the consumer.

> **Case history**
>
> **Shareholder activism goes Green: corporations increasingly called to account for environmental issues**
>
> Frustrated by legislation that is often compromised or not enforced, and legal challenges that can take years to resolve, environmental and social justice groups are challenging corporations head-on through the use of boycotts, direct action and shareholder activism.
>
> Shareholder activism is uniquely suited for a direct approach to corporations since it provides a formal channel of communication between management and shareholders. Shareholder activists use the power of stock ownership to file resolutions, raise awareness, build coalitions and exert pressure to 'create change' from the inside.
>
> While the corporate world sometimes disregards the criticism of grassroots groups, it pays serious attention to its own peer group and financial community.
>
> Shareholder activism has traditionally been organized by religious groups such as Interfaith Centre for Corporate Responsibility (ICCR) – a coalition of more than 300 religious and social investors with $150 billion in stock. Recently, environmentalists have begun to add this tactic to their activist toolbox.
>
> In 2000, Greenpeace received strong support for its resolution asking BP Amoco not to drill in the Arctic and to increase its solar energy programme. The National Wildlife Federation votes in its proxies on environmental resolutions and the Sierra Club is to initiate shareholder activism through shareholder campaigns in 2002.
>
> Some key resolutions that shareholder activist groups and collaborative groups will undertake in 2001 are to influence the environmental practices of organization such as Coca-Cola, in order that they will recycle elements of their containers, and BP Amoco on global warming and Hershey on genetically modified foods.
>
> For more information see www.asyousow.org or www.socialfunds.com/sa.
>
> Source: Lexis-Nexis

Legislation

Perhaps one of the most dynamic areas for the major political parties when in power has been the introduction of legislation to protect the consumer. This provides external constraints on business, the most significant being that of government policy itself.

The manufacturer and supplier have legal duties to consumers and a number of laws have been passed over the years to protect the latter, notably:

- The Trade Descriptions Acts 1968 and 1972
- The Consumer Safety Act 1978
- The Consumer Credit Act 1974.

These are just three of the most important areas of legislation.

The rise in consumerism

A major element of social responsibility is considering the impact of consumerism. Although consumers have had rights, enforceable by law, for many years, they have not really been effective because of the cost of taking legal action. The consumerist movement is a way of taking agreed action for specific purposes, such as opposing the building of another runway at Manchester or Birmingham Airport, and similar schemes elsewhere.

Such schemes are often associated with local initiatives, but the group which is known nationally is the Consumers' Association, famous for the publication *Which?*

The consumer movement is a diverse collection of independent individuals, groups and organizations seeking to protect the rights of consumers.

It may be useful to consider at this stage two definitions of consumerism.

> **Definition**
>
> **Consumerism**
>
> Consumerism is an organized movement of concerned citizens and government to enhance the rights and powers of buyers in relation to sellers. P. Kotler, *Marketing for Non-Profit Organizations* (1996).
>
> Consumerism is a social force designed to protect the consumer by organizing legal, moral and economic pressures on business. (D. Cravens and G. Hills, *Consumerism: A Perspective for Business*)

In both of these definitions there is a suggestion of an alienation from business and industry, and a feeling that the consumer's point of view is neglected.

Social response to consumerist pressure

Companies have responded in many different ways to the consumer movement and the individual consumer. Some have resisted and actively lobbied against consumerist pressure; others have ignored it and gone about their business as if the consumerist movement did not exist. However, evidence from the USA suggests that those companies which reacted to the consumerist movement positively, increased their market shares and profits quite substantially, and it is now recognized that most companies have to respond to environmental and social issues and accept the new buyer's rights, at least in principle.

It is quite interesting to consider the differing responses of organizations to social and environmental pressures. Below are some of the responses of businesses:

- *Ignore consumerism* – a reaction that encourages legislation in the marketing area, as companies believe/hope that the consumerism movement is a passing phase.
- *Counter consumerism* – the stronger elements in the business sector will endeavour to resist consumerist pressures by lobbying government. This is really a delaying tactic, as a government wins more votes from consumers than from big business generally.
- *Profit from consumerism* – to respond to consumerist pressures by creating new means of profit is the most acceptable alternative long-term strategy for business.
- *Voluntary adaptation* – this is, in fact, treading the tightrope – meeting consumerist demands, but over a longer period than the government would want. This approach could misfire, indeed backfire.

- *Accept government intervention* – business has traditionally resisted government interference, but it is now becoming more acceptable, and certain politicians talk of a government/business partnership.

There is one thing, though, that is certain and that is that consumerism is here to stay. Increasingly it demonstrates against the building of more roads or airport runways, and it shows that people have a high level of determination that can no longer be ignored.

The same applies to the 'Green' movement, which aims to preserve the natural order of things to reduce pollution. Quite often the improvement of processes, which is necessary to reduce pollution, is a once-only capital cost and the process runs at lower cost after improvements.

It is clear that the ideas of consumerism and anti-pollution make some sense, even if manufacturers do not like the details of some of the claims, and it is essential to have a policy on these matters.

Reduction of pollution is a social responsibility, and can often be achieved either through factory processes or in lower-cost wrappings, and this, in turn, is a matter which can be used as a topic for favourable publicity.

For many organizations, it would make sense to run a social audit, in the same way that they may run a marketing audit. The difference would be that the results could be used for publicity purposes, either to show existing good practice, or to report progress on matters that need attention.

Most important of all, though, is a declaration of company policy regarding consumerism and social responsibility. When all members of staff at all levels have a clear directive to which they can work, they will feel happier to do the little bit extra that is often needed to work more cleanly. This may look like a matter of ethics and social responsibility, but it will often result in the production of economies and a reduction in selling costs.

Ethical issues for consumers and marketers

We have very much focused on social marketing, of which ethical marketing is an important part. Taking social responsibility often means being ethical in behaviour. We must briefly consider the importance of ethical issues relating to the role of marketing.

Some of the matters that are highlighted by the consumer movements are often taken up because they impinge strongly on the livelihoods of people who are closely involved with the industry. Farmers have to work the land efficiently and effectively, yet intensive farming methods spoil wildlife habitats. These methods include the growth of GM (genetically modified) crops, even when these crops threaten to upset the ecological balance of the agricultural environment.

Instead of just fighting farmers, organizations such as the Royal Society for the Protection of Birds have investigated a range of activities and produced a book to show farmers how they can benefit from looking after wildlife as well as their crops. The government has found itself with a moral and ethical obligation to consider the impact of GM crops more closely also. In turn, codes of practice or legislation will be introduced on the future inclusion of GM crops in the marketplace and the development of associated food products.

This is probably a more acceptable view of consumerism, but at times there are excessive demands from consumers, who continue to bring the consumer movement into disrepute. Therefore, it is necessary, where appropriate and indeed possible, to have codes of ethics by which industry can operate.

Ethical implications for the marketing mix

Should a company be quite serious about acting responsibly at a social and ethical level, then it is likely that there may be some adoption of the marketing mix. Key issues in the mix are:

Product

- Meeting safety standards
- Dangerous products modified or removed
- Ethical issues relating to planned obsolescence should be considered
- No further testing on animals

Price

- Consideration given to what is a fair price
- Monopolies and mergers more closely monitored to prevent monopolistic power on prices

Promotion

- Ensuring that advertising standards are upheld and not brought into disrepute

---

Case history

'Swedes urged to re-think advertising policy aimed at children': A case of commercial ethics versus social responsibility

The Swedish EU Presidency was urged by a number of advertising chiefs to re-think its plans for a ban on advertisements aimed at children.

The Culture Minister told a Stockholm Conference that children were a 'special group of society in need of special care and attention' and called for barriers against harmful content.

The Minister insisted that Sweden would press for further discussions to pursue this in the future.

The advertising industry was quick to respond. Andrew Brown, Director-General of the UK Advertising Association, suggested that there was no evidence to suggest that there was a need for binding legislation or a ban.

He went on to say 'Children are not the naïve, gullible and exploited sector of society, who can be isolated from the commercial pressures of the real world, those who believe in bans suggest.'

Within the EU, Sweden and Greece already have bans on advertising aimed at children. Denmark, Ireland, and Flemish regions of Belgium are said to support further restrictions. The UK, Germany and France support the status quo.

Place

- A duty to ensure that products are available to all, on a equal cost basis
- Environmental transportation concerns are considered

Question 9.5

Explain with examples the difference between ethics and social responsibility.

Codes of ethics

The Chartered Institute of Marketing, of which you are now probably a member, worked very hard to achieve the Royal Charter, which was granted by the Queen in February 1989, and members are rightly proud of the achievement of this status. Subsequent to this, in 1999 they managed to gain approval by the Privy Council to award Chartered Status to individuals who met with the professional charter criteria.

Most professional bodies publish codes of conduct, which set out the minimum standards of conduct considered necessary for their members, and the punishments for members who are found to have contravened the code. Few members even bothered to read the codes because they consist of normal good behaviour, and most people work that way. It is worthwhile giving you the CIM Code in detail, however, not because you are likely to break the rules, but just to add to your knowledge.

Chartered Institute of Marketing's Code of Practice

Marketing's professional responsibility

This is a code drawn up by the Institute, which sets out guidelines for its members to ensure that the practice of marketers is carried out ethically.

The professional marketing executive has responsibilities to his employer, to customers – both ultimate and intermediate – to his colleagues and to the public. The Institute requires its members, as a condition of membership, to recognize these responsibilities in the conduct of their business, and to adhere to the following Code of Practice. All members shall be answerable to the Council of the Institute for any conduct, which in the opinion of the Council is in breach of this Code, and the Council may take disciplinary action against any member found to be in breach thereof.

The CIM code of ethics

General: a member shall at all times conduct himself as a person of integrity and shall observe the principles of this Code in such a way that his reputation, that of the Institute and that of marketing shall be enhanced.

Instruction of others: a member who knowingly causes or permits another person or organization to act in a manner inconsistent with this Code or is party to such action shall himself be deemed to be in breach of it.

Injury to other members: a member shall not knowingly, recklessly or maliciously injure the professional reputation of another member.

Honesty: a member shall at all times act honestly and in such manner that customers – both ultimate and intermediate – are not caused to be misled. Nor shall he in the course of his professional activities knowingly or recklessly disseminate false or misleading information. It is also his responsibility to ensure that his subordinates conform with these requirements.

Professional competence: it is expected that, in the exercise of a member's profession as a marketing executive, he shall seek at all times to ensure that he attains and retains the appropriate levels of competence necessary for the efficient conduct of such tasks as are entrusted to him by his employers. He shall seek to ensure that all who work with him or for him have the appropriate levels of competence for the effective discharge of the marketing tasks entrusted to them and where any shortcomings might exist he will seek to ensure that they are made good as speedily as possible.

Conflict of interest: a member shall use his utmost endeavour to ensure that the provision of this Code and the interests of his customers are adequately and fairly reported to his company in any circumstances where a conflict of interest may arise.

A member holding an influential personal interest in any business, which is in competition with his own employer, shall disclose that interest to his employer.

A member having an influential personal interest in the purchase or sale of goods or services as between his own company and another organization shall give his company prior information as to that interest.

Confidentiality of information: a member shall not disclose, or permit the disclosure of, to any other person, firm or company, any confidential information concerning a customer's business without the written consent of the customer except where required by statute.

A member shall not disclose, or permit the disclosure of, to any other person, firm or company or use to his own advantage, any confidential information concerning his employer's business without the written consent of his employer except where required by statute.

Securing and developing business: no member may seek to obtain or obtain business in a manner, which, in the opinion of the Council of the Institute, is unprofessional. In determining whether or not any behaviour is unprofessional, the Council will be guided, inter alia, by this Code and by any professional Codes of Practice in effect at the time the behaviour occurs. The Council of the Institute will always, unless it has determined to the contrary and so informed members, accept such other Codes of Practice as a minimum level to be expected of members of the Institute.

The Council of the Institute also issues from time to time Schedules for the Guidance of Members on facets of the marketing process to supplement such Codes of Practice. These Schedules for the Guidance of Members are statements of minimal expected practice and do not preclude the Council from concluding that behaviour not covered in such Schedules is, in fact, unprofessional.

Other relevant codes of practice: members should be aware of other relevant Codes of Practice. The most important amongst these are:

- *Advertising*: British Code of Advertising Practice (Advertising Standards Authority); International Code of Advertising Practice (International Chamber of Commerce).
- *Sales promotion*: International Code of Sales Promotion Practice (International Chamber of Commerce).
- *Market research*: Code of Conduct (Market Research Society/Industrial Marketing Research Association).
- *Public relations*: Code of Professional Conduct (Institute of Public Relations).

The enforcement of the Code of Practice within CIM

- *Role of the individual member*: it is the duty of all members to assist the Institute in implementing this Code and the Institute will support any member so doing.
- *Misuse of the code*: unfair, reckless or malicious use of this Code by members or others to damage the reputation and/or professional practice of a member and/or his organization shall be deemed a breach of this Code.
- *Procedures for handling complaints*: the Council of the Institute may nominate, at its discretion, a person or persons whose task will be to decide if there is a prima facie case to answer. If there is such a case, the Council shall initiate the necessary procedure for its investigation.

- *Sanctions for breach of this code*: if the Council of the Institute, having duly and properly examined an alleged breach of this Code by a member, finds that member in breach of the Code, it shall be empowered to take such disciplinary action as it shall deem appropriate. If the Council decides to expel a member from the Institute, it shall act in strict accordance with the provisions of the Articles of Association of the Institute, of which Article 19 is set out below:

    Any member of any class who shall fail in observance of any of the regulations or by-laws of the Institute or whom the Council in their absolute discretion deem an unfit or unsuitable person to be a member of the Institute may be expelled from the Institute by the Council. Such member shall have seven clear days' notice sent to him of the meeting of the Council at which the proposal for his expulsion is to be considered and he may attend and speak at the meeting, but shall not be present at the voting upon such proposal nor (except as aforesaid) take part in the proceedings otherwise and as the Council allows. A member so expelled shall forfeit all claims to the moneys paid by him to the Institute, whether upon admission or for fees or subscriptions or otherwise and shall cease to be a member of the Institute.

The marketing associations of other countries have similar codes of conduct.

Proactive, reactive or passive strategies for deploying ethics and social responsibility at a corporate level

Reaction strategy

This usually means that an organization will go on letting a situation continue, until the public learns about it. The situation may be known or unknown, but the normal stance is to deny knowledge, then deal with the consequences, continue to do business and ensure a high level of PR to minimize the negative impact. Here you will immediately see the use of the marketing communications mix to rescue a situation.

Defence strategy

This is where an organization will try to avoid or indeed minimize any additional obligations linked to a problem. Strategies will include taking legal action, seeking support of trade unions, playing for time, etc.

Accommodation strategy

A business using an accommodation strategy assumes responsibility for its actions. It may take on board an accommodation strategy when special interest groups are encouraging a particular action or when the business perceives that if it fails to react the government will pass a law enforcing the issue. A good example of this was when McDonalds developed an advertising campaign around the nutritional values of its products. A further example is the government enforcing a more detailed approach to ensuring that contents of products, nutritional information, etc. is on all food articles purchased.

Proactive strategy

A business that uses a proactive strategy is assuming social responsibility and ultimately responsibility for its own actions, and will therefore respond to any complaints or accusations made against it without outside pressure or threat from government intervention. A proactive strategy requires management to redefine its strategy. BMW is a good case in point. They are setting up recycling plants across Europe to enable them to use materials and components from existing cars to be recycled and used for future cars.

A company that supports both socially acceptable moral philosophies and individuals who act ethically, are likely to make decisions that have a positive impact upon society.

Social responsibility, in the words of Dibb, Simkin, Pride and Ferrell (2001), is:

> *The obligation of an organization to maximize its positive impact and minimize its negative impact on society. Thus social responsibility deals with the total effect of marketing decisions in society. These two concepts work together; a company supports socially acceptable moral philosophies and individuals who act ethically are likely to make decisions that have a positive impact upon society.*

Social responsibility and ethical behaviour is a critical mix. Added to this, legislation then tightens the loop considerably.

As a marketer, it is critical, therefore, for you to develop a broad working knowledge of social, ethical and legal issues in order to meet with the ongoing approval of your local community and your customer base.

Social and ethical marketing may require a corporate culture change; building a culture that is morally, ethically and socially responsible will undoubtedly have a positive impact upon society.

The relationship marketing plan

It is essential that an organization manage the scope and range of relationships within the marketing environment, in order to achieve all-round success.

As the management of relationships in each of the markets we have defined is critical to the achievement of the overall customer-retention objectives, there must be crystal-clear linkages that bridge the objects and the markets (see Figure 9.7).

Figure 9.7 The relationship marketing plan (Adapted from Payne, Christopher, Clark and Peck, 1998)

In order to achieve a meaningful relationship marketing plan, you have to consider the needs of each of the individual markets in order for it to be successfully implemented. The linkages between each audience should be clear, and they should all be directed towards the same overall purpose. The successful implementation of such a plan will most likely impact upon the achievement of retention goals.

Summary

The move from transaction marketing to relationship marketing has meant that the marketing planning process has now taken on a new set of dynamics. It is no longer purely based around developing a marketing mix to meet organizational goals, it is much broader in perspective, and the task much bigger.

Essentially, organizations who are truly committed to developing a relationship marketing approach will need to be supported by a structure, culture and overall organizational climate that will enable each of the functional business units within the organization to align and co-ordinate themselves to develop an integrated approach to the achievement of the overall marketing objectives of every market.

Principally, the role of the relationship marketing plan is to ensure that there is a synergy, consistency, coherence and cohesiveness, and a 'pan-company' approach, to the implementation of the marketing plan.

Further study and examination preparation

Study tip

The subject of relationship marketing and customer retention, as you will have seen earlier in this unit, was the subject of the mini-case study for the December 2000 paper. The move from transactional marketing to relationship marketing is growing in importance and is now acknowledged as a necessity by industry in order to achieve sustainable customer relationship and competitive advantage.

Therefore, you would be advised to concentrate some effort on ensuring that you have a broad understanding of the subject and its importance in the role of marketing today.

Extending knowledge

Recommended reading

There are some useful articles that appear from time to time in *Marketing Business* in respect of relationship marketing and customer retention.

Other reading comes from *Relationship Marketing for Competitive Advantage* by Payne, Christopher, Clarke and Peck (1998) – Chapters 1, 4 and 8.

Question 9.6

June 2000, Question 6

Go to www.marketingonline.co.uk or www.bh.com/marketing to access Specimen Answers and Senior Examiner's advice for this exam question.

Question 9.7

June 2001, Question 5

Go to www.marketingonline.co.uk or www.bh.com/marketing to access Specimen Answers and Senior Examiner's advice for this exam question.

Unit 10
Industrial/business-to-business and services marketing

Objectives

This unit is one of three units looking at the application of marketing in a number of given contexts, to help you understand the broad diversity of marketing, given different situations, different markets and different customers.

The indicative content of the syllabus is as follows:

- Characteristics of business versus consumer markets
- Business buyer behaviour, factors affecting buyer behaviour and business decisions
- Marketing mix differences
- Basic characteristics of services
- The extended marketing mix
- Importance of service quality.
  (Syllabus reference 1.4.1 and 1.4.2)

This unit will be separated into two parts – one for business-to-business and the other reflecting upon services marketing.

Business-to-business marketing

Introduction

There are varying terms to describe the business-to-business markets, however, one of the more commonly used ones is 'organizational markets'. Principally, this is where the buyers within the organizations, buy on behalf of them. This could include a range of different products from computer equipment, forgings, welding, stationery, various plant and equipment that might be needed in order to get the job done.

Organizational markets include organizations such as manufacturers, hotels, hospitals, conference centres, wholesalers and sometimes retailers, local authorities, government bodies to name but a few.

There are many implications of organizational markets, but in short they include:

- Geographical diversity – they can be spread very far and wide
- Size of the decision-making unit
- The issue of 'preferred supplier status'
- Size of purchase
- Frequency of purchase
- Negotiation of contracts
- Lead time between order and delivery.

One of the most important factors that you must identify with, particularly from a forecasting position, is that industrial demand in business-to-business markets is derived from consumer demand. This may be difficult to follow at first, but if you think of any consumer product you should be able to work out that the need for the production factory, the raw material supply and the transportation services all depend on the demand for the product. They would disappear if the consumer demand for the product actually declined.

An obvious example of this would be cars. You may not be overly familiar with the level of manufacturing, components and raw materials that go into the building and production of cars, you must have some concept of the size of the enterprises that make cars and deliver them to their customers throughout the world. A further example of this was the potential demise of the Rover factory early in 2000. There was massive concern about the impact of factory closure in the West Midlands if another buyer was not found for the Rover plant. Essentially you would have been looking at the demise of the Rover car and the associated demand, and the impact would have been a loss of towards 100,000 jobs in the UK motor parts industry.

The same applies to every industrial product, although it is often difficult to visualize the extent of supply chains, with the different manufacturers and their network of suppliers and distributors.

Characteristics of business/industrial buying behaviour

There are many characteristics of organizational markets, which will ultimately distinguish their buying behaviour and decision-making unit in comparison to consumers and service-based decisions. They include:

- *Organizational size* – this will be a vitally important factor as organizational buyers will often be placing high volume or high price orders. The size, order capacity and nature of the organization will reflect the buying potential.
- *Nature of products purchased* – essentially, many organizational buyers have to buy items, which the consumer would not have any use for.
- *Buyer behaviour* – affects the organization not the individual's motivation.
- *Size and influence of the decision-making unit* – this can be considerable and involve many individuals or groups of individuals.
- *Customer relationships* – tend to be closer and more involved than in a typical business-to-consumer relationship. The level of involvement will most likely be high.
- *Power of buyers (Porter's Five Forces)* – the buying capacity and employment opportunities provided by organizations are often of major importance in a community, so the organization has some local, and maybe national, power, which can influence politicians.

Organizational buying

Organizational buying behaviour, like that of a consumer, will be very much influenced by a range of different factors:

- The amount of money available
- The size/volume of purchase
- The level of risk involved
- The timeframe for decisions
- The buying situation
- The purpose of the purchase
- Competitive offers
- Credit terms and conditions of purchase
- Delivery lead times

- Packaging
- Environmental factors
- Supply and demand
- Inelastic demand
- Fluctuation in demand
- SLEPT influences
- Organizational objectives
- Individual and interpersonal.

As a marketing manager, it is essential that you understand the different degrees to which you could find yourself involved, within organizational markets. You will find that in many organizational markets by and large products are bought on a repeat purchase basis, possibly the same order sizes, qualities and quantities. There is little difference between these transactions and the consumer buying, and the selling situation will be very much based upon 'order taking' perhaps rather than order making.

However, for some re-buys, in particular modified re-buys, the process will often be more involved and perhaps require more technical advice, sales support and negotiations. Past experience will have a big effect on the decision and the DMU will be strongly affected by technical matters.

It is in the 'new buy' or 'new task', which involves perhaps the buying organization embarking upon a new project or a new job, that marketing must be used to its full effect, so we shall look closely at the information required, the time and resource involvement the contract might require, and the level of technical support. Essentially, as a marketer you will need to identify the level of involvement the contract will entail.

While it is vitally important to understand all of these influences, it is also essential that you are aware that one of the key influences in the buying process is the actual buyer themselves.

Understanding the nature of business-to-business buyers

Quite clearly the role of an industrial buyer in an organizational market is going to be poles apart from that of a typical consumer. Their objectives and motivations are going to be entirely different, as they are based around the organization, its function and its customers. Generally they are better informed, more demanding, more technically minded, and they also manifest more rational behaviour than consumer buyers.

However, while their focus might be the organization, as a marketing manager you should be aware that sometimes their own personal goals and hidden agendas might actually influence the purchasing decision. While the motivation is supposed to be organizationally focused some buyers do gain psychological satisfaction from the purchase process. Essentially, they are human and their human and personal feelings will on occasions influence the decision.

The organizational/industrial buyer will be very interested in the overall value proposition; they have a duty and responsibility to the organization and stakeholder alike, to execute the best deals for their business. For a typical buyer, the key considerations in relation to the value proposition will include quality, delivery, service and price. The range of products available and the level of innovation an organization demonstrates will also play a role in influencing their thinking.

For large and more specialized products, you should expect a buyer to require significant amounts of data, market information, performance specifications, technical specifications, and it is also likely they will require a great deal of consultancy style support in order that they have the complete picture and can make a fully informed decision.

Because of the nature of their role, they will also involve themselves with competitor organizations and therefore will be fully aware of different options and alternatives available. As a marketing manager, you will therefore need to understand clearly the nature, scope and threat the competition will provide.

When all is said and done, organizational buyers are probably far more rational than individual buyers, they are less likely to be compulsive buyers, but what they will be is informed, demanding and focused upon achieving the best deal for the organization.

To give you a somewhat clearer picture of the high-level involvement in the organizational marketing context the Howard Sheth Model of Industrial Buying might be helpful (Figure 10.1).

Figure 10.1 Howard Sheth model of industrial buying behaviour

Question 10.1

With your knowledge of the selling process gained in Unit 5 'Promotional operations' of this text, outline the nature of the sales relationship that would be developed in the purchase of motorway maintenance contract, which would be managed and co-ordinated by a large civil engineering consultancy.

Market segmentation for organizational marketing

As many companies supply to a wide range of industries it is wise to segment the market so as to serve a specific market segment more thoroughly. It is equally essential to specifically target your products at special groups in organizational markets as it is in consumer-based markets.

Segmentation criteria may include:

- *Type of industry* – it may be possible to specialize, but even if this is not possible there may be common characteristics in some industries. For instance, aircraft manufacturers need specific certificates, which can only be supplied by approved companies; other industries have their own special needs.
- *Size of company* – by turnover, number of employees, output or capital employed; many large companies have professional buyers, so they tend to evaluate their suppliers differently.
- *Type of product* or service required.
- *Type of buyer* – some big companies allow their branch factories to buy, others do not. Some companies put limits on the value to which the branch factory buyer can go without asking for higher authority.
- *Geographical location* – there may be some parts of the country which have specialist needs, in which case you can segment them on that basis.

For gaining a clearer insight into both geographic factors and demographic factors, a look at the following additional factors might be of assistance:

- Standard Industrial Classifications (SICs)
- Census of the population (most recently in April 2001).

To understand the nature of the organizational requirements you will need to know:

- The nature of the benefits sought
- The degree of formality of the buying organization
- The people involved in the buying process.

Segmentation, however, is not perhaps as commonly used in organizational markets, and while it is an ideal, often the markets are limited in size, which makes it perhaps a little less appropriate.

The buying and decision-making process in organizational markets

It is here that the most important difference between industrial and consumer buying becomes almost self-evident. Traditional consumer-based markets aim directly at the customer or consumer, i.e. the end-user, and therefore understanding customer satisfaction levels is essential. However, in organizational markets the motivations are different. The key to customer satisfaction is on-time delivery, quality of the products, arriving undamaged in order to meet production deadlines. It involves heavy-duty distribution requirements, stock handling, serious packaging and, of course, tightly negotiated deals.

The sales lead is likely to originate from a requirement within the company that emerges as a result either of the buying organization tendering for work (and therefore needing technical specifications and prices), or orders that have been placed by customers, and the buyer may have to buy raw materials, components, services, machines and even, perhaps, some design work.

There are a number of problems relating to organizational decision-making that perhaps put some of the above into focus:

- *Precipitation* – why is the decision being made, what is it supposed to achieve, what are the benefits, what are the cost cuttings available?
- *Product specification* – quality, quantity, characteristics, attributes, service levels, pricing.
- *Preferred supplier* – it is likely that supplier selection will be based upon a short-list of known suppliers, creating a major barrier to entry for new suppliers. They will almost definitely have some key criteria that they will work on based upon past experience of their supplier base.
- *Commitment* – will the chosen supplier be committed to the process, deliver on time, understand the nature of the problem?

Within the buying process there are a number of roles that might emerge based upon the level of technical specification being presented. Therefore, in a highly technical specification sale the following roles might be very significant:

- Supplier relationship management
- Supplier sourcing
- Evaluating tenders
- Negotiation
- Financing
- Order placing
- Performance evaluation
- Purchasing.

From the internal perspective of a supplying organization, i.e. a supplier to the organization market, you will additionally be involved in liaison with production and engineering division:

- Research and development processes and findings
- Financial – assessing return on investment, managing methods of financing, costing and any borrowing in relation to the purchase
- Marketing of the products.

The process of the supplier/buyer relationship is quite a complex web and does in the main require a level of mutual understanding and co-operation and support on both sides.

The decision-making process

You will be familiar with the consumer decision-making process, as explained in Unit 4, 'Theories of communication', therefore Figure 10.2 will need little explanation. However, what it does do is explain which elements are relevant to new tasks, modified re-buys and straight re-buys (repeat purchases).

	Buy classes		
	New task	Modified re-buy	Straight re-buy
1 Problem recognition	Yes	Maybe	No
2 General need description	Yes	Maybe	No
3 Product specification	Yes	Yes	Yes
4 Suppliers' search	Yes	Maybe	No
5 Proposal solicitation	Yes	Maybe	No
6 Supplier selection	Yes	Maybe	No
7 Order-routine specification	Yes	Maybe	No
8 Performance review	Yes	Yes	Yes

Figure 10.2 Buy grid – Source: Marketing Operations – Worsam

The buying centre – the decision-making unit

Like consumer markets, organizational markets have a decision-making unit, or a buying centre. However, the dynamics and scope of the task are considerably higher.

The roles of a typical decision-making unit for an organizational market are as follows:

- *User* – the machine operator – the person who actually uses the product.
- *Influencer* – typical influencers will be users, suppliers, research and development staff, accountants, buyers, sales representatives, external consultancy representatives.
- *Decider* – on this occasion it is more likely to be 'deciders'. These might include a management team, a tendering committee, an individual buyer, shareholders - this really will vary depending upon the extent and financial involvement of the decision.
- *Buyer* – the person who will handle the internal supplier sourcing, information seeking, handle negotiations with the suppliers.
- *The gatekeeper* – this is likely to be a member of the secretarial or administrative staff, handling the flow of information inbound and outbound through the organization.

Question 10.2

What are the distinctive differences between a consumer decision-making unit and an industrial decision-making unit. (Refer to your studies in Unit 4, 'Theories of communication' for information about the consumer DMU).

Relationship marketing in organizational markets

In Unit 9, 'Managing marketing relationships' you will have gained an insight into the challenges and complexities of relationship marketing. In an organizational market, the strength of relationship between a buyer and seller is vitally important, as often there is a high level of involvement during and after the buying process is concluded.

A poor purchasing decision from an organizational buying perspective could be fairly catastrophic and therefore every opportunity has to be taken to ensure that the risk inherent in the decision, and therefore in the relationship, is reduced.

The history and previous experience of the organization will be an imperative to the final choice of supplier that an industrial buyer will make, amid other key factors, however, gaining preferred supplier status gives a positive stance, so that when the tendering process has a close outcome, the strength of the preferred supplier relationship secures the deal.

There are three key components linked to the relationship marketing stance:

- The durability of the relationship, i.e. the length of time over which a supplier/buyer relationship will continue (in some industries a purchase can take 12 months and above to secure)
- Economics – the investment of time and money in the relationship actually enhances relationships and preferred supplier status opportunities
- Social dimensions – because of the duration of the relationship it is likely that it might take on some form of social dimensions. While this is inevitable, mixing business with pleasure can sometimes cause conflict. Having said this, some supplier/buyer relationships, according to research, extend beyond 20 years.

Essentially there are likely to be two approaches to managing the supplier: adversarial and collaborative.

Adversarial – the characteristics pertinent to this approach include:

- Regular price quotes
- Little co-operation
- Quality and delivery thresholds meet lowest denominator
- Emphasis on lowest unit price
- Multiple suppliers.

Collaborative – the characteristics of this approach will include:

- Few suppliers
- Long-term and long-standing relationships
- Partnerships
- Frequent planned communications
- Integrated approach to operations
- Quality and timescales designed in and met
- Emphasis on the value proposition but the key being value for money – i.e. the lowest cost for the highest quality.

Question 10.3
Why is it important for a supplier to establish a strong relationship with the buyer, and what are the benefits overall?

Competitive tendering

The nature of organizational markets lends itself to being involved in a significant amount of tendering work, particularly for local authority work, government work, major contracts, special projects or partnering agreements. The primary purpose of this type of tendering will relate to the potential price of the purchase and the level of public interest, when the buying process consists of inviting selected companies to bid for the work, then opening all the bids at once and choosing the lowest price (or best value for money).

For example, some tenders are based on both quality and cost, and will be tendered for in two separate parts. The enquiry for a big public works project, such as a new section of motorway or a big bridge, will go only to companies that have qualified to get their name on the list of approved suppliers. Qualification often involves an examination of resources, equipment, staffing levels and jobs completed satisfactorily.

In theory, this ensures that every competent company can ask for the drawings and specifications for the design so that they can then prepare their bid for the work. The selection of the lowest price then seems to be the way in which the 'owners' of the project – the population in general or the people who live in a town – will get value for their money.

This type of buying is only sensible for very large contracts where big resources are needed, and the bid (or 'tender') documents usually say that the lowest price is not necessarily the one that will be chosen.

The stages in the process will vary, but the following steps are common criteria for tendering processes:

- *Step 1* – acquire expression of interests from potential suppliers, perhaps through advertising in relevant trade magazines or making it known to preferred suppliers that a potential tender is available. This is known as pre-qualification stage, i.e. the stage that confirms the appropriateness of the organization/supplier who will submit the tender.
- *Step 2* – those who qualify for the tender process now submit a formal tender document, against tender criteria, based usually on the key components of product/service, quality, timing, resources, pricing, etc.
- *Step 3* – tender assessment stage – once the tenders have been received by the buying organization, a tender assessment process is undertaken, where each bid is measured against the criteria determined by the buyer. It is likely that each of the bids will then be weighted, possibly in two categories, price and quality.
- Sometimes before the final award is made further information is required or even negotiation is required before the contract is awarded.

Essentially the key stages are the pre-qualification and evaluation/assessment of the tender.

The marketing mix for organizational marketing

As with any consumer products, there is a need to tell the organizational buyer that your product exists, just as in any other type of marketing, and the specific nature of most organizations makes it fairly easy to segment the total market. However, telling the customer that your products exist is a different matter when dealing with these buyers: they are usually professional people, probably having or aiming to have a qualification as good as yours, and they are just as ambitious as you are.

Some advertisements will be useful 'to put the company on the map', but the organizational buyers will be more interested in brochures/catalogues or complete information packages explaining the company's portfolio of products and services, and price lists for standard products.

Product

The product may range from tiny components through to massive projects such as a ship or airline. Obviously, there is quite a difference between marketing small screws, in packs of several hundred each, and the marketing activities that go into a large construction of a car park or motorway.

For a product that has been designed for a specific customer, all the features required are already there, and the marketing manager can concentrate on other things. There are also products that are built to agreed international standards so that they can be interchangeable, at least in theory, because the standards usually specify the dimensions and minimum performance ratings.

Place

The demand for a distributor can be very challenging, particularly with very large products, or indeed very heavy products. There is likely to be a wide distribution network, which will be similar in many ways to the wholesaler/retailer system used in consumer marketing. Therefore, some of the key areas of managing a distribution channel covered in Unit 8, 'Place promotions' will be comparable in this situation.

In addition, some manufacturers will make their products so that they exceed the minimum performances shown in the standards. This added value does distinguish the product from the rest, and can be a valuable selling point if your distributors are trained to use it.

Price

Pricing will take on a different dimension, and will be based around a variety of different methods, from negotiation through to tendering. It is often quite complex and highly competitive. You will find that there is less likelihood, however, of organizational markets switching due to price, as reliability is equally important.

In respect of available budget, this will of course vary from business to business, but it is likely that the scope of the budget will be limited and not as significant as in some consumer-based markets.

Promotion

The promotional mix itself is shown in Figure 10.3 and its major uses in Figure 10.4.

Figure 10.3 Role of the promotional mix – Source Organizational Behaviour – Hill and Hillyer

Types	Use
Public relations	As in all forms of marketing, to secure favourable mention and restrict and/or counter unfavourable. With trade press and industry specific features in the major newspapers there is ample opportunity to create PR opportunities.
Press advertising	National press is broadband and not often cost-effective, with the obvious exceptions of those organizations who operate in the customer markets and thus allow the industrial marketer to ride along if brand extension has been achieved.
Trade press	Highly targeted. Most effective for awareness and to stimulate a first response perhaps via a reader's enquiry service. Major oppotunity for linked advertising and PR. Quality of trade journals varies widely.
Direct marketing	Mainly direct mail because many lists exist. Need to be careful to select with care and shorten where possible. Can be very important to develop one's own list and protect it rigorously.
Directories	Very valuable for services in paricular. *Yellow pages* and *Talking pages* are extremely effective for certain businesses. Beware not to subscribe to an unknown directory and never pay for space without having ordered it first.
Exhibitions	Most valuable in many areas. An opportunity to display product, to meet with existing customers, to develop and qualify leads and to sell (many forget that they can sell from a stand!). Also a valuable opportunity for competitive contact and research. Should be used positively, never simply to 'show the flag'.
Brochures, sales literature	Educational and informative, they should supplement, not be expected to carry the whole message. A range of mix and match, targeted literature will be needed in most areas.
Audio-visual	Can be simply educational and ephemeral but can also be used to positive effect if designed to achieve something that is otherwise difficult, such as a visit to a remote location. Can be mounted in the buyer's office using easily portable equipment as part of a sales pitch.
Computer	Few salespeople are today properly equipped without the ability to interrogate a database whilst with the buyer. Quotations can be printed on the spot, as can contracts. Via a modem a link to a senior manager can be established and a deal struck. Computers will support audio-visual presentations that can easily be tailored to need ahead of each visit.
Sales promotion	It is possible in some markets to add a 'temporary inducement at point-of-sale'. Not to be confused with discounts, however, unless SP gifts are of low value they may be perceived as bribes. It is better to target them on benefits to the organization or the department, not on the buyer.
Give-aways	Can be useful as reminders of phone numbers, etc. They also provide an opportunity to make contact. Probably the best are the long-lasting ones such as desk pads and diaries – but these benefit from tailoring to need rather than simply being bought off the sheff with the buyer's initials added (i.e It is better to invest quite heavily and do a proper job because the give-away says a lot about you and your organization).

Figure 10.4 Major uses of the promotional mix

There are many sources of support and things that can be done to help the sales representatives and these usually involve the provision of quality catalogues, where they are appropriate, or such items as films to show your products in use. Such films and brochures can give clients a better idea of how to use the products and some of them will be flattered if you can feature their products along with your own.

The role of the salesforce could be quite intensive and involved, from actually establishing the lead through until the order placement. This might involve qualifying leads, sorting and evaluating them against an established criterion.

Quite often the promotion consists simply of the knowledge of the salesperson, and he or she must be able to help designers or get someone in who can.

For the large construction projects, which take months or years to complete, the marketing team must match the DMU in terms of rank and status, in the early stages at least.

Summary

In the organizational marketing sector, marketing takes on a totally different meaning. Many organizations still do not embrace marketing in the same way and do not necessarily have organized or structured marketing activity. This often means that marketing can be random and ad hoc in nature.

Some parts of the industrial sector suffered heavily in the late 1990s and early 2000 due to the economic strains put upon them by the strength of sterling. The effects of this are still being felt among many organizations. This is particularly relevant for organizations trading internationally, with a potential downturn in the economy being predicted as a result of the economic slowdown in the USA.

Industrial organizations will need to develop a competitive advantage, indeed a competitive edge. Therefore, in many sectors a serious cultural change may need to be initiated in order for those sectors to impact seriously upon the competitors and maintain their stake within the marketplace.

Marketing is a complex and costly process, with high levels of involvement, requiring significant financial and time investment. Many buyers will be subject to significant influences, as seen earlier in this unit. Those which you must be specifically aware of relate to four key categories:

- The business environment
- Organizational structure
- Interpersonal relations
- Individual buyer characteristics.

The critical component of any business buying situation is to ensure that a long-term sustainable relationship is established, in order that some form of buyer preference can be achieved. This, combined with the right value proposition, could potentially have a dynamic impact upon marketing success.

Question 10.4

RWS Environmental Services Ltd has decided to exploit its strengths in water treatment by targeting public authority contracts. Competitive tenders are required in this market; because RWS does not have experience, it has employed you as a Consultant. Provide a guidelines document for the company on how to prepare competitive tenders.

Marketing of services

Delivering services is people's business: only great customers and great employees can guarantee great service quality. (Hans Kasper)

There are a number of problems and challenges associated with the management and implementation of service organization, relating to a wide range of factors such as the gap between expectations and what is delivered, evidence on the service proposal being limited and different perspectives on what constitutes quality service.

In order that an organization can deliver any form of service, they will need to recognize what that actually means in practice.

The purpose of this part of the unit is to address the particular issues associated with service delivery and how the process of continuous improvement is essential to the successful implementation of service offerings.

Services defined

Dibb, Simkin, Pride and Ferrell (2001) define a service as:

An intangible product involving a deed, a performance or an effort that cannot be physically possessed.

You may recall that when examining the 'product' element of the marketing mix, we briefly looked at the intangible element of the product and noted that the product itself was normally tangible, i.e. had a physical dimension to it.

Services are usually divided into two main sectors, consumer services and business services.

- *Consumer services* include marketing in non-profit making organizations such as education, health, charities and government. Profit-making sectors include financial services, personal and professional services, leisure, entertainment and tourism.
- *Business services* include repairs and maintenance, consultancy, leasing/contract hire, transportation, recruitment, advertising, marketing research, financial services, to name but a few.

The structure of the services sector

A good benchmark of the significance of services marketing both home and abroad is the number of people employed in various service jobs.

The service sector is growing and evolving rapidly. For example, in the UK, over 64 per cent of the workforce are employed in a services related industry and, in Europe alone, over 61 per cent of the workforce are also in the services industry.

One of the main reasons for the significant growth in the services sector is related to lifestyle. It would appear that while a potential economic slowdown might be looming, the services sector will possibly suffer a little less than areas such as manufacturing, as services are now a core part of everyday existence.

In the main, people are spending more of their income on insurance packages, financial services packages, convenience services, travel and leisure and many organizations provide employees with private health packages. People now buy time. In 1999 there was an article in the *Observer* relating to families' 'purchasing time'. To enable time-starved families to spend quality time together many more people were buying services such as laundry, cleaning, gardening, take-aways, etc.

Service characteristics

The difference between product and services

There is a distinct difference between the marketing of goods and services. The one common factor is that customers purchase goods and services for one reason only – they want the benefits a product can provide. Having said that, it is critical that you understand the difference between the two.

Services have four main characteristics:
- Intangibility
- Inseparability of production and consumption
- Perishability
- Heterogeneity.

Let us look briefly at each characteristic in turn.

Intangibility

Services are intangible, because there is no physical product, nothing to be touched, tasted, smelled or heard before being purchased. The difficulty being, therefore, that the customer will be unable to perceive, imagine, or fully understand the nature of what they are to receive.

The challenge for the service provider, therefore, is to ensure that they determine the extent of intangibility and how, if necessary, tangible elements could be included to aid the understanding and expectation on the part of the customer.

A key characteristic of intangibility is that once that service performance has taken place, it cannot be used again. The performance was for that occasion only. For example, the training that you have undertaken cannot ever be delivered in exactly the same way again, it will never be repeated word for word in the same way, because effectively you have consumed the service. If the quality was poor or the standard of the course director was poor, nothing can be done about that particular performance. It could be improved for the next time, but the service would then be a different service.

Inseparability

There is a definite distinction between products that are bought and used over and over again by the same customer, and that of services which are essentially consumed as they are purchased. A simplistic example of this might be having your hair cut or staying in a hotel. Should you decide to have your hair cut by one particular stylist, then it is not possible for another client to have the same hair cut at the same time, because you have purchased it and consumed it. Another example of this would be the use of a hotel room. If you use the hotel room on the night of 1st June then nobody else can use it that night; you have consumed the service the hotel provided on the occasion.

The implication for this particular component is that the involvement of the customer in the production and delivery of the service means that the service provider must take care in what is actually being produced.

Perishability

Because services are produced and consumed at the same time, they are perishable, i.e. they cannot be stored for later sales or later usage. If the service is not used then, it cannot be used again. Again a hotel is a good example of that. If you did not use that room on the night of the 1st June and nobody else booked in the room it could not be used again on that night, because that night has now gone. If the hair appointment isn't filled, and the time passes by, then effectively that appointment has perished, gone forever.

The implications of this relate to fluctuations in demand. Those which were unexpected pose a serious threat to the organization, in that they actually lose potential income, as a result of the time of use of the service passing by.

This is quite a serious problem for the service sector. Should the appointment not be booked, the bed not slept in, the car not hired or the flight seat remain empty, each of the providers of that service have seen the service perish and therefore they cannot gain any income from time not used. This is why you can purchase last minute flights or holiday deals, as organizations would rather take less income for the provision of the service than no income at all.

Heterogeneity

Heterogeneity, or variability, effectively means difference. Going back to the example of a training course, there could be two training courses running on the same day, the same materials are being used and the rooms being used are exactly the same. The difference comes in the delivery. Each of the course directors will be different. They will have different appearances, different personal characteristics and different styles. It is unlikely that you would ever receive exactly the same service twice.

From a business perspective, the implication is that marketing services then becomes a difficult task, as each time you sell a service, there is no real guarantee that the service will be as good as you may say it is, as it is often down to human behaviour, or unfortunately and all too often true, human error. It is difficult to determine the quality and level of service provided as the service is not a product that can be quality assured before dispatch, it is produced as it is consumed. This also makes pricing the service very difficult.

The main difference between products and services is the tangible versus the intangible. Tangibility does to a degree give you guarantees of performance, of quality and of value for money. Therefore, marketing a tangible product enables you to balance the marketing mix more successfully and you are then able to deliver a key set of standards to the customer.

The uncertainties of service

As we have established, delivering service quality presents a tremendous challenge to the marketer on a day-to-day basis. From a customer's perspective, it is can be very difficult to qualify what you expect from a quality service because your personal expectations will quite often differ from others. However, from a marketing point of view, it is you and your perspective as a customer that will define how the service quality expectations are defined and delivered.

It is therefore necessary to stop for a moment and consider the interface between the service and the customer.

The main characteristics of this process can be identified thus:

- The customer is physically present, i.e. the place where the service is delivered
- The service and delivery process are interdependent (simultaneous production and consumption).

Within this interface it becomes clear that a potential 'uncertainty' arises between what the customer actually wants and what the customer is actually going to be provided with.

According to Mudie and Cottam (1999), this uncertainty arises for a number of reasons, but mostly because service deliverers fail to understand, for example, the following key customer inputs:

- Physical state of body (e.g. for a fitness clinic)
- Mental state of mind (e.g. for an education service)

- State and complexity (e.g. of a car for detecting faults during a service)
- Capacity (e.g. of clothing and carpet fabrics to withstand chemical treatment)
- Amount and nature of customer information (e.g. for medical diagnosis).

Essentially what happens is that in the above situations it becomes clear that the service provider is unsure about the customer's state of mind, which in turn, can affect their preparedness for creating and delivering an effective service.

During the service delivery, the customer can actually be portrayed as posing problems for an organization by being disruptive, rude, ignorant or even arrogant and essentially fail to comply with the service demands. Principally this is due to the lack of understanding in the interface situation and potentially the wrong fit being delivered – i.e. the wrong service to the right customers.

> **Question 10.5**
> Explain your understanding of 'customer uncertainty'

It is very rare that organizations ever supply either a pure product or a pure service, it is more often a combination of the two. For example, if you buy a new car or TV, you rarely just buy the product. It is normal for products to have warranties and customer services support as part of the value-added element of the product. This essentially means that there are two components to consider, the core service and the peripheral service.

The *core service* relates to the core technical feature of the service; for example, if you are travelling by train, the service will be to get you to your destination in a safe and reliable manner. By the same token you are taking the CIM Advanced Certificate in Marketing Course, and the service is to provide you with a learning package that provides career enhancement, self-achievement and actualization. Essentially, therefore, the core service is what is at the heart of the package, and every effort should be made to communicate this to your customers.

The *peripheral service,* however, is almost like the distribution channel, it is the way in which the service is supported or implemented, i.e. the check-in desk at the airport, the ticket office at the railway station. Therefore, the peripheral service relates to the facilitation of and support of the core service.

Meeting customer expectations

Understanding customer expectations is the same as understanding customer buying behaviour. However, on this occasion understanding the behaviour and perceptions before and after the event is essential, in order to understand whether the service either exceeds expectations, meets expectations or indeed fails to meet expectations.

According to Mudie and Cottam (1999), service organizations need to understand and recognize the importance of the first law of services, which states:

Satisfaction = perception − expectation

However, as you can imagine, this is likely to be quite a subjective measure, as everybody's interpretation is probably different.

Measuring consumer perceptions in the service industry is essential in order that continuous improvement can be adopted, and that the appropriate market mix is designed. Essentially, the role of the organization will be to determine the views of the customers, against the perception of the organization.

The services mix

The marketer has a full tool bag when it comes to marketing services; there are the traditional 4Ps: product, price, place and promotion. In addition to that there are the physical environment, the people and processes – the other 3Ps that ultimately give the opportunity to establish a high-quality service provision on behalf of the organization.

The physical environment – physical evidence

The physical element of the marketing mix relates to the physical environment, the place from where the services are prepared and delivered. For example, the restaurant where you go to have a meal out is the physical environment. The restaurant is where the service is delivered and consumed.

From a marketing perspective it does help support the marketing of services as the physical element of the service brings some consistency and guarantee of quality and does enable the basis for a brand to be established and built upon. There are many examples of this, for example with chain restaurants such as Pizza Hut, BeefEaters, Brewers Fayre, etc. They are all well-known brands where the physical environment has played a significant role in relation to service delivery.

The physical environment can be represented in quite simple ways, through staff wearing uniforms, similar interior design and often the same menus, special offers and promotions. This is reassuring for the customer, to know that the brand is meaningful and familiar.

Therefore, when establishing a marketing mix for services, the physical environment plays a significant role in stabilizing the quality perception of the organization, similar to the way in which a product can.

People

I am sure that you are aware that services can be administered both mechanically, e.g. on the Internet, or through automated voice handling mechanisms, but also through a physical human contribution.

The people element of the mix is quite complex in that the one big inconsistency in planning for the marketing mix is human nature. The role of customer-facing personnel is very difficult and demanding and at times extremely frustrating. Therefore, it is difficult not to let that frustration show and affect the level of customer service then being delivered.

The people element of the marketing mix in today's marketing environment is critical, as customer service is seen to be one other major value-added component of the customer's overall purchasing experience.

Managing the people's aspect of the marketing mix requires a high degree of interpersonal skills and a strong internal marketing programme, whereby the internal members of staff, 'people', have their roles and responsibilities and overall contribution to the purchasing process communicated to them. For them to be effective and for the organization to go some way towards guaranteeing quality, the people's aspect of the mix must include:

- *Investing in staff and training* – product and organizational training.
- *Empowerment of staff* – encouraging staff to be involved to make a contribution.
- *Internal marketing* – communicating to them and motivating them to achieve.
- *Decision-making capacity* – to enable staff, within their empowerment factor, to make decisions relating to the delivery of the service.

Sadly, one of the most significant impacts upon the service industry, the Internet, is reducing the number of people involved in customer service delivery and is effectively very process-oriented.

Process

The process element of the marketing mix will always need to be managed with the customer in mind, what are their expectations, their needs and wants in relation to the service experience?

Process is about developing processes for the delivery of service that will add value to the customer experience. For example, when staying in a hotel, you would expect the booking in and out process to be concise, fast and efficient. To add value to the customer experience when staying in hotels, many of them put your bill under the door for your information, overnight, which makes checking out faster and efficient.

The process of booking a holiday or flight should be the same. The customer requires the whole service to be a positive experience; therefore, processes are critical to that value-added aspect of the product or service.

The impact of the Internet upon process

One of the reasons that many organizations are being drawn to the Internet is for the advancement and continuous improvement in customer services, but also to ensure that customer service is more cost-effective to deliver.

Currently, on the process side of the marketing mix, the Internet is still causing many aggravations and frustrations. You have probably heard of or experienced the process of filling your shopping basket on-line, only for the server to go down and 30 minutes shopping input to be lost. While this is a technological problem it is also a service process problem, which means that organizations need to understand the technology requirements, time-out settings, etc. on personal computers and give more guidance and advice on purchasing a service through this mechanism.

A further example of process is automated voice handling. Many financial services organizations have developed a process for enabling customers to ring through, giving them a number of options to choose from. This then means that they can go through to the right department and not waste time working their way around the organization trying to find the correct person to speak to. Clearly there are disadvantages with this process, for example waiting for long periods to get answers, but the process is now becoming common practice.

E-mail looks like an exchange of letters. In reality it is a form of speech – it is conversation. But it is speech without gestures. No smiles to take the edge off tough statements or nods.

Question 10.6
Explain with examples the importance of the 3Ps of the services mix.

The marketing mix in the context of services

The marketing mix does play a role, as has been suggested now on a number of occasions but the lack of tangibility poses a serious problem to its design and implementation.

Product

You have to convert this to think in terms of benefits, but there also are often products associated with services and the products may have a big influence. The 'product' of dry cleaning is the cleaner clothing, or the benefit of clean curtains that would not fit in your electric washing machine. The benefit may also be psychological rather than physical.

Price

Price reflects quality levels, whether we like it or not. The basic idea of charging as much as customers will pay may be reasonable for products where customers have a choice of whether or not to buy the product, but would that be reasonable for essential services, such as business consultancy, secretarial services, medical and dental treatment? This is actually like asking a question 'How long is a piece of string?' The price charged for a service will be based around the service value proposition, the levels of tangibility that might offset concerns about levels of intangibility. Therefore, when the delivery of a service provides a tangible benefit, pricing becomes more objective. Of course other factors such as demand and market forces will play a significant role.

At the end of the day, evaluating value in terms of price is highly subjective, however, the price of a service can create demand and entice customers.

In a more traditional manner, travel companies do charge according to demand – if you travel by rail at peak periods you pay a lot more than you would if you went later in the day. The same applies to electricity – there are much lower 'off-peak' charges in the night because the demand is lower then but the generators still have to run.

Place

One of the key characteristics of services is that the actual service provider may deliver them directly to you. However, there are a lot of services that do not involve the customer being present. You can transfer money via the Internet or telephone banking, you can order flowers, all of which are away from the place of service delivery. However, physical evidence can play an important part in this, for example within a bank, hotel or restaurant, when the role of the place becomes quite important.

Promotion

We have already given several examples of the promotion of services, such as those offered by Egg, Lufthansa and easyJet. Promoting services is more difficult the higher the level of intangibility, and there is a likelihood of customer uncertainty being aroused.

We are all subject, on a daily basis, to a surge of advertisements, promotions and direct mail in relation to financial services, pensions, holidays, flights, rail travel – the list is endless. There is probably a close correlation between the levels of advertising for services and that for products. The justification of the core service has to be at the heart of the message for customers to listen, retain and respond.

Service positioning will be a big issue in establishing the core values of the service and therefore this will need careful consideration in the context of any promotional activity.

Principally, whatever the promotion, 'don't promise what you can't deliver'.

The key components of designing a services mix

While we have looked at the importance of the 7Ps in relation to the marketing mix, we also need to consider the eleven design elements that run in parallel with the 7Ps. Mudie and Cottam (1999) suggest that the following design principles are considered:

- *Customer contact* – what is the level of contact between the organization and the customer during the delivery of the service?
- *Service mix* – how many service offerings will there be, how effective will they be, what will the services portfolio consist of?

- *Location* – should the service go to the customer, or the customer be drawn to the service?
- *Design* – practical design extends from basic logos and letterheads through to uniforms, physical structures and therefore is a component of the 7Ps.
- *Technology* – what technology will be required for the delivery of the service – will it be reliable, what are the customer expectations and what will the impact be?
- *Employees* – success will hinge on the organizational culture, the level of support, the strength of internal marketing, the appropriate and adequate resource base to support them in their work.
- *Structure* – the structure will go a long way towards determining the organizational culture and establishing lines of command.
- *Information* – good MIS systems will be useful in ensuring appropriate levels of information are available to support the service delivery and understand customer expectations.
- *Demand* – the level of demand for a service will affect the standards of delivery.
- *Procedures* – as in process – it is essential to understand the nature of the processes required for successful execution of the service.
- *Control* – the only way in which continuous improvement can be understood and quality standards measured is through a range of monitoring and control processes.

The importance of service quality

People, physical evidence, process – these three elements of the marketing mix are critical to the delivery of exceptional service quality. They are responsible for reducing waiting times, long check-in lines at the airport, getting quick answers on financial services packages, to name but a few.

It will always be difficult for service-related organizations to deliver 100 per cent quality, but with the complete marketing mix at its disposal, service should be improving all the time.

When it comes to marketing a service versus a product the considerations are the same for delivering service quality (see Figure 10.5). Service-related organizations should always consider:

- What the customers expects
- Service specifications (in the same way as there are product specifications)
- Employee performance – quality of their delivery, training needs
- Managing customer service expectations – making sure quality is achieved.

```
┌─────────────┐  ┌─────────────┐  ┌─────────────┐  ┌─────────────┐
│ Understand  │  │   Service   │  │  Employees  │  │  Managing   │
│  customer   │  │specifications│  │   (people)  │  │   service   │
│expectations │  │             │  │             │  │expectations │
└──────┬──────┘  └──────┬──────┘  └──────┬──────┘  └──────┬──────┘
       └────────────────┴────────┬───────┴────────────────┘
                                 ▼
                ┌────────────────────────────────┐
                │       Service Quality          │
                │         Reliability            │
                │       Responsiveness           │
                │         Assurance              │
                │          Empathy               │
                │ Tangible/intangible dimensions │
                └────────────────────────────────┘
```

Figure 10.5 The dynamics of service quality – SERVQUAL

Managing the differing levels of quality in services is, as we have established, more difficult than for goods overall, as a result of issues relating to levels of tangibility and intangibility.

Quality management has to be based around the three key elements of the services marketing mix: the people, the physical evidence and the process. Analysis of performance in each of these areas would help the organization ascertain their position both from a customer perspective and a competitive perspective. High scores or rating in each of these is likely to be a positive factor. If it is the reverse, there are some severe financial penalties to face.

Quality measurements and quality objectives are highly important and will be the basis in establishing customer perception and achieving customer satisfaction. Principally, promises that are made should be kept.

Performance relates to the delivery of the product by staff, and it is essential in that respect that there is strong internal marketing support in order that the ethos of the organization shines through, that staffs are highly motivated and influence the basis of consumer perceptions of the service.

Implementing a quality culture

Quality can be used as a tool for competitive advantage, and can be a powerful strategic weapon within the organization. This would include addressing the following elements:

- Innovation
- Status
- Leadership
- Rewards
- Values
- Developments of a learning organization
- Empowerment to achieve challenging goals.

The successful measurement of a quality culture may manifest itself in the following ways:
- People see for themselves the needs for quality management tools
- Motivators and champions start to emerge
- People talk of processes and not of functions
- People volunteer to take on tasks, which previously have involved considerable management intervention.

The quality guru Claus Moller suggested that there are 12 golden rules to aid quality implementation and improvement, all of which are particularly pertinent to the delivery of good quality service:
- Set personal and corporate quality goals
- Establish personal accountability
- Check how satisfied customers are with your efforts
- Regard the next link as a valued customer
- Avoid error
- Perform task more effectively
- Utilize resources well
- Be committed
- Learn to finish what you have started
- Control stress
- Be ethical
- Demand quality.

Moller emphasized the need for administrative procedures to improve rather than an improvement in the delivery process, as it is often the one that lets the other down. He further emphasized the need to use checklists, personal performance standards, ideal performance levels and actual performance levels (Moller, 1988).

Essentially, quality is the key to success, and in the context of services people are the key to achievement.

Monitoring and evaluating service

There are a number of key issues that impact upon quality measurement:
- The difference in perception between employees and customers
- The inseparability of production and consumption
- The individuality of employees' performance and customers' perceptions.

There is a proposed formula for measuring these components:
- *Customer expectations – service organizations' perceptions of customer expectations*
- *Customer experience – service organizations' perceptions of customer experience.*

This is based on the different expectations of 20 customers receiving the same service, and is probably very subjective as each of them will feel differently and therefore the analysis could be rather inconclusive. However, while the feedback might be diverse, it is likely that some useful information might manifest itself in order that future improvements might be made.

To be able to continuously improve the level of service offered, to understand the gaps, the confusion, the customer uncertainties, the following monitoring and evaluation processes could be implemented:
- Marketing research – to gather information about services, and delivery of them
- Data collection – frequent reviews

- Observing respondents as they receive the service
- Interviewing respondents to understand their perceptions and expectations versus their experience
- Customer satisfaction surveys – questionnaires to monitor customer satisfaction
- Mystery consumer experience – include a mystery person in the delivery of the service
- Evaluating dissatisfaction – examine the main causes of customer dissatisfaction
- Monitoring image – how is the image of the service perceived
- Performance appraisals – of staff involved in the delivery of the service
- Employee group discussions – internal marketing practice.

There is a particular model known as SERVQUAL that aids the measurement of service delivery.

SERVQUAL seeks to measure quality within the service sector and looks closely at five factors as listed below:

- Reliability – ability to perform the promised service dependably and accurately.
- Responsiveness – willingness to help customers and provide a prompt service.
- Assurance – knowledge and courtesy of employees and their ability to inspire trust and confidence.
- Empathy – caring, individual attention the organization provides its customers.
- Tangibles – physical facilities, equipment, appearance of personnel.

SERVQUAL measures the gap between customer and management perceptions of the quality issue.

The gaps, highlighted by B. G. Dale, *Managing Quality* (1994) are as follows:

Gap 1 – Consumer expectations – managers' perceptions of consumers' expectations

Gap 2 – Managers' perceptions of consumer's expectations – service quality specifications actually set

Gap 3 – Service quality specifications – actual service delivery

Gap 4 – Actual service delivery – external communications about the service

Gap 5 – Resources.

Quality and reliability are often used synonymously. Part of the appeal and acceptability of a product or service will depend on its ability to function satisfactorily over a period of time, and also a measure of reliability.

You will be familiar with the meaning of each one of these through your work in Management Information for Marketing Decisions and the Marketing Customer Interface and Effective Management for Marketing. In addition to this, evaluation tools have been continually discussed throughout the text.

> **Question 10.7**
> Why is it important to evaluate the delivery of services?

Summary

Marketing to organizations and industries is different in practice from consumer marketing, but uses the same principles. The demand is managed differently and the buying process has to be accepted as it is. Quite often the delivery in the time promised is more important than price alone.

The range of marketing opportunities is very wide and the range of products can be bewildering. The buyers are professionals, and their motives for buying are quite different from those of consumers. Instead of looking at their own individual needs they will be accountable to the organization for making the right purchase decision in order for the supply chain to function satisfactorily.

The 4Ps can still apply to marketing to organizations but with a different emphasis. Distribution of some products is similar to that for consumer goods, but there are also some quite big differences.

There is a stronger need to maintain a competitive edge, because of the professionalism of the buyers and the competitors.

The importance of services in the modern economy is shown by the fact that Britain, and most other developed countries, are now service economies, with more than 50 per cent of gross spending being on services and 64 per cent of the workforce employed in services.

Services have to be marketed but there are more differences than similarities with the marketing of products. The problems arise from the features of services – their intangibility, inseparability from the provider, perishability and the impossibility of stocking up for future sale. There is also the potential variation of quality due to the fact that people, who vary in performance day by day, provide the services.

The marketing mix for services includes the 4Ps of product marketing, with the addition of people, physical evidence and the process or methods of providing the service. However, the importance of the eleven elements of design should not be underestimated.

Ultimately, as with all marketing strategies, plans and implementation of various marketing mixes, the quality of the product and service provision should be a matter of 'excellence'.

Further study and examination preparation

Study tip

Because of the growing importance and influence of services in the economy, it is natural that this should be reflected in the syllabus and the examination. Therefore a total grasp of the subject will be vital.

In the same token, business-to-business applications play a major role and are frequently the source of exam questions.

The test will be of your ability to apply marketing in a variety of different contexts, this means organizational marketing, services marketing, international marketing and not-for-profit-marketing. In doing this you will develop very versatile marketing skills that will make your transition from one industry to another a little smoother than perhaps it might be.

Extending knowledge

Recommended reading

In addition to reading your recommended text, you will find it useful to gain a more in-depth understanding of some of the services issues by reading the following chapters from *The Management of Marketing Services* by Peter Mudie and Angela Cottam – Chapters 1, 3, 5, 10, 11 and 12

Question 10.8

June 2000, Question 7

Go to www.marketingonline.co.uk or www.bh.com/marketing to access Specimen Answers and Senior Examiner's advice for this exam question.

Unit 11
Charity and not-for-profit marketing

Objectives

This unit looks at the role of marketing within charities and not-for-profit organizations. The profile of charities and the work that they undertake has risen significantly in the last 10 years. Originally charities did not involve themselves heavily in the function of marketing. However, as there is more and more work to undertake, and more and more competition in respect of gaining charitable donations and grants, they have had to implement a more marketing-oriented approach, and take a competitive stance in order to survive and undertake the work they feel destined to do.

The indicative content of the syllabus underpinning this learning outcome is:

- Objectives differ from consumer/industrial markets
- Target markets (donors, volunteers, clients)
- Marketing mix differences (product usually ideas and services rather than goods, short distribution channels, approach to pricing, promotion emphasis on PR and face-to-face fund raising)
- Performance hard to measure.

(Syllabus reference 1.4.3)

Charities – non-business marketing

One of the certainties in life is that we need money to survive, as few things in this world can be either acquired or achieved without money. The key role of any charity therefore, has to be to generate income in order to achieve the aims and objectives defined by the board and management of the charity. Increasingly, charities are recognizing the value of marketing, and there has been a distinct change, as more and more charities emerge into the arena of different forms of retailing, sponsorship and event organizations. However, their approach to retailing takes on very different dynamics to that of a traditional retailer.

Charities as retailers work very much on a non-business-marketing basis. The shops are stocked with goods that mainly have been donated, and therefore the necessity to purchase stock does not exist at the same level. In addition to this, charity shops are manned by volunteer workers, therefore payroll costs are a minimum in comparison to mainstream retailers.

Many of the bigger charities involve themselves in 'high-profile charitable events', for example Children in Need, Red Nose Day and the London Marathon, or various 'party in the park' type events, or major rock/pop festivals, probably the most significant event of this type being 'Live Aid' run by Bob Geldof. In hosting and managing these events the benefits include considerable publicity, both in terms of TV and press coverage, and usually fairly significant donations.

One of the major differences between profit-making and non-profit-making businesses is that their perspective on life provides for an interesting range of dynamics. As profit-making business are very focused on making money, charities are focused and dedicated to changing people's lives and really making a difference in the most horrendous situations.

> ## Case history
>
> **Ronald McDonald House Charities**
>
> *New Ronald McDonald Care Mobile Programme*
>
> To help address the growing need for access to health care for millions of children worldwide, Ronald McDonald House Charities announce the launch of a fleet of Ronald McDonald Care Mobiles, mobile paediatric healthcare units that deliver free medical and dental care directly to underserved children in their own neighbourhoods. Plans call for 12 mobile healthcare programmes in operation by the end of 2001 and a projected 40 by the end of 2005, making this one of the most extensive mobile healthcare programmes ever undertaken.
>
> Ronald McDonald House Charities will launch the first Ronald McDonald House Care mobile outside of the US later this month in Buenos Aires, Argentina. Through the Ronald McDonald Care Mobile Programme, McDonalds see that they can be part of the solution to the serious healthcare access problem facing children today.
>
> The Ronald McDonald Care Mobile helps reduce reliance on expensive and inappropriate health resources, such as hospital emergency departments. The programme also provides continuity of care by providing follow-up services and referrals to primary care physician, dentist or paediatric sub-specialists and helping eligible families enrol in a government assisted health insurance programme such as 'Insure Kids Now'.
>
> *Background of Ronald McDonald Charities*
>
> 166 Ronald McDonald House Charities in 33 countries around the world, 207 Ronald McDonald houses in 18 countries and a legion of more those 25,000 volunteers. Ronald McDonald House has helped millions of children and their families in local communities around the world.
>
> Ronald McDonald House Charities, a not-for-profit organization, creates, funds and supports programmes that directly improve the health and well being of children. The Charity makes grants to not-for-profit organizations and provides support for all Ronald McDonald Houses and Mobiles. To date they have contributed some $300 million to children's programmes.
>
> www.rmhc.org
>
> Source: Lexis-Nexis

Typically the Board for a charity will comprise of a number of professionals who will be ultimately responsible for the effectiveness of the organization in supporting appropriate causes. They will be responsible for allocation of funds, utilization of resources and a number of specialist activities that the charity might be planning to embark upon.

The source of funds for not-for-profit organizations will come from a range of government bodies, lottery funds, trust funds and in some instances corporate funds from large organizations who support the specific work of the not-for-profit organizations, particularly if there is vested interest in their work.

That covers all the services we mentioned above, but it could also cover a lot of the most visible charities, such as the Red Wings Horse and Donkey Sanctuary, which runs a thriving mail-order business. Profits from the mail order business are reinvested directly back into the business for future care and development work.

Marketing planning for charities

Setting objectives

You will have noticed by now that all marketing activities start with some measurable objectives, and so it is with charities and non-profit-making organizations, although the measurement of achievement is not always so straightforward.

The prime objective of charities will reflect their desire to enhance the quality of lives. For example, a typical objective might be 'To serve the needs and wants of the "users" through the financial contributions, time and support of the public donor'.

The objectives in general terms tend to be used as an umbrella for several more specific objectives, which deal with problems that occur from time to time. This makes the measurement of achievement of the objectives, in the marketing sense, difficult. Marketers are used to dealing in money terms, or units sold, but that is not possible for the work of, say, helping to save sea birds from polluted seas, or of saving an old building so that future generations can enjoy the view from the balcony.

Essentially, the most likely objectives that charitable organizations will seek to achieve is to gain surplus funds through donations and sales of merchandised products, so that they can use the income generated to achieve their objectives. Therefore, the role of the Charitable Trust Board and its members will be to ensure that the income is properly and appropriately managed.

The objectives set will very much be formed on basis of the nature and purpose of the marketing audit undertaken. This auditing activity will be essential in determining the scale of the charitable needs in the 'users marketplace' to gain a full understanding of the level of donations required and how they might be appropriated in the future. This essentially allows organizations to clearly define their 'marketing opportunities'.

Typical auditing will obviously be upon a SLEPT basis, but with a particular focus on some of the following areas:

- Other similar charitable activities (competitive charities)
- Research into focused areas of needs
- Breadth and depth of the situation
- Economic situation of area of country involved
- Taxation benefits for charitable giving
- Facts and figures in relation to the number of potential users in one market
- Resources available
- Scale of user needs
- Levels of charitable giving in these areas previously
- Level of publicity in relation to user problems
- Political influence and involvement in particular area of need and available funding
- Social responsiveness to charitable giving
- Legal loopholes for charities
- Trends on the most popular forms of attracting donations.

These are just a few ranges of information that might be needed to underpin the objective-setting and strategy development of the charitable organization.

Marketing segmentation and targeting for charities

The market segmentation process for charities consists of closely targeting individuals who are able to support the charity through donations of money, equipment and time in order to assist them in meeting the objectives of the charity and meeting the needs of their users.

The key targets for charities will include:
- *Donors* – those who give funds and equipment
- *Volunteers* – those who will give their time and effort to support the charitable cause
- *Clients* – i.e. users of the charitable trusts, funds and services.

Obviously in mainstream marketing of profit-making organizations the segmentation process is very scientific, and focuses on the whole range of marketing mix activities, such as targeting customers for different variations of the marketing mix.

Charity marketing has to offer some benefit, and that is not always easy to visualize. The flag days have the answer – you put some money in the box, and in return get a flag to stick on your clothing to show that you have paid up. Because the feeling of well being that comes from donating some of your hard-earned money soon wears off, it is essential for the charity to provide a tangible indicator of your generosity, usually in the form of a flag or sticker, which serves as a tangible reminder of your willingness to support the charity concerned.

That is one aspect of the marketing activities of charities, but there is a further vast 'target market' in companies. If some of the profits made by companies can be donated to charities, the improvement in funding might be quite dramatic. This is rather different from appealing to the individual – the company has no conscience and cannot get the benefit of 'feeling good' because of having donated some money.

Marketing planning and control

Planning is as vital to charitable organizations as it is to any commercial venture, as it is necessary to take a structured approach to implementation in order to achieve the objectives defined by the charitable board.

However, planning takes on two dimensions:
- To generate high levels of income from donations
- To allocate and apportion funds to particular products efficiently and effectively.

It is essential that considerable control be implemented over the planning process, in order that levels of accountability can always be achieved. Therefore, monitoring and control processes should be implemented in order that evidence of fund management can be provided. Objectives will be SMART in the same way as commercial objectives are.

While there has been a focus on voluntary workers earlier on, there are paid staff who deal with corporate fund-raising and therefore have played a different role, because they have to show the public and charitable stakeholders that they are above reproach in the way in which they manage charitable funds. However, there are also donors who like to gain high profile coverage of their donations, and who like to see that there is a measurable commercial benefit in giving money, or lending facilities to a charity.

It is likely that many of the significant donors will want ultimate recognition for their contributions, as this is a way of reaping commercial benefits. Therefore, publicity of this nature has to be jointly managed by the charity and the organization for mutual benefit and gain. Charitable managers must therefore ensure that the credibility of the donor is satisfactory in order that there is no backlash of public support, due to the dubious nature of donors.

However, the approach taken to marketing planning is slightly different in nature, while the marketing mix does have similar characteristics. Therefore, it is essential at this time to look at the nature of not-for-profit organizations and compare and contrast them with profit-making organizations, before looking at the combined approach to the marketing mix. In respect of control, there will be a number of key areas that the charities should involve themselves in the measurement of:
- The environment in which they operate
- Consistency and quality in the level of service offered

- Customer satisfaction
- Competence of staff and ability to manage and implement programmes effectively
- Effects of internal and external communications.

> **Question 11.1**
>
> Explain three key methods of acquiring donations for charities?

> **Question 11.2**
>
> Who are the three important audiences a charity needs to target and why are they so important?

What is a non-profit-making organization?

While there are a number of definitions for non-profit-making organizations they are not universally agreed.

> **Definition**
>
> **Non-profit-making organization**
>
> An organization whose prime goal is non-economic. However, in pursuit of that goal it may undertake profit-making activities.

> **Definition**
>
> **Alternative non-profit-business marketing**
>
> Activities conducted by individuals and organizations to achieve some goal other than ordinary business goals of profit, market share or return on investment. Source: Dibb, Simkin, Pride and Ferrell

Charity is not the only form of 'not-for-profit-marking' organization. There are many other types of organizations. Bodies such as the armed forces, police, probation service, ambulance service and a number of support societies are also not-for-profit marketing organizations.

The determination of non-profit-making realistically relates to the focus and objectives of the business. The whole ethos of not-for-profit organizations relates to the use of funds for particular reasons; they are accountable for the specific allocations of funds against objectives. Accountability in not-for-profit organizations is a serious business.

Not-for-profit marketing versus profit marketing

A not-for-profit marketing organization typically faces a very different range of challenges in terms of both managing and marketing their business. In the absence of a product or service to sell in the same way as profit-making organizations, its marketing focus is primarily to provide a range of products and essential support services for little or indeed no charge to the user. It will usually have multiple objectives and multiple publics, to whom it offers multiple services, but the funder of the service is different from the receiver.

Principally, profit-making organizations focus their attention on a number of profitable markets that have very tightly defined profitable targets. This purpose of the profit-making will not only be to cover their overhead costs from the income generated from the sales of products and services, but to provide a dividend for shareholders and to generate funds for investment in growth and diversification opportunities. Profit-making organizations such as business-to-business, consumer, industrial or services-related industries have in the main been the focus of marketing in the context of this book.

While the focus of profit-making organizations customer base is customers and consumers, the focus of a charity will be on the receivers, the people who benefit from their services, who indeed then effectively become the 'user'.

For not-for-profit organizations, marketing is now playing a pivotal role in raising considerable funds that will not only serve the 'receivers' end of the service, but also fund the management and resourcing of the charity. There has, however, been a lot of controversy about mismanagement and misuse of funds within charities.

Therefore the focus of marketing for non-profit-making organizations will principally be on attracting substantial donations, equipment and voluntary support in order that they can achieve the defined objectives of the organizations.

Many non-profit-making organizations have very scarce resources and often struggle to achieve their corporate objectives, but the challenges they face are very demanding and very different, as the stakeholder audience is often extensive.

Case history

New organization to raise profile of British Seed Industry

Seed producers and merchants have a new voice to promote homegrown seed in Britain. The British Association of Seed Producers has been established to raise the profile of the British seed industry in the face of growing competition from multinationals.

The BASP, which has evolved from the WHD Seed Growers Ltd, aims to maintain high seed quality standards and liaise with other national bodies such as the Ministry of Agriculture, the British Society of Plant Breeders and the National Institute of Agricultural Botany.

Chief Executive David Buttle said the *non-profit making* seed organization would be recruiting a national core membership of growers and merchants, plus support from organizations covering the whole spectrum of industry.

Source: Lexis-Nexis

The motivational factors influencing not-for-profit marketing and profitable organizations

All organizations, both profit and not-for-profit, will benefit from having a clearly defined understanding of the customer base, i.e. consumers or users. Therefore, in that respect, there are many similarities in the motivation of both profit-making and non-profit-making organizations, in that they both need income to survive.

The profit-making organization needs income to enable it to survive, to aid continuous improvement, and to meet profit objectives and shareholder objectives. The non-profit-making organization also needs income to survive, and to continue to provide a considerable service to needy and worthy causes, but the income is channelled in different directions.

The main difference in respect of motivation is the use of the word 'profit'. Both organizations are committed to generating as much money as possible, but effectively the use of that money is very different.

The non-profit-making organization does not make a profit in the same sense that perhaps a profit-making organization does. Whatever the source of income, it will be directly invested back into the organization whereby all money will go into supporting the work of the business.

Therefore, while motivational factors may be similar to a degree, the word 'profit' creates different dynamics for the diverse nature of the organizations. So while profit motivates profit-making organizations, the focus of delivering a range of invaluable services is the main motivation of not-for-profit organizations.

Marketing planning for not-for-profit marketing

Setting objectives

The nature and dynamics of objectives for this particular sector differ again. For example, the objectives of a church might be to 'inform the public about the doctrine of the church and encourage a growth in church membership'. This is particularly relevant as recent statistics have shown a drastic reduction in church membership of the last 10 years.

The most likely source of funds in the case of not-for-profit organizations may be from government sources, lottery funds, and local authorities or industrial support for the purpose of the project. In addition to this, income might be generated by membership subscriptions and charitable donations. In the Church of England, for example, the money will come from church offerings, donations and tax benefits, among others.

Setting objectives and controlling them may prove difficult for the marketer working in not-for-profit organizations. A marketing manager employed by a charity may have the same type of ambitions as his or her opposite number in a profit-making organization, and he or she may not think that the objectives which are aimed at by the charity will provide the career advancement opportunities that he or she wants, and so perhaps may think they should be changed.

Marketing planning and control

It is essential that in order to control the achievement of objectives, through the implementation of the marketing plan, not-for-profit managers use the range of information that they should have collected through undertaking some form of marketing audit, to define objectives and implement a range of controls.

Controls will be based around the product/services mix, in order that quality is maintained and standards delivered. In addition to this, financial controls must be in place to ensure that funds are pulled in, in order to achieve the objectives defined by the organization.

While the principles are the same, sometimes, because of the nature of the organization, and the number of volunteers involved, the waters become a little muddied, and the overall objectives of the organization fail to be achieved.

Objectives, while SMART, can be difficult to measure. While objectives might be related to creating an awareness, it will be difficult to determine the level of awareness as perhaps advertising is not measured in the same mechanical way as it is with commercial organizations.

However, in organizations such as universities, a very business-like approach is now taken to planning and control, with an increasing emphasis on accountability, quality and service levels. They have had no choice but to change the way they operate to be much more business-oriented and focused.

> **Question 11.3**
>
> In what ways do not-for-profit organizations differ from mainstream commercial organizations?

Managing the marketing mix – charities and not-for-profit marketing organizations

Charities and non-profit-making organizations are more similar to services than to manufacturers, and it may put their marketing into perspective if we try to see how the 7Ps of service marketing fit in with their activities. However, one thing that should be considered in developing and optimizing the effect of the marketing mix is the ability for each charity to retain some form of competitive advantage, in terms of gaining preference for charity giving to their own organization.

- *Product* – is equivalent to the benefit that charities provide to donors; the feeling of well being, either for the individual or the staff and management of the commercial enterprise. A similar 'benefit' is gained from the efforts of those involved in the British Seed Growers Association in the case study, but this is less obvious.

- *Place* – you may think that 'place' is not important to the collectors of money for charities, because all money is of equal value wherever it comes from. However, in some instances it is vitally important, with the need for charity shops to play a significant role in income generation. For Oxfam in particular, this is a vital source of income, therefore distribution of stores on an intensive basis as possible is desirable.

- *Promotion* – is very relevant, as has been seen earlier in the text, with sponsorship, publicity and PR playing a major role in the marketing activities. There is a heavy involvement in direct marketing and specifically targeting homeowners to donate to charities on a regular basis.

    Promotion of non-profit-making organizations is increasing and becoming much more high profile in order that they may gain support, membership and potentially donations to further enhance the work they undertake. This may be more focused in terms of specialist journals, relevant to the organizations, and direct mailing base.

- *Price* – as a concept will vary between both charities and non-profit-making organizations. For charities, price will hold two interests, the amount of money generated and the cost of programme implementation.

    However, the not-for-profit-making local authority assesses the amount of money they will need for the next year, then works out the amount to be charged to each household.

- *People* – certainly matter in charities and in non-profit-making organizations: the charities depend on lots of non-paid-for help from volunteers, and the work that they do, in marketing terms, is very much 'people-oriented'. All the various non-profit-making organizations are people-oriented too. There are people involved in the interface with the public, naturally, and the characteristics of these people can make the marketing activities more, or less, effective depending on how well they relate to other people.
- *Physical evidence* – is needed – if you know what a charity will achieve with your donation you may feel disposed to give more money, and when you have to pay for the services of the local authority, without much choice, you do expect to see some physical evidence of the use of the money.
- *Process* – in charity and non-profit-making organization terms is making it easy to donate your money. The charities collect money from you in the street, or at your home, and they all show you how to make your contribution more effectively. The days of the street collection may be numbered, as people complain that there are too many of them.

The non-profit-making organizations seldom have to ask the public to be donors, because their funds come directly or indirectly from some form of public source, but their dealings with the public must still be smooth and efficient. The public are often in the position of customers and owners, although the ownership is indirect.

Case history

Charities' attitude to communication

A survey of 100 not-for-profit making organizations, mainly charitable trusts, was undertaken by Oasis Media in order to ascertain their attitude towards media. This research was revealed exclusively to *PR Week* by Oasis Media (April 2001).

The results of the survey clearly indicated that charities are approaching communications more professionally and far more sharply than ever before. It would appear that charities recognize the need for the brand to be seen and therefore communications are becoming brand-led.

Some of the findings were as follows:

- The most used technique was *promotional material* used by 98 per cent of the charities surveyed
- The *Internet* is the next most popular method used, by way of reaching target audiences and is now used by over 89 per cent of charities, with an average of 12 per cent of the marketing budget being spent on the Internet. Two million pounds was raised through the Internet on Red Noise Day in 2001, believed to be the largest amount ever raised online by one single charity; 46 per cent of charities suggested they now have a web-strategy
- Pure *media relations* as a tool was used by 85 per cent of charities surveyed
- *Public affairs* used by 58 per cent
- *Direct marketing* was used by 76 per cent
- *Sponsorship* by 65 per cent.

> However, the majority of this work is still undertaken in-house in many instances as many not-for-profit marketing organizations still view with some caution and indeed scepticism, believing that the charity culture is too big a leap for agencies to make. It is perceived that educating an agency team in the ways of charity marketing is possibly too time-consuming and could be less-cost effective in the short term.
>
> Source: Lexis-Nexis

It is appropriate to mention the changing nature of some of the non-profit-making organizations. I have mentioned the way in which some charities have taken up marketing activities, with good effect, and it is evident that since the 1990s there has been a growing move to make the non-profit-making organizations more accountable for the money they spend.

Different marketing adoption in not-for-profit organizations

In Table 11.1 you can see the variety of ways in which the adoption of marketing has been implemented in a range of different not-for-profit organizations.

Table 11.1 Marketing's adoption

Colleges and universities	1. The product range is under constant review, the physical environment is of concern and more efficient methods of teaching are being devised. 2. Promotion has sharpened and the importance of internal marketing is being recognized. 3. Staff needs, both teaching and support, are identified using HRM techniques; recruitment ads are more professionally produced and placed; selection is more concerned with effectiveness than qualifications. Training is budgeted and encouraged. 4. Funding sources are targeted and marketing plans developed to maximize the probability of achievement. Trans-EU funding requires a long-term commitment. Commercial sponsorship needs activities targeted to meet the sponsor's needs.
Hospitals	1. Excess demand and budgetary constraints are causing hospitals to allocate their resources very carefully. 2. Sponsorship and the aid of voluntary groups such as 'Friends of the Hospital' has to be solicited and the benefits be seen to be valued.
Doctors	1. Excess demand and budgetary constraints are causing doctors to consider which patients they can afford to accept on to their lists. 2. There is a growing resentment in the population because the tradition of open access is now restricted. This presents a serious need for doctors to use marketing to show that they are not responsible for Government actions.
Charities	1. Funds must be solicited from a variety of sources. 2. Beneficiaries of the charity must be located and encouraged to apply and/or accept support.

	3. Internal marketing must co-ordinate and motivate the individuals who work for the charity either in an employed or voluntary capacity.
Social organizations	1. Many long-standing organizations such as the YMCA, the Scouts and the Churches are losing members and suffering from lack of income. Marketers face the twin problems of redefining mission and corporate policies to provide what people require today and securing the necessary funds to generate an upturn in membership.

Case history

Charities facing a crisis of their own

A phrase that sums up a problem facing many charities when it comes to marketing their cause is 'out of sight – out of mind'.

International disasters often attract an initial flood of donations, but when the media spotlight disappears the flow of money slows, just as the clear-up or redevelopment operations begin in earnest.

When picture of the Indian earthquake in January 2001 hit the TV screens, money poured into the coffers of aid charities. Donations topped £100,000 in January, February and March according to figures from the Charities Aid Foundation, but in April they were reduced to £43,000.

Although the level of charitable giving has reached a plateau of £7 billion to £8 billion per year, the number of people dipping into their pockets is declining.

Homeless charity, Crisis, was once guaranteed exposure for its cause by constant highly visible presence of homeless people sleeping on the streets. Now, following the decline in the number of people sleeping rough, the longer-term problems associated with homelessness are easier to ignore.

Some charities such as Barnardo's, have produced controversial advertising campaigns in order to raise awareness of their cause.

The director of Citigate, which handles the advertising for Sue Ryder Care, Arthritis Care and the British Legion Poppy appeal suggested that 'you may have one hundred people who know who you are but not very well, and it is unlikely that you will get one of those to donate. You could have 20 people who think you are good and get one to donate, but if you have ten people passionate about your cause they are all likely to give'.

Therefore, in targeting the appropriate audience, the message also has to be right. Creating messages aimed at existing supporters may help charities raise much-needed funds, but in the longer-term they will have to think about extending their reach to recruit new and younger people to the charitable cause.

Source: Lexis-Nexis

Question 11.4

You are a marketing manager for a well-known charitable organization. You have been asked to justify to the Board the reasons why the charity should not employ an advertising agency to undertake promotional work on their behalf.

Summary

Planning and controlling go together, and in this respect there is no basic difference between the activities of normal commercial organizations and those of charities and non-profit-making organizations.

The big difference for charities is their dependence on the unpaid work of volunteers; you cannot make the same demands on volunteers that you can on employees. Also, you do not have the power to threaten them with dismissal – many employees tolerate the job because they need the money, either now or in the future, so they cannot walk out. It is almost impossible to estimate the value of volunteer workers, and controlling them is a matter of good organization and the appropriate expressions of gratitude for their help. If you see a charity putting on a big party, don't grumble – the people in there probably deserve a lot more than they get.

There is more need for charities to be seen to be using their money wisely than there is for commercial companies, as a donor who thinks that money is being wasted may not feel like giving money next time round. Donations to such television marathons as Children in Need improved when some of their successful projects were shown in the course of the programme.

The marketing philosophy is now becoming a permanent feature of not-for-profit organizations. It has been necessary to introduce marketing gradually, so as to highlight a 'customer-centred' focus, which had not previously been noticeable.

Typically, all customers are better educated, better informed and are not shy about asserting their 'rights and entitlements' – therefore in the context of charities and not-for-profit organizations the power of the customer (Porter's Five Forces) is not to be underestimated. Introducing a marketing philosophy into charities and not-for-profit organizations is now of primary importance.

The most significant benefits that marketing can give the public sector organization are in the provision of managed information – effective use of the promotional mix. The value of advertising, PR and sponsorship have already shown great success in increasing the availability of funds. We have seen this in the case of Red Nose Day and the Children in Need Appeal, where millions of pounds are generated in a one-day event.

The total income for charities and not-for-profit organizations is significant (in the case of McDonalds, $300 million, has been given to improve medical support and aid for children in need). Therefore to plan and control the use of these funds is vital.

The same applies to smaller local charities, as locally involved participants will want to see their donations appropriately used, in order that they might be encouraged to contribute to these organizations in the future.

Further study and examination preparation

Study tip

The importance of not-for-profit-marketing has grown in significance over the past years within the marketplace, and a reflection of this might emerge in the exam paper. In recent years, this particular topic has been the centre of the mini-case study, therefore it is essential to understand the concepts and context of charities and not-for-profit and how they have emerged and become much more marketing focused.

Question 11.5

December 2000, Question 2

Go to www.marketingonline.co.uk or www.bh.com/marketing to access Specimen Answers and Senior Examiner's advice for this exam question.

Unit 12
International marketing

Objectives

With the ongoing evolution of global markets, it is of primary importance that the function and practice of marketing in an international context is considered.

The learning outcome underpinning this module is demonstration of the adaptation of marketing in a variety of contexts.

The underpinning indicative content, i.e. the syllabus areas to be covered, include:
- Identifying marketing information needs
- Marketing environment, managing the differences
- Structure choices: exporting, licensing, joint ventures, trading companies and direct ownership
- Necessary adaptation to the marketing mix.
(Syllabus reference 1.4.4)

Introduction

In order to survive in the marketing environment in the 21st century, alternative methods of growth, expansion, diversification and differentiation are playing an increasing role in everyday business. Expansion into international markets is one of the more common ways of fulfilling growth and market development objectives.

Around the world managers are realizing the increasing necessity for their organizations to develop skills, awareness and knowledge to enable them to manage the international market development process. That knowledge and understanding includes an insight into the expectation of international customers, their cultures and their existing levels of awareness of products and services that you might offer.

As an international marketing manager the demands on you will present an interesting challenge as you strive to understand the cultural diversity of doing business in other countries.

One of the many misunderstandings in the business environment is that international marketing is exclusively for large organizations. This is a great misconception, as the whole world is a marketplace, presenting many profitable marketing opportunities for all. Every country and every region offers new and exciting challenges, and a different range of marketing opportunities, which in essence will arise from its own particular needs. Understanding these needs as a marketer is of pivotal importance. Marketing after all is the process of identifying, anticipating and satisfying customer requirements profitably.

Why go international?

For many organizations going 'international' will ultimately be to fill a gap that will affect the organization's ability to expand in the long term. These gaps in organizational performance will be due to a number of reasons:
- *Intensity of the competition* – an organization may expand, first, because there may be less intensity of competition overseas, or second, because some organizations are finding

the intensity of competition so virulent in their own country, that they are unable to survive without an alternative strategy.

- *Saturated domestic market* – as competition continues to intensify it is likely that businesses can no longer sustain the level of competitive advantage and market share, therefore the alternative is to look for market growth and market development opportunities elsewhere.
- *Product life cycle differences* – as a product moves through its life cycle it is subject to many levels of change, in functionality, style and quality. However, in order to avoid deletion from the product range, international markets provide new opportunities for the same product, perhaps for a different use, or alternatively there is a cultural and time lag in the country. For example, the Hillman Minx has long been obsolete in the UK but they are a common sight on the roads of Tehran, Iran. So while they have expired in most of the western world, there has been life thereafter.
- *Excess capacity* – where an organization is operating successfully in the domestic market, but operating below optimal capacity, then there is excess capacity available to produce more products for different markets. Particularly important here would be issues relating to marginal costing. If economies of scale were appropriate, marginal costing could reduce the price significantly in order to overcome the barriers of entry into new markets.
- *Comparative advantage* – organizations may establish, as a result of their research, that they actually have comparable advantage over their international rivals, perhaps in their own domestic market. The advantage might be skills based, technology based, access to raw materials, etc.
- *Financial reasons* – there are a number of financial reasons why an organization may decide to take the international route. These might include investment incentives, availability of venture capital and grants from local authorities.
- *Organizational issues* – on many occasions early entries into international markets can almost happen by default. Organizations involved in mergers or acquisitions may find that their partners in the product have international operations, of which they then become a part.
- *Geographical diversification* – this will likely happen as a result of some of the other factors covered. To avoid competitive intensity, saturated markets, etc. The organization will expand geographically into new areas.

Levels of international marketing

The decision to exploit international marketing opportunities will be a strategic one, it will be linked to corporate and financial goals and will involve considerable financial risk. Therefore the decision must be an informed one. Strategic evaluations will be considered and the exploitation of any opportunities will have to be justified, with the provision of a high level of substantiating information.

The key to making the right decision will be gaining understanding of the different levels of international development available backed by market research into the chosen countries in order to ascertain the strategic fit between the hosting nation and your own organization.

The various levels for international marketing are as follows:

Domestic/regional marketing – which involves the company manipulating a series of controllable variables such as price, advertising, distribution and the product in a largely uncontrollable external environment that is made up of different economic structures, competitors, cultural values and legal infrastructure within specific political or geographic boundaries. For the United Kingdom, this is a challenging issue, particularly with the very close links relating to our relationship with continental Europe through the European Union. While in normal domestic or regional settings, there is only one common language to deal with, for example within the United States of America, Europe has the situation where in some respects there is no one dominant language and while English is widely spoken, it most certainly is not a prerequisite for joining the EU. This immediately erects cultural barriers.

International marketing – which involves operating across a number of foreign country markets in which not only do the uncontrollable variables differ significantly between one market and another, but the controllable factors in form of cost and price structures, opportunities for advertising and distributive infrastructure are also likely to differ.

Global marketing management – which is a larger and more complex international operation. Here a company co-ordinates, integrates and controls a whole series of marketing programmes into a substantial global effort. Here the main objective of the company is to achieve a degree of synergy in the overall operation so that by taking advantage of different exchange rates, tax rates, labour rates, skill levels and market opportunities, the organization as a whole will be greater than the sum of its parts.

Export marketing – is where the organization trades its goods and services across all national and political boundaries. There are two types of exporting, direct and indirect.

Direct exporting – is where an organization sells their goods and services directly to a host country. This will mean that they will need to invest much resource, time and effort in establishing business links within international markets. This may mean establishing a physical presence in the marketplace.

Indirect exporting – is where an organization with limited resource, trades internationally through the most simple and low-cost method available. Quite often their profile will be raised through a number of market entry methods, for example the use of an agent, or an export house.

To clarify this a little more, let us look at the differences in domestic and international marketing, as shown in Table 12.1.

Table 12.1 Domestic versus international marketing

Domestic Marketing	International Marketing
Main language	Many languages
Dominant culture	Multi-culture
Research straightforward	Research complex
Relatively stable environment	Often unstable environment
Single currency	Exchange rate problems
Business conventions understood	Conventions diverse and unclear

The international marketing environment

International marketing carries with it a high element of financial risk, as there are many uncertainties, some of which are significant and often many times greater than those facing a company operating in just one marketplace. Therefore, it is of primary importance that before entering any overseas marketplace, the organization has a thorough understanding of the nature and characteristics of the marketplace. This is effectively undertaking a marketing audit, but in an international context.

Earlier in this book within Unit 2, 'The marketing audit', there was some discussion about the nature and extent of the external marketing environment. The environmental influences that should be considered in the context of international marketing are still the same, namely SLEPT, but let us look at how it balances out for international considerations.

Figure 12.1 illustrates some of the considerations of international marketing.

Technological
Satellite communications
ISDN
Internet websites
Superhighway

Economic
Developed economies
Emerging economies
Lesser developed countries
Currency

Political
Operating restrictions
Discriminatory restrictions
Physical actions

Environmental influences on international marketing

Social/cultural
Language
Religion
Aesthetics
Values & attributes
Social organization
Material culture

Legal
Local domestic laws
International law
Home domestic laws

Figure 12.1 Cultural framework

Social/cultural factors

Cultural differences are apparent from one end of the UK to the other, or one end of China to the other, but between different countries it would appear that in some instances they are enormous. You will find a range of different social interests and a variety of different customer behaviour patterns. Failure to understand them on the part of the organization could end in disaster, as it did several years ago when McDonalds moved into Iran. That country was less than delighted at Western intervention and it resulted in Iranians doing significant damage to the buildings.

Cultural differences are very significant, with considerations of religion, languages, education, symbols – these differences are often termed as cultural gaps. Clearly these will cause operational problems with the marketing mix and the ability to develop global brands. For example, Pepsi-cola had to change its 'Come Alive with Pepsi' campaign theme as in Germany it was translated as 'Pepsi Out of the Grave'!

These factors present many challenges for marketers, in terms of their ability to meet such a broad range of customer needs under the social and cultural banners. While product specifications, the tangible element of the mix might be almost identical, the services mix, the level of customer services and technical support required may be very diverse, dependent upon the infrastructure and expectations of the host country.

The challenges will be across the whole range of the marketing mix, not just the traditional elements of pricing, distribution and advertising, but also the 3Ps of the services mix, which will present significant challenges for the marketer.

Religious cultures present a very interesting challenge, particularly in Middle Eastern countries, where the role of women is different to the Western world. Marketers must be very sensitive to the varying levels of cultural diversity if they wish to be successful in international marketing terms.

> **Question 12.1**
>
> Identify two countries that you are familiar with and draw up a list of potential social/cultural differences. You should do this by identifying four cultural characteristics and then compare and contrast them across both countries.

Legal environment

Legal systems will invariably be different, both in context, content and meaning. You may have to think of law as being the 'rules of the game' for international trading.

There are four key considerations for international law:

- *Domestic laws in the home country* – at the same time as working within international law requirements, you also have to consider your own country's legal requirements.
- *Local domestic laws* – these are all different. The only way to survive through the legal systems abroad is to employ external agents, experts in the country, to manage the legal side of the business for you.
- *International laws* – there are many international laws that affect the marketing of products and services overseas. For example international conventions and agreements, trade embargos, International Monetary Fund (IMF) and World Trade Organization regulations, treaties, patents, trademarks, etc.
- *Laws and international marketing activity* – these laws will affect each element of the marketing mix in different ways; it could be product patents or advertising restrictions, many of which exist in the Middle East.

There have been many interesting legal cases relating to international marketing and also cases of major organizations giving up on on trying to achieve new market entry strategies because the red tape has been too difficult to get through. For example, Mercedes and Kellogg's both were interested in pursuing entry into India, but it was just too difficult to broker their way through the endless bureaucracy and red tape.

Economic environment

There are fairly wide extremes in relation to the economics of varying countries. For example, Ethiopia, where average earnings are considerably less than $100 per annum, through to North America, where the average *monthly* earnings are in excess of $2000. The differences between Southern American economies and those of the Asia Pacific Rim are considerable. A further example of differences in economies is that in Tokyo you have to work for less than 25 minutes to buy a Big Mac from McDonalds, whereas in Mexico City you have to work for 80 minutes to buy exactly the same product.

Three categories of the economic environment

Developed countries – the majority of the Western world would be classified as developed, e.g. Japan, Europe and the USA. The NAFTA (North America Free Trade Areas) countries, the

European Union and Japan account for over 80 per cent of trade in the Triad economies. The Triad being a global triangle within which trade exists – three different groups of cultures and economies coming together.

Emerging economies – countries such as India, China, South America (in particular Brazil) are defined as emerging because of the successful change in direction of their internal economic policy which has in turn produced a growing demand for every type of Western product, e.g. mobile phones, cars, computers.

All of these present significant marketing opportunities, but also significant marketing mix challenges, as the marketer deals with the wide range of international trade issues.

Less developed countries – typically this means that the per-capita income is extremely low, which in turn inhibits the amount of disposable income for regeneration in the economy. Common characteristics of such countries are poor communications networks, poor transportation system, high levels of poverty, low levels of education and health care.

> ### Case history
>
> **Iran back in touch!**
> **Iran unveils its business plan**
>
> For over two decades Iran's relationship with Western business has often been highly hostile. Now, though, it wants UK investors to look at it afresh – and help to plough £50 billion into its beleaguered economy.
>
> After 20 years of political and economic isolation Iran is now thrusting its way back onto the international stage, with a very ambitious investment programme.
>
> Iran now wants to position itself as a regional economic power – a 'Persian tiger'. Plans include massive expansion of its oil and gas industries, exploitations of its huge yet barely tapped mineral wealth, improving agriculture, manufacturing and major infrastructure works.
>
> But to achieve economic renaissance Iran must attract finance and expertise from overseas, after first regaining confidence of an outside world.
>
> In the last 20 years Iran's economy has been decimated, and gradually broken down, now with the help of the Western world they have big plans for shaping and forming a more robust and solid infrastructure.
>
> www.tradepartners.gov.uk or www.iraniantrade.org will provide an insight of how Iran plans its re-emergence on to the international business stage.
>
> Source: *New Civil Engineer*, October 2000

Currency/interest rate risks

World economic instability and currency variations are potentially very damaging to organizations. A rapid drop in one particular currency can wipe away almost immediately the benefit of doing business abroad, in fact it can be the difference between organizations managing to sink or swim.

Rises or falls in interest rates can also have significant effects, as we have seen in the UK in the past, where high interest rates make international trading difficult, as UK products and services are expensive.

Then you have the single European currency, monetary union within Europe, with the objective of bringing stability to the European economy.

Political

In Unit 2 of this text, we explore the volatile nature of politics in respect of the external environment. As we watch world events unfold it is only too clear to see that international markets can be significantly erratic and volatile politically. For example, the events of 'September 11' found the USA forging very close ties with countries from within the European Union. However, in March 2002, there has been a political eruption over the exporting of steel into the USA, as they seek to enforce tariffs on the importation of European steel. This has created significant backlash.

Technological environment

The biggest single influence of recent times on international trade has to be the Internet and the technological revolution. Principally, the effect of the Internet has manifested itself by reducing the world to a global village, with trade, communication and information being easily and readily available.

With the evolution of satellite and digital and mobile phone technologies, the marketplace has become much more accessible, without there necessarily being a physical presence. The continuing levels of innovation may go some way in the future to easing some of the burdens on international trade, as there may be a sharp decrease in trade barriers as a result of the Internet. As we saw in the case of Lufthansa, it will see a sharp reduction in marketing costs.

The Internet and the World Wide Web have completely changed the way both individuals and organizations trade and by the end of 2001 over 175 million people worldwide will be able to trade on the Internet.

> **Question 12.2**
>
> List five ways in which the Internet will aid international trade.

Know your markets

Marketing research is critical in all markets, but when trading overseas, and effectively operating in a vacuum, the need for comprehensive information is essential. There are two components to marketing research:

- The need to understand customers and their buying behaviour
- The need to understand the marketing and operating environment.

International research is complex and difficult to manage. It is very costly and time-consuming and the outcome is not always very meaningful. The consequences of collecting incorrect or inappropriate information could be immeasurable.

Organizations failing to carry out effective marketing research could find themselves missing significant market opportunities, or alternatively finding that the supposed opportunities identified do not exist. Either way, without the right information on the proposed market, the organization could lose out.

The role of the international researcher for the organization will be to produce a clear overview of the current state of the marketplace. This should include examining issues such as the SLEPT factors, demand for products, ability to pay, levels of competitor activity, ability to meet the political and legal requirements of the host country and, of course, the technological ability of the country concerned.

There are three key functions an international market researcher should undertake:

- *Scanning international markets to identify and analyse the opportunities* – this will include looking at accessibility, profitability and market size of existing markets, latent markets and potential markets.
- *Building marketing information systems to monitor international environment trends and patterns of trade* – this includes the collection of primary and secondary data and ongoing external audits to monitor the pace of change or the stability of the host economy
- *Carrying out primary research for specific reasons* – this would include potentially carrying out test marketing and measuring the feasibility and viability of trading in the host country as well as the impact that this trade would have on the marketing mix and the implications of changing the mix to meet a range of different customer needs.

The key to successful market entry is to ensure that markets are scanned and analysed, and comprehensive market profiles are built up and detailed country studies undertaken.

Understanding the external marketplace

We have already looked at the intricacies of analysing the external environment, through the use of PEST or SLEPT. However, there are some specific market performance indicators in relation to key economic indicators that you might need to ascertain the position of. They include:

- Population size and growth
- Population density and concentration
- Population age and distribution
- Disposable income and income distribution
- Economic activity – where is the concentration of economic/financial generation?

These indicators will highlight to you the economic position of the country and its status in relation to its level of development, e.g. emerging economies or less developed economies, such as Iraq.

Other indicators include areas such as:

- Natural resources
- Topography
- Climate
- Energy and communication
- Urbanization
- Differential inflation levels.

Clearly, understanding these indicators will give you a broad brush picture of the state of the host nation you are considering, which provides a sound basis on which to judge the level of perceived risk in market entry.

As you move onto the Postgraduate Diploma in Marketing, you may have the opportunity to study in more depth the nature and context of international marketing. This will expand upon some of these key points.

Understanding consumer and business buying behaviour

Business buyer behaviour is something you will have covered in Unit 10, 'Industrial/business-to-business and services marketing', but in an international context is it essential that you understand the key principles and structures behind business-to-business buying.

From a domestic perspective, the typical focus would be:

- The structure and composition of the DMU (decision-making unit)
- Organizational influences upon purchasing
- The role of technology
- The business/industrial buyer process
- The personal characteristics of the buyers.

These factors, combined with an understanding of the marketing environment, would provide you with a robust management information system that would serve to underpin any decisions that might be made in respect of international expansion.

Ultimately, before a market entry strategy can be considered you need to be aware of the market potential:

- Market size
- Competition
- Resource
- Customer demands and the ability to purchase
- Accessibility
- Barriers to entry.

International research

As with domestic marketing research, there is a need to take a very structured approach to solving the marketing problem (see Figure 12.2).

STAGE 1 Set survey objectives - identify what you need to know

STAGE 2 Decide who, which group of customers to survey

STAGE 3 Decide how to undertake the survey

STAGE 4 Design the questionnaire or focus group needs

STAGE 7 Interpret and report the findings

STAGE 6 Process the data

STAGE 5 Collect the data

Figure 12.2 The marketing research process

The research process, while needing to be formal, must have key objectives to be achieved. In the instance of international marketing research, the key questions and objectives, as recommended by Carter, Fifield and Lewis (2001) are:

- Where to go?
- How to get there?
- What shall we market?
- How do we persuade them to buy it?

Table 12.2 is an abbreviated list of key challenges that marketing research will need to address.

Table 12.2 The task of global marketing research: what should it determine? Adapted from Terpstra and Sarathy (1997)

The marketing environment	The competition	The product	Marketing mix	Firm-specific historical data
Political context: leaders, national goals, ideology, key institution	Relative market shares, new product moves	Analysis of users Who are the end-user industries?	Channels of distribution: evolution and performance	Sales trends by product and product-line, salesforce and customer
Economic growth prospects, business cycle stage	Pricing and cost structure, image and brand reputation	Industrial and consumer buyers; characteristics: size, age, sex, segment growth rates	Relative pricing, elasticities and tactics	Trends by country and region
Per capita income levels, purchasing power	Quality: its attributes and positioning relative to competitors	Purchasing power and intentions	Advertising and promotion: choices and impacts on customers	Contribution margins
End-user industry growth trends	Competitors' strengths: favourite tactics and strategies	Customer response to new products, price, promotion	Service quality: perceptions and relative positioning	Marketing mix used, marketing response functions across countries and regions
Government: legislation, regulation, standards, barriers to trade		Switching behaviour, role of credit and purchasing Future needs, impact of cultural differences	Logistics networks, configuration and change	

While the research needs to focus on the environment, and the customer, it also needs to focus on the necessary adaptations that might be required to the marketing mix. Therefore, it will be necessary to involve the organization in research that will ascertain the position of the product, and its appropriateness for the market, the threshold for pricing and market sensitivity, and the most appropriate distribution channels.

Developing an international marketing information system

A typical information system would potentially look very similar to the one in Figure 12.3, and is something that you will essentially concentrate on in the early part of your studies in Management Information for Marketing Decisions.

Secondary sources of information

Databases
Keynote
Mintel
Euromonitor etc.
Government statistics
National press
Trade press
Internet
Trade associations

Marketing decisions

Defining data needs, analysing and distributing data for the purpose of decision-making

Marketing information

Database - Central information point
Collecting and sorting of data and information

Internal sources

Sales information
Products, prices, outlets, regions, distribution channels

Customer information
Types of purchase
Frequency of purchase
Volume/value of purchase

Marketing communications
Communications spend
Performance to plan

Sales force information

Market research studies commissioned

Decision support system

Analysing data

Figure 12.3 MKIS Framework – Adapted from Principles and Practices of Marketing – Bassington and Pettitt

However, with every information system there need to be criteria for essential information to be collated in order that an informed decision might be made. To assist with this, Doole and Lowe (1999) refer to the 12C analysis model for creating an information system:

- **Country**
  - General country information
  - Basic SLEPT data
  - Impact on environmental dimensions.

- **Choices**
    - Analysis of supply
    - International and external competition
    - Characteristics of competitors
    - Import analysis
    - Competitive strengths and weaknesses.
- **Concentration**
    - Structure of the market segments
    - Geographical spread.
- **Culture/consumer behaviour**
    - Characteristics of the country
    - Diversity of cultural grouping
    - Nature of decision-making
    - Major influence on buyer behaviour.
- **Consumptions**
    - Demand and end-use analysis of economic sectors that use the product
    - Market share by demand sector
    - Growth patterns of sectors
    - Evaluation of threat of substitute products.
- **Capacity to pay**
    - Pricing
    - Extrapolation of pricing to examine trends
    - Culture of pricing
    - Conditions of payment
    - Insurance terms.
- **Currency**
    - Stability
    - Restrictions
    - Exchange controls.
- **Channels**
    - Purchasing behaviour
    - Capabilities of intermediaries
    - Coverage of distribution costs
    - Physical distribution infrastructure.
- **Commitment**
    - Access to market
    - Trade incentives and barriers
    - Custom tariffs
    - Government regulations
    - Regulations on market entry.
- **Communication**
    - Promotion
    - Media infrastructure and availability
    - Which marketing approaches are effective

- Common selling practices
- Media information.
- **Contractual obligations**
  - Business practices
  - Insurance and legal obligations.
- **Caveats**
  - Factors to be aware of.

Acquiring secondary data

Typical sources of secondary data might include:

- Specialist trade press
- Quality press, journals and magazines
- Trade associations
- Directories – Kompass and Euromonitor
- Major universities and business schools
- Public libraries
- Local chamber of commerce
- Bankers
- International consultancies
- Electronic media
- Published research
- Competitors' published research
- Export houses and freight forwarders
- Embassies, both domestic and that of the host country.

In the past, marketing research into international markets has been difficult and at times completely unreliable. When a local national agency carried out research projects on behalf of potential international marketing organizations quite often the information collected and then presented, could give the organization a very biased view of the state of the nation.

The biggest inhibitors of international research are language and culture. Both these characteristics can be interpreted very differently depending upon the country of origin.

Lack of appropriate marketing information, on any geographical area, is dangerous, but to commence trading overseas without a thorough investigation of the opportunities and threats is completely negligent of the organization.

With the use of modern technologies, the standard and availability of market research information is much improved. There are databases and CD ROMs, in addition to the banks of information stored on the World Wide Web. Due to the ongoing emergence of a significant range of international trading organizations, both commercial and political, more reliable information is starting to emerge, some of which has been collected through worldwide research initiatives.

However, while the situation is improving considerably, researching international markets is an enormous task.

Acquiring primary research

Primary research in international markets can be a very difficult process. Obvious difficulties include:

- Costs associated with primary data are traditionally high
- Language and cultural differences

- Sampling – geographical diversity
- Non-response
- Social organization
- Terminology.

Of course primary research can be undertaken through the traditional routes of questionnaires, focus groups, experimental and observation research.

Once the data have been accessed and analysed, the organization is then in a position to start making decisions in relation to entering the market and how to enter the market, i.e. what international channel options are open to them.

> **Question 12.3**
>
> What are the implications of collecting primary data from less developed countries?

Market entry strategies

Market entry strategies are based around a strategic decision taken to trade internationally. Ultimately it will form part of the overall corporate and marketing strategy. However, it is useful to understand the basis of the different entry strategies.

Having established the following facts, the organization should be able to choose the most appropriate method of international expansion:

- The company objectives in relation to the size and value of the market
- The financial resources required to commence trading
- The existing marketplace
- The level of competition that exists
- The nature and characteristics of the market
- Pricing issues
- The nature of the product/service
- Timings.

Answering these questions should enable the organization to decide on the most appropriate method of trading internationally.

- *Licensing* – the positive side to licensing is that it requires relatively low levels of investment. Licensing is usually based around a contract that enables a second party, the licensee, to produce products or services, have technological know-how, research and development information and trade marks that belong to another organization, namely the licenser. Both parties sign an agreement that then outlines terms and conditions for the use of the above.

    The advantages include a low level of commitment, reduced market entry costs and the ability to enter smaller markets in a more cost-effective way.

    Disadvantages could include being tied into a long-term relationship, particularly if conflict evolves, and competition from the licenser.

- *Agents* – agents are effectively overseas sales personnel, who operate in a range of markets on behalf of different organizations. Agents will usually work on a retainer basis with commission or on a commission basis. Their role is to create an awareness of your organization and the products and services it has to offer, ultimately with the view to securing a sale.

Agents are often very successful as they will operate in their local marketplace which then reduces some of the barriers to entry that organizations often face when trying to gain entry into new markets.

Agents should be selected for their financial strength, their contacts within the host country, the nature and extent of their relationships with organizations and their skills, abilities and resources.

- *Franchising* – franchising was covered in Unit 4 'Theories of communication', under Distribution, which you should read again to refresh your mind. Franchising is a very common way of operating overseas. Think about how many McDonalds, KFCs, and Pizza Huts, etc. there are around the world. You can probably see from those very examples the success of franchising on a global scale.
- *Company acquisition* – this actually refers to gaining market entry by buying an existing company in the country where you wish to trade. The advantage of this is that you are buying an existing going concern and therefore the infrastructure is in place, but the financial risk involved is considerable.
- *Wholly-owned subsidiary* – probably one of the most expensive methods of international business is setting up a wholly-owned subsidiary, which means that the organization will effectively set up a fully-fledged business overseas. This will include very significant overheads and is therefore a very costly option.
- *Joint venture* – is really a variation of the above, but instead of a total investment into another country, your organization may choose to buy into another country, through a joint venture, potentially buying up to half of a compatible business. This is a very common practice. There are many advantages of this process, as organizations share market research, product development, marketing planning and implementation, capital and resources both human and financial. You will often find that organizations join forces for competitive reasons, or even for technological know-how.

There are also many disadvantages, such as trust with the other partner, differences in aims and objectives and strategies. One partner may hold a greater stake than the other; that in itself can cause much conflict.

Question 12.4

Explain the differences between international and export marketing.

Case history

Cathay Pacific seeks closer ties with Chinese Airlines

Hong Kong's flag carrier Cathay Pacific Airlines Ltd wants closer ties with China's largest airlines so it can cash in on the country's rapid industrial growth.

A director of Cathay Pacific, Raymond Yuen, was cited by *South China Morning Post* as saying 'that such an alliance would help the regional airlines become more competitive with links in outbound traffic'.

Yuen said that the huge demand in China's aviation industry had prompted the need for more co-operation with mainland companies. He said closer co-operation could take the form of code sharing and joint selling of air tickets, partnership cargo operations, pilots training and other back-up services.

> From now until the year 2006, China will need a total of 1,600 Boeings and Airbuses, an average of 4.5 pilots are needed for each plane.
>
> Source: Lexis-Nexis

Potential barriers to entry

While these are potential market entry strategies, there are a number of barriers to entry that organizations must consider and how they will overcome them.

Barker and Kaynack (1992) listed the following important areas:

- Too much red tape
- Trade barriers
- Transportation difficulties
- Lack of trained personnel
- Lack of export incentives
- Lack of co-ordinated assistance
- Unfavourable conditions overseas
- Slow payment by buyers
- Lack of competitive products
- Payment defaults
- Language barriers.

By selecting the right market entry channel, many of these barriers may possibly be overcome; therefore careful consideration of the most appropriate entry method, for the most successful outcome is crucial. The more informed the organization, the clearer the country profile, the easier it will be to identify the best method for the organization.

> ### Question 12.5
> What do you think the principal barriers to entry would be for a clothing manufacturer to enter into Iran?

The implications on marketing plans

Again, from your earlier studies you should be very familiar with marketing plans and the marketing mix. What you need to consider now, looking at them in an international context, is how in some instances organizations may need to amend their plans and mix to meet the needs of the particular market.

One thing you must be clear on is that it does not matter where in the world you operate, or have a physical presence, the concept of marketing and customer orientation are exactly the same.

When trading internationally, organizations will clearly need to break their markets down into a number of different segments, which in turn become target markets.

While the organization may have one set of corporate objectives, which include international marketing, it is highly likely that they will have a number of varying plans and strategies to reflect the local demands of each country. In turn this means that the marketing mix could also be different.

The organization produces products or services for the benefits their customers want to gain. Therefore, it is critical to ensure that the organization's product offering fits the requirements of the host country. For example, almost every country in the world uses irons or hairdryers. While the main functions, characteristics and mechanisms are the same, the power supplies and sockets are different. Therefore, an organization must reflect on this element and amend their products accordingly. Should they do this, it would flag up a change to the product element of the marketing mix.

The key question the organization should then ask is should their product offering be standardized or differentiated?

Product life cycles and product positioning will also vary according to the country of operation. This will be due to issues such as market demand, market growth, the pace of change and competitive activity.

Under 'product' the issue of branding will also have to be considered. Organizations will need to consider the benefits of branding and whether or not their brand is meaningful in the country in which they operate.

Product

New products for international markets will effectively need to go through the same new product development process as within the domestic country setting. Product opportunities should be referenced against aspects relating to its development such as:

- Manufacturing requirements – home and abroad
- Marketing research
- Ability to purchase the product
- Customer needs, wants and expectations in relation to the product
- Fit with existing product portfolio
- Trade mark and patenting agreements for overseas
- Local and international safety standards
- Technology demands
- Technical support
- After-sales support
- Whether or not it should be standardized or adapted for local use.

Pricing

Clearly pricing will be an issue where there could be significant variances. This could be because of currency exchange rates, international or local legislation, distribution and storage costs, as well as the cost of manufacturing the products.

In many instances organizations could be subject to varying taxes and tariffs, which will affect their pricing policy. Obviously the method of payment and speed of payment will also be a critical issue.

The influences on price will be very similar to the ones highlighted in the 'Price operations' unit of this text, but careful consideration must be given to the economic situation and economic indicators within the host country.

Being able to control the pricing strategy in international markets will depend upon the degree of regulation employed on a local basis. However, controlling prices will be an essential activity in order to sustain market share, competitive positioning and a degree of continuity within the chain.

Issues of price sensitivity will vary from country to country, but cultural diversity will have an influence on the perceived value proposition.

Place

The big factor in this area will be accessibility and the cost of accessibility. There are many logistical challenges with distribution, including warehousing, storage, transportation network, etc. The selection of the appropriate market entry strategy will influence the way in which distribution can effectively be managed.

Clearly, with the growing impetus of the Internet, the dynamics of distribution are sure to change in the coming years, and while there is some instability, currently organizations such as Amazon have proved it can work.

Management of channel members will require serious consideration and could prove to be a logistical nightmare. However, the following points should be taken into account:

- Set-up costs of the channel and members
- Level of investment required
- Level of incentive required
- Synergy with the local/domestic channels
- Management and control of the overall process.

Promotional mix

This area is possibly the most interesting and the most complex to deal with, because of the nature of social/cultural differences from country to country. There are many challenges to be faced under this banner. These include:

- Language
- Image
- Relationships
- Corporate identity
- Product image
- Company image
- Methods of advertising
- Tolerance of advertising
- Marketing ethics
- Available media
- Adult literacy levels
- Accessibility of information
- Agencies.

As a result of so many different facets of culture within so many different countries it is highly likely that the organization will need to develop a range of different marketing and promotional mixes to match the host country's market.

Again the importance of defining a good country profile is highlighted. This should be based around a wide range of issues critical to the successful development of a marketing strategy. This then ensures that the organization achieves a true marketing and customer-oriented focus, producing products they want, where they want, when they want, at a price they want to pay and responding to promotions that are meaningful.

> **Question 12.6**
> Choosing a country of your choice, discuss how you perceive the effects of economic and environmental trends on international product development.

Globalization

In the final part of this unit, we consider the advantages and disadvantages of global marketing, and discuss whether plans and mixes should be global and whether we should be thinking global and acting local.

For a long period of time we have heard terms such as the global village, the borderless world. This was an idealism of the 1990s but the surge towards standardization has been considerable as organizations see the potential for cost saving through economies of scale. Organizations constantly struggle to find the balance of just how far they should go, how much they should standardize, how much should they adapt to meet the needs of the global market.

So far there has only been limited success in developing a standardized global marketing strategy. It has been suggested that the only likely place for this type of strategy to really succeed is on the Internet, where the world is a global village. The same product, price, distribution channel and promotional campaign are used across the globe.

Often people associate organizations such as McDonalds or Coca-Cola with being truly global. While their brand is global, they do have variations on a theme to meet the customer expectations of the market they operate within. While they are global in market coverage, they localize in both tastes and language; they are global, but local.

Globalization is often characterized by the standardization of the marketing mix, and while this in essence would seem the most cost-effective and efficient way to move forward, it may not be the most competitive.

The marketing mix and standardization

An organization seeking to globalize would have to consider standardizing almost all of the following elements:

- Market access
- Industry standards
- Technology
- Products
- Services
- Promotion
- Distribution
- Customer requirements
- Competition
- Communication.

The implications of standardizing the organization's approach present the marketer with a significant challenge, as moving towards a standardized marketing mix has no guarantee of success in all markets.

Benefits of globalization

There are number of advantages and disadvantages associated with globalization. The advantages are that globalization is more straightforward, in that it seeks to use one set of tools to meet one global set of customers. This provides economies of scale, supposed fairness and equity and potentially greater accessibility, and could potentially lead to the organizations being very competitive on a cost basis. But you may ask yourself: do we want one product for all?

Clearly, there are a number of disadvantages associated with standardizing the mix, as it could prove to be a very inhibitive practice that could cause immense difficulty when trying to meet the needs of so many different facets and such extreme target markets.

The key success factor in achieving any marketing strategy, including globalization, is to ensure that the organization keeps a constant watch on the global marketing environment.

Organizations should monitor change, identify strengths and weaknesses, opportunities and threats and then aim to build a strategy based around customer satisfaction, increasing profitability, head marketing share and achieving global competitiveness.

As the world becomes a smaller place through the power of information communication technology then true globalization and complete standardization may one day be achieved. In the meantime, thinking global and acting local is the most customers and marketing-oriented focus an organization can achieve.

Summary

The issues relating to international marketing and globalization are considerable. But the key to its success is to remember the purpose of marketing. It is critical to the organization not to see international markets as a special project or view them in isolation.

Critical to any decision in relation to international marketing is sufficient information on which to base a decision. Organizations should never underestimate the power of market research in giving them a snapshot of the bigger picture. That picture will show the many different facets of the target country, which is when the organization identifies whether to globalize or localize.

Because marketing is dynamic and ever-changing and because of the growing participation of the Internet in the marketing environment today, globalization will continue to be an objective for which many organizations should strive.

To remain competitive the organization will need to make a number of major decisions based on who their market is, where their market is, the status of the economy of their markets and the opportunities they present.

Staying ahead of the competition will be critical, therefore for may years to come, organizations will increasingly need to develop and use a range of marketing information, market entry strategies and overall marketing strategies to keep the balance between globalization and localization, and customer satisfaction.

Further study and examination preparation

Study tip

As a result of the growth in international marketing, clearly it is playing a more prominent role in our everyday lives. The examination of Marketing Operations is no exception. One of the key tips to consider, is that whenever the situation permits you to, include reference to internationalization, globalization, as being key market driving forces in the economy. Virtually every exam paper has an international marketing question on it, and this should be a good indicator to you to highlight its importance.

Extending knowledge

Recommended reading

In addition to reading this text, and your recommended text, you may find it helpful to read some of *International Marketing Strategy* by Isobel Doole and Robin Lowe, in particular Chapters 3, 4, 9, 10, 11 and 12. This book is the recommended text for International Marketing Strategy and the Postgraduate Diploma level.

You will see from the exam question below that you are asked to provide an example of excellence in respect of continuous assessment. It is therefore advisable that you actually follow the press, *Marketing*, the *Economist*, among others, to observe the nature of international marketing and also the successful implementation of international marketing strategy across the world.

Question 12.7

June 2000, Question 5

Go to www.marketingonline.co.uk or www.bh.com/marketing to access Specimen Answers and Senior Examiner's advice for this exam question.

Question 12.8

June 2001

Go to www.marketingonline.co.uk or www.bh.com/marketing to access Specimen Answers and Senior Examiner's advice for this exam question.

Appendix 1
Guidance on examination preparation

Preparing for your examination

You are now nearing the final phase of your studies and it is time to start the hard work of exam preparation.

During your period of study you will have become used to absorbing large amounts of information. You will have tried to understand and apply aspects of knowledge that may have been very new to you, while some of the information provided may have been more familiar. You may even have undertaken many of the activities that are positioned frequently throughout your Coursebook, which will have enabled you to apply your learning in practical situations. But whatever the state of your knowledge and understanding, do not allow yourself to fall into the trap of thinking that you know enough, you understand enough, or even worse, that you can just take it as it comes on the day.

Never underestimate the pressure of the CIM examination.

The whole point of preparing this text for you is to ensure that you never take the examination for granted, and that you do not go into the exam unprepared for what might come your way for three hours at a time.

One thing's for sure: there is no quick fix, no easy route, no waving a magic wand and finding you know it all.

Whether you have studied alone, in a CIM study centre, or through distance learning, you now need to ensure that this final phase of your learning process is tightly managed, highly structured and objective.

As a candidate in the examination, your role will be to convince the Senior Examiner for this subject that you have credibility. You need to demonstrate to the examiner that you can be trusted to undertake a range of challenges in the context of marketing, that you are able to capitalize on opportunities and manage your way through threats.

You should prove to the Senior Examiner that you are able to apply knowledge, make decisions, respond to situations and solve problems.

Very shortly we are going to look at a range of revision and exam preparation techniques, and at time management issues, and encourage you towards developing and implementing your own revision plan, but before that, let's look at the role of the Senior Examiner.

A bit about the Senior Examiners!

You might be quite shocked to read this, but while it might appear that the examiners are 'relentless question masters' they actually want you to be able to answer the questions and pass the exams! In fact, they would derive no satisfaction or benefits from failing candidates; quite the contrary, they develop the syllabus and exam papers in order that you can learn and then apply that learning effectively so as to pass your examinations. Many of the examiners have said in the past that it is indeed psychologically more difficult to fail students than pass them.

Many of the hints and tips you find within this Appendix have been suggested by the Senior Examiners and authors of the Coursebook series. Therefore you should consider them carefully and resolve to undertake as many of the elements suggested as possible.

The Chartered Institute of Marketing has a range of processes and systems in place within the Examinations Division to ensure that fairness and consistency prevail across the team of examiners, and that the academic and vocational standards that are set and defined are indeed maintained. In doing this, CIM ensures that those who gain the CIM Certificate, Advanced Certificate and Postgraduate Diploma, are worthy of the qualification and perceived as such in the view of employers, actual and potential.

Part of what you will need to do within the examination is be 'examiner friendly' – that means you have to make sure they get what they ask for. This will make life easier for you and for them.

Hints and tips for 'examiner friendly' actions are as follows:

- Show them that you understand the basis of the question, by answering *precisely* the question asked, and not including just about everything you can remember about the subject area.
- Read their needs – how many points is the question asking you to address?
- Respond to the question appropriately. Is the question asking you to take on a role? If so, take on the role and answer the question in respect of the role. For example, you could be positioned as follows:

    'You are working as a Marketing Assistant at Nike UK' or 'You are a Marketing Manager for an Engineering Company' or 'As Marketing Manager write a report to the Managing Partner'.

    These examples of role-playing requirements are taken from questions in past papers.
- Deliver the answer in the format requested. If the examiner asks for a memo, then provide a memo; likewise, if the examiner asks for a report, then write a report. If you do not do this, in some instances you will fail to gain the necessary marks required to pass.
- Take a business-like approach to your answers. This enhances your credibility.
  Badly ordered work, untidy work, lack of structure, headings and subheadings can be off-putting. This would be unacceptable in the work situation, likewise it will be unacceptable in the eyes of the Senior Examiners and their marking teams.
- Ensure the examiner has something to mark: give them substance, relevance, definitions, illustration and demonstration of your knowledge and understanding of the subject area.
- See the examiner as your potential employer, or ultimate consumer/customer. The whole purpose and culture of marketing is about meeting customers' needs. Try this approach – it works wonders.
- Provide a strong sense of enthusiasm and professionalism in your answers; support it with relevant up-to-date examples and apply them where appropriate.
- Try to do something that will make your exam paper a little bit different – make it stand out in the crowd.

All of these points might seem quite logical to you, but often in the panic of the examination they 'go out of the window'. Therefore it is beneficial to remind ourselves of the importance of the examiner. He/she is the 'ultimate customer' – and we all know customers hate to be disappointed.

As we move on, some of these points will be revisited and developed further.

About the examination

In all examinations, with the exception of Marketing in Practice at Certificate level and Analysis and Decision at Diploma level, the paper is divided into two parts.

- Part A – Mini-case study = 40 per cent of the marks
- Part B – Option choice questions (choice of three questions from seven) = 60 per cent of the marks

Let's look at the basis of each element.

The mini-case study

This is based on a mini-case or scenario with one question, possibly subdivided into between two and four points, but totalling 40 per cent of marks overall.

In essence, you, the candidate, are placed in a problem-solving role through the medium of a short scenario. On occasions, the scenario may consist of an article from a journal in relation to a well-known organization: for example, in the past Interflora, EasyJet and Philips, among others, have been used as the basis of the mini-case.

Alternatively, it will be based upon a fictional company, and the examiner will have prepared it in order that the right balance of knowledge, understanding, application and skills is used.

Approaches to the mini-case study

When undertaking the mini-case study there are a number of key areas you should consider.

Structure/content

The mini-case that you will be presented with will vary slightly from paper to paper, and of course from one examination to the next. Normally the scenario presented will be 400–500 words long and will centre on a particular organization and its problems or may even relate to a specific industry.

The length of the mini-case study means that usually only a brief outline is provided of the situation, the organization and its marketing problems, and you must therefore learn to cope with analysing information and preparing your answer on the basis of a very limited amount of detail.

Time management

There are many differing views on time management and the approaches you can take to managing your time within the examination. You must find an approach to suit your way of working, but always remember, whatever you do, you must ensure that you allow enough time to complete the examination. Unfinished exams mean lost marks.

A typical example of managing time is as follows:

Your paper is designed to assess you over a three-hour period. With 40 per cent of the marks being allocated to the mini-case, it means that you should dedicate somewhere around 75 minutes of your time to both read and write up the answer on this mini-case. Some students, however, will prefer to allocate nearer half of their time (90 minutes) on the mini-case, so that they can read and fully absorb the case and answer the questions in the context of it. This is also acceptable as long as you ensure that you work extremely 'SMART' for the remaining time in order to finish the examination.

Do not forget that while there is only one question within the mini-case, it can have a number of components. You must answer all the components in that question, which is where the balance of times comes into play.

Knowledge/skills tested

Throughout all the CIM papers, your knowledge, skills and ability to apply those skills will be tested. However, the mini-cases are used particularly to test application, i.e. your ability to take your knowledge and apply it in a structured way to a given scenario. The examiners will be looking at your decision-making ability, your analytical and communication skills and, depending on the level, your ability as a manager to solve particular marketing problems.

When the examiner is marking your paper, he/she will be looking to see how you differentiate yourself, looking at your own individual 'unique selling points'. The examiner will also want to see if you can personally apply the knowledge or whether you are only able to repeat the textbook materials.

Format of answers

On many occasions, and within all examinations, you will most likely be given a particular communication method to use. If this is the case, you must ensure that you adhere to the requirements of the examiner. This is all part of meeting customer needs.

The likely communication tools you will be expected to use are as follows:

- Memorandum
- Memorandum/report
- Report
- Briefing notes
- Presentation
- Press release
- Advertisement
- Plan

Make sure that you familiarize yourself with these particular communication tools and practise using them to ensure that, on the day, you will be able to respond confidently to the communication requests of the examiner. Look back at the Customer Communications text at Certificate level to familiarize yourself with the potential requirements of these methods.

By the same token, while communication methods are important, so is meeting the specific requirements of the question. This means you must understand what is meant by the precise instruction given. **Note the following terms carefully:**

- **Identify** – select key issues, point out key learning points, establish clearly what the examiner expects you to identify.
- **Illustrate** – the examiner expects you to provide examples, scenarios and key concepts that illustrate your learning.
- **Compare and contrast** – look at the range of similarities between the two situations, contexts or even organizations. Then compare them, i.e. ascertain and list how activities, features, etc. agree or disagree. Contrasting means highlighting the differences between the two.
- **Discuss** – questions that have 'discuss' in them offer a tremendous opportunity for you to debate, argue, justify your approach or understanding of the subject area – *caution* it is not an opportunity to waffle.
- **Briefly explain** – this means being succinct, structured and concise in your explanation, within the answer. Make your points clear, transparent and relevant.
- **State** – present in a clear, brief format.
- **Interpret** – expound the meaning of, make clear and explicit what it is you see and understand within the data provided.
- **Outline** – provide the examiner with the main concepts and features being asked for and avoid minor technical details. Structure will be critical here, or else you could find it difficult to contain your answer.
- **Relate** – show how different aspects of the syllabus connect together.
- **Evaluate** – review and reflect upon an area of the syllabus, a particular practice, an article, etc., and consider its overall worth in respect of its use as a tool or a model and its overall effectiveness in the role it plays.

Source: Worsam, Mike, *How to Pass Marketing*, Croner, 1989.

Your approach to mini-cases

There is no one right way to approach and tackle a mini-case study, indeed it will be down to each individual to use their own creativity in tackling the tasks presented. You will have to use your initiative and discretion about how best to approach the mini-case. Having said this, however, there are some basic steps you can take.

- Ensure that you read through the case study at least twice before making any judgements, starting to analyse the information provided, or indeed writing the answers.
- On the third occasion read through the mini-case and, using a highlighter, start marking the essential and relevant information critical to the content and context. Then turn your attention to the question again, this time reading slowly and carefully to assess what it is you are expected to do. Note any instructions that the examiner gives you, and then start to plan how you might answer the question. Whatever the question, ensure the answer has a structure: a beginning, a structured central part of the answer and, finally, always a conclusion.
- Keep the context of the question continually in mind: that is, the specifics of the case and the role which you might be performing.
- Because there is limited material available, you will sometimes need to make assumptions. Don't be afraid to do this, it will show initiative on your part. Assumptions are an important part of dealing with case studies and can help you to be quite creative with your answer. However, do explain the basis of your assumptions within your answer so that the examiner understands the nature of them, and why you have arrived at your particular outcome. **Always ensure that your assumptions are realistic.**
- Only now are you approaching the stage where it is time to start writing your answer to the question, tackling the problems, making decisions and recommendations on the case scenario set before you. As mentioned previously, your points will often be best set out in a report or memo type format, particularly if the examiner does not specify a communication method.
- Ensure that your writing is succinct, avoids waffle and responds directly to the questions asked.

Part B

Again, with the exception of the Analysis and Decision case study, each Part B is comprised of six or seven more traditional questions, each worth 20 per cent. You will be expected to choose three of those questions, to make up the remaining 60 per cent of available marks.

Realistically, the same principles apply for these questions as in the case study. Communication formats, reading through the questions, structure, role-play, context, etc. – everything is the same.

Part B will cover a number of broader issues from within the syllabus and will be taken from any element of it. The examiner makes the choice, and no prior direction is given to students or tutors on what that might be.

As regards time management in this area, if you used about 75 minutes for the mini-case you should have around 105 minutes left. This provides you with around 30 minutes to plan and write a question and 5 minutes per question to review and revise your answers. Keep practising – use a cooker timer, alarm clock or mobile phone alarm as your timer and work hard at answering questions within the timeframe given.

Specimen examination papers and answers

To help you prepare and understand the nature of the paper, go to www.marketingonline.co.uk or www.bh.com/marketing to access Specimen Answers and Senior Examiner's advice for these exam questions. During your study, the author of your Coursebook may have on occasions asked you to refer to these papers and answer the questions. You should undertake these exercises and utilize every opportunity to practise meeting examination requirements.

The specimen answers are vital learning tools. They are not always perfect, as they are answers written by students and annotated by the Senior Examiners, but they will give you a good indication of the approaches you could take, and the examiners' annotations suggest how these answers might be improved. Please use them. You can also access this type of information through the Virtual Institute on the CIM website using your student registration number as an access code.

Other sources of information to support your learning through the Virtual Institute are 'Hot Topics'. These give you scope to undertake a range of associated activities related to the syllabus and study areas, and will also be very useful to you when you are revising.

Key elements of preparation

One Senior Examiner suggests the three elements involved in preparing for your examination can be summarized thus:

- Learning
- Memory
- Revision

Let's look at each point in turn.

Learning

Quite often students find it difficult to learn properly. You can passively read books, look at some of the materials, perhaps revise a little, and regurgitate it all in the examination. In the main, however, this is rather an unsatisfactory method of learning. It is meaningless, shallow and ultimately of little use in practice.

For learning to be truly effective it must be active and applied. You must involve yourself in the learning process by thinking about what you have read, testing it against your experience by reflecting on how you use particular aspects of marketing, and how you could perhaps improve your own performance by implementing particular aspects of your learning into your everyday life. You should adopt the old adage of 'learning by doing'. If you do, you will find that passive learning has no place in your study life.

Below are some suggestions that have been prepared to assist you with the learning pathway throughout your revision.

- Always make your own notes, in words you understand, and ensure that you combine all the sources of information and activities within them.
- Always try to relate your learning back to your own organization.
- Make sure you define key terms concisely, wherever possible.
- Do not try to memorize your ideas, but work on the basis of understanding and, most important, applying them.
- Think about the relevant and topical questions that might be set – use the questions and answers in each of your Coursebooks to identify typical questions that might be asked in the future.
- Attempt all of the questions within each of your Coursebooks since these are vital tests of your active learning and understanding.

Memory

If you are prepared to undertake an active learning programme then your knowledge will be considerably enhanced, as understanding and application of knowledge does tend to stay in your 'long-term' memory. It is likely that passive learning will only stay in your 'short-term' memory.

Do not try to memorize parrot fashion; it is not helpful and, even more important, examiners are experienced in identifying various memorizing techniques and therefore will spot them as such.

Having said this, it is quite useful to memorize various acronyms such as SWOT, PEST, PESTLE, STEEPLE, or indeed various models such as Ansoff, GE Matrix, Shell Directional, etc., as in some of the questions you may be required to use illustrations of these to assist your answer.

Revision

The third and final stage to consider is 'revision', which is what we will concentrate on in detail below. Here just a few key tips are offered.

Revision should be an ongoing process rather than a panic measure that you decide to undertake just before the examination. You should be preparing notes *throughout* your course, with the view to using them as part of your revision process. Therefore ensure that your notes are sufficiently comprehensive that you can reuse them successfully.

For each concept you learn about, you should identify, through your reading and your own personal experience, at least two or three examples that you could use; this then gives you some scope to broaden your perspective during the examination. It will, of course, help you gain some points for initiative with the examiners.

Knowledge is not something you will gain overnight – as we saw earlier, it is not a quick fix; it involves a process of learning that enables you to lay solid foundations upon which to build your long-term understanding and application. This will benefit you significantly in the future, not just in the examination.

In essence, you should ensure that you do the following in the period before the real intensive revision process begins.

- Keep your study file well organized, updated and full of newspaper and journal cuttings that may help you formulate examples in your mind for use during the examination.
- Practise defining key terms and acronyms from memory.
- Prepare topic outlines and essay answer plans.
- When you start your intensive revision, ensure it is planned and structured in the way described below. And then finally, read your concentrated notes the night before the examination.

Revision planning

You are now on a critical path – although hopefully not too critical at this time – with somewhere in the region of between four and six weeks to go to the examination. The following hints and tips will help you plan out your revision study.

- You will, as already explained, need to be very organized. Therefore, before doing anything else, put your files, examples, reading material, etc. in good order, so that you are able to work with them in the future and, of course, make sense of them.
- Ensure that you have a quiet area within which to work. It is very easy to get distracted when preparing for an examination.
- Take out your file along with your syllabus and make a list of key topic areas that you have studied and which you now need to revise. You could use the basis of this book to do that, by taking each unit a step at a time.
- Plan the use of your time carefully. Ideally you should start your revision at least six weeks prior to the exam, so therefore work out how many spare hours you could give to the revision process and then start to allocate time in your diary, and do not double-book with anything else.
- Give up your social life for a short period of time. As the saying goes 'no pain – no gain'.

- Looking at each of the subject areas in turn, identify which are your strengths and which are your weaknesses. Which areas have you grasped and understood, and which are the areas that you have really struggled with? Split your page in two and make a list on each side. For example:

| Planning and control ||
Strengths	Weaknesses
Audit – PEST, SWOT, Models Portfolio analysis	Ratio analysis Market sensing Productivity analysis Trend extrapolation Forecasting

- Break down your list again and divide the points of weakness, giving priority in the first instance to your weakest areas and even prioritizing them by giving them a number. This will enable you to master the more difficult areas. Up to 60 per cent of your remaining revision time should be given over to that, as you may find you have to undertake a range of additional reading and also perhaps seeking tutor support, if you are studying at a CIM Accredited Study Centre.
- The rest of the time should be spent reinforcing your knowledge and understanding of the stronger areas, spending time testing yourself on how much you really know.
- Should you be taking two examinations or more at any one time, then the breakdown and managing of your time will be critical.
- Taking a subject at a time, work through your notes and start breaking them down into subsections of learning, and ultimately into key learning points, items that you can refer to time and time again, that are meaningful and that your mind will absorb. You yourself will know how you best remember key points. Some people try to develop acronyms, or flowcharts or matrices, mind maps, fishbone diagrams, etc., or various connection diagrams that help them recall certain aspects of models. You could also develop processes that enable you to remember approaches to various options. (But do remember what we said earlier about regurgitating stuff, parrot fashion.)

Figure A1.1 Use of a diagram to summarize key components of a concept (Source: Adapted from Dibb, Simkin, Pride & Ferrell, Marketing Concepts and Strategies, 4th edition, Houghton Mifflin, 2001)

Figure A1.1 is just a brief example of how you could use a 'bomb-burst' diagram (which, in this case, highlights the uses of advertising) as a very helpful approach to memorizing key elements of learning.

- Eventually you should reduce your key learning to bullet points. For example: imagine you were looking at the concept of Time Management – you could eventually reduce your key learning to a bullet list containing the following points in relation to 'Effective Prioritization:'

  - Organize
  - Take time
  - Delegate
  - Review

  Each of these headings would then remind you of the elements you need to discuss associated with the subject area.

- Avoid getting involved in reading too many textbooks at this stage, as you may start to find that you are getting confused overall.
- Look at examination questions on previous papers, and start to observe closely the various roles and tasks they expect you to undertake, and importantly, the context in which they are set.
- Use the specimen exam papers and specimen answers to support your learning and see how you could actually improve upon them.
- Without exception, find an associated examination question for the areas that you have studied and revised, and undertake it (more than once if necessary).
- Without referring to notes or books, try to draft an answer plan with the key concepts, knowledge, models and information that are needed to successfully complete the answer. Then refer to the specimen answer to see how close you are to the actual outline presented. Planning your answer, and ensuring that key components are included, and that the question has a meaningful structure, is one of the most beneficial activities that you can undertake.
- Now write the answer out in full, time-constrained and written by hand, not with the use of IT. (At this stage, you are still expected to be the scribe for the examination and present handwritten work. Many of us find this increasingly difficult as we spend more and more time using our computers to present information. Do your best to be neat. Spidery handwriting is often offputting to the examiner.)
- When writing answers as part of your revision process, also be sure to practise the following essential examinations techniques:

  - **Identify and use the communication method** requested by the examiner.
  - **Always have three key parts to the answer** – an introduction, middle section that develops your answer in full, and a conclusion. Where appropriate, ensure that you have an introduction, main section, summary/conclusion and, if requested or helpful, recommendations.
  - **Always answer the question in the context or role set.**
  - **Always comply with the nature and terms of the question.**
  - **Leave white space.** Do not overcrowd your page; Leave space between paragraphs, and make sure your sentences do not merge into one blur. (Don't worry – there is always plenty of paper available to use in the examination.)
  - **Count** how many actions the question asks you to undertake and double-check at the end that you have met the full range of demands of the question.
  - **Use examples** – to demonstrate your knowledge and understanding of the particular syllabus area. These can be from journals, the Internet, the press, or your own experience.

- **Display your vigour and enthusiasm for marketing.** Remember to think of the Senior Examiner as your customer, or future employer, and do your best to deliver what is wanted to satisfy their needs. Impress them and show them how you are a 'cut above the rest'.
- Review all your practice answers critically, with the above points in mind.

Practical actions

The critical path is becoming even more critical now as the examination looms. The following are vital points.

- Have you registered with CIM?
- Do you know where you are taking your examination? CIM should let you know approximately one month in advance.
- Do you know where your examination centre is? If not find out, take a drive, time it – whatever you do don't be late!
- Make sure you have all the tools of the examination ready. A dictionary, calculator, pens, pencils, ruler, etc. Try not to use multiple shades of pens, but at the same time make your work look professional. *Avoid using red and green as these are the colours that will be used for marking.*

Summary

Above all you must remember that you personally have invested a tremendous amount of time, effort and money in studying for this programme and it is therefore imperative that you consider the suggestions given here as they will help to maximize your return on your investment.

Many of the hints and tips offered here are generic and will work across most of the CIM courses. We have tried to select those that will help you most in taking a sensible, planned approach to your study and revision.

The key to your success is being prepared to put in the time and effort required, planning your revision, and equally important, planning and answering your questions in a way that will ensure that you pass your examination on the day.

The advice offered here aims to guide you from a practical perspective. Guidance on syllabus content and developments associated with your learning will become clear to you as you work through this Coursebook. The authors of each Coursebook have given subject-specific guidance on the approach to the examination and on how to ensure that you meet the content requirements of the kind of question you will face. These considerations are in addition to the structuring issues we have been discussing throughout this Appendix.

Each of the authors and Senior Examiners will guide you on their preferred approach to questions and answers as they go. Therefore where you are presented with an opportunity to be involved in some activity or undertake an examination question either during or at the end of your study units, do take it. It not only prepares you for the examination, but helps you learn in the applied way we discussed above.

Here, then, is a last reminder:

- Ensure you make the most of your learning process throughout.
- Keep structured and orderly notes from which to revise.
- Plan your revision – don't let it just happen.
- Provide examples to enhance your answers.

- Practise your writing skills in order that you present your work well and your writing is readable.
- Take as many opportunities to test your knowledge and measure your progress as possible.
- Plan and structure your answers.
- Always do as the question asks you, especially with regard to context and communication method.
- **Do not leave it until the last minute!**

The writers would like to take this opportunity to wish you every success in your endeavours to study, to revise and to pass your examinations.

Karen Beamish
Academic Development Advisor

Appendix 2
Answers and debriefings

The answers that follow are indicative and are not intended to be complete. Some of the answers to the activities are embedded in the course materials, the essential text, in web sites or simply in the mind of the reader.

Unit 1

Debriefing Question 1.1

Marketing would have required to define the level of service Egg would be required to offer. They would have been involved in the service development stage, taking Egg as a brand from conception to reality. In order to do this the marketing function would have had to consider the 'people, process and physical' elements of the marketing mix process. This would have been developed in association with the human resources function.

Human resources would have been responsible for considering resource implications, developing appropriate recruitment and selection strategies, enabling training and skills development and assigning the correct personnel to the job in order to achieve high performance levels.

The two functions would need to understand the concepts, the resources, the processes and the physical environment requirements. This could not be achieved while working in isolation or in a vacuum.

Egg's success is clearly as a result of an integrative strategy worked through from the top of the strategy and planning hierarchy down to the bottom. The success for marketing was the rapid rate at which brand recognition grew and the significant number of hits on the websites within a short period of time.

Debriefing Question 1.2

Specific barriers might include:

- General resistance to restructuring
- Lack of co-operation due to scarce resources
- Breakdown in communication
- Obstructive behaviour
- Political barriers
- Cultural barriers
- Functional barriers – lack of co-operation and agreement among business units
- Employee relations issues
- High turnover of staff
- Political infighting
- Management not prepared to change.

Barriers might be created as a result of:

- Lack of communication (one of the biggest single factors in creating barriers to change)
- Lack of consultation
- Autocratic management style
- Failure to address the resourcing issue can force complete lack of co-operation
- Inappropriately skilled staff
- Fear of the unknown

- Unrealistic targets
- Lack of top-down commitment to the planning process.

Debriefing Activity 1.1

Typical changes might include:

- New information systems
- Restructuring/reorganization
- New management
- New products/service offerings
- Diversification – change in direction
- Mergers/acquisitions
- Downsizing.

These are just a few of the modes of change organizations frequently encounter.

Drivers for change might include:

- Efficiency drivers
- Stakeholders
- Competitive forces
- Evolution of information communication technology (ICT)
- External drivers of change
- Political or economic forces.

Unit 2

Debriefing Question 2.1

Potential opportunities might include:

- Anti-ageing products
- Provision of nutrients and vitamin supplements
- Provision of food supplements
- Opportunities to provide medical bandages, stockings
- Incontinence pads, etc.

The key to this is that while the example is a healthcare products company, there are so many opportunities available as the demographic trend is that the 'grey market' is living for longer. There are opportunities to provide products that both enhance that life cycle and support it practically.

Debriefing Question 2.2

The long-term effect on Exxon of consumer pressure and demonstrations by stakeholder audiences could go two ways:

1. They will respond to consumer pressure and adhere to the requirements of the Kyoto summit, but effectively they will reduce their bottom line and overall profitability quite significantly. This will bring pressure from shareholders, and will ultimately mean that they will fail to fulfil their long-term profit objectives.
2. If they fail to respond to consumer pressure, it is likely that consumer pressure will grow, that competitors will take the opportunity to attack Exxon in its moment of weakness and that the results could potentially be catastrophic.

It is likely that whichever way Exxon go, this particular demonstration will do them untold damage in the short to medium term and that a range of marketing and PR activities will be required to start to undertake damage limitation.

Debriefing Question 2.3

A SWOT analysis of your own organization or one you will know well should present many of the components listed within the SWOT analysis grid (Figure 2.4). Clearly recommendations to overcome weakness should highlight a transferring of a weakness into a strength, which would potentially see a change in internal marketing objectives to remedy some of the situations your weaknesses currently present.

For example:

- Lack of resources should be converted into a strength, by taking a planned approach to increasing the current resource base, through organizational growth and investment.
- Aged technology – this could become a strength again, through planned investment.
- Weak supplier relationships can also be converted into a strength, by changing the basis of their agreement, incentivizing them, managing them closely and effectively. Be aware of opposing competitive forces, and divert their attention into alternative areas.

Unit 3

Debriefing Question 3.1

SWOT effectively identified the key components in relation to the internal and external environment.

It draws a substantial amount of the marketing audit together and provides the basis of the decision-making process by giving a clear insight into the dynamics of the marketing environment.

Strengths of the organization	What the organization does well
Weaknesses of the organization	What the organization could improve
Opportunities for exploitation by the organization	Where the organization can go to
Threats that face them	The inhibiting factors of growth

It provides the basis of strategy development and acts as an indicator when establishing market entry strategies, growth strategies, marketing penetration strategies, new product development, etc.

Debriefing Question 3.2

Some of the key benefits of a gap analysis might include:

- It provides an insight into how much there is to achieve between where the organization is now and where they are going
- It provides an insight into exactly how much marketing activity the organization may need to undertake in order to meet the corporate goals
- It provides the basis for strategy development such as market growth, or market development strategies that might fill the gap
- It will provide the basis on which to consider the resources required in order the fill the gap
- It forces the organization to consider carefully the realism of the objectives they have set, versus what is realistically achievable
- It identifies the potential for competitive activity and being prepared to be proactive in order that the competitor does not fill the gap in place of the organization.

In essence it gives the basis on which to formulate a strategy and develop a planned approach.

Debriefing Question 3.3

Differentiation is a highly significant way of establishing a long-term competitive advantage, in order to retain market share. Therefore it is essential that the business looks for a number of ways to add value to the product/service offering in a way that makes their offering more attractive than that of their competitors. The value, however, has to be perceived as such by their customers.

Differentiation therefore provides the foundation on which to compete on price, promotions, product benefits and distribution options.

Debriefing Question 3.4

Benefits of being a market follower are:

- Less perceived risk
- Allowing the leader to make the mistakes
- The organization works on a follower basis, therefore strategies are generally reactive
- Wherever the leader goes you can follow – therefore entry strategies, etc. are usually already defined and the groundwork is done for the follower.

Debriefing Question 3.5

Segmentation and targeting are crucial to the success of any organization. It is a necessary process that enables the organization to understand who their customers are, how they buy, what they buy, their lifestyle and their expectations.

It is important to know where they are, their characteristics, their beliefs and values, in order that you can specifically target their needs and expectations directly through your marketing offering.

The benefits are significant.

Failure to undertake this activity could be catastrophic as you could lose market share, competitors will move in and attack your inability to target the market specifically and ultimately will erode your competitive advantage in the marketplace.

Failure to undertake segmentation and targeting will mean that the organization is planning in a vacuum, targeting and positioning to an audience who do not necessarily exist.

Therefore it is essential that the organization fully researches the market and understands it in order that they can respond to its needs.

Debriefing Question 3.6

Positioning statements should reflect issues relating to:

- Quality
- Service
- Price
- Accessibility
- Brand image
- Benefits/characteristics.

Think of the perceptual map and how you would explain the positioning of British Airways against Virgin Express – links to quality, price, service, delivery, etc., spring to mind.

Debriefing Question 3.7

Communications is the vital component of internal marketing. It is the bridge between the organization and its employees. It is the very channel that will not only inform and communicate change, but also the channel that will indicate to the organization the employees' willingness and commitment to change.

Furthermore, communication is a vital component to all members of the organization in order that they understand the vision and mission, and what their responsibility and contribution is towards achieving the corporate goals.

Good internal marketing will erode some of the barriers to the implementation of the marketing plan, in order that effectiveness and efficiency can be achieved.

Communications can act as a motivator to the organization, it can act as a tool that conveys inspiration, encouragement and commitment and leadership.

The list of benefits of communication internally is endless, but ultimately to achieve organizational success, you need to take the 'internal customer' with you. Therefore communicating values, commitment, vision, empowerment and the mission, effectively and efficiently, proactively, not reactively, might enable a smoother transition to new working practices and processes.

Internal marketing should be targeted and planned in order to gain the most success.

Unit 4

Debriefing Question 4.1

Key differences between opinion leaders and opinion formers:

Opinion leaders

Key characteristics include:

- People who are predisposed to receiving information and using it to influence others
- Social class equivalence to those who are influenced
- People who express negative or positive comments in relation to organizations and their products.

They can include specialist interest groups, lobbying groups, etc.

Opinion formers

Key characteristics include:

- Subject knowledge specialisms
- Expert judgement and expert witness skills
- Shape the opinions of others from their knowledge of particular situations
- They are often lobbied by organizations for support in a particular context
- Often credible sources.

The overall differences relate to the fact that opinion leaders can exert influence on opinion formers, they can shape and influence from a position of strength and experience. Each can make a valuable contribution and if their contributions are cross-fertilized through the multi-step process then the organization has the benefit of two influential groups feeding their communications process.

Debriefing Question 4.2

The two-step communication model only takes into account the potential influence of the opinion leaders and therefore is likely to target those leaders in order that they can assert a positive influence on the target audience, i.e. the customer.

The multi-step communication model creates an opportunity for an interactive approach to communication with the potential for all members of the group, the organization, the opinion leaders, opinion formers and the customer, to inform the communications process.

Therefore the multi-step model provides a basis for more effective communication and an interactive relationship between all parties concerned. However, targeting communications for all parties could potentially be a complex process, should the parties be different enough to require tailored communications for each group.

Debriefing Question 4.3

1–3 Cognitive

4–6 Affective

7–10 Behavioural

11–15 Corporate

Unit 5

Debriefing Question 5.1

Objectives provide definition and direction for the advertising campaign, but they also put it into context of the marketing strategy and plan in respect of implementation.

Setting of objectives ensures that there is value to the advertising programme, that is measurable, achievable, realistic and timebound.

It is essential that the objectives also relate to other elements of the promotional mix, so that the advertising is relevant and complementary to the promotional mix strategy.

Debriefing Question 5.2

While advertising on its own can work, to optimize effectiveness it is essential that either the advertising, associated sales promotions and direct marketing, provide the opportunity for customers to respond, to take action to either trial the product or adopt the product.

Due to the technical nature of some products, it might be that while advertising provides the awareness, personal selling, aided by direct marketing, might actually provide the information required to solve the problem of purchase, inducing early adoption of the product and associated services.

Debriefing Question 5.3

Advertising acts as a support mechanism for the remainder of the promotional mix, in order to create the awareness, interest, desire. Other elements of the marketing mix might then create the incentive to act, or inducement to adopt, indeed take the decision to purchase.

With more emphasis on direct response advertising, there is perhaps less of a necessity for some other promotional mix activities, but in the main it is helpful to optimize as many tools as possible for reinforcement of the message.

Debriefing Question 5.4

Full service agencies provide a full suite of skills including:

- Creative skills
- Artwork
- Media buying
- Public relations
- Direct marketing
- Market research

under one roof, or the umbrella of the organization. Therefore in respect of standards, full service provision, integration and co-ordination, it is possibly more beneficial to select a full service agency.

A limited service agency, while they might be experienced in specific elements of advertising, do not offer the full suite of skills in-house, and therefore have to rely on outsourcing the remainder of the work. In this situation, the brief is being passed on, and the quality assurance issues of standardization might be diluted by introducing a third party to the client.

Debriefing Question 5.5

Pre-testing advertisements is a useful process, whereby organizations have the opportunity to test on a small sample of the market, therefore ascertaining answers to questions such as 'Is it usable? Does it meet with customer expectations? Would you buy it? Why would they buy it?' etc.

It is therefore essential that pre-test is undertaken to ascertain appropriateness for the target audience. Should it appear to be unsuitable, unclear, or ineffective then the organization will have the opportunity to adapt prior to the major launch.

Debriefing Question 5.6

Typical sales promotional activities from manufacturer to consumer includes elements relating to a pull strategy, pulling the products up through the supply chain for adoption and purchase:

- Encouraging trial – samples, gifts, trial drives of vehicles – allow customers to decide for themselves
- Disseminating information – information packs on a door-to-door basis, perhaps closely linked with a direct marketing campaign (again utilizing the integrated marketing communications approach)
- Trading up – encouraging customers to trade-up from their existing models – a typical activity of car manufacturers and white goods manufacturers.

Debriefing Question 5.7

Typically sales promotion adds value to advertising by providing the incentive to purchase and the response mechanism, to trial, gain more information, increase sales, encourage repeat purchase and for competitive responses to competitive activities.

Advertising therefore creates the awareness; promotion is the means by which customers have the incentive to respond.

Debriefing Question 5.8

PR complements the promotional mix in a number of ways – these are just some ways to point you in the right direction:

- Creates a broader awareness of the brand and the organization
- Increases coverage to principal events and draws further attention to the corporate brand and profile
- It represents the organization fully in both a negative and positive response to events
- It provides the basis for securing greater awareness of product developments, products launched
- It is a form of advertising
- As a function it might run sales promotion campaigns
- It covers a broader potential audience than perhaps advertising and therefore creates awareness in new markets.

Debriefing Question 5.9

The promotional mix should take an integrated approach to ensuring successful achievements of the marketing objectives and implementation of the strategy. Therefore, advertising, sales promotions and direct marketing present the opportunity for an awareness-raising, incentive-boosting, informative communications campaign.

As previously suggested, advertising creates the awareness, sales promotion creates the incentive and the direct mail (direct marketing) provides the channel for communication in relation to the promotion, possibly including a voucher.

The three of these promotional mix mechanisms are very compatible promotional tools.

Unit 6

Debriefing Question 6.1

The core of the BMW business is the base-line car for the purpose of this question. To take the product from the core to the augmented product, will include the development of a range of added value extra components, such as stereos, car alarms, superior finish, computerized traffic systems, etc.

Augmenting the product provides the manufacturer with an opportunity to differentiate their products, target different groups of customers, with the same core model, but with specification differences, to meet the needs of all customers within the appropriate market segments.

Debriefing Question 6.2

Brand loyalty and customer retention are significant priorities of organizations today. It is a known fact that retaining customers is more cost-effective than gaining new ones.

The basis of brand loyalty, therefore, is through market research, aligning and associating your brand, its values and mission, with your customers.

One of the benefits of brand values is that customers will associate them with inbred and inherent values of their own lives and those of the organization. In a business sense these values should be exploited in order to achieve brand loyalty and ultimately develop a brand preference.

Therefore the brand, all that it stands for, image, association, values, assets, should be highly targeted and customer characteristics closely matched.

Debriefing Question 6.3

Packaging clearly is a hybrid function as it is multifunctional from a product and promotional perspective.

From a product perspective it provides:

- Security
- Safety
- Protection
- Information.

From a promotional perspective it provides:

- Brand awareness
- Brand recognition
- Advertising
- Promotions.

From a corporate perspective, as in the case of EarthShell, it provides an opportunity for ethical, environmental and legal support which can ultimately be designed and included as part of the corporate and brand value process.

Debriefing Question 6.4

The contents of the briefing should focus on cars, in particular:

- Vehicle modifications – including quality, functionality and style
- Differentiation activities, brand and product differentiation
- Potential repositioning or re-branding

- Increase in promotional activities – advertising, sales promotions, direct mail
- A range of different pricing strategies, very specifically targeted for maximum effect
- Increase in competitive activity – therefore prepared attacks required.

Debriefing Question 6.5

The BCG matrix is a highly useful tool in ascertaining the position of both products and their competitive positioning in relation to market share, and potential growth opportunities.

In terms of its overall use, it is an extremely useful planning tool, whereby plotting the position of products on the matrix provides you with information to underpin the planning process. Some of the information provided will be:

- Competitive position
- Stage in the product life cycle
- Potential for growth
- Necessity for deletion
- Level of investment required to sustain market share
- The need for repositioning
- Market development opportunities
- Market penetration strategies
- Level of expected profitability from products.

All of the above information, in addition to many more elements, will be fed into the marketing audit process, which ultimately feeds into the marketing strategy. At this stage the contribution that the product will make, proposed changes, new product development strategies, modification programmes, etc. will be decided. Therefore BCG is a planning tool to support both strategic level decision-making and future product planning opportunities.

Unit 7

Debriefing Question 7.1

The following are some of the key points to be discussed:

- Seasonal variation
- Business market rates
- Services issues of intangibility – if the room is not filled on a particular night the income from that room is lost for ever – should a lower price be charged in order that the room might be filled?
- Time influences
- Regional variances
- Income – state of economy – boom or bust
- Disposable income levels
- Customer perception
- Competitive activity.

Debriefing Question 7.2

Justifying the value proposition will be quite a challenge and therefore the following marketing activities could be undertaken – these are only some of the activities you could undertake:

- Product positioning – perceptual mapping
- Brand development – brand association – establishing brand preference
- Advertising – promoting benefits and functionality of the products – creating high levels of awareness
- Market testing
- Trial programmes

- Product differentiation
- Defining tightly targeted groups through the segmentation process
- Establishing quality measures with quality being perceived as a visible component of the purchase
- Price skimming – sometimes pricing might justify quality (however this can be precarious overall)
- Competitive positioning
- Distribution strategies – availability of product, exclusivity of outlets, etc.

Debriefing Question 7.3

The overall impact of competitive pricing in the 21st century is:

- Intense rivalry
- Competitor warfare
- Profit margins narrowing
- Price reductions unsustainable in the long term
- Industry infrastructure suffering
- A route to mass unemployment
- Saturated markets
- High levels of innovation to overcome competitiveness
- Shorter life cycles – less opportunity for maturity and profit
- High quality/low price.

Debriefing Question 7.4

It is essential that pricing objectives reflect marketing objectives, in order that the marketing plan can be successfully implemented.

If marketing objectives are based on growth, then pricing objectives have to reflect the ability to achieve growth through appropriate pricing strategies. Similarly, if market penetration is the focus of the marketing strategy, then market penetration activities should be undertaken.

Price will be a key influence in meeting profitability goals (ROI goals) and therefore key influences, costs, and external drivers, combined with the marketing strategy, should shape closely pricing objectives in order for successful execution and implementation of the marketing plan.

Unit 8

Debriefing Question 8.1

Changes in lifestyle have impacted upon distribution in some of the following ways:

- Less time/time-starved individuals
- The need for more convenience products
- The necessity to shop out of hours
- More choice and selection in retail outlets
- Shopping is a highly significant leisure activity
- Direct marketing becoming increasingly desirable
- The strength and power of the customer and consumer pull the product to market
- Increasing customer demands
- Customers more clued into value propositions
- Increasing debt
- More flexible payment systems.

Debriefing Question 8.2

The producer can achieve cost-effectiveness through introducing intermediaries into the channel, in the following way. They should be encouraged to facilitate, undertake logistical management and provide transactional management.

Incentivizing organizations to undertake this level of activity, i.e. through promotional support, merchandising support, profit share, etc., can cost significantly less than resourcing and managing the following functions:

Marketing information	Analyse information such as sales data. Carry out research studies
Marketing management	Establish objectives, plan activities and manage, co-ordinate financing, risk-taking. Evaluate channel activities
Facilitating exchange	Choose and stock products that match buyers' needs
Promotion	Set promotional objectives, co-ordinate advertising, personal selling, promotions etc.
Price	Establish pricing policies, terms and sales
Physical distribution	Manage transport, warehousing, materials handling, stock control and communication
Customer service	Provide channels for advice, technical support, after-sales service and warranties
Relationships	Facilitate communication, products, parts, credit control etc. Maintain relationships between manufacturer and retail outlets, and customer/consumer

Debriefing Question 8.3

The basis of your decision and justification should include the following points:

- It is likely that this will be the basis of selective distribution in the medium term. While palm-tops are highly popular, the diffusion process is relatively slow with the overall prices still being moderately expensive. Therefore, costs of associated valued-added components are also relatively high at this stage.
- The concept of palm-tops and portable keyboards is excellent, but again diffusion will be slow.
- Currently this product is not widely available and while it is not sufficiently exclusive to fall under 'exclusive distribution', it is nowhere near a mass market, low price product.
- In terms of market segmentation and targeting, the likely contenders for the use of this product will be Bs and C1, middle, junior and supervisory managers.
- Essentially the uses of these products and the associated technicalities of using palm-tops will require some level of technical support and know-how, which would not typically match against the requirements of an intensive distribution strategy.

Debriefing Question 8.5

- Disintermediation refers to the process of selling directly between the organization and the customer, without the assistance of traditional intermediaries and more in line with the association of cybermediaries.
- The benefits of this method of selling, as in the case of Lufthansa, are that the cost of physical and human resources are considerably reduced and the need for significant building of bricks and mortar is less likely.
- It speeds up the process of transaction considerably, it closes a sale more effectively, and it provides growth opportunities and cost reductions.

- The cost of marketing activities is reduced and the necessity for marketing support to intermediaries will cease to exist.
- The process of disintermediation may bring the producer/supplier much closer to their customers. In doing this, with the electronic footprint method of collecting information on an underpinning database, the organization can potentially get much closer to targeting specific customer needs and expectation.
- The list is endless, but these are some of the key points.

Unit 9

Debriefing Question 9.1

You will very likely be surprised at the extent of relationships that you are currently involved in the workplace, however the challenge will be to manage them successfully in the true context of relationship marketing.

Debriefing Question 9.2

- *Organizational markets* – require high levels of relationship management due to the intensity and time dimensions of the process of purchase. The market is essentially less fickle and more rational, which provides the basis of establishing closer links.
- Closer links mean working towards gaining preferred supplier status. Achieving this will ultimately mean long-term supplier/buyer relationships, effectively putting a relationship on a strong footing.
- Essentially relationship marketing is about collaborative relationships, working together, optimizing opportunities and maximizing potential.

(Taken from within the text – this should form the basis of your answer.)

Debriefing Question 9.3

The value of key account management is based on the concept of interrelated key account management – where there is almost a partnership concept between the supplier and the buyer exhibiting some of the following points:

- Both organizations acknowledge importance to each other
- Preferred supplier status could be achieved
- Exit from the relationship is more difficult
- High level of information exchange – some information sensitive
- Wider range of joint and innovative activity between supplier and buyer
- Larger number of multifunctional contacts
- Streamlined processes
- Both sides are prepared to invest in the relationship
- High volume of sales achieved
- Better understanding of the customer
- Developing social relationships
- Development of trust
- Cost savings
- Proactive rather than reactive
- Joint strategic planning and focus on the future
- Opportunity to grow business.

Debriefing Question 9.4

Highly motivated personnel are an essential ingredient and should be developed by the organization in order that their skills and abilities are optimized, particularly as they are the frontline people with whom customers actually interact.

Their ability to help, support, guide and service, will hopefully turn them from customer into client, client into advocate and advocate into partner, and will be crucial to the achievement of customer loyalty and customer retention within the organization.

Debriefing Question 9.5

Ethical issues are those that are moral principles that define right and wrong behaviour in the context of marketing. Therefore, there are key activities that an organization should avoid, change their direction in or ensure that there is no ethical controversy within the organization. It is essential that codes of ethics from all associated organizations are adhered to and that no harm should come to anybody within the organization or its customers and stakeholders as a result of their marketing activities.

Social responsibility, however, is a moral obligation to maximize positive impact and minimize negative impact upon society. This is essentially like being a good corporate citizen, contributing towards the environment, the community and assisting the improvement in the quality of life and the quality of the environment.

Unit 10

Debriefing Question 10.1

The following activities are likely:

- Once the original interest had been registered by the buyer, it is likely that the consultancy would spend some time understanding the nature and complexity of the project – highlighting that this will likely be a high involvement sale.

The process might include some of the following as an illustration of high-level involvement:

- The consultancy would then spend some time drawing up provisional specifications in consultation with the buyer, prior to entering the formal tendering process.
- This would involve further meetings, references and information being provided by both organizations, in order to gain a mutual understanding of the situation.
- The consultancy is likely to be one of many involved within the tendering process, therefore it will be essential that they understand the full details of the requirements before proceeding to tender.
- It is likely that the tenderer will work on partnership arrangements with contractors in order to actually be able to fully price the work, estimate lead times, and draw up resource specifications that will deliver the technical support.

Debriefing Question 10.2

Typical differences will include:

- The consumer process could be more impulsive
- Individual decisions can be made without reference to others
- Complexity of the purchase is less
- Number of decision-makers may be one or even a family of four – but not a huge team of decision-makers
- Purchaser is the person who pays for the product
- The user is probably the same person, or passes it on as a gift to the end-user or consumer
- The influencer – this will vary, but will relate to cultural, social and personal influences rather than organizational.

Debriefing Question 10.3

Establishing sound and robust relationships with buyers is essential in order to achieve some of the following:

- Gain preferred supplier status
- Gain trust
- Collaborate and establish partnership agreements that are mutually beneficial
- Flexibility
- Respect, honesty
- A stronger likelihood of quality and delivery.

Debriefing Question 10.4

June 2000 – Question 4a

Debriefing Question 10.5

Customer uncertainty relates to the gap between understanding the customer and their expectation and what the service deliverer actually provides.

The gap, so to speak, can cause a range of different behaviour in the customer as a result of the gap in delivery and their expectation, thus highlight 'customer uncertainty' in respect of what they have received, as opposed to what they expected.

Debriefing Question 10.6

The additional 3Ps of the marketing mix are an imperative in order to enable the successful execution of the services marketing campaign. The original 4Ps of the marketing mix fail to take into account the service deliverables, i.e. the people, the processes, and where appropriate, the physical evidence. As services are very people oriented, these mix elements need to be introduced.

They are vital to enabling service delivery, service success, and give a basis on which to develop a service-based strategy.

However, the 4Ps do have a function, indeed the elements are complementary to the 3Ps in order that the mix may be priced, promoted, and delivered.

Debriefing Question 10.7

The basis of evaluation of services delivery could be along the lines of the following points. These are some suggestions that you might find consolidate your learning:

- To ensure that quality delivery is taking place
- To identify the gaps in delivery performance and delivery goals
- To identify the gap in expectations between the consumer and the delivery
- To be able to implement a programme of continuous improvement
- To ensure that quality prevails as a core denominator in the programme
- To ensure that customer uncertainties do not continue to arise and that the perception gap is filled
- To be a learning organization
- To understand customer dissatisfaction
- To ascertain levels of satisfaction
- To ensure that the design criteria were successful
- To measure the effectiveness of administrative and peripheral elements of the services mix.

Unit 11

Debriefing Question 11.1

Three methods of gaining funds for charitable donations might include some of the following:

- Charitable event organization
- Door-to-door collections
- Selling of merchandise
- Internet
- Major appeals – Red Nose – Children in Need
- Sponsorship of participants in major events (London Marathon)
- Corporate sponsorship
- Corporate donations
- Bequests from wills.

Debriefing Question 11.2

Targeting for Charities

Target donors – this is in order to continually remind them of the need for their donations; they are in the main the backbone of the financial support needed in order that the charitable objectives can be achieved.

Target volunteers – in order that fund allocations can be maximized, charitable work is therefore carried out by volunteers. The more volunteers, the less funds are committed to the running costs of the charities.

Clients/users – they are targeted in order that the organization can carry out their works to a target audience who need their services, their support and their financial contributions. Therefore clients might be homeless, disabled, suffer from MS, starving, blind, to name but a few. They need to be aware that there are resources available to make their life easier.

Debriefing Question 11.3

Not-for-profit organizations differ from commercial organizations in the following ways:

- Not for profit, means profit is not the focus of their business, however income generation is
- Objectives will be based around making people's lives better, rather than making money to benefit shareholders and the board
- Highly accountable to their members and donors
- Less resources available to do the job well
- Target market very broadly based (geographically diverse and culturally diverse nations)
- Measurement and control less easy to implement and monitor
- The nature of the marketing audit will focus on very specific areas
- Heavy reliance on stakeholders
- Donors give money for nothing in return, rather than receive anything for their contribution.

Debriefing Question 11.4

You should be thinking along these lines:

An advertising agency would be inappropriate for the following reasons:

- Too costly, this might be an inappropriate use of funds – agency costs historically high
- Work can be done by professional volunteers without a fee attached
- Agencies would need to understand the nature and culture of charities, this could be time-consuming and possibly not achievable
- Charity work is capable of achieving its own publicity, and can be managed in-house more satisfactorily overall.

Unit 12

Debriefing Question 12.1

As this question is based upon a country of your choice you should identify key differences such as

- Religion
- Education
- Place of women in society
- Work ethics
- Social behaviour
- Leisure persuits
- Language barriers
- Values
- Political affinity.

Look at the cultural framework in Figure 12.1 and identify at least two possible options of cultural diversity and discuss them.

Debriefing Question 12.2

The Internet will aid trade in some of the following ways:

- Opening up more markets
- Reducing barriers to entry on a country-by-country basis
- Make companies more competitive
- Cost-effective
- Reduces the need for high investment in marketing
- Creates opportunities to establish a more direct relationship with the customer
- Potentially a less risky venture, depending upon the distribution channel
- Reduces the implications of channel management
- Price competitive and price sensitive
- Enables fast response times to transactions
- No time barriers.

The list could go on – see how many you can get.

Debriefing Question 12.3

The implications for collecting primary data from lesser developed countries:

- Very expensive
- Not easily accessible
- Language barriers
- Terminology
- Geographic diversity within the host country
- Cultural differences
- Reliability and bias in the data collection
- Lack of response (non-response).

Debriefing Question 12.4

International marketing is an overall strategy that initiates international trade from a strategic level. The process of international marketing then devises appropriate marketing strategies based upon robust market research.

Export marketing is a distribution option available to the organization, i.e. as opposed to actually having bricks and mortar in a country, exporting is an alternative channel option.

Debriefing Question 12.5

Principal barriers to entry in Iran would be:

- Western cultures
- Western businesses
- Position of women in society
- Religion (Muslim)
- Cultural diversity
- Economic stature
- Less developed country
- Political intervention.

These are just some of the potential barriers to entry.

Debriefing Question 12.6

- *Economic* indicators would include the ability to afford the product being produced
- The exchange rate
- Cost of development in international markets
- Technology – costs of implementing appropriate levels of economy
- Market share
- Disposable income
- Per capita income
- Cost of raw materials
- Availability of raw materials
- *Environmental* – Kyoto Agreement and other similar agreements in relation to the use and disposal of materials and chemicals
- Packaging
- Transportation restrictions
- Positioning of plant in respect of environmentally friendly zones.

These are just an example of the possible answers you might come up with.

Appendix 3
Curriculum information and reading list

Syllabus

Aims and objectives

- To build on the knowledge of marketing fundamentals which the student is already expected to have gained.
- To encourage students to test and apply modern marketing theory to the understanding and solution of practical marketing problems and situations. This will enable them to perform effectively in any single functional area of marketing at junior management level.
- To provide students with a sound understanding of the process of marketing planning (analysis, strategy and implementation) and underpinning knowledge for the Diploma subject Planning and Control.
- To provide students with a sound understanding of the marketing mix tools that contribute towards the effective implementation of marketing strategy.
- To be able to evaluate the relative effectiveness and costs of elements of the promotional mix providing underpinning operational knowledge for the Integrated Marketing Communications module at Diploma level.
- To encourage students to explore the multiple relationships which need to be formed and maintained to enable successful and ongoing marketing exchange.
- To examine the need to adapt marketing operations in a variety of contexts; business-to-business, services, not-for-profit and international.

Learning outcomes

Students will be able to:

- Conduct a basic marketing audit considering internal and external factors.
- Understand the process of marketing planning at an operational level.
- Develop marketing objectives and plans at an operational level.
- Understand the need to integrate marketing mix tools to achieve effective implementation of plans.
- Select an appropriate integrated mix (4 Ps or 7 Ps) for a particular marketing context.
- Select and justify the use of one or more promotional techniques for a particular marketing context.
- Demonstrate the adaptation of marketing operations principles in a variety of contexts.
- Understand and appreciate the marketing operations process and how it can be delivered through multiple relationships.
- Communicate ideas effectively in a variety of formats; report, article, presentation.

Indicative content and weighting

1.1 The Marketing Planning Process: An Overview (15%)

1.1.1 Conducting a marketing audit
- Analysis of an organization's marketing environment Macro: political, legal, economic, socio-cultural, technological Micro: market size/trends, customers, competitors, suppliers, distributors, publics.
- Analysis of organization's internal capabilities. Financial resources, human resources, manufacturing, operations, R & D and marketing (strategy, mix, organization, systems, productivity).
- SWOT analysis and key issues.

1.1.2 Developing marketing objectives and strategies
- Marketing objectives as simple goal statements, links to mission statement.
- How marketing strategy defines target markets (from segmentation bases and profiles), differential advantage and desired brand positioning.
- Gap analysis and Ansoff matrix.

1.1.3 Implementing the marketing plan
- Implementation barriers.
- Allocation of budgets, tasks, responsibilities.
- Control implications.
- Alternative ways of organizing marketing activities; by function, product, region, type of customer, matrix.
- Internal marketing implications; gaining commitment for the plan.

1.2 The Marketing Mix (50%)

Theories of communication: single step, two step and multi-step communication models, adoption models.

1.2.1 Promotional operations (20%)
- Advertising techniques: campaign planning, developing creative and media briefs, message content, evaluation.
- Sales promotion techniques: objectives, mechanics (sampling, price-offs, in-pack etc.), evaluation.
- Public relations techniques: establishing publics, press relations, lobbying, crisis management, evaluation.
- Direct and interactive communications: objectives, database marketing, direct mail, telemarketing, Internet, evaluation.
- Sponsorship: objectives, types (sport, arts, community etc.), evaluation.
- Personal selling techniques (sales force, sales support and sales literature).

1.2.2 Pricing operations (10%)
- The importance of price and its determinants.
- Pricing models for decisions based on cost competition and demand (including basic break-even analysis, marginal costing and price elasticity).
- Pricing objectives and methods (cost-plus, perceived-value, competitive parity etc.).
- Adapting the price (discounts, promotions, product-mix etc.).

1.2.3 Product operations (10%)
- The nature of products, components and life cycles.
- Brand management; brand values, brand planning and threats to the brand.
- Product portfolio, product mix (product line breadth and depth).
- New product development (idea generation, screening, concept development and testing, marketing strategy, business analysis, launch, evaluation and development).

1.2.4 Place operations (10%)
- Distribution channels; consumer and business-to-business, new direct channels of distribution such as the Internet.
- Criteria to select and evaluate alternative channels of distribution.

1.3 Managing Marketing Relationships (15%)

1.3.1 Relationships with customers
- Defining the concept, types of relationships; degree of importance.
- The recognition of distributors, intermediaries, agents and franchisees as customers.
- Customer retention planning; relationship marketing mix.
- Managing customer relationships.
- Key account management techniques.

1.3.2 Relationships with outside suppliers
- Briefing, working, control and review of agencies and consultancies (specifying needs/time span/budgets).
- Working with distributors, franchisees and agents; building relationships and controlling performance.

1.3.3 Relationships with the wider public and society
1.3.4 Internal marketing relationships
- The importance of marketing ethics and social responsibility.
- Ethics for marketing executives and within the marketing mix.
- Codes of ethics.
- Social responsibility issues: consumer, community, green.
- Proactive, reactive or passive strategies to social responsibility.
- The concept, organizational structures and cultures.
- Effective internal marketing techniques (recruitment, training, communication, cross-functional team working etc.).

1.4 Marketing Operations in Context (20%)

1.4.1 Industrial/business to business marketing applications
- Distinguishing characteristics of business versus consumer markets.
- Business buyer behaviour, factors affecting buying decisions and buying process.
- Marketing mix differences (service component, bid and negotiated pricing, role of personal selling, use of distributors and agents).

1.4.2 Services marketing
- Basic characteristics (intangibility, inseparability, perishability, heterogeneity).
- Extended marketing mix (people, process, physical evidence).
- Importance of service quality.

1.4.3 Charity and not for profit marketing
- Objectives differ from consumer/industrial markets.
- Target markets (donors, volunteers, clients).
- Marketing mix differences (product usually ideas and services rather than goods, short distribution channels, approach to pricing, promotion emphasis on PR and face to face fund raising).
- Performance hard to measure.

1.4.4 International marketing
- Identifying marketing information needs.
- Marketing environment, managing the differences.
- Structure choices: exporting, licensing, joint ventures, trading companies, direct ownership.
- Necessary adaptations to the marketing mix.

Reading list

Core texts
Kotler, P., Armstrong, G., Saunders, J. and Wong, V. (2001) *Principles of Marketing*. 3rd European Edition. Harlow, FT/Prentice Hall.

Syllabus guides
CIM (2002) *CIM Companion: Marketing operations*. Cookham, Chartered Institute of Marketing.

BPP (2002) *Marketing Operations*. London, BPP Publishing.

Beamish, K. (2002) *Marketing Operations Coursebook*. Oxford, Butterworth-Heinemann.

Supplementary reading
Brassington, F. and Pettitt, S. (2000) *Principles of Marketing*. 3rd revised edition. London, FT/Prentice Hall.

Chapman, D. and Cowdell, T. (1998) *New Public Sector Marketing*. London, Pitman.

Dibb, S., Simkin, L., Pride, W. and Ferrell, O. (2000) *Marketing: Concepts and strategies*. 4th revised edition, Abingdon, Houghton Mifflin.

Doole, I. and Lowe R. (2001) *International Marketing Strategy: Analysis, development and implementation*. 3rd revised edition. London, Thomson Learning.

Fill, C. (2001) *Marketing Communications*. 3rd edition. Harlow, FT/Prentice Hall.

Hatton, A. (2000) *Definitive Guide to Marketing Planning*. Harlow, FT/Prentice Hall.

Jobber, D. (2001) *Principles and Practices of Marketing*. 3rd edition. Maidenhead, McGraw-Hill.

McDonald, M., Rogers, B. and Woodburn, D. (2000) *Key Customers*. Oxford, Butterworth-Heinemann.

McDonald, M. (2002) *Marketing Plans*. 5th edition, Oxford, Butterworth-Heinemann.

Payne, A., Christopher, M., Clark, M. and Peck, H. (1998) *Relationship Marketing for Competitive Advantage*. Oxford, CIM/Butterworth-Heinemann.

Woodruffe, H. (1998) *Services Marketing*. London, Pitman.

Wyburd, G. (1998) *Competitive and Ethical?* London, Kogan Page.

BPP (2002) *Marketing Operations Practice and Revision Kits*. London, BPP Publishing.

Marketing Operations: Success tape. Learning cassettes by BPP Publishing.

Index

Symbols

4Ps 143, 248, 255
7Cs model 82

A

Accenture 78
Accommodation strategy 228
ACORN 58
Adoption process 88
Advertising 98, 124
  and market mix 103
  influence in price 104
  media characteristics 99
  objectives 98
  role in product life cycle 101
Affective objectives 90
Agencies 109
  a la carte 110
  full service 109
  limited service 109
Agency
  brief 216
  relationship management 111
  selection criteria 110
Agents/brokers/facilitators 186
AIDA model 90
Anderson Consulting 78
Annual reports 124
Ansoff matrix 36
Attitude 126
Augmented product 145
Automobile Association (AA) 197
Awareness 126

B

Balance of power 190
Balanced scorecard 44
Barriers to entry 285
BCG matrix 159
Behaviour segmentation 60
Behavioural objectives 90
Benchmarking 67, 76
Benefits of globalization 289
BHP 30
Black and Decker 91
BMW 21, 92, 146, 221, 228
Boston Consulting Group
  matrix 66, 158, 160

Brand
  advantages and disadvantages 150
  extension 150
  loyalty 149
  management 151
  planning 149
  strategies 149
  threats 150
  values 147
Branding 146
Break-even analysis 176
British Airports Authority (BAA) 126
British Airways 55, 65, 126, 130, 150, 213
British Association of Seed Producers 262
British Telecom 104
Budget 126
Budgetary control 78
Building supplier relationships 217
Business analysis 164
Business/industrial buying behaviour 233
Business/marketing function 26
  competitive factors 27
  financial factors 27
  managerial factors 27
  technical factors 27
Business-to-business (B2B) marketing 232
Business-to-business segmentation 60
Business-to-consumer (B2C) 195

C

Campaign
  evaluation 113
  planning 107
Cash cows 159
Cathay Pacific 65, 284
Channel 85
  effectiveness evaluation 199
  members 185
  of distribution 189
  strategy 191
Charities 257
Chinese Airlines 284
CIM code of ethics 226
Code of practice, enforcement of 227
Codes of ethics 226
Cognitive objectives 90
Communication
  loop 84
  process 83
  theory 84

Company acquisition 284
Competitive
 analysis 28
 marketing strategy 50
 positioning 55
Competitor performance 79
Competitors 28
Concept testing 163
Confusion marketing 104
Consumer and business buying
 behaviour 277
Consumer audits 121
Consumer decision-making unit 89
Consumerism 223
 social response 223
Context of services, marketing mix in 249
Control and evaluation 217
Control process 75
Core and peripheral values 148
Core product 145
Corporate planning 8
Corrective action 79
Cost leadership 50
Cost-plus pricing 180
Creative advertising 105
Creative process 108
Crisis management 126
Currency/interest rate risks 275
Customer loyalty 205
 schemes 119
Customer retention
 consumer markets 209
 not-for-profit markets 210
 organizational markets 209
Customer retention management 208
 marketing mix 213
 techniques to aid 210
Customer-oriented advertising 106
Customers 33
 perspective 45

D

DAGMAR 89
Data Protection Act 128, 130
Database marketing 129
Decider 89, 238
Decision-making unit (DMU) 89
Decline 102, 154
Decoding 85
Defence strategy 228
Demographic segmentation 58
Designing services mix 250
Developed countries 274

Development 154
Differential pricing 179
Differentiation 51
Diffusion 165
Direct and interactive marketing 127
 evaluation 135
 objectives 128
 techniques 130
Direct
 exporting 272
 mail 130
 response advertising 131
Distribution channels 185
 and customer 188
Distribution marketing issues 185
Distributors/dealers 186
Diversification 36, 54
DMU 89
Dogs 159
Domestic laws 274
DRIP 84
Dun and Bradstreet 131, 140
Durable products 145

E

Early
 adopters 165
 majority 165
EarthShell Corporation 164
Easy Group 3, 37, 54
EasyJet 3, 27, 33, 54, 65, 78, 99, 149, 250
Economic
 environment 274
 factors 22
 intelligence 20
Electronic point of sale 115, 194
Emerging economies 275
Encoder 84
Environmental
 analysis 19
 assessment process 19
 scanning 19
Environmentalism 221
EPOS 115, 127, 194
ESSO 24, 25, 171
Establishment of price 180
Ethical issues
 consumers and marketers 224
 marketing mix 224
Evaluation criteria 114
Events 124
Exclusive distribution 191
Export marketing 272

External marketplace 277
Exxon 21, 24, 25, 34, 221

F

Family branding 149
Feedback 85
Financial performance 44
Financial resources/budgets 74
Focus 51
Franchisee 186
Franchising 284
Functional organization 73

G

Gap analysis 47
General Electric (GE) 160
Geo-demographic segmentation 58
Geographic segmentation 57
Geographical diversification 271
Global marketing management 272
Globalization 288
Green issue 21, 221
Green marketing 221
Grey market 21
Growth 101, 154
Growth strategies 52

H

Häagen-Dazs 97
Haji-Ioannou 3
Heinz 101, 102, 149
Heterogeneity 246
Hierarchy of effect 90
Higher prices, setting 180
Horizontal channel integration 193
Human resources 8, 42, 45, 68, 74

I

Idea generation 163
Impact of internet on process 249
Independent Television Commission (ITC) 138
Indirect exporting 272
Influencer 89, 148, 238
Influences on
 distribution 184
 price 170
Information processing model 90
Innovation and learning perspective 46
Innovators 165
Integrated marketing communications 97
Intensive distribution 191
Intermediaries 187

Intermediary selection criteria 190
 optional 190
 strategic 190
Internal marketing 70
 relationship management 218
Internal perspective 45
Internal public relations 125
 acceptability 126
 feasibility 125
 suitability 125
Internal relationship marketing techniques 219
Internal stakeholders 218
International laws 274
International marketing
 environment 272
 levels of 271
International marketing information system 279
International Monetary Fund (IMF) 274
International research 278
Internet marketing 133
 advantages 134
 business benefits 134
 disadvantages 135
Internet on channel decisions 195

J

JICNAR 58, 91
Joint venture 183, 270, 284
Just in time (JIT) 194

K

Key account management 212
 characteristics 212
 characteristics of interdependent 212
Key opportunities 36
Key success factors (KSF) 53

L

Laggards 165
Late majority 165
Launch 164
Leadership, strong and committed 68
Legal environment 274
Legal factors 21
Legislation 222
Less developed countries 275
Licensee 186, 283
Lifestyle segmentation 59
Lobbying 125
Lufthansa 197, 250, 276

M

Macro environment analysis 20
Managing marketing relationships 2
Marginal costing and pricing
    177, 179
Market
    challengers 54
    development 36, 53
    entry strategies 283
    followers 55
    intelligence 20
    leaders 54
    nichers 55
    penetration 36, 52
    positioning strategies 54
Market segmentation 55
    achieving effective 61
    monitoring 61
Marketing
    environment assessment 19
    mix and standardization 288
    mix effectiveness 79
Marketing adoption in non-profit
    organizations 266
Marketing audit
    conducting 16
    to planning process 41
Marketing mix in context of marketing
    operations 82
Marketing objectives
    aims and objectives 4
    indicative content 5
    learning outcomes 4
Marketing operations examination 6
    approaching 6
    importance of reading 6
Marketing operations in context 2
Marketing oriented and
    customer-focused culture 69
Marketing plan 66
    implementation 67
    implications 285
Marketing planning
    for charities 259
    process 1
Marketing relationships, scope of
    204
Marketing segments, profiling 92
Marketing strategy
    declining products 157
    growth 156
    maturity 156
Marketing strategy formulation 48

Marketing structure, effective 71
Marketing versus corporate public
    relations 122
Maturity 102, 154
Media coverage and tone 126
Media relations 124
Merchandiser 187
Mergers/acquisitions intelligence 20
Micro environment 18
    analysis 26
Monitoring 253
MOSAIC 59
Motivational factors 263
Multi-branding 150
Multi-step communication model 87

N

New product development 162
    process 163
Noise 85
Non-business marketing 257
Non-durable products 145
Non-profit versus profit marketing 262
Non-profit-making organization 261
North America Free Trade Areas
    (NAFTA) 17

O

Objectives
    functional 42
    marketing 43
    non-financial 42
    primary 42
    programme/subsidiary 43
Opening and closing a sale 140
Organizational segmentation 60
Outsourced relationships, types 214
    agents 214
    distributors 214
    franchisees 214
Outsourcing, merits and demerits 215
Own branding 150

P

Packaging 96, 98, 152, 163, 183, 194, 221, 234
PC World 29
PDM 193, 194
People 248
Perceptual positioning map 64
Personal selling 138
    task of 139
PEST 17

Physical distribution management
    (PDM) 193
Physical environment 248
Place 225
Planning 11
  barriers 13
  for relationship management 205
  framework 93
  horizons 40
Planning process
  backdrop 7
  influence of change 13
Political
  environment 276
  factors 23
  intelligence 20
Porter's five forces 28
  bargaining power of buyers 31
  bargaining power of suppliers 31
  threat for competitive rivalry 30
  threat for potential entrants 32
  threat for substitutes 32
Positioning 63
  alternatives 65
  role of marketer 66
Post-testing 115
Potential product 145
Press conferences 124
Press releases 124
Pre-testing 113
  approaches to 113
Price and organization, perspective of 169
Price 225
  perception and customer 169
  sensitive markets 174
  with value correlation 171
Pricing
  in relation to demand 169
  objectives and strategies 177
Primary research 282
Proactive strategy 228
Process 248
Product
  management 153
  operations 143
  oriented advertising 106
  portfolio planning tools 158
  range 153
Product adoption process 165
Product development 36, 53, 163
Product extras 213
Product life cycle 153
  management 156
Product-based organization 73

Promotion 225
Promotional communications process 94
Promotional mix 96
  tools 96
Promotional operations 93
  in context of marketing mix 82
Prudential 9, 24
Public relations 121
  aims and objectives 122
  attitude change 123
  evaluation 126
  techniques 124
Publications 124
Publicity 121
Pull strategy 92, 194
Push strategy 93, 194

Q

Quality culture 252
Quantity discounting 179
Question marks 159
  problem children 159

R

Reaction strategy 228
Recall testing 115
Receiver 85
Recognition tests 115
Reinforcing promotions 214
Relationship ladder 206
Relationship marketing 202
  based on trust 207
  dimensions 206
  with wider public and society 220
Relationship marketing plan 229
Relationship pricing 213
Relationships with outside suppliers 214
Repositioning through advertising 103
Response generation 127
Responsibility, marketing and social 221
Retail audits 121
Retailers 186
Return on investment (ROI) 101, 169
Richard Branson 3, 148
Ronald McDonald House Charities 258

S

Sales
  information 121
  performance evaluation 140
Sales force
  feedback 121
  objectives 139

Sales promotion techniques 117
  manufacturer to consumer 118
  retailer to consumer 118
  trade promotions 117
Sales promotion 116
  evaluation 120
Saturated domestic market 271
Screening new ideas 163
Seasonal fluctuations 117
Segmentation of consumer markets 57
Segmenting markets, basis for 57
Selective distribution 191
Service product 146
Service quality 251
Service uncertainties 246
Services mix 248
SERVQUAL model 254
Share price 127
Single-source data 115
Single-step communication model 84
SLEPT 17
SMART 42
Social factors 21
  culture 21
  demography 21
  society 21
Specialized distribution 213
Sponsorship 136
  evaluation 138
  objectives 136
  regulations governing 138
  role of 137
  types 136
Stakeholders 34
Standard Industrial Classifications (SIC) 60, 236
Stars 159
STEEPLE 17
Strategic pricing 178
  debtors and creditors 176
  demand 172
  determinants 172
  product life cycle 176
  product positioning 176
Strategy and planning hierarchy 7
Substitutes 32, 172

Supplier selection 215
Suppliers 33
Supply chain intelligence 20
SWOT analysis 35

T

Tactical pricing strategy 178
Tangible/actual product 145
Target audiences and public 122
Targeting 62
  decision makers 91
    for charities 259
Technical intelligence 20
Technological
  environment 276
  factors 25
Telemarketing 131
  scope 132
Tendering 236, 238, 239, 240, 241
Territory-based organization 73
Test marketing 164
Timberland Boots 53
Time Computers 29
Toyota 106, 112
Tracking studies 115
Transactional to relationship marketing 202
Two-step communication model 85

U

Unique selling point (USP) 209

V

Variance analysis 77
Vertical channel integration 192
Virgin Megastores 108
Voucher/coupon redemption 121

W

Walkers Crisps 97
Wal-Mart 25, 80, 175, 190, 192, 193
White goods 117, 118, 153
Wholesalers 186
Wholly-owned subsidiary 284
Wise and Lovey 131
Wyvern Direct Response 131